NOT JUST A HOUSEWIFE

A Volume in the Series
Culture and Politics in the Cold War and Beyond

Edited by
EDWIN A. MARTINI AND SCOTT LADERMAN

JON COBURN

NOT JUST A HOUSEWIFE

WOMEN STRIKE FOR PEACE AND THE COLD WAR WOMEN'S PEACE MOVEMENT

UNIVERSITY OF MASSACHUSETTS PRESS
Amherst and Boston

ISBN 978-1-62534-887-6 (paper); 888-3 (hardcover)

Designed by Deste Relyea
Set in Garage Gothic and Minion Pro
Printed and bound by Books International, Inc.

Cover design by adam b. bohannon
Cover photo by Dorothy Marder, *Women Strike for Peace Die-In Outside of ITT Building*, New York, New York, April 12, 1972.
Courtesy Swarthmore Peace Collection.

Library of Congress Cataloging-in-Publication Data
A catalog record for this book is available from the Library of Congress.

British Library Cataloguing-in-Publication Data
A catalog record for this book is available from the British Library.

The authorized representative in the EU for product safety and compliance is Mare-Nostrum Group.
Email: gpsr@mare-nostrum.co.uk

Physical address: Mare-Nostrum Group B.V., Mauritskade 21D, 1091 GC Amsterdam, The Netherlands

For Mum, Dad, Paul, and Sarah

CONTENTS

ACKNOWLEDGMENTS

This book culminates thirteen years of my life. It began with me lucking my way into a PhD program in American Studies at Northumbria University in 2012, with a vague project outline, no clue where to begin, and a strong sense of intimidation. But the PhD saved my life. It let me spend time and build relationships with the most incredible people. Those four years made me who I am, and I will be forever indebted to Northumbria University and the people there for giving me that opportunity. I completed the PhD in 2016 and spent the next nine desperate years trying to snatch minutes here and there to complete this book. Immense change, disruption, and growth are behind it—nine homes, six jobs, two emigrations, one global pandemic. The predictable awfulness of higher education mismanagement means this book may be my last opportunity to contribute something academic to the world. I hope that isn't the case. But if it is, I am proud of this—my little contribution.

Everyone in my life was essential for this book. So many people read drafts, offered advice and support, their vital time, and I can never begin to repay that in thanks. But more importantly, everyone sustained me personally, without question or condition. I can only name-check some of them, and I'm absolutely certain I've left people out. If that's the case, and you think you should receive a shout out, get in touch—I owe you a drink. Similarly, if you're named personally but don't think you should be, let me know—I'll cross your name out of my copy.

Everyone at University of Massachusetts Press has been wonderful. I had constant doubts about the value of this project, especially as it took so long to complete, but the decency, honesty, general all-around goodness of everyone at UMass has been a joy. Thanks particularly to Matt Becker for the initial positivity towards this work—it meant a lot. The peer reviewers were unbelievably thoughtful, insightful, and supportive, especially given how burdensome the academic research and publishing enterprise is these days. This book is so much better because of them. I am also especially grateful for the incredible time, patience, and advice Ellen Goldstein provided in editing the unwieldy nightmare of a draft I initially completed. Thank you!

My PhD supervisor, Michael Cullinane, remains the most important factor underpinning all of this work. He took this scared lad's ill-informed ideas and patiently guided me toward something better. This exploration of women and peace would not have begun without Mike, and his charismatic nurturing ensured it progressed. Mike was exactly what I needed. I am a historian because of him. And I will always try, badly, to not use the verb "to be."

I'm so lucky to have shared space at Northumbria with such a fantastic group of people. Sylvia Ellis's expertise as a second supervisor was invaluable. I adored the scholarly environment cultivated by people such as Brian Ward, Charlotte Alston, Daniel Laqua, David Gleeson, Henry Knight Lozano, James McConnel, Joe Hardwick, Laura O'Brien, and Tanja Bueltmann, among countless others. I thank Joe Street especially for his contributions throughout my PhD, and I was privileged to have had him as one of my examiners. I am proud to have been a brief part of American Studies at Northumbria University, and to the wider community of postgrads, including, but by no means limited, to André Keil, Cao Anh, David Hope, Jen Kain, Lara Green, Lee Collins, Maria Cannon, Megan Hunt, Megan Holman, Peter O'Connor, Rachel Ramsey, Sarah Hellawell, Stan Neal, Stef Allum, and Stephen Bowman. It was the honor of a lifetime to work alongside them. PhD Eindhoven is also due a trophy (thirteen years of hurt.)

It goes without saying that the research was only possible due to the incredible skills and knowledge of archival staff. Thanks especially to Wendy Chmielewski and all the staff at Swarthmore College Peace Collection; Melissa Lindberg at the Bender Library of American University; the Bancroft Library of University of California, Berkeley; the Allen Library at the University of Washington, Seattle; the Chicago History Museum; and the Wisconsin Historical Society in Madison. Jonathan Manton at the Stanford Archives of Recorded Sound helped with frequent tedious requests. Judy Adams's generosity secured my best research. Thanks also to Judith Lipton for generously offering her reminiscences. Catherine West's insight during my time in Seattle will always stay with me. I also thank Katie Henry for her kindness while I was in Madison. They had more influence on me than they'll ever know. But I know I've lost touch with so many others who supported my research endeavors, and I am so sorry for that. I'm grateful to the British Association for American Studies for their funding.

I am indebted to a huge community of historians for their support over the years. Jonathan Bell offered wonderful insight and critique as my external examiner and in the years since. Involvement in the Society for the History of Women in the Americas in the early months of my PhD gave me an essential foundation as I took my first nervous steps into academia. Huge thanks to Rachel Ritchie, Sinead McEnaney, Helen Glew, Charlie Jeffries, Eilidh Hall, and all of the kind contributors to the Postgraduate Writing Workshops. Amy Schneidhorst's encouragement during my first few years and beyond was invaluable, and I'm so grateful for her wisdom and help. Jessie Frazier's kind advice and reassurance as I found my way post-PhD is something I'll always appreciate. Jan Kempe was immensely charitable with her time as I pieced together aspects of Alice Herz's life. She is an amazing person. Many thanks also to Lara Track, whose work on Women Strike for Peace I particularly admire. I value our all-too-irregular conversations and I'm delighted that she published her own history of WSP prior to mine (read it—it's better than this one!). Congratulations!

It's not just that this book could not have been completed without the support of friends and family—that's obvious. More importantly, without them, the work doesn't matter anyway. I would devote more words than I'm able to thank Betsy Kalin for her influence on my life. Betsy renewed my passion for this history—I hope we get to work together on an Alice Herz project soon! Ben Houston remains an essential and reliable guide for me, and I'm grateful for the assured support and occasional pints he provides. Ellie Rolls will remember what I was like trying to finish the first draft of this during our late-night library shifts. Some of my happiest memories are of our time working in the Marj together. I'm so thankful to her, for so much.

I'm lucky to have found such a life-affirming community in the School of Humanities and Heritage at the University of Lincoln. Tom Bishop and Adam Page are immense historians, great people, and indispensable friends. We never actually won a FIFA World Cup—good gravy catch ups though. Michael Wuk is the most decent, honest, and reliable friend I've ever had. But more than that, he is a very strong and handsome man. I am so thankful that, in Begüm Ulusoy, I had an ally in Lincoln as we both navigated everything that the people in that city have to offer. Which was *a lot*. I miss hanging out and laughing at vaytis. And Natasha Barnes's extraordinary kindness and nurturance helped me rebuild and find myself again. Thank you so much.

Back up north, I'll always treasure the first tentative post-PhD steps I took at Newcastle University alongside Dr. David Hope and Dr. Jen Kain. I feel that's when we truly came of age as academics (and ne'er-do-wells). Thanks, bosses. Nick Moore shared my time in the archives of Washington, DC, mainly so we could enjoy the night life afterward. Which we did. I think. Union Jack's remembered us being there at least. Simon Dick, Jon Dodds, and Carl McVeigh kept me sane with derby days and nights in Chester-le-Street, partying with people whose names I forget. I'm fortunate to share the same appreciation for good comedy as Dan Cain, who I'm sure will help write a book about *The Simpsons*. Thanks to Jen Buck for the regular Instagram reels. I'm overwhelmed to have remained friends with Russ Shaw since our first year of school. Steve Gillespie continues to provide fantastic insight about all things politics and has done so since undergraduate. I'll never be able to say enough good things about Lee Houghton and Prudence Seed. They kept me fed with Sunday dinner and pounds of sticky toffee pudding while we watched and scored every single James Bond movie. I am proud of this book, but not nearly as proud as I am of the calendar we made. To the 'guv, in particular, you're my brother. Thanks for everything. Put some chocolate on it. We'll get into a practice room again. Peace and . . . love ya.

There are too many of my extended family to name here—literally the most loving family in the world, and I love you all. Karen has become like an older sister to me. Kevin and Agnes gave incredible love, support, and packed lunches as I tried to survive on the very few hours of paid work I was lucky to get in my first teaching position. It led to everything else, and I am indebted to them. Obligatory mention of the various animals whose love sustained me throughout the last thirteen years too—Toby, Ralf, Pavel, Mia, Prudence, Winnie, Thomas, and Enzo. I won't say too much about them because the humans in my life will get jealous and weird, but we all know who the most important beings are.

To my Andrea, who came into my life just in time to experience the final year of pain and mental toil as I pieced this book together. Such wonderful timing for her; she's very lucky! Andrea is the patient, positive, affirming influence I've always needed. She rode this final year out with me, and I really could not have got this book together without her. I laugh more than I ever have before, and she makes me happier than I ever thought possible. I love you (more).

Finally, to Mum, Dad, Paul, and Sarah, to whom this book is dedicated. Paul was my first hero, and will always be the man I aspire to be. Sarah should someday see herself as we all see her—as an inspiration, an awe-inspiring icon of a woman. And Mum and Dad, who have always given all of themselves to their family. You are proud of your kids no matter what—we are prouder still to have you as our parents. This book is for you most of all.

INTRODUCTION

NO ONE PERSONIFIES THE intricate history of women's peace group Women Strike for Peace (WSP) quite like Bella Abzug. When she witnessed WSP's second demonstration in November 1961, the fiery progressive lawyer gleefully joined the New York branch to contribute to its campaign against atmospheric nuclear weapons testing. Abzug saw in WSP an opportunity to inspire a "folksy" collective of housewives and mothers to a more direct political initiative than their "moralistic performance of respectable motherhood."[1] This wish reflected her wider efforts to draw the energy of social movements into the sphere of legislative politics. In this regard, she was among a coterie of experienced progressive activists, leftist radicals, community organizers, and women's rights advocates who tried to lead their more inexperienced WSP peers into making the "strength of women's political power felt."[2] Abzug forged a particularly assertive presence among WSP's New York–based leaders. She created a role for herself as WSP's national legislative chairwoman and, being seen as the organization's "principal political director," worked to professionalize its informal operations. Abzug's political lobbying initiatives proved instrumental to cementing WSP's presence and influence among the social movement landscape of the early 1960s.

Yet many of her WSP contemporaries resisted Abzug's forceful promotion of "new politics."[3] Furthermore, she encountered opposition from those who felt she did not embody the "correct" image of their group—one rooted in traditional ideals of apolitical white American motherhood. Having rallied around the group's reticent founder, Washington, DC, children's illustrator Dagmar Wilson, many WSPers proudly emphasized their political neutrality, lack of activist experience, and their motivation, which was only to protect the world's children from the harms of nuclear war. Describing herself as a "mere housewife," Wilson ensured WSP's popularity by exploiting the moral authority of motherhood, declaring that her group was "appalled at our own audacity, for we're just ordinary people, not experts."[4] For her part, Abzug recognized that she "was not reflective of the typical Women-Strike-for-Peacer." Judging the Washington, DC, founders "to be political amateurs," she grew frustrated with her colleagues' unwillingness to embrace a more avowedly feminist perspective on women's political agency.[5]

By the 1970s, however, WSP had transformed, and Abzug's reputation with it. In the interim, radical feminists confronted WSP and criticized its reliance on "traditional motherhood" to make a case against war.[6] In response, WSPers realigned their image and rhetoric to suit the new upsurge of public feminist politics. Meanwhile, the group's continual opposition to rampant American militarism led previously moderate activists to embrace increasingly militant acts of political dissent. A change in leadership, forced by Dagmar Wilson's withdrawal in late 1968, caused WSP's more charismatic and politically energetic elements to rise in influence and visibility. To navigate this social and political landscape, WSPers repositioned themselves, their group, and their history.

WSP lessened their emphasis on motherhood as a motivation for political action and instead emphasized a feminism that extolled women's agency more directly. As a result, WSP changed its perspective on Abzug's contributions. When she announced her candidacy for the US Congress in 1970, WSPers nationally threw themselves into Abzug's campaign. The campaign slogan—"This Woman's Place is in the House . . . The House of Representatives!"—illustrated not only Abzug's own political zeal but also the newly discovered feminist sentiments of growing numbers of WSP participants.[7] As they began the important but less visible work of writing their own history, WSP's activists overlooked their earlier strained relationship with Abzug. They now endorsed her enduring vision for a comprehensive, feminist peace praxis and celebrated Abzug, inaccurately, as one of WSP's original founders. Despite their previous reservations about her political sensibilities, WSP now used Abzug to symbolize their character. She became equal in historical importance to Dagmar Wilson, someone whose almost mythical status among her supporters represented an entirely different image of WSP.[8]

WSP's evolution reveals the clashing politics, vibrant personalities, and intense contributions that characterized the Cold War women's peace movement.[9] What is more, Bella Abzug's particular journey shows how activists re-situated themselves and their history to suit new organizational identities. This phenomenon is overlooked in women's peace histories that discount the profound developments in experience, identity, and historicism typical of long-standing women's movements. Accordingly, *Not Just a Housewife* provides a new history of WSP, illuminating the group's complexity to show that it was more than just a static peace organization railing against war in the name of traditional motherhood.[10] Although some WSPers were neither housewives nor mothers, the group's activism was informed by the identity and expected roles associated with white, middle-class American motherhood. This essentially depoliticized women's protest in favor of a moral appeal centered on the protection and nurturance of the health and wellbeing of children and the family as a whole. However, while participants were commonly underestimated as "just a housewife," WSP's maternal peace activism was ideologically charged, geographically disparate, radically militant, and responsive to change.[11] The group's longevity—it functioned as a national body from 1961 until 1990—allowed thousands of activists to successfully navigate periods of significant social and cultural dislocation. The group's survival also proved the robustness and flexibility of maternal activist identity.

WSP's history shows that framing WSP as a group of respectable, modest, and conventional housewife activists is false. *Not Just a Housewife* argues that such historicism has prevented a broader understanding of maternal peace activism. Similarly, to depict WSP as embodying an ideological duality between women such as Abzug and Wilson oversimplifies the group's complexity, and an accurate account must balance the wide range of activist identities contained in the group. A more comprehensive history of WSP demonstrates the unique significance of the Cold War–era women's peace movement, as it brought together and maintained many kinds of organizing through periods of profound transformation. This book takes inspiration from recent studies that have repaired and refreshed histories of the American women's movement, applying their approaches to women's maternal peace organizing.[12] To make its case, *Not Just a Housewife* draws upon a repository of autobiographical, collective, and organizational memory to cast WSP's history in activists' own terms. It uses this trove of activist memory to consider WSP's significance as a meaning-making organization for its participants. This book therefore illuminates how maternal peace activists asserted their own place within social movement history, navigated fluctuations in activist identities, and understood peace and feminism during the transformative decades of the Cold War. In doing so, *Not Just a Housewife* repositions maternal peace activism as a force within the social movement landscape of the twentieth century.

WSP grew from modest beginnings at a cocktail party in Georgetown to become one of the most effective peace groups in American history. Its first public demonstration, held on November 1, 1961, drew thousands of women to "Strike for Peace" across the United States in a coordinated effort against atmospheric nuclear weapons testing. This upsurge was not just a reaction to heightened Cold War tensions, but also dissatisfaction with women's limited opportunities to lead dynamic political action in organizations controlled by men. Under Dagmar Wilson's stewardship, WSP initially leveraged American reverence of motherhood to assert a moral responsibility on behalf of their children.

It evolved from a one-off demonstration to become a dynamic network renowned for spontaneous action, autonomous local campaign groups, and maternal expressions of concern for life on earth.[13] The dynamism of its gender expression, and its assertion that housewives were radical political actors, drove interest in WSP by contrasting sharply with existing organizations such as the Committee for a Sane Nuclear Policy (SANE) and the Women's International League for Peace and Freedom (WILPF). Branches formed in cities and towns across the US, adopting their own leaders, projects, and monikers: Women Strike for Peace (WSP) in some cities, Women for Peace (WFP) in others, and still more idiosyncratic versions elsewhere (e.g., Seattle Women Act for Peace, or SWAP). WSP's fingerprints can be found on most of the major arms control treaties and successful antiwar efforts of the Cold War. WSP overpowered the feared McCarthyite House Un-American Activities Committee (HUAC) during their famous 1962 hearing. WSP catalyzed public support for the landmark 1963 Nuclear Weapons Test Ban Treaty, and brokered conferences between American women and their international counterparts, all while receiving glowing praise from journalists and political leaders who encouraged people to "listen to mother."[14] As historian Petra Goedde depicts, WSP's "even-handed common sense" rehabilitated the politics of peace amid the absurdity of Cold War nuclear strategy and a turbulent social movement landscape.[15]

Public conformity with gendered social expectations did not amount to a surrender of values, and WSP's expression of maternal outrage concealed a vibrant political militancy that became more visible over time. The political value of maternalism appeared in various forms throughout the early twentieth century, and many WSP activists took immense pride in their roles as housewives and mothers. They adopted the maternalist ideals of women's movement luminaries such as Jane Addams and believed that their "primary responsibilities" for nurturing the family necessitated their entrance into public politics. In this way, WSP was typical of a long American tradition of housewife activism.[16] But, as Michelle Nickerson writes, the "seemingly timeless designation" of housewife took on renewed value in the mid- twentieth century. It came to imply "ordinariness, anonymity, and community" amid a polarizing domestic sphere charged by Cold War tensions.[17] Both progressive and conservative housewife movements impacted the American political space, finding natural entryways into debates over public schooling, traffic safety, environmental health, and, more visibly, atomic weapons, civil defense, and nuclear war strategy.[18]

WSP benefitted from the initiatives of participants to these actions: experienced leaders of the postwar American left (known as the Popular Front); younger supporters joining from the broader, student-led counterculture movement of the New Left; radical internationalists acting in solidarity with resistance leaders around the world; and reluctant mothers taking part in their first demonstrations.[19] The positive social identification of motherhood allowed WSPers to assume authenticity and experience while shielding themselves from criticism for radical, anti–Cold War political action. Historian Amy Schneidhorst writes that WSP's leading participants, therefore, emphasized women's maternal roles tactically, to navigate a febrile political environment.[20] Drawing upon their identities as housewives and mothers, WSPers positioned themselves as what Cynthia Stavrianos terms "accidental activists," to ensure their success on the political scene.[21]

Although WSP's approach to maternal activism often heightened the effectiveness of their contemporary campaign, it also led to condescension in histories that demean the political conviction of maternal activism. Peace movement historians in particular took the group's proclaimed domesticity at face value and ignored the complex politicism and activist lineages underpinning it.[22] This "historical amnesia" motivated former New York WSP leader and history professor Amy Swerdlow to spend two decades writing the history of WSP, which culminated in the publication of her definitive history *Women Strike for Peace: Traditional Motherhood and Radical Politics in the 1960s*.[23] Her work encouraged an upsurge of interest in women's peace history, providing new recognition for WSP's campaign against nuclear weapons testing and the Vietnam War. However, *Women Strike for Peace* remains foundational for historians of women's peace activism largely because, thirty years since its publication, it is still the only dedicated historical account of WSP's exploits. Marian Mollin's 2009 plea that historians renew studies of women's identities in peace and pacifist movements did not succeed, and depictions of WSP continue to mistakenly place it as a fixture only of the 1960s.[24] This overlooks the evolution in activist identity—what Jill Greenlee describes as the "dynamic process," ensuring that even motherhood "is not a stable, static state."[25]

Depicting maternity as the driver of women's antiwar work meant that peace activism was excluded from histories of the American women's movement, especially those that centered radical feminism.[26] Traditionally, women's rights activism worked in tandem with peace causes. Suffrage activists saw violence and militarism as obstacles to women's equality, and the campaign for voting rights notably merged with pacifism during World War I. Women continued their antimilitarism throughout the interwar era, epitomized by the formation of WILPF, whose leaders Jane Addams and Emily Greene Balch separately won Nobel Peace Prizes. As fear of nuclear war thrust women's domestic duties to the forefront of civil defense preparation in the early years of the Cold War, a new set of gender-based arguments against war percolated among American activist groups.[27] But by the end of the 1950s progressive campaigns did not address a coalition of issues and connections between peace, feminism, and social justice broke apart.[28] Forming in 1961, WSP had a single-issue focus on nuclear weapons, which decoupled peace from campaigns for gender and racial equality. Individual activists still balanced peace and broader social justice campaigns, and WSP made bigger contributions to antipoverty initiatives, environmentalism, and Black freedom movements toward the end of the 1960s.[29] By this time, however, a burgeoning generation of radical feminists painted WSP's movement of housewives and mothers as reinforcing an oppressive gender order. In this view, although women's liberation similarly comprised radical anti-imperialism, antimilitarism, and critiques of masculinist violence, peace activism guided by maternalism undermined women's freedom. Reconnecting peace and feminist activism remained fraught throughout the 1970s and 1980s, despite radical grassroots initiatives such as the Women's Pentagon Action, liberal organizations such as the Women's Action for Nuclear Disarmament, and sprawling ecofeminist women's peace encampments, all of which demonstrated the sustained strength of women's peace activities and their influence on the development of American feminism.

The story of the American women's movement has been told and retold, and recent scholarly interventions have diligently corrected what historian Melissa Estes Blair identified as the historical "dominance of radical feminism."[30] Challenges to the so-called conventional view of feminist history acknowledge an increasingly broad definition of women's movement activism while de-emphasizing the pervasive metaphor that rights activism comes and goes in waves. Such developments should also have shown that "there was no period in the last century when women were not campaigning" for an end to militarism.[31] However, women's activism for peace remains curiously absent from stories of the women's movement, save for studies that focus specifically on that area. But even in scholarship addressing women's contributions as peace activists, the histories of groups like WSP and WILPF are siphoned into distinct segments that prevents their consideration as a connected part of the wider social movement landscape.[32] New personal and organizational archives, oral histories, autobiographies, and transformative works of scholarship have spurred more complex analysis of WSP in recent years.[33] Nevertheless, there remains uncertainty over exactly where a successful maternal peace organization should lie in histories of American social movements.[34] In her illuminating work on WSP's radicalization across the 1960s, Andrea Estepa argues that "it is likely that WSP's neglect at the hands of second-wave historians has less to do with their politics and more to do with the fact that mothers and motherhood in general are largely invisible in this literature."[35] This not only limits appreciation for this particular avenue of women's work; it abridges the history of women's movement activism generally. Maternal peace activism, it seems, remains on the periphery of studies on Cold War–era social movement organizing.[36]

Not Just a Housewife reinterprets WSP's story to assert the significance of maternal peace activism in American women's history. It describes WSP's influential and active role in what historian Andrea Estepa terms "mainstream" social movement history.[37] WSP carried forward multiple historic streams of women's organizing.[38] Its activists politicized daily life as much as any organization of the student New Left or the women's liberation movement, urging American women to see their routines of child-rearing and consumerism as complicit in the arms race, while also highlighting women's immense political and societal power. At the same time, WSP's more radical participants helped others understand how their personal actions fit into broader systems of militarism, violence, and inequality. Active engagement with women from the Soviet Union and Vietnam globalized the Cold War American peace movement. WSP's operational structure, or "unorganization"—a term used by WSPers to describe their loose coordination characterized by local autonomy, a lack of centralized leadership, and decision-making by consensus—set its most significant and overlooked precedent.[39] It predated the appeal for participatory democracy made more famous by young New Leftists and directly inspired the form of gathering that later typified women's liberation.[40] These contributions require maternal peace activism to be put back into a historical context from which it has been removed, and it also forces a reconsideration of American student and feminist movements: when they began, and who participated in them.

Not Just a Housewife extends WSP's chronology beyond the 1960s, which was only a third of the group's life, to chart its entire history in detail.[41] This contradicts the founding story depicting WSP as having "emerged from nowhere" in November 1961.[42] *Not Just a Housewife* instead reveals WSP's origins in a persistent lineage of anti-imperialism, labor activism, school advocacy, civil rights work, and other postwar progressive movement causes. This was galvanized into a global antinuclear movement by the emerging crisis of atmospheric nuclear weapons testing toward the end of the 1950s. These diverse precursors remain unacknowledged in accounts that foreground the arguably more newsworthy image of apolitical housewives resisting nuclear Armageddon with baby strollers in hand.[43] Charting this vibrant scene challenges activists' own rendering of WSP's historical significance, but actually heightens, rather than erodes, the group's importance. It shows WSP as an overlooked convergence of multiple activist streams that sustained progressive activism at an inflection point in the history of American women's organizing, providing a vital channel for continuing activism when movements for gender equality had receded from public view.[44]

Advancing WSP's story into the 1970s and 1980s, *Not Just a Housewife* provides a unique exploration of the transformation in collective identity that occurred among maternal activists as they encountered and confronted the resurgence of American feminist activism.[45] Challenged by women's liberationists who criticized the maternal frames used to justify WSPers' entry into politics, WSP reconsidered the form, relevance, and value of its maternalism.[46] Its activists began applying generalized feminist rhetoric and altered the language of their protests while engaging with contemporary women's movement politics more robustly than before. Nevertheless, WSP never fully conceptualized its version of feminism. The peace politics of this period did not significantly differ from its earlier iterations of women's role in antiwar initiatives—women were different than men, in particular, more nurturing, and should therefore exert their political power to ensure peace. This book uses maternal peace feminism to describe WSP's rhetoric and attitudes as expressed in the 1970s and 1980s, but deliberately leaves the concept ill-defined to reflect the group's own ideological flexibility.

Nevertheless, the feminist bent of WSPers became more pronounced over time. Recent approaches to feminist history offer innumerable justifications for describing WSP, as former activist and historian Amy Swerdlow did, as "basically a feminist organization."[47] Both Jo Reger's description of "*submerged feminist identity* that puts feminism at the core of all issues" and Alison Dahl Crossley's conceptualization of "waveless feminism" support such an assertion.[48] However, both WSP's archives and a public record detailing the ambivalence to feminism among many leading figures in the early 1960s complicates this determination. Rather than relitigating the debates over WSP's feminist credentials, this book instead seeks to illuminate the fluidity and contradictions of maternal peace activists' political identities. WSPers were not just housewives and, despite their maternal peace politics, not just mothers either. Instead, WSP subtly repackaged traditions of women's social movement organizing to suit the fractious social, political, cultural climate of the Cold War, which attests to the malleability, appeal, and sheer staying power of its maternal organizing. In this way, *Not Just a Housewife* explains that WSP established unheralded consistent connections among communities of feminists across the social movement landscape, successfully navigating activist transformations to forge an unbroken lineage from the 1950s to the 1990s.

The vibrancy of WSP's constituency and activities appears in the political militancy that complemented its more moderate elements. An ideologically radical leadership guided WSP from its founding, which was embodied by figures such as Bella Abzug, Shirley Lens, and Mary Clarke. Its grassroots participants initiated some of the most radically combative actions ever performed by American social movement activists. In 1965, 82-year-old Detroit branch leader Alice Herz performed a shocking act of self-immolation in protest of the Vietnam War, the first of its kind in the western world.[49] Meanwhile, WSPers travelled to North Vietnam to hold a high-profile meeting with Vietnamese women in direct contravention of the US government at a time of war.[50] These instances contradict the framing of maternal peace activism as distinctly "respectable," while also forcing a more consequential rejection of a trend in historical scholarship that pits respectability as the opposite of radicalism in women's activism.[51] Such framing has pernicious effects. Radicalism has been used by both activists and historians to determine authenticity in movement circles. It has been used to set organizations against one another in clashes over values and legitimacy.[52] In WSP's case, the binary forced activists and historians to contort, flatten, and homogenize their descriptions of social movement organizing to reconcile these apparently conflicting ideas. Its expansive collection of women participants led to persistent tension, and often disagreement, over appropriate image, campaigns, and organizing strategy, particularly with regards to the use of militant civil disobedience and radical political critiques. The force of WSP's traditional motherhood reveals militancy, radicalism, moderation, and respectability complementing one another.

Not Just a Housewife looks at regional and city-specific studies of American feminism to overcome "sweeping nationally-based narratives" and instead capture the contexts and the "nuance and texture" that characterize maternal peace activism at a local level. The celebrated autonomy of WSP's operations encouraged branches to celebrate separate founders, distinctive logos, independent campaigns, and unique activist subcultures. WSPers believed their group represented different things, different ideologies, and different tactics. Branches therefore developed their own lore to understand their pasts, often with meaningful departures from the national script. Experiences of local activists demonstrate the multiplicity of WSP's work across the country, while also revealing a fraught, but vitalizing story of difference, fissure, and fracture among branches. These individual branch histories are commonly undervalued, subsumed as they are into narratives that prioritize the experience of influential hubs on the East Coast. Historian Stephanie Gilmore observes the perceived "hegemony of a US women's history rooted in the lives of eastern elites" and uses the term "grassroots" to "refer to women whose activism was not represented in the dominant sites of activism on the East Coast."[53] Following this approach, *Not Just a Housewife* provides renewed focus on West Coast WSP branches, especially those in the San Francisco Bay Area, which were among the most collaborative, energetic, and substantive of all WSP branches. Indeed, its story cannot be told in isolation from the city's WILPF branch, with whom it shared membership, office space, and the cosponsorship of most activities during the Vietnam War. Activists working in the Bay Area did not simply experience "a local variant of a national story." They had their own kind of activism, rooted not in WSP's organizational identity but in their specific local context.[54]

The mobilization of thousands of people across three decades makes WSP worthy of historical reassessment, but the outsized influence and import of its participant-observer accounts also demands attention. The lack of scholarly interest afforded the group, acknowledged by Amy Swerdlow throughout her academic life, prompted WSP activists to assume the upkeep of their historical legacy. Individual efforts began in the 1960s when founding member Eleanor Garst compiled thousands of archival records and drafted innumerable pages for her informal but immersive history of the group's early years.[55] History-making stepped up in the 1970s, as leaders supported the public dissemination of commemorative journals to mark milestones. Anniversary gatherings provided further opportunities for key figures to historicize the organization's rise, its successes and failures, and link plans for the future to its efforts in the past.[56] During the 1980s, WSP activists instigated historical exhibitions and oral history projects, often run by women peace activists themselves, an example of which is Judith Porter Adams' initiatives with WILPF. WSPers compiled thousands of documents for various collections and museums, much of which remain in the historical archives at Swarthmore College, the American University, the University of California, Berkeley, the University of Washington, and the State Historical Society of Wisconsin.[57] Even following the closure of their National Office, WSPers continued to offer their recollections in memoirs and retrospective features about their experiences.[58] This collection of writing, oral recollections, correspondence, branch records, and other ephemera amassed by WSPers remains the significant source of information regarding the group.

WSP was only one group among many—and its brand of maternal peace activism was not a component of many other women's peace groups—but its historical consciousness and memory making had such an impact on the field of women's peace history that WSP became synonymous with the women's peace movement. As such, *Not Just a Housewife* observes that WSP's story is not just a WSP story, and the intricacies of its activists' version of history therefore requires interrogation. As Lara Leigh Kelland emphasizes, the widespread practice of history-creation among social movements of the 1960s and 1970s reveals the power of narrative and memory for the development of activist identity.[59] By invoking the past in speeches, anniversary celebrations, and commemorative journals, WSP created a cultural memory that used its activists' sense of self to inform their historical perspectives. As *Not Just a Housewife* depicts, WSP's longevity affected these memories as the group necessarily responded to new societal and political pressures with new perspectives of its past. The field of women's peace history has, therefore, portrayed an ever-changing, often conflicting sense of WSPness.[60]

The expansion of WSP's story—chronologically beyond the 1960s, thematically beyond its maternal antiwar activism, methodologically toward feminist archiving and activist history-making—provides the comprehensive historical reassessment that the group deserves. A renewed accounting of WSP's contributions and evolutions demonstrates how maternal peace activists carried forward a broad range of progressive causes following a postwar period that saw the decline of campaigns built around more than one issue. Exemplified by WSP, women's peace activists made unheralded contributions to the American peace and feminist movement throughout the tumultuous decades of the late twentieth century. Such recognition allows an examination of women's successful navigation of the social and cultural dislocations of the Cold War. It also corrects ruptures in the historicizing of women's peace organizing. Charting WSP's contributions to myriad social movement campaigns over three decades, the chapters that follow assert the continual presence of women's peace activism throughout the twentieth century.

CHAPTER ONE

Founding Stories and the Roots of Women Strike for Peace

THE STORY GOES THAT on a warm September night in 1961, six friends gathered in a Georgetown living room and talked of nuclear war. The women were horrified by the resumption of atmospheric nuclear weapons testing, which broke a fragile moratorium between the Soviet Union, United States, and the United Kingdom. Previous tests dispersed radiation over vast distances, contaminating the land and its inhabitants. They also polluted milk supplies, which caused the radioactive compounds strontium-90 and iodine-131 to appear in the bones and teeth of children. Called together by Dagmar Wilson, a Washington, DC–based children's illustrator and mother of three, the six women felt that a "special responsibility" to protect the health and wellbeing of the world's young required them to act. Disillusioned with a complacent predominantly male antinuclear movement and the lack of opportunity for women to lead organizing efforts, they decided to make a bold, unprecedented, and unpopular stand by directing a one day "strike for peace." The housewives drafted a Call to Strike exhorting that the grave urgency of the moment overrode their lack of activist know-how. They spread their simple appeal throughout the country by word of mouth, telephone trees, PTA acquaintances, and Christmas card lists. Just six weeks later, on November 1, 1961, fifty-thousand people across the country "took off their aprons," and came out of their homes to march in the streets. The small band of politically inexperienced mothers organized one of the largest public demonstrations in US history. Women Strike for Peace was born.[1]

The stories activists tell about their beginnings become what peace movement historian Robert Benford describes as "sacred narratives."[2] They provide an accessible, shared account that establishes collective identity, relationship to history, and agreed goals around which social movements can unify. Scholars often describe such founding stories as "myths." This is not to imply inaccuracy or falsehoods but rather, as historian of social movement memory Lisa Tetrault explains, to emphasize "a venerated and celebrated story used to give meaning to the world."[3] WSP's founding story informed its activists and outside observers for decades. Participants proudly narrativized their group's beginnings throughout their lives, asserting the importance of their work by juxtaposing later triumphs and successes against a humble start.[4] The tale of six friends, unfamiliar with political activism but determined that "it was time for women to speak out" for the sake of their children, invoked a modest application of political activism that suited a widely accepted postwar American ideal.[5] According to WSP's founding story, its participants had no prior activist experience and were uninvolved in the divisive politics of the 1950s. Furthermore, the founding story claimed that no comparable initiatives existed: that American women had never publicly demonstrated the way WSP women did. The subsequent success of WSP's first strike, with its widely reported attendance of fifty thousand, established the group's knack for spontaneous acts of dissent among a prevailing consensus that frowned upon such activities. Crucially, this success affirmed WSP as a new, spontaneous rising with no precursors and no attachment to traditions of women's movement organizing. WSP's story made the group appear apolitical, authentic, and destined to succeed.

Such founding stories are designed for public consumption and by conveying an image of a particular kind of activist they distort and obscure historical complexity. In WSP's case, participants downplayed their decades of political organizing and the contemporary antinuclear scene in order to portray themselves as an apolitical collective of housewives and mothers who embodied an idealized perception of the white American middle and upper class. A significant motivating factor was the anticommunist hysteria that they had seen destroy US movements for social and political change, such as the Congress of American Women, or, in the case of organizations such as SANE and Women's International League for Peace and Freedom (WILPF), caused leadership to purge their membership of those vulnerable to suspicion of communism. Downplaying politicized roots was a sensible response to such harsh lessons. But WSPers' version of their beginnings also epitomized what historian Verta Taylor termed the "immaculate conception view" of the origins of 1960s social movements, in which organizations "seemingly emerged out of nowhere and represented a sudden shift from the quiescent 1940s and 1950s."[6]

As such, WSP's founding story did not just simplify its own origins—it unwittingly interrupted the perceived timeline of women's peace history. Such was its influence, WSP's founding story continues to inform historical assessments of the era that posit late 1961 as a watershed in history, rather than as a strong and logical continuation of precursors.[7] Just observing the nature of WSP's founding story reveals how maternal peace activists tailored themselves to the reactionary climate of the Cold War, advocating their newness as a pivot in the era's approach to anticommunism.[8] Activists also conveyed their version of WSP's founding to heighten the group's importance. However, disputing this narrative does not undermine the significance of their efforts.[9] Recontextualizing WSP's emergence repairs the fractured chronology of women's organizing initiatives that meant that early 1960s maternal peace efforts were not connected to the lineage of women's postwar activism.

This chapter charts the circumstances and narrativization of WSP's founding, recovering the group's roots to assert its significance to histories of women's postwar organizing. It begins by detailing the extensive scene of postwar women's peace organizing that prefigured WSP's formation before telling individual WSPers' life stories, finding the influential contributions of Dagmar Wilson, Margaret Russell, Eleanor Garst, Mary Chandler, Jeanne Bagby, and Folly Fodor within a maelstrom of Cold War organizing that characterized women's activism in the 1950s. Far from the political neophytes commonly depicted, WSP's founders brought with them years of experience in peace, labor, environmental, civil rights, and women's rights activism. Despite branding themselves as a movement of housewives and mothers, many WSP participants did not have children, nor did they fulfill the ideal of the demure housewife. The extent of WSPers' prior activism is worth highlighting on its own merit, but it also shows how WSP was a convergence point of multiple activist trends. The first strike culminated years of tireless work from activists across the United States. With this lineage, WSP's participants could have taken on the mantle as legitimate heirs to the American women's movement and certainly as the latest stage in the historic women's peace movement. However, they planned and executed their first strike by firmly distancing themselves from this context, using apolitical maternal outrage to head off anticommunist and misogynistic attacks, and to carve space for themselves amid combative antinuclear activism.

This chapter traces the subsequent narrativization of WSP's founding story through branch meetings, personal correspondence, speeches, and comments to the press. WSPers immediately celebrated their strike and retold the circumstances guiding it. This was particularly noticeable in the inflated, but universally accepted claim that fifty-thousand women in sixty communities took part in the first strike. As WSP's antinuclear campaign continued through the Cold War, activists promoted their histories with autobiographies and public addresses that retold the group's founding story. These contributions resulted in distorted histories, as participants championed their own activist pasts while also suggesting that WSP was their first foray into politics. Not only does recognition of WSP's roots revise its own origin story, it illustrates the power of historical consciousness as a force in political identity formation and reveals the influence of WSP's history in women's peace scholarship in general.

The women who would make up WSP acted on a range of socially progressive and pacifist compulsions to force change in the interwar era. They were daughters of suffragists, Communist Party activists, or Jewish working-class parents; first-generation descendants of European refugees or refugees of war themselves; and citizens justifiably concerned for the health and well-being of family and friends. Some cut their teeth as union organizers and labor movement activists; these included Ruth Pinkson of New York WSP or East Bay WFP's Madeleine Duckles, who credited the beginning of her "political education" to a labor strike at the University of California, Berkeley, during the 1930s.[10] Others put together support drives for the Republicans fighting the Spanish Civil War, with Amy Swerdlow describing that her first "strike for peace" happened while in high school.[11] Philadelphia activist Ethel Taylor described her fervent campaigning in the American Jewish Congress. Such was her energy, the organization suspected her of harboring communist sympathies and asked her to leave, citing, in her words, the "serious charges that I became active immediately upon joining" and her "highly suspicious ability to speak without notes."[12] Still more railed in earnest against the rise of fascism and Nazism that led to the Second World War, whether protesting individually, in community groups, or as part of international organizations such as WILPF.[13] When former Vice President Henry Wallace launched an electoral challenge to Harry Truman in 1948, future WSPers flocked to his Progressive Party to lend their support.[14]

As the affluent white suburban ideals of the postwar era provoked a return to domesticity for many American women, future WSPers exerted fulsome resistance to anticommunist conformity and the accusatory environment of the domestic Cold War. WSP's forebearers suffered while attempting to exercise political dissent amid the pervasive conservatism and anticommunism of the early Cold War era. The Congress of American Women was torn apart by red-baiting, and anticommunist hysteria disrupted WILPF.[15] But the women who would become WSP persevered throughout this period and had long expressed "scathing" attacks on American militarism, saw the Cold War "as a distraction," and found popular support for "respect for cultural differences in foreign policy."[16] Shirley Lens, the future area leader for Chicago WFP, courted the media's attention in 1955 when she controversially and defiantly resisted the Broyles Loyalty Oath for the Chicago Teacher's Union. Described as a "publicly positioned" radical, Lens made activist connections around the world, travelling with her husband and fellow labor and peace activist Sidney.[17] Anci Koppel and Thorun Robel, the future leaders of Seattle Women Act for Peace, resisted state Representative Albert Canwell's red-scare paranoia that "swept over" the city in 1948, a "precursor" to Senator Joseph McCarthy's efforts.[18] Robel later aided a Supreme Court case that successfully overturned part of the McCarran Act after the FBI arrested her husband at his shipyard job.[19] A decade before WSP's famously triumphant 1962 battle with the House Un-American Activities Committee (HUAC), its future participants were resisting the committee's persistent harassment.[20] In California, Alice Hamburg appeared before the State Un-American Activities in 1951 for her public support of Paul Robeson.[21] Hamburg and Hazel Grossman, members of WILPF who would become key organizers for WFP in the San Francisco Bay Area, first worked together to protest against HUAC on the steps of San Francisco City Hall in May 1960.[22] San Francisco's HUAC opposition, decentralized and able to spontaneously mobilize thousands of supporters, bore all the hallmarks of WSP's later organizing initiatives in the area.[23]

Women's attention turned toward antinuclear efforts after the US dropped bombs on Hiroshima and Nagasaki in 1945. By Mother's Day in 1951, American Women for Peace (AWP) mobilized two-thousand women to march against nuclear weapons in Los Angeles.[24] It took the public recognition of atmospheric nuclear weapons testing to move the American peace movement out of its postwar malaise. In 1954, the ill-fated Castle Bravo nuclear test vastly exceeded its predicted explosive yield, the thermonuclear device vaporizing the northwestern part of Bikini Atoll. Radioactive fallout spread across the Pacific Ocean and rendered parts of the surrounding

Marshall Islands uninhabitable. Twenty-three unfortunate Japanese fishermen sailing fourteen miles outside of the designated danger area succumbed to radiation sickness. One died. The test proved a watershed moment for the antinuclear movement. Twenty million people signed a petition demanding a nuclear test ban as international support rallied to the cause.[25] New peace organizations formed, spearheaded by SANE, the Committee for Nonviolent Action, and the Campaign for Nuclear Disarmament.[26] Historic organizations also recouped their strength, groups such as the War Resister's League, the American Friends Service Committee (AFSC), and WILPF recovering to recruit new members.

The histories of most women's peace groups are closely intertwined, but WILPF was a predecessor and foil for WSP. As an international band of feminist-pacifists, WILPF persevered against fraught circumstances throughout the twentieth century. Emerging in response to World War I, it brought together an international band of women campaigning against war and for women's suffrage. Under the guidance Jane Addams, Gertrude Baer, and Emily Greene Balch, WILPF successfully navigated a fraught interwar climate to grow into one of the largest international women's organizations in the world. It set its members to work in struggles for social justice and global disarmament, through which both Addams and Greene Balch received a Nobel Peace Prize. As fascism rose in Europe, WILPF mobilized to help Jewish refugees fleeing Germany. However, the US section's resistance to American intervention into World War II proved wildly unpopular. As atomic bombs dropped on Hiroshima and Nagasaki, WILPF activists "were faced with a whole new international trauma," but lacked the vitality and membership to act.[27] As it stumbled into the 1950s, WILPF found itself besieged by McCarthyite attacks, turning individual activists and branches on one another in vain attempts to redeem credibility.[28]

The organization recouped its prestige and status as the decade progressed. It achieved the status of a nongovernmental organization and consulted with the Economic and Social Council of the newly formed United Nations, through which it attained steady successes. WILPF influenced the creation of the UN International Children's Emergency Fund in 1950, as well as the passage of the UN Declaration of Human Rights. It remained steadfast in its call for "substantive and strictly monitored decrease in *all* armaments." It was WILPF's Gertrude Baer who, through the UN, pushed the World Health Organization to investigate the radioactive fallout dispersed by atmospheric nuclear weapons tests in 1956.[29] WSP leaders who were previously or concurrently members of WILPF is an exhaustive list: Alice Hamburg, Hazel Grossman, Madeleine Duckles, and Frances Herring in San Francisco; Ethel Taylor in Philadelphia; Thalia Stern in Miami; Ruth Gage-Colby in New York; and Shirley Lens in Chicago. Indeed, the extent of WSPers' prior involvement challenges efforts to tell a streamlined history about just one of these organizations, and an examination of WSP's roots overlaps the history of WILPF activists' postwar activism.

Women from all walks of life campaigned against nuclear arms in this period. Elite women, such as Eleanor Roosevelt, characterized the ranging and profuse antinuclear initiatives upon which "eminent members" of American society embarked. Historian Dario Fazzi calls Roosevelt a "voice of conscience" for the transnational antinuclear movement, not only because of her use of political connections but also the sheer scale of her technical understanding, communication skills, and mass education efforts.[30] Other elite women, such as future Los Angeles WSPer Ava Helen Pauling, sought to consolidate an international community of antinuclear figures.[31] Although her husband, the Nobel Peace Prize–winning chemist Linus Pauling, received the plaudits for his antinuclear work, it was Ava's unrelenting commitment to women's rights, human rights, and peace initiatives that guided Linus. Together they organized the 1961 Conference of Sixty Scientists Against the Spread of Nuclear Weapons in Oslo, Norway, at which the assembled group of international scientists demanded the end of nuclear weapons testing.[32]

Another figure of elite society often overlooked in antinuclear histories is Anne Eaton, future coordinator for WSP in Cleveland and wife of the philanthropist and industrialist Cyrus Eaton. Anne "swept into worldwide notoriety" for her statements favoring greater cooperation with the Soviet Union, and she accompanied Cyrus to meetings with Russian Premier Nikita Khrushchev and Minister of Foreign Affairs Andrei Gromyko. Anne enthusiastically retold the story of her "being lost once in the Kremlin gardens while top Soviets and Americans searched for her" and "happily remembered a dinner in her Washington hotel suite in September 1959, at which she was a hostess to such notable Russian women as Mrs. Nikita Khrushchev," along with their daughter, Rada Khrushchev, and the wife of Andrei Gromyko. But Anne Eaton's most important contribution to the antinuclear cause came in her painstaking arrangements for the famous 1957 Pugwash Conference on Science and World Affairs, founded by Cyrus and held at his ancestral home in Nova Scotia. The conference drew twenty-two scientists from around the world with the goal of channeling efforts toward peace and disarmament, leading to the founding of the Pugwash group, which made decades-long contributions to international security.[33]

The daring, dangerous public protests of women of color fighting racial injustice further elevated the scene of postwar women's organizing out of which WSP emerged. Danielle McGuire's extraordinary history of the Civil Rights Movement reclaims the women's leadership that almost single-handedly prompted and sustained the Montgomery bus boycott.[34] Lesser-known events, such as the 1959–63 Tex-Son garment workers' strike in San Antonio, highlight Mexican American women's determined public militancy in opposition to unfair labor practices. Using identical descriptors of WSP's later antinuclear campaigns, historian Lori A. Flores writes that the Tex-Son strikers "won support for their 'unladylike' labor protests by creatively using contemporary Cold War ideologies of femininity and domesticity to their advantage."[35] Although embracing similar motivations of "the American home as metaphor for a tidy postwar order," as white progressives and later WSP did, Black women developed a "more complicated understanding of the concept. For them, the African homeland and the American home were sites of contradiction, representing haven and hazard."[36] As Jacqueline Castledine writes, leftist Black women therefore developed more radical critiques of the intersecting forces of colonialism, racism, sexism, and nuclear arms that "linked the US military's actions overseas to white supremacy and racism within the country's borders."[37]

The presence and scale of Black women's radical anti-imperial work in the postwar era is similarly undervalued in histories of WSP's rise. Two years before WSP's first strike, Juanita Nelson and Eroseanna Robinson refused to file federal tax forms in an ongoing protest against the military budget.[38] While Amy Swerdlow rightly reasserted the importance of the Congress of American Women as a precursor to WSP, Dayo F. Gore's illuminating *Radicalism at the Crossroads* emphasizes how CAW's leadership integrated a Black civil rights agenda into their campaigns for peace that is often overlooked by histories of maternal women's peace organizing. Meanwhile, AWP adopted statements on "Negro-white unity" and boasted of Thelma Dale Perkins, Beulah Richardson, Alice Childress, Claudia Jones, and Halois

Moorhead among its leadership. Gore's description of AWP could easily be transposed onto WSP, as "putting forth a mother-centered vision of peace activism, AWP supported uniting women of all races, ethnic backgrounds, and classes in a struggle that represented their 'natural responsibility' to preserve life." The organization's declaration stated that "because the privilege of giving birth is uniquely the labor of women, it becomes the natural responsibility of all women to preserve life, and especially to protect it from the dangers of useless and criminal warfare."[39] Overlooking this lineage not only fractures the history of women's postwar organizing, it encourages the abridgement of Black women's antiwar efforts that has taken half a century to even partially resolve.

The emphasis on women's protective duties allowed peace protesters to leverage their social roles and craft damning, engaging criticisms of Cold War militarism without transgressing beyond the expected place of white middle-class American women. Historians such as Elaine Tyler May observe that the nuclear arms race solidified traditional gendered notions of women's domestic role.[40] Civil defense programs called on the public to "prepare your home and your family against attack" and, as housewives, it fell on women to take the lead and do the work.[41] Katherine Howard of the Federal Civil Defense Administration suggested that preparing the home for war was "merely a prudent extension" of women's maternal responsibilities.[42] Leo A. Hoegh, Director of the Office of Civil and Defense Mobilization, urged women to "recognize and foster civil defense action." Failure to do so was, according to Hoegh, to gamble with the safety of both their family and their country.[43] McCarthyite social politics and, for women of color, the added scourge of racial discrimination, ensured greater costs for women who stepped beyond the conformist elements of postwar American society. However, as Laura McEnaney explains, the same "maternalist-domestic ideology" used to encourage women's civil defense efforts allowed mothers to become politicized against war.[44] They turned civil defense justifications on their head, highlighting the hypocrisy of being ordered to take responsibility for the protection of their children while arms buildups threatened the very existence of humankind.

While political identities based on "maternal sensibilities" did not inevitably entail organizing for peace and disarmament, Marian Mollin's comprehensive examination of gender in the American antinuclear movement portrays the effective use of maternal and familial denunciations of the arms race in the postwar era.[45] WILPF, while cautiously navigating McCarthyite attacks from critics, sponsored radio ads encouraging "traditional housewives and mothers" to protest against the arms race. American Women for Peace, active between 1950 and 1953, advocated the "natural responsibility of all women to preserve life" and protect children "from the dangers of useless and criminal warfare." A women's conference in 1960 explained that the "heavy responsibility" for nuclear disarmament fell on women because of "the special frame of reference of women as mothers, breadwinners, citizens. Participants will consider what disarmament means to them individually and their families in this period when personal security and the survival of the human race are one and inseparable."[46] The multifaceted scope of women's activism demands bringing "mother and housewife" antinuclear campaigners into a more tangled account of postwar-era feminist and gender activism. As Emily E. LB. Twarog explains, women "intentionally invoked their housewife identity" to assert political power throughout the postwar period.[47] In this way, women's antinuclear campaigners continued the strategic use of maternal image previously deployed by labor, welfare, civil rights, and consumer activists.

At the turn of the 1960s, increasing numbers of women directed public demonstrations, dressed "respectably" in coats and high heels while clutching handbags.[48] However, a burgeoning militancy and impatience took hold, and civil disobedience increasingly became a part of individual activists' repertoire. In March 1959, Dorothy Hutchinson, future leader of WILPF, held a fast at the headquarters of the Atomic Energy Commission. In the aftermath, she wrote a report of her experience titled "How a Mother spent Mother's Day far from her children—for the sake of all children."[49] In April, future WSP participants Mary Sharmat and Janice Smith, young mothers who did not previously know each other, set out to "intentionally break the law" by refusing to participate in New York City's annual "Operation Alert" civil defense drills.[50] A part of WSP's founding, Sharmat was subsequently referred to as "one of the true originators of the Women's Peace Movement" by its activists.[51] Declaring that she protested out of frustration with male colleagues in the peace movement, Sharmat presaged WSP's approach by crafting a "respectable" appearance in order to offset potential criticism for her civil disobedience while conveying her fears for children by bringing her young son to protest.[52] Sharmat united with Smith the following year to organize further resistance to the drill, drawing more than a thousand people, among them five-hundred "well-groomed mothers and children," to Central Park. Notions of respectable motherhood shaped the protests. Sharmat recalled, "our skirts gave them courage. We loaned out extra babies to bachelors who had the misfortune to be childless." Historian Dee Garrison argues that Smith and Sharmat transformed "non-violent direct action, once the province of a small band of radicals, into an effective weapon of ridicule used by angry mothers to discredit the nuclear policies of the militarist state" some time prior to WSP's first demonstration. Famed conscientious objector, radical pacifist, and civil rights activist Jim Peck described it as "the biggest civil disobedience peace action [ever] to take place in the United States."[53]

Further activity throughout 1960 drew more women into antinuclear organizing, with efforts dispersed throughout the United States. The presence of women on peace marches in Chicago "rose substantially" throughout the year, until they comprised nearly half of all marchers.[54] In April 1960, the Easter Walk for Peace in Manhattan saw three-hundred people march on the United Nations.[55] That same month, in California, a group of women sponsored by the AFSC held "a women's conference" to discuss "Your Family's Stake in Disarmament." Over five-hundred paid registrants attended, representing thirty separate organizations. Pat Nixon and Eleanor Roosevelt "sent greetings" to the California conference.[56] In July 1960, a group of Canadians formed Voice of Women (VOW) to oppose nuclear weapons "in the cause of a universal motherhood."[57] In Portland, Oregon, Carol Urner marshalled two-hundred women into a "non-organization" called Women for Peace that called on each individual to act as a "human dynamo." Urner's group demonstrated publicly, met the governor of Oregon, and wrote to Congress to protest nuclear weapons testing.[58] National newspapers extensively documented the successes of Portland's women.

Peace historian Amy Schneidhorst explains that these efforts "foreshadowed the women's peace groups" that followed.[59] In the months before WSP's formation, University of California, Berkeley, professor and peace activist Frances Herring wrote to friends that a burgeoning "communication network" of women's peace activists existed in the San Francisco Bay Area that, she hoped, would soon coalesce into a formidable campaign group.[60] In September 1961, following a three-year moratorium, the US and Soviet Union restarted atmospheric test of nuclear weapons. Women across the United States were primed for a peace strike.

WSP owed its formation to the individual efforts of Georgetown artist and political activist Dagmar Wilson. Born in New York City in January 1916, Wilson grew up in Europe. Her father, Cesar Searchinger, worked as a German-based foreign correspondent for CBS radio before moving to the UK, where Wilson attended a "progressive school." She recalled dissenting "against traditional ways of doing things" in her youth, and Wilson's "upper-class British accent" delivered an air of calm grace and respectability to her later public addresses.[61] Her self-description as a "mere housewife" disguised Wilson's lifelong involvement in activist politics. Wilson's parents were directly involved in the women's suffrage movement and were best friends with militant suffragist Betty Gram Swing.[62] Her father proved a particularly important influence.

Cesar Searchinger was a naturalized American citizen from Germany and had an impressive intellect. Mastering the English language within a year of his arrival in the United States, Searchinger worked as a journalist for the *New York Post* and published a well-reviewed book that explored the practicalities of peace in Europe.[63] Her father's work exposed Dagmar to intellectual political discourse from an early age, and she reflected that she often "heard journalists talk in her house" about contemporary political issues.[64] In his weekly radio broadcasts for CBS, a forerunner to Edward R. Murrow's show "Hear It Now," Searchinger presented broadcasts informing the American public of international news, politics, and culture. He often covered "political events," such as the visit of Mahatma Gandhi to London, and allowed his daughter access to such occasions. Gandhi's visit "made a deep impression" on the sixteen-year-old Dagmar. She recalled being impressed with his "principles for peace" and forever remained proud of an English essay she wrote about Gandhi's pacifism.[65] After attending the Slade School of Fine Art in London, Wilson moved back to the United States with her husband, Christopher, just prior to World War II. They settled in Washington, DC, where Christopher worked at the British Embassy as a commercial attaché. Dagmar pursued an artistic career, first as a teacher and graphic artist, and then as an illustrator of children's books. They had three daughters, Sally, Clare, and Jessica.

Wilson remained immersed in politics into her adult life. In the PTA she founded the Action Committee for School Libraries that, under her leadership, brought about the promotion of a library school program. She organized an annual two-week book fair with *The Washington Post* as part of the Children's Book Guild and frequently gave "Chalk Talks" in local schools and neighborhoods.[66] Wilson worked for the campaign to expand DC residents' ability to govern their own affairs—so-called Home Rule—while turning her artistic talents to politics by working for Nelson Rockefeller's Committee for Inter-American Affairs. She converted statistics into graphics, charts, and diagrams for use in board meetings.[67] Christopher's position in the British Embassy exposed her to the intrigues of international relations, while Dagmar's pacifist compulsion directed her to the antinuclear movement.[68] She joined SANE on its founding in 1957, serving as secretary for the Washington, DC, branch and taking part in lobby initiatives.[69]

Wilson's frustrations with SANE and WILPF provoked the first stirrings of the new group. Writing a letter to *The Washington Post* in 1959, she expressed her concerns for the "disturbing" state of debate over nuclear weapons testing.[70] While many future WSPers admired the commitment of WILPF's "grey-haired stalwarts," they saw the organization as outdated and treated it "with mixed respect and amusement."[71] Meanwhile, SANE alienated its members in 1960 when, following Senator Thomas Dodd's accusation that communists had infiltrated the group, its leaders moved to expel suspected communist sympathizers from its ranks. The situation confirmed Wilson's belief that existing peace groups lacked the seriousness, inclusiveness, and urgency required to prevent nuclear catastrophe.[72] Experiences of sexism also disgusted women members, future WSP founder Donna Allen explaining that SANE appeared "unwilling to move in the direction its women members wished it to go."[73]

Frustration with SANE's male-led hierarchy sparked Dagmar Wilson's determination to act. In early 1961, she gathered some of her female colleagues to propose a robust public campaign on the dangers of radioactive fallout in milk. However, SANE's Executive Director Sanford Gottlieb declined to support it. The Soviet Union's decision to resume atmospheric nuclear weapons testing, followed by the US government's reciprocal response in September 1961, marked the reemergence of nuclear tensions. The danger was further crystalized in the public imagination when British public intellectual and pacifist Bertrand Russell was arrested while peacefully protesting in London. Russell's act of civil disobedience compounded Wilson's concerns. She remembered that it seemed "an unnecessary thing for a man of his stature, his reputation, and his wisdom to have to do."

On a "beautiful autumn, mild evening" in September, Wilson and her husband Christopher held a cocktail party in their Georgetown garden, during which Dagmar aired her antinuclear concerns to the pair's visiting

English friends. Wilson recalled that "as often happens, I find, when people are uncomfortable with a subject, they were rather turning me off with jokes, making sort of rather cynical wisecracks." Sensing his wife's increased distress, Christopher "threw out a casual line, he said, 'Well, you know, women are very good at getting their way when they make up their minds to it.'" Wilson "realized that that was a signal to me to cut it out and I did. But it stayed with me, that phrase." The following day she called SANE's leadership to take a more direct, confrontational stand against nuclear arms. She was, again, rebuffed, as SANE wished to pursue a more conciliatory approach towards the US government. The call was a defining moment in Wilson's life. She recalled pondering her frustrations by the phone. "I thought, I thought, I thought." The failed attempt to rouse action from SANE was, for Wilson, "the last straw." She now realized that "we were in a desperate situation" Wishing to deviate from the sluggish activities of her other organizations, Wilson asked herself "well, what about a women's action?"[74]

A few days later, on September 21, 1961, Wilson held an "exploratory meeting" in her living room. In attendance were the six women who would become known as WSP's founders—Dagmar Wilson, Margaret Russell, Folly Fodor, Eleanor Garst, Mary Chandler, and Jeanne Bagby. However, the meeting had a larger attendance. In correspondence with Amy Swerdlow, Wilson confided that, prior to the meeting, she had only ever met Russell, Fodor, and Chandler.[75] While Wilson arranged the meeting, "all the names to call" came from her SANE colleague Margaret Russell, someone Wilson described as "much more politically active than I."[76] Russell sourced the majority of the meeting's participants from her immediate SANE network and asked her contacts to bring anyone else they felt could aid the cause. Eleanor Garst responded to a specific invite from Russell, as did Folly Fodor.[77] A fellow SANE member, Fodor subsequently spread word around her Quaker acquaintances in the Philadelphia area. She persuaded influential peace activist Lawrence Scott to come along. The former leader of the American Friends Service Committee, Scott had, for several years, aimed to recruit more women into disarmament protest. Scott recognized the "symbolic importance of having mothers as well as fathers on the front lines of protest," less out of a commitment to gender equality than, as historian Marian Mollin argues, an emphasis on "motherly duty" to "children yet unborn."[78] Scott, in turn, asked Jeanne Bagby to attend. In total, Russell invited seventeen people, of whom ten attended.[79]

In addition to the six commonly referred to as WSP's founders, Mary Sharmat attended the meeting, fresh from her Operation Alert protests.[80] Janet Neuman, a director of WILPF who assisted in the resettlement of Jewish German refugees during World War II, and Edith Villastrigo, a former Communist Party USA activist and friend of Dagmar Wilson's in SANE, also contributed to the initial planning.[81] Donna Allen, another influential member of SANE, was unable to make WSP's first meeting, but considered herself a founding member nonetheless given her subsequent input.[82] Many of those who gathered had never previously met, but knew of each other as members of political campaign groups.[83] According to Los Angeles WSP participant Patricia Kempler, most of the women belonged to "half a dozen of the usual organizations," including WILPF, SANE, the League of Women Voters, and the United Nations Association.[84] Such was the activist makeup of the initial group that Allen claimed the intention was for WSP to be an "outgrowth of SANE" that drew from existing activist efforts.[85]

The background of WSP's founders reveals extensive experience underpinning the new group's formation. In her 1963 study of WSP participants, sociologist and peace campaigner Elise Boulding concluded that, "the respondents themselves are not hopelessly atypical of women for peace generally."[86] Folly Fodor had previously formed an "antinuclear mothers' group" in California following the birth of her daughter in 1956.[87] She joined SANE after moving to Washington, DC, when her husband began working for the US Department of Labor. Eleanor Garst described Fodor as one of the more "politically oriented" of the initial group.[88] Mary Chandler also worked for SANE. Heavily pregnant at the time of WSP's founding, she directed her leadership skills toward her work as an international representative of the group over the next ten years.[89] An "early hippie," Jeanne Bagby was a white woman who deliberately lived in integrated areas to show solidarity for civil rights and railed against "man's threat to the natural environment." She too contributed her talents to SANE—her environmentalism having moved her "naturally" to antinuclear activism. Swerdlow noted that Bagby had long been "active in foreign policy dissent and other social justice causes" prior to her involvement in WSP, and Bagby occasionally wrote and published incisive articles for *Liberation* magazine. She attended the first meeting having already participated in pacifist direct action during weeks-long vigils outside the White House.[90]

Margaret Russell and Eleanor Garst were the most instrumental in forming WSP. A Canadian national with an illustrious background in academia, Russell promoted grassroots liberal democracy in the Halifax Co-Operative Society before a "world tour" between 1936 and 1937 led her to adopt "an increasingly critical antiwar view of international affairs." She married in her late forties before settling in Washington, DC, and began serving on the local SANE executive committee soon after. Historian Ian McKay describes her as "a seasoned political historian long fascinated with empire, democracy, and grassroots mobilization." He explains that Russell never became the docile housewife of 1950s stereotypes and never "wavered in her life-long reverence" of and public campaigning for liberal rights and freedoms. She became an integral organizing figure for WSP, using her activist network to bring the first WSPers together and ultimately taking charge "of all arrangements" for the group's first march.[91]

Like Russell, Eleanor Garst brought a lifetime of activist experience to WSP. Describing herself as "a pacifist at the age of ten," Garst actively opposed World War II. As assistant director of the Committee to Oppose the Conscription of Women (COCW), she worked closely with WILPF luminaries Mildred Scott Olmstead and Dorothy Detzer, as well as stalwarts of the peace movement, such as A. J. Muste and Dorothy Day. COCW foreshadowed WSP in several ways, with maternalist opposition to conscription while also seeking to "transform motherhood from women's primary private responsibility into public policy." It was not a women-only body, but 147 of 155 people on its governing board were women. Garst was a key spokesperson for COCW, writing letters and newspaper editorials throughout the war. COCW's "Quaker-style" meetings influenced Garst's later approach to organizing WSP.[92] Following World War II, Garst took executive positions for the American Association for the UN, the United World Federalists, the International Centre, the Race Relations Council, and the National Conference of Christians and Jews. She founded the Los Angeles branch of SANE before moving to Washington, DC, and joining the branch there. Garst wrote relentlessly throughout the 1950s, lamenting the inability of Congress and the Atomic Energy Commission to curb the arms race.[93] She took immense pride in her "self-education," researching and producing her own pacifist and antidraft materials and writing articles for the *Saturday Evening Post*, the *Reporter*, and the *Ladies' Home Journal*.[94] She drafted WSP's initial call for participants that arose out of the September meeting and took credit for writing much of the "essential methodology" that influenced the group's stance. Later, Garst sought the major credit for forming WSP.[95]

Those assembled in Wilson's living room came together hoping to break from the perceived passivity and ineffectiveness of existing antinuclear efforts, but they could not escape the influence of their peers. Presumably unaware of previous organizations such as American Women for Peace, Wilson initially suggested that their group label themselves "Women for Peace," but "everyone groaned." Garst recalled that initial ideas did not "sound very dramatic, or very different" from what Quaker groups, SANE, or the WILPF were currently doing.[96] Having continued their activism in what Leila Rupp and Verta Taylor termed the "doldrums" of feminist activism in the 1950s, the attendees recognized the importance of grasping favorable media treatment in order to press their case to the general American public.[97] "What we need," Garst commented, "is something that will jar people out of their lethargy."[98] Attendees passed around newspaper clippings of Carol Urner's Women for Peace success in Portland as inspiration. Her efforts left a glowing impression on Garst in particular, who became enamored with the dynamic approach to grassroots organizing. Having tried to start her own antinuclear protest action a month earlier, Garst claimed that it was she who "was able to suggest" to the women gathered in Wilson's living room "that it might be possible to stage a one-day protest action."[99]

However, the action that became WSP's hallmark arose from Lawrence Scott's admiration for students' civil rights protests in the South. Historian Marian Mollin explains that Scott hoped that antiwar activists could take the "active nonviolence" of the Montgomery bus boycott and the Greensboro lunch counter sit-ins and apply it to developing a "highly publicized use of mass nonviolent resistance" in the struggle for disarmament.[100] Having previously organized the Committee for Nonviolent Action's (CNVA) Hiroshima Day demonstration and vigil at Nevada's nuclear test site, Scott believed a women's strike might energize the public.[101] Amy Swerdlow acknowledged that the CNVA's antinuclear activism created "a model for direct action by ordinary citizens in opposition to nuclear testing that would be followed by WSP."[102] Sensing the "dramatic impact and the media potential of such an action," the exploratory meeting quickly rallied behind the idea of a one-off, one-day strike for peace.[103]

WSP's founders possessed peerless experience and expertise and could have legitimately declared themselves as the latest phase in a historical line of women's activism. Instead, partly reflecting the lingering McCarthyism of early 1960s American politics and partly a desire to separate themselves from peer groups, WSP's leadership crafted a story of themselves as new, unique, inexperienced, and detached from history. This was exemplified by the manner with which Dagmar Wilson became the group's figurehead. Wilson's importance to WSP's lore goes far beyond her initiative in the group's founding. WSPers across the United States identified with Wilson because of her measured demeanor and calm assertion of maternal concern about nuclear weapons. They venerated her opinion on the issues they faced and foregrounded her in their campaign literature to prove an association with the national network. Although WSP tried to resist hierarchy and structured leadership, Wilson was undoubtedly its de facto national figurehead. She herself later acknowledged becoming a "mythical" figure within WSP.[104]

But stories of Wilson's leadership neglect the careful selection process the founders went through to appropriately head their protest. Initially reluctant to install any leadership of the strike, the Washington, DC, women eventually buckled to the demands of media and members that "there should be a spokesman. Someone who's colorful, good copy."[105] Wilson's shyness originally ruled her out of leadership. She also feared the possible "jail, loss of income, and ostracism" that such a position could bring. However, Eleanor Garst believed that every other potential leader brought something that would prevent any attempt to appear apolitical. Folly Fodor's feminism was too overt; Jeanne Bagby appeared too much of a "hippie." Pre-empting negative press reaction, Margaret Russell was deemed by the group to have too "masculine" an appearance while Garst, whose determination and political convictions made her an ideal candidate, felt her status as an unmarried, twice-divorced woman would detract from the group's message. Ultimately, Wilson "came closest to fulfilling the late fifties/early sixties ideal of nuclear family wife and mother."[106] Garst called her "ideal: with a handsome husband, three pretty daughters, a house in the 'right' area, Georgetown." Wilson remained reluctant. She disliked the spotlight and was "scared to death of having to speak." The others reassured her that she had "something vital to say. You're photogenic, with a good voice and manner. What more do you need?"

"Confidence!" she retorted. After "some sleepless nights," and with an absence of a comparable alternative, Wilson decided reluctantly to accept the responsibility.[107]

The founders reinforced their detachment from the surrounding context in their first public appeal for participants. Deftly written by Garst, WSP's Call to Strike anticipated anticommunist suspicion by downplaying political rhetoric or ideological protests against the Cold War. It likened conflict between the US and Soviet Union to that experienced by "husbands and wives, parents and children" and made clear that individuals could exert themselves in politics the same way mothers intervened in family disputes.[108] Significantly, WSP did not require that participants be housewives or mothers. This speaks to the power of the maternal political identity at the time WSP formed. In this way it mirrored terms set by previous groups such as American Women for Peace and Voice of Women, who expressed the belief that "it is the special responsibility of women—who bear the children and nurture the race—to demand for their families a better future than sudden death."[109] However, WSP's appeal went further, asserting its founders were "appalled at our own audacity, for we're just ordinary people, not experts."[110] Though some of those present at Wilson's house believed that WSP would be an affiliated offshoot to SANE and WILPF, the appeal explicitly refuted links to any other contemporary organizations, emphasized individual action, and affirmed that "we're not asking anyone to sign anything, join anything. Details in your town are up to you." The appeal then explained how the founders wanted word to spread, asking every recipient to "join in a Women's Strike for Peace—and to get her friends and neighbors to do likewise."[111]

WSP's founders set the date for their first demonstration as November 1, giving themselves only six weeks to spread word of their demonstration and recruit nationwide participants. It was an unenviable task, but reflected a pervasive urgency among the antinuclear movement. Investigating why women flocked to WSP, social scientist Elise Boulding found that participants joined partly out of specific concern for fallout, testing, and civil defense, and partly out of fear for nuclear war that were raised by ongoing tensions between the US and Soviet Union. Yet women mainly joined out of "an increasing sense of urgency about the total world situation and a feeling of need to make a declaration of personal responsibility." Boulding wrote that "WSP was born out of a nationwide rush of demonstrating women."[112]

Circulating their appeal after the Soviet Union had unilaterally broken the moratorium on atmospheric nuclear weapons testing, WSP capitalized on a global context of acute and specific international tension, a trigger missing from earlier protests that offered a generalized discomfort with nuclear arms. Further crises over the next six weeks reached their apex just as WSP was about to strike. Conflict over access through the Berlin Wall peaked in late October 1961, leading to direct stand-offs between American and Russian tanks armed with live munitions. Military police twice intervened to rescue American embassy official E. Allen Lightner from East Berlin.[113] Then, on October 30, just two days before WSP's planned first strike, the Soviet Union tested the 50-megaton Tsar Bomba nuclear bomb. The largest manmade explosion in history broke windows as far away as Norway and Finland. The resulting fireball was visible one thousand kilometers away. Significantly, as one of the three parties to the previous testing moratorium, the UK denounced the test as "a crime against humanity" at the United Nations.[114] The Tsar Bomba test catalyzed worldwide public revulsion of nuclear weapons testing and the Cold War arms race. Protest swiftly followed, and thousands around the world demonstrated the day before WSP's strike.[115] In New York City, a protester threw a brick through a window of the Soviet Mission to the UN, "painted with a skull and crossbones on one side," and "50 MG" on its edge.[116] Campaigners for SANE prefigured WSP's language by invoking the threat to children while picketing the Soviet Embassy in Washington, DC.[117] Mothers, pregnant women, and children attended marches in London.[118]

The next day, November 1, 1961, thousands emerged across the country in support of the Women's Strike for Peace. In Washington, DC, *The Washington Post* observed "some 500 schoolgirls, government workers, mothers and grandmothers together with a score of children, half a dozen men and a Collie named 'Candy.'"[119] They picketed the White House and the Soviet Embassy and presented identical letters to Jacqueline Kennedy and Nina Khrushchev imploring them to pressure their husbands into banning all atmospheric testing and developing a more cordial relationship. Although the Washington, DC, strike served as a focal point, events around the country dwarfed activities in the Capital.

The day's largest demonstration took place In Los Angeles as two-thousand women gathered for a public demonstration, assembling at the State Building to confront Attorney General of California Stanley Mosk. Extra police were called to supervise the gathering as demonstrators "spilled onto the lawns and into the street."[120] San Francisco strikers confronted their elected officials; and hundreds from around the Bay Area visited the governor in Sacramento. In Illinois, six-hundred women attended a series of meetings in Winnetka Community House, wrote letters to Republican congressperson Marguerite Stitt Church, and sent telegrams to the UN, President Kennedy, and other political representatives. More than a thousand North Side and South Side Chicago women came together to march through the city, a delegation of whom presented their list of demands to Mayor Richard Daley. Responding favorably, Daley told the Chicago marchers that he would "do everything he could to assist the cause of peace."[121] Women in Philadelphia held a televised debate with their senators in a city courtroom and chastised them for their ineffectiveness.[122] In New York City, two-hundred activists staged protests at the building for the Soviet delegation to the UN and the Atomic Energy Commission offices.[123]

WSPers believed that the success of their initial demonstration rested on their carefully crafted appeal and public image, which persuaded otherwise reluctant supporters to gather behind their cause. However, as social movement theorist Sidney Tarrow explains, the presence of an explicable grievance is, alone, not sufficient to trigger collective action.[124] WSP's achievement instead was a result of the skillful planning of the group's experienced organizers.[125] Each community that staged a WSP demonstration benefitted from the organizational acumen of key individuals who had, from previous endeavors, acquired the expertise necessary to arrange permits, host speakers, and set up meetings with elected officials. Others exploited their networks to secure favorable publicity for the peace strike. Janet Neuman and Donna Allen, key organizers in New York and Washington, DC, used their connections in the news media to cultivate eager support from journalists such as Art Hoppe of the *San Francisco Chronicle*, *London Observer* correspondent Joyce Eggington, and *The Guardian* journalist Sophia Wyatt.[126] Their reporting reached a large audience, building interest in the lead up to the strike and conveying significant publicity afterward.

Frances Herring and Ruth Gage-Colby informed their contacts in governments around the world of WSP's plans, including the British Member of Parliament Anne Kerr and future Secretary-General of the United Nations U Thant. Gage-Colby used her affiliations to deliver a speech to the United Nations in which she extolled the virtues of WSP. Embellishing the group's influence somewhat, Gage-Colby affirmed that she sought "to expand round the world the marvelous grass roots movement WSP begun by Dagmar Wilson of Washington and already spread to the major American cities and London, Paris, Moscow, Delhi and Tokyo to name but a few cities abroad."[127] Frances Herring later spoke of her embarrassment at the way in which Gage-Colby reported on the organization, "because it was so glowing that I felt it was very misrepresentative of our strength."[128]

Delighted with the response, leading WSP figures immediately narrativized the first strike into its founding lore: the perfect example of the irreverent and spontaneous display of maternal outrage that came to epitomize the group. "We can congratulate ourselves on a beginning," declared a mailer sent in the strike's aftermath, urging participants to consider what had taken place as equivalent to a suffrage demonstration. "For the first time since women went out to get the vote 41 years ago," it read, "the New York newspapers have given a women's movement front page coverage."[129] Ads reinforced the domestic identity of WSP's founding members, with a "Women for Survival" leaflet explaining that the strike was "spearheaded by Dagmar Wilson, a DC housewife."[130] An official report of the strike, sent to marchers throughout the United States, said "it is obvious that November 1 has come to be regarded as only the beginning of a truly massive grassroots effort to turn toward peace and a different kind of world."[131]

The first strike was certainly significant, but WSP can be depicted as a conventional response to the circumstances of the Cold War. The strike reflected majority public opinion and supported existing government policy. In a contemporary survey of public opinion, Eugene Rosi argued that the original 1958 moratorium on nuclear weapons testing existed because of the sheer visibility of public antinuclear sensibilities.[132] Responding favorably to Los Angeles WSP's strike, Governor Edmund G. Brown wrote that "peace is everybody's business" and explained that "your demonstration today serves as an expression of public support for our president's determination to achieve a just peace."[133] In fact, memos between American cabinet officials in August 1961 suggested the government encourage "peace paraders, ban the bomb platoons, organization and propaganda of every kind" to publicly castigate the Soviet's breaking of the testing moratorium and demonstrate global support for a weapons test ban.[134] WSP's family oriented, white middle-class image, alongside its specific warning over contaminated milk supplies and appeals to protect American children, echoed the antinuclear priorities of existing social movement organizations and government.

The surge in public and political opposition to nuclear weapons both aided WSP's recruitment and allowed observers to understand its actions as part of a broader context of protest.[135] It was not strange to see large numbers take to the streets in protest of nuclear arms. Peace protest by groups of mothers was a global phenomenon. On the day of WSP's strike, *The Washington Post* reported that the group "followed the pattern of previous outburst against the Soviet tests of the last two months."[136] In fact, WSP's strike was not even the only reported incident of women's peace protest on November 1. Anne Stadler, executive secretary of the Platform of Peace in Seattle, reportedly "stole a march" on WSP by delivering a plea for the cessation of nuclear testing to the Soviet Embassy before their demonstrations. Accompanied by SANE's Sanford Gottlieb, Stadler even met with Special Assistant to the President Arthur Schlesinger, Jr, and utilized the same maternal rhetoric espoused by WSPers who marched later.[137] Subsequently, five-hundred mothers with their children marched to the Soviet and American embassies in London on November 5.[138]

What made WSP's strike more significant than comparable instances of women's antinuclear demonstrations was its narrativization by activists. Frequent references to the first strike in later reminiscences reveal how activists used the strike story as a linchpin. The founding story remained constant, ensuring activists maintained their sense of individual and organizational identity even during transformative change. It also affected historical consciousness and perceptions of WSP's place in history. Keynote addresses at national conferences from 1962 onward invoked the November 1 strike to depict WSP's unique daring and the audacity of the demonstration.

Recalling the first strike two decades later, a 1980 retrospective explained that "in 1961–1962, when WSP began to bring the nuclear issue to public attention, we were daring dissenters, a lonely minority." WSPers believed they therefore deserved "credit for helping to create the climate of opinion" that subsequently sparked both the peace and women's movements.[139] Amy Swerdlow depicted WSP's first action as "something absurd."[140] "The women seemed to have emerged from nowhere," she wrote.[141] Her assessment reflected the attitudes of many activists involved in the group's founding. Philadelphia WSPer Ethel Taylor believed that, given contemporary events and attitudes, WSP embarked on an "unpopular" protest.[142] Eleanor Garst believed that the "small remaining peace movement" was "silenced" before

WSP, and that the group allowed direct action demonstrations to become "routine; but in 1961 they were startling."[143] In 1985 Madeleine Duckles concurred, explaining that demonstrations were "kind of undignified" in the fall of 1961, but that "now, of course, everybody does it."[144]

Even a cursory acknowledgment of McCarthyism explains contemporary attempts to depoliticize postwar activism—and postwar women's activism specifically. Indeed, subsequent attacks on WSP's strike homed in on the prior affiliations of some strikers to suggest that communist infiltrators had "made dupes" of the otherwise "sincere" housewives and mothers of WSP.[145] Had WSP not asserted itself as a spontaneous, unaligned movement of apolitical housewives, these attacks would surely have been worse. Similarly, journalists unaccustomed to reporting such scales of activism also needed to report the WSP story through a comprehensible frame, with the latent sexism of the era's news only being able to accept and transmit a women's action if respectable, white, middle-class mothers spurred it. This influenced how women projected their political identities, and civil rights and women's equality protesters frequently concealed their backgrounds to deflect charges that they were controlled by communist outsiders.[146]

Amy Swerdlow explained that "WSPers believed that their political credibility depended on projecting a ladylike, ordinary image," and journalists and commentators reinforced this belief through coverage that articulated "intrigue with the contradiction between domesticity and political activism." Aware that they needed publicity, "the WSP women were delighted to be described as amateurs" and continued to project themselves as such.[147] The enduring influence of this Cold War paradigm continued to influence historical understanding long after WSP's first demonstration. As Stephanie Coontz argues, recent public reflections of the postwar period still fall into a "nostalgia trap" that emphasizes domesticity and uniformity over stories of dissent.[148] Historian Francisca de Haan similarly observes that pervasive anticommunism caused a historical devaluation of postwar-era women's activism that continues to require correction.[149]

Yet another crucial factor influencing this narrativization of the first strike was founding members' desire to mark WSP as distinct amid a thriving antinuclear scene. Activists knowingly distanced themselves from previous and contemporary antinuclear initiatives to mark WSP as a decisive new addition to the social movement landscape. By invoking their founding as a spontaneous event detached from ongoing initiatives, WSPers created a unique "organizational identity claim" to set their group apart from peers and inform activists' collective identity.[150] WSPers were, after all, aware of links between their actions and previous campaigns for suffrage, peace, and civil rights.[151] Shortly after the first strike, Dagmar Wilson wrote to female members of the UK's Campaign for Nuclear Disarmament and thanked them "for having started a movement which was largely responsible for the birth of the WSP here."[152] However, they did not want to be seen as a continuation of efforts undertaken by others; they did not want to be seen as just another peace organization; and they did not want to be associated with the failures of previous efforts. These factors were part of WSP's identity claim, which required a specific version of the group's founding, based on the publicity needs of its infancy.

The effects of these imperatives can be seen in activists' consistent attempts to maximize their perceived significance by overstating how many attended the first strike.[153] Initial reports struggled to gauge the number of people involved, but organizers exclaimed their astonishment that turnout everywhere "far exceeded expectation." Eventually WSPers settled on an oft-quoted figure: fifty-thousand women in over six-hundred cities, a statistic Amy Swerdlow used to frame her historical study of the group.[154] WSPers embellished this number in later recollections. In 1965 Dagmar Wilson claimed that, actually, "half a million mothers" poured into the streets for the marches.[155] A "highlights of WSP history" list from 1980 claimed that "100,000 women from 60 cities came out of their kitchens and jobs to demand 'END THE ARMS RACE—NOT THE HUMAN RACE,' and WSP was born."[156] A twenty-fifth anniversary celebration for Women for Peace in the San Francisco Bay Area raised the number of cities from sixty-one to seventy.[157] Still further escalation occurred in a 1997 retrospective of WSP history, as Seattle Women Act for Peace claimed that the "national strike brought out one million women."[158]

Even the figure of fifty thousand was a known inflation of the strike's turnout. Through her research, Amy Swerdlow "tallied the highest numbers I can find reported by the strike organizers." Even with "this most generous method of estimation," she could only arrive at a figure "no higher than twelve thousand." While acknowledging this significant disparity in figures, Swerdlow nevertheless continued to describe the first strike with reference to fifty-thousand marchers and consigned her findings to the endnotes of *Women Strike for Peace* where she explained, candidly, that "the number fifty thousand became part of the founding legend of WSP." Beyond the endnote, she never directly refuted the accuracy of that figure.[159] The figure of fifty-thousand women on the first strike, accepted by Swerdlow as incorrect, remains the universally accepted attendance, frequently recited in descriptions of WSP's history.[160] WILPF historian Catherine Foster demonstrated the power of WSP's founding narrative in a single, telling sentence. Narrativizing WSP's first strike, she wrote that "hundreds of thousands of women" left their jobs and homes and take to strike for peace on November 1, 1961.[161]

The impact of WSP's founding story reveals itself in the contortions required to accept activists' version of events. In writing her history of WSP, former leader and historian Amy Swerdlow tried to correct the record surrounding WSP's founding and used the second chapter of her profile to chronicle the extensive history of women's peace activism that served as a "prelude" to her group's formation. Swerdlow's masterful recounting of women's peace history indeed acknowledged and affirmed WSP's continuance of historic organizing initiatives. However, she continued to represent WSPers' "newness" and affirm that WSP participants had no connection to this history. "The WSPers," she explained, "would have been astounded to learn that they were following in the steps of millions of their foremothers who had, for over a century, petitioned, lobbied, and demonstrated against America's major wars and military interventions."[162] But WSP activists not only knew of previous peace and women's activist initiatives—they had actively contributed to them.

In their autobiographies, private correspondence, and public speeches, WSP's founders proudly declared their extensive involvement in peace activities stretching before World War II.[163] Branch records show activists' sustained awareness for the efforts of their predecessors in groups such as the Women's Peace Party. Curious discrepancies therefore appear between the individual autobiographical accounts of activists and the group's organizational memory, as activists claimed extensive personal activism prior to 1961 while simultaneously declaring that WSP was the first thing they ever did. When talking about their own lives, WSP activists told stories of their activism and political campaigning. However, when talking about their lives in relation to WSP, activists changed tack, relegated their prior experiences, and spoke of the group as the first meaningful foray into political activism. Ethel Taylor, despite acknowledging her leadership of various organizations in the 1950s, simultaneously wrote of her political innocence in the years preceding her leading role in WSP. Dagmar Wilson similarly claimed to have "never been in any way politically active before in my whole life" before she began WSP.[164]

WSP's organizers accomplished a significant feat with their first strike, drawing thousands of women in support of a new women-led antinuclear group that drew praise from the press, the public, and politicians. The strike galvanized a vibrant cohort of activists around a simple, moral appeal for life on earth, but its most consequential result was the establishment of a founding image that shielded experienced activists from potential criticism while appealing to a mass constituency. WSP's founding story underscored the group's success, but at the expense of subsequent perceptions of women's history. Despite emerging from a thriving activist scene, WSPers continued to reiterate their spontaneity, rupturing the lineage of women's social movement organizing. As WSP moved from a one-day action into an ongoing concern, it further refined its organizational identity by continuing to separate itself from the historical and contemporary actions of its peers. How WSP positioned itself would continue to have consequences for its place among the broader context of 1960s social movement activism.

CHAPTER TWO

Unorganization

Maternal Organizing, Participatory Democracy, and Black Women's Peace Protest in the Early 1960s

ON THE EVENING AFTER their first strike, East Bay Women for Peace gathered in a school classroom in Berkeley, California, and celebrated the day's success. As she "happened to be the oldest person there," local coordinator Frances Herring commandeered a blackboard and chaired the impromptu meeting.[1] Earlier that day, hundreds of women throughout the San Francisco Bay Area marched as "an army of housewives and mothers" to demand "an immediate cessation to the nuclear arms race."[2] The Berkeley women learned that they had joined thousands of fellow strikers across the country who had taken their appeal to "centers of government throughout the nation." The strike drew fulsome support from public officials. The *San Francisco Examiner* reported the glowing reception WSP marchers received from California Governor Edmund Brown, who exclaimed "I hope your message rings around the world."[3]

Their cause was taken up as elected representatives wrote to President Kennedy in support of the "outstanding women" for their "sincerity, their dedication" to the antinuclear cause.[4] The WSPers sensed their momentum. Herring recalled that "we talked about the fact that we must go on in some definite way here. We can't just have this meeting. We will have a group start now."[5] Berkeley women's enthusiasm was reflected by their colleagues around the country who were "determined to go on working."[6]

WSP experienced remarkable success in its first two years. The enthusiasm sparked by the first strike carried women into continuous operations, as they made space for themselves in the antinuclear landscape with dynamic protests that encouraged thousands to form branches throughout the United States. While navigating this formative period, WSP scored a victory against the House Un-American Activities Committee, took their campaign directly to arms negotiators at the Eighteen Nation Disarmament Summit in Geneva, and celebrated the momentous conclusion of their banner campaign with the passage of the Partial Test Ban Treaty in 1963. Such was WSP's broad popularity that it mobilized thousands of new activists among its grassroots, while also securing the personal endorsement of President John F. Kennedy and UN Secretary-General U Thant. Achieving such success in just two years secured the group's reputation within the antinuclear movement. Yet its most important feat was the development of a distinctive organizational style that encouraged participation without formalizing operational structure, dubbed "unorganization" by its activists. WSP's informal daily functions were deemed so integral to understanding the group that former national leader and historian Amy Swerdlow devoted a chapter of *Women Strike for Peace* to describing how it worked. Activists reflected positively on their loose coordination and autonomous work, with lack of formal hierarchy and leadership becoming a marker of the group's collective identity. While activists were undoubtedly proud of their legislative achievements, the way in which they worked with one another became most significant in their memories.[7]

This chapter chronicles WSP's operations during its formative years to detail unorganization's centrality to activists' collective identity. Following their momentous first strike, WSP activists sought to distinguish themselves in a busy social movement landscape and deliberately dissociated themselves from other activist groups. Constant discussion about branch functions found throughout local archives reveals that WSP's unstructured operations became the most significant locus for this activity.[8] However, this chapter explains that unorganization made WSP a more representative example of the contemporary social movement milieu than its activists wished to acknowledge. The chapter relocates WSP in a broader culture of experimentation with participatory democracy that characterized early 1960s activism, demonstrating a kind of maternalism in a scene more commonly associated with the student-led New Left and later women's liberation collectives.

Nevertheless, unorganization was not without its limitations. Key women struggled with the contradiction of an unorganized operation that required careful management of message, image, and bureaucracy. Meanwhile, WSP's dogged commitment to a single-issue antinuclear campaign complicated its commitment to political inclusivity. Starting in its first few months and continuing throughout the 1960s, WSP expressed wavering solidarity toward Black participants' civil rights concerns. Documenting this history, this chapter reveals lingering limitations of women's peace scholarship that uncritically accepts maternal peace activists' public avowals of inclusive organizing.

WSP navigated a hectic formative period, growing from a loose collective into a coherent apparatus while maintaining an urgent challenge against rapidly escalating nuclear tensions. The group's Washington, DC, founders did not intend to continue their activities beyond the first strike and had not considered that their efforts would lead to a sustained organization.[9] Strike participants similarly lacked an organizational vision. They only knew what they did not want—a repeat of the bureaucracies that, they felt, paralyzed the antinuclear movement.[10]

WSPers similarly had concerns about the reactionary exclusion of suspected communists. Many had been members of SANE when, in 1960, Senator Thomas Dodd, chair of the Senate Internal Security Committee, charged that communists had infiltrated the organization. SANE's leadership panicked and embarked on a purge, demoralizing members, and significantly damaging the organization. WSPers did not want to apply such aggressive suspicions toward their own group.[11] As women in Washington, DC, explained, those who attended the women's strike for peace wanted to continue "on the same loosely-knit basis," only "on a national scale."[12] An early meeting of national leaders emphatically declared that no one wanted "TO BECOME ANOTHER ORGANIZATION."[13] Los Angeles participants affirmed that other groups "get so involved in tinkering with the machinery" they lose sight of their purpose. "Let us communicate and even coordinate," they exclaimed, "but let us never 'corporate.'"[14] At a large WSP gathering the month after the first strike, Dagmar Wilson emphasized "the need to keep the movement loosely structured."[15]

What emerged, in Frances Herring's words "as a side-effect" of the strike, was an unguided cooperative so lacking in formal structure that activists dubbed it "unorganization." In the absence of national direction, local collectives rolled the spontaneous informality and liberty of their first strike into ongoing operations. Each branch of WSP acted distinctly, aligned with one another but not formally organizing together. Starting a WSP action required only two things. First, that participants prioritize a singular purpose to "End the Arms Race, Not the Human Race." WSP made no other political or cultural test for its possible recruits and did not wish to divert attention away from this cause by tackling other social justice issues. Second, to maintain contact and affiliations with their peers elsewhere, planners only had to communicate details of their spontaneous actions with the wider network.[16] Everything else was left for local activists to determine for themselves. Since there was no organization, WSP contributors did not need to sign up for membership, pay any fees, or accept ongoing affiliation.

WSPers also balked at appointing leaders or spokespeople. They wanted their unorganization to empower individuals to protest the arms race however, whenever, and wherever they saw fit. As such, WSP promoted all women as authoritative spokespeople for their area's activities, encouraging participants to assume leadership and educate themselves, and others, on the apocalyptic threat posed to life on earth. Such was the lack of centralization that WSP did not even require branches to use the same moniker. Various names emerged in the weeks after the first strike—from Women Strike for Peace, to Women for Peace, to Women Act for Peace. Activists on the East and West Coasts nevertheless aligned, as did local and national figures.[17] Historian Rhodri Jeffreys-Jones' aptly described WSP as an "organism more than an organization."[18]

WSP broke onto the activist landscape at a time of "effervescent liberalism," described by historian Lisa McGirr as "a climate of change boosted by the energy, dynamism, and youth of the Kennedy administration and a blossoming civil rights movement. It was a time when a deepening atmosphere for reform promised change on the horizon."[19] While the previous decade had demonstrated the power of social movement organizing, by the early 1960s young Americans frustrated with a slow pace of change sought to free themselves from stifling organizational bureaucracy to enact more direct and urgent opposition to a variety of social ills. Black students discarded what they deemed as the ponderous passivity of older civil rights organizations and initiated a sit-in movement that spread, in the words of sociologist Francesca Polletta, "like a fever" across the United States. In the aftermath of the sit-ins, students continued their efforts under the Student Nonviolent Coordinating Committee (SNCC), revitalizing the Civil Rights Movement with dynamic, direct action, and rejection of stifling leadership from ministerial elders.[20] Meanwhile, the Students for a Democratic Society (SDS) shook off its proximity to union organizations to make "a forceful protest against many of the complacent ideas and stolid institutions that seemed so well rooted in Cold War America."[21] This New Left, breaking from the old, seemed inherently youthful.

More mature in comparison, WSP nevertheless fell into the zeitgeist. Its participants' resistance to formalized operations was a rational response to the anticommunism of government authorities that could, and did, use organizational structure as evidence of seditious intent. But unorganization also reflected the mood of WSPers, among leadership and the grassroots, who longed for the freedom to personally direct their own actions. Their experimental process merged with a widespread understanding that previous generations of peace women had failed in their task. "We saw ourselves as new" recalled Amy Swerdlow, as her WSP colleagues distanced their group from previous organizing efforts.[22] Yet, as an initiative "rooted in the networks of everyday life," WSP also took inspiration from earlier generations of women's activists and a range of organizational strategies converged under its banner.[23] Historian Jacqueline Castledine shows that WSP "provided an outlet" for former Progressive Party activists, revealing that these activists' previous experiences influenced how the group designed its organizing strategy. WSP's "maternalist rhetoric, nonhierarchical organization, loose networks of communication led by 'key women,' and refusal to purge Communists or former Communists from its ranks" was one that Progressive women had sought to employ for years prior. Helen McMartin, one such former Progressive Party activist who contributed to WSP's formative years, wrote about her experiences in leftist magazines and portrayed the group "as a peace organization in the tradition of the Popular Front and the natural home for former Progressives."[24]

Much of WSP's organizational flexibility arose because its WILPF-affiliated participants wanted it. WILPF historian Catherine Foster indicates that her group used WSP as a useful alternative outlet for "rapid action in a crisis" when their own bureaucratic process prevented it.[25] WSP's approach to organization was replicated in women's groups across the political spectrum. For example, despite their political differences, WSP shared its informal organizational setup with the conservative women of the John Birch Society. As Michelle Nickerson writes, the Birchers emulated "a grassroots networking pattern that was already expansive because women had been devoting hours of their unpaid labor to its development for several years," having "relied on members to expand the organization through their own friendship networks."[26]

Unorganization reflected the social movement experimentation of the era, but it remains exceptional for its ability to balance the amateurish disorder that enthused inexperienced recruits and the professional, prestigious legacy of women's peace activism represented by a strata of "key women" that emerged in WSP's first few weeks.[27] Described by Amy Swerdlow as an "informal leadership clique," this group did not exert formal authority, but their influence remained fairly static throughout the organization's existence.[28] "Recognized standing in WILPF or other peace groups" granted women influence, as did "personal friendships with the Washington founders or other national leaders, professional standing or media recognition, powerful husbands, and personal economic resources for travel and communication."[29] Yet, unorganization also demonstrated WSP's ability to overcome interpersonal friction. Younger and inexperienced activists were, in fact, eager to allow more experienced women to coordinate activities, especially as they could simultaneously assert that they were not being led, since hierarchy did not officially exist.[30] WSPers entered constant dialogue over their administrative processes, incorporating "movement relations, concepts and practices into their everyday lives" and having every participant acknowledge and limit how they exercised authority.[31] Even as branches gradually adopted more formal structure over time, they retained an animation that led WSP founder Jeanne Bagby to describe unorganization as "the lifeblood of the movement."[32]

Bagby's characterization reflects what social movement scholars call "identity work," the process by which individuals in a group "overcome dissonance between themselves and the groups to which they belong" to "bring the collective identity into correspondence with individual members."[33] Maryann Barasko's illuminating study of social movement governance in the National Organization for Women (NOW) reveals that activist groups rarely derive identity from organizational process in this way.[34] This can be seen in WSPers' bullish admonishment of their peers, whose hierarchical bureaucracies they considered "as a roadblock" to progress.[35] In early 1963, Los Angeles WSPer Kay Hardman wrote to then SANE National Executive Homer Jack to assert that other peace organizations were destined to fail. Referring to SANE, she said that it "may be in the tradition of the unfortunate groups, whose purpose was so politically limited, philosophically narrow and expediently-based that a change in the political balance of power in the world caused immediate death." For Hardman, the manner of WSP's organizing made it exceptional. She saw it as nothing less than "an advance in inter-human relations."[36] WSP leader Lyla Hoffman concurred. Writing in WSP's newsletter, *Memo*, in 1963, she observed that "WSP was born into an already crowded field—SANE, WILPF, CNVA, FRIENDS and many others were actively functioning." And yet the women of WSP saw their movement as something new—something urgently needed within US society. Hoffman added, "[W]e had our own reason for being. We filled a void."[37] Eleanor Garst, in her own unpublished draft of WSP's history, remarked that WSP made other pacifists "scornful of the enjoyment the average woman gets from her peace work." WSPers, she wrote "are joyful—they do enjoy peace work—because it relieves them from the dreadful frustrations of waiting, passively, for destruction. They can cheerfully throw themselves into a cause which is constructive and life-oriented."[38]

The influence of unorganization on WSPers' identity separated both activists and their group from the surrounding social movement landscape. To sustain this separation, WSPers adopted terms to describe themselves and their organizational functions as clearly distinct from any other group. Categorically denying characterizations that they were simply members of an organization, they instead asserted that WSP was, in and of itself, an entirely separate movement of women.[39] In Eleanor Garst's account for the September 1962 edition of the *Magazine for the Fellowship of Reconciliation*, WSP was not just another movement but "*the* women's peace movement" itself. WSP "is a movement and not merely another organization," she wrote.[40] WSPers did not identify as peace activists per se, but as women going through a transformative experience in their political lives. Nevertheless, they similarly resisted identifying as participants in the women's movement. Neither a peace group, nor a women's group, nor willingly a part of a wider women's peace movement, WSPers challenged traditional social movement analysis.[41] WSP's claim of being a different kind of movement made it difficult for allies, the public, and the press to situate the group—both contemporaneously and historically. This complicates historians' attempts to connect WSP to contemporary allies. It also fractured the lineage of women's peace history, of which the group was a part, by making WSP appear to have emerged from nowhere rather than being a continuation of previous efforts. Peace historian Harriet Alonso took issue with this characterization, importantly observing that WSP represented one organization within a broader movement. However, descriptions of WSP as a movement persist, which negates the robust history of women's peace activism that existed before 1961, fragmenting women's peace history in the process.[42]

This distinction also affected how WSPers related themselves to women's peace history, as reflected in Amy Swerdlow's revealing lament of her own attitude toward past efforts. She recounted meeting WILPF's international security Gertrude Baer at the Eighteen Nation Disarmament Conference in Geneva in 1962 and opined that she had not given her "the respect and admiration I have since come to feel for her important role in women's peace history." Initially dismissing Baer as "an opinionated old woman," Swerdlow's later studies educated her about such events as the 1915 International Congress of Women at the Hague and WILPF's 1932 Geneva conference, in which Baer played a significant role. She used this incident to explain WSPers' attitude toward activist history, one in which her own "ignorance" continued to cause her "shame and pain."[43] There was more to this attitude than just a lack of historical knowledge. WSPers were aware of the past; they understood their place in a lineage of women's peace activism. However, "we regarded history as irrelevant," explained Swerdlow, as WSPers disparaged their forebearers for failing to achieve disarmament.[44]

Acknowledging that WSP functioned as one organization within a broader social movement milieu forces a reconsideration of its links to other organizations, most notably among the New Left. For their part, leading New Lefters and WSPers distanced themselves from one another. Amy Swerdlow recalled a meeting during which SDS leaders Tom Hayden and Rennie Davis criticized WSP's participants. "We're going to be around a lot longer than Amy Swerdlow," she remembered Hayden saying, "like, 'you older women don't count'" while Jerry Rubin dismissed the "little old ladies" as "timid and scared."[45] Swerdlow responded by distancing WSP from the New Left context. She observed that it grew "around the same time" as other antihierarchical organizations, but explained that WSP was "exceptional." "The women of WSP," Swerdlow argued, "unlike the young men in SDS, gloried in their 'outsider' standing."[46] Despite observing WSP's growing leadership clique, Swerdlow furthermore asserted that WSP had an altogether different attitude toward leadership that set it apart from SDS and SNCC, which she believed "made much of their named and acclaimed leaders." While Amy Schneidhorst notes the appreciative support WSP activists provided younger students, these moments of generational discord evoke a sense that WSP was not, at the time, considered a part of the New Left community.[47]

WSP's organizational form nevertheless made it more like the New Left than activists claimed.[48] Decision-making by consensus was an essential function that WSP shared with contemporary New Left groups.[49] Andrea Estepa argues that WSPers expressed dissatisfaction with the lack of attention that nuclear strategists paid to the voices of individual Americans and proclaimed that participatory democracy was an important tool for including the public in the antinuclear debate. In its Call to Strike, WSP avowed that women should upend public deference towards the government by involving themselves in military matters, and they repeated this appeal throughout its early years.[50] Such a declaration of participatory democracy presaged SDS's more acclaimed and "profoundly influential" 1962 political manifesto, the Port Huron Statement.[51] The broad critique of the American political and social system was celebrated as forming "the essence of the New Left and the Movement throughout the High Sixties," and continues to spur rigorous analysis of its intellectual foundations and legacies.[52] WSP's views, argues Estepa, "would have fit comfortably" with that foundational text, but are not afforded such rigorous analysis, nor celebration.[53]

In fact, participatory democracy perhaps came more naturally to the experienced housewife activists of WSP than to student groups. As Sylvie Murray finds in *The Progressive Housewife*, women activists in suburban Queens understood the term "good citizen" to mean "the people of a community who are consistently engaged in public affairs . . . public meeting-goers and joiners of voluntary organizations who discuss and deliberate with others about the politics that will affect them all."[54] In this sense, as it allowed women to transition from the Progressive activism of the 1950s into the unorganization of the 1960s, WSP provided a direct, unbroken link between the housewife-organizing of the postwar era and the student New Left. Although the direct influence of WSP's Call to Strike on the Port Huron Statement is difficult to ascertain, SDS leaders were encouraged by the group's example. In her illuminating exploration of democracy in social movement organizations, Francesca Polletta noted that the leading influences in SDS took their cues directly from WSP. "Some among

SDS's leaders had had exposure to consensus-based decision making," she writes, with "the contingent from Swarthmore College, students who had been involved with the Congress of Racial Equality (CORE) and Women Strike for Peace, and some others."[55] SDS leader Mickey Flacks thought of WSP as "the most participatory organization of its time." At twenty-one, she joined WSP alongside SDS because it offered "a new vision of how to operate politically."[56]

Indeed, WSP's promotion of informed citizen participation in democracy was not just a platitude. Within a few months of forming, it set up numerous research committees designed to liberate women's "creative ideas for peace" and democratize the science of nuclear weapons testing and radioactive fallout. Through its research committees, WSP produced independent research reports to educate the wider public about the various dangers of US militarism.[57] A memo from June 1963 demonstrates the range and depth of WSPers' work, listing a Committee on Disarmament, Economic Reconversion, Peace Education—Schools, Peace Education—General, a Committee on Political Action, a Committee on Radiation Hazards, and an Anti-Shelter Committee.[58] Southern California WSP declared that "we women are acutely aware that the education of our children will determine their ability to deal wisely with the affairs of our small planet."[59] Through its suite of research groups, WSP published numerous in-depth reports based on the diligent investigations of its activists.[60] Journalists and editors sought out WSPers for their knowledge of nuclear issues, and WSP took pleasure in educating the nation's opinion-makers.

Although it is difficult to measure tangible effects on policymakers, WSP had a definite influence on the manner with which test ban negotiations took place. Much as Richard Rothstein recognized SDS' reputation for being "the intellect of the student left," WSP's committee work places it among the intellectual drivers of the 1960s peace movement. WSP's reach is certainly comparable to SNCC's Freedom Schools or SDS's work through its Economic Research and Action Project. Historian Andrew Ross writes that, through its research committees, WSP "articulated a sense of civic duty that focused on independently vetted information, public education, and a factually balanced discourse" that it deemed essential "for the civilian-state relationship to function well." Ross points to WSP activists Marion Brown and Margot Feuer, who wrote that "an informed citizenry is an effective citizenry. We need your brains, your heart, and your action for

PEACE." Ross's claim that WSP created an informational network builds on the understanding of WSP as a communication network, which is also indicative of the civic responsibility unorganization intended to foster in the lives of its participants.[61]

WSP's contributions to contemporary women's rights organizing are more difficult to ascertain. Throughout the 1960s, its participants did little to challenge the traditional, White, middle-class expectations that kept many American women as housewives. The group in fact exploited this expectation by protesting in floral dresses, white gloves, and high heels, accompanied by children in baby-strollers to heighten the legitimacy of women's antinuclear views. But WSP's participants, as a whole, did not express a desire for greater political involvement. When speaking to the press, they publicly declared that they would happily return to their "pots-and-pans" once they had achieved their aims." Dagmar Wilson assured the public that "we are not striking against our husbands. It is my guess that we will make the soup that they will ladle out to the children on Wednesday."[62] Historian Catherine Foster explains that WSP's eschewing of feminist politics reflected the approach of other contemporaries such as WILPF, and contemporary peace organizations generally refrained from aligning themselves with the aims of the women's rights movement, even if individual participants did.[63]

Yet WSP's influence on women's rights is uncertain. Historian Petra Goedde contextualizes the gender politics of WSP's rise through the contemporary disagreement between feminist philosopher Simone de Beauvoir and the anthropologist Margaret Mead. Whereas de Beauvoir negatively cast maternal protest as self-sacrifice and asserted that housekeeping "condemned women to servitude," Mead positively paralleled "peacekeeping" and "housekeeping," arguing that maternal antinuclear protests demanded "the patience and fortitude and the endless unremitting efforts that are so much more characteristic of a woman's than a man's role in society."[64] To Goedde, WSPers reflected Mead's side of the issue. But de Beauvoir's condemnation of maternal protest aside, she supported WSP's campaign against nuclear proliferation and wrote a message to WSP in 1964 to "align myself with all the women campaigning" and to "assure the women of the 'Strike for Peace' of my solidarity."[65] WSP's popularity and public avowals of inclusivity, juxtaposed with its reluctance to embrace the women's rights agenda of some of its own leaders made its non-feminist public image particularly noteworthy.

When Betty Friedan published her 1963 treatise *The Feminine Mystique*, she directed particular scorn toward WSP and Dagmar Wilson directly, asking "why does the professional illustrator who heads the peace movement say she is 'just a housewife,' and her followers insist that once the testing stops, they will stay happily at home with their children?" Women in the peace movement, Friedan pointedly remarked, "must make their contribution not as 'housewives' but as citizens."[66] On the one hand, Friedan's criticism of WSP was hypocritical, as she herself downplayed her own activist past to make her feminist critique more palatable to the general public, as revealed by historians such as Daniel Horowitz.[67] On the other hand, while Friedan chastised WSP's maternal peace activism, WSP's key women such as Bella Abzug, Shirley Lens, and Mary Clarke expressed a more politically advanced and comprehensive understanding of feminist agency than contained in the pages of *The Feminine Mystique*. Historian Leandra Zarnow explains that Abzug in particular saw the book "as purposely avoiding a racialized class critique of domesticity in which Friedan was well schooled."[68] At the time, Abzug's influence was certainly less persuasive or influential, or impactful on the political sensibilities of WSP activists, and was not visible publicly. However, its presence is obvious retrospectively.

Recognition for WSP's contributions to feminist organizing can be found more clearly in absentia, through historical and scholarly analysis of comparable organizations that emerged later in the decade. Examining the influence of WSP's unorganization shows its reach. In Francesca Polletta's thorough analysis of American experiments with participatory democracy, she writes that "more than any of the movement groups I have treated thus far, feminists in the late 1960s and early 1970s made the internal life of the movement the stuff of political experimentation." But WSP's archival record and activists' own declarations demonstrate that the group's maternal activists performed this experimentation much earlier. Even Polletta's contention that feminist groups suffered internal pressures, unintended side effects of nonhierarchical organizing, is evident in WSP.[69] Similarly, writing about both the National Organization for Women and the Women's Marches of 2017, Kelsy Kretschmer explains that "activists and scholars alike have argued that the ideal type of feminist structure is closer to nonbureaucratic, nonhierarchical, participatory, with democratic decision-making" and a nonhierarchical "horizontal approach to leadership" that prides itself on organic, grassroots efforts and inclusivity.[70] Such descriptors map seamlessly onto WSP's own system of unorganization. Not only did WSP's welcoming environment entice and politicize thousands of women, but its unorganizational methods remain an overlooked contribution to women's organizing strategies of the twentieth century. "It was never given enough credit for this," SDS' Mickey Flacks told Amy Swerdlow in 1980.[71] That remains the case.

Unorganization facilitated dynamic action. Free to move quickly and decisively following their first strike, WSP activists continued to hold demonstrations in their communities on the first of every month and maintained national visibility through large profile-raising actions. "Milk Day" demonstrations on December 1, 1961, scheduled in seventy cities, drew thirty-five hundred women to protests at the UN in New York.[72] Smaller, local initiatives kept grassroots figures engaged in cities unrenowned for progressive activism, an example of which was the protest outside the Indiana statehouse, which brought thirty women together on a cold Saturday afternoon on December 30.[73] WSP came into its own the following year, fortifying its presence in the US peace movement while extending its global reach. Its first international action on January 15 brought WSP women from across the United States on a "peace pilgrimage" to the capital, coinciding with similar visits to capital cities by peace women around the world in the First International Women's Peace Action. Nearly two thousand WSPers from New York, Connecticut, New Jersey, and Pennsylvania traveled to Washington DC aboard a Peace Train chartered by the women themselves, described in news reports as "the longest ever" to leave New York City's Pennsylvania Station.[74] They picketed the White House for hours in pouring rain. Having watched the demonstration from a White House window, President Kennedy praised the "great number" of WSPers and acknowledged that they should consider "that their message was received."[75]

News of WSP's protests carried internationally and its leaders built relationships with peace organizations around the globe. In March 1962, WSP's national body arranged for a delegation of fifty women to confront the Eighteen Nation Committee on Disarmament that was meeting in Geneva. Sponsored by the United Nations, the conference aimed to curtail nuclear weapons testing and build trust between the US and the Soviet Union. WSP was chagrined that the US government had appointed no women to its negotiating team and so set out to "make their presence felt."

Women embarked on silent marches and vigils outside the conference, while also taking opportunities to challenge diplomats directly. Dagmar Wilson lectured US diplomat Arthur Dean "like a schoolmistress" while Amy Swerdlow, pregnant at the time, recalled that her "particular confrontation" with Soviet UN Security Council Representative Valerian Zorin was "one of the most significant moments of my life."[76] Returning via the United Kingdom, WSPers spoke publicly with their British disarmament counterparts, securing their status as reputable and energetic participants in the international movement. WSPers formed an ongoing partnership with the British MP and disarmament proponent Anne Kerr, inviting her to picket in front of the White House during talks between President Kennedy and British Prime Minister Harold MacMillan later that year.[77] In July 1962, a selection of WSP's leaders organized a controversial but productive exchange with counterparts in the Soviet women's peace movement. A documentary, narrated by San Francisco WFP leader Frances Herring, gave a month-by-month account of all activity undertaken by her branch, highlighting the ongoing attempts of activists to raise public awareness and lobby their elected representatives.[78] WSP's achievements set it apart as a decisive new addition to the international antinuclear movement. Indeed, such was its impact that the RAND Corporation think tank investigated the upsurge of peace activism, claiming that the growing support for "non-military alternatives" among "more influential people in our society" deserved serious consideration.[79]

WSP's early visibility and effectiveness arose from the inclusiveness and accessibility of its dynamic protests, which were billed as welcome to all who wished to join. Some key women determined that any demonstration organized by WSP had to capture women who had never acted politically before. An event "wasn't successful," New York WSP's Cora Weiss stated, "if it wasn't a first for lots of people."[80] While wishing to mobilize newcomers, WSP also ensured that experienced activists were not ostracized from antinuclear activism because of their political affiliations. A policy paper from 1963 declared that the most important factor in WSP's success was "the all-inclusiveness of the movement. You don't have to be a Christian, or a Jew, or a Buddhist; you don't have to be religious at all. You don't have to be a Democrat, a Republican, an anti-Communist amateur or professional, a Communist, Fascist, Socialist."[81] Eleanor Garst's commentary served as a seamless conclusion to this statement: "you just have to be a human being."

Garst continued her avowals of WSP's inclusivity in her unpublished history of the group, explaining that it was "the simplicity of the philosophy that binds the women together. It is the profound belief that mankind deserves a future. There are those who criticize the movement's lack of dogma—but this is precisely its strength. Deliberately geared to the lowest common denominator of agreement among the world's women, it concentrates on unification rather than hair-splitting." WSP did not demand a particular ideological view—all one needed to become a WSPer was to "shout NO! to annihilation of the species. Presto you're a Women for Peace. The women, of course, have expanded the peace movement by promoting the discovery that peace is not just for pacifists."[82] Historian Andrew Ross concludes that WSP achieved nothing less than the expansion of "the parameters of American democracy."[83]

WSP's committed resistance to anticommunist fervor helped recruit participants but also made it an easy target for government suspicion. Over ten years, the FBI accrued 49 volumes of reports containing eyewitness accounts and organizational documents about WSP.[84] Suspicion that some women may have been FBI informants bred paranoia, but WSP participants adeptly dismissed anticommunist attacks by unashamedly declaring their inclusivity.[85] Far from hiding what they were doing, activists sought to publicly declare their views as much as possible. A clergyman once confronted New York WSPer Esther Newill and, taking issue with her politics, claimed, "I'm going to tell people what you're doing." Newill shot back, "Good! That's what I'm trying to do! I want people to know about our activities!"[86]

A crucial moment came in December 1962, when the House Un-American Activities Committee held three days of hearings to try and expose the extent of communist infiltration in the peace movement generally, and WSP specifically. Usually, the suspicion from HUAC alone caused targets to cower. However, WSP responded defiantly. Over three days of hearings its activists publicly, politely ridiculed HUAC's histrionic questioning.

The HUAC affair became a defining episode in WSP's history for its display of maternal resistance to Cold War hysteria. In the *Washington Evening Star*, Mary McGrory described how Blanche Posner lectured "the committee members as though they were recalcitrant boys at DeWitt Clinton High School in the Bronx, where she had taught."[87] Dagmar Wilson's appearance drew particular praise from Russell Baker of *The New York*

Times, who explained that she treated Counsel Nittle "exactly as if he were a rather trying dinner partner."[88] Amy Swerdlow interpreted the HUAC hearings as a battle between "male, HUAC" perceptions of social movement organizing "and those of the female, WSP."[89] For Swerdlow, the HUAC hearings' importance lay in its demonstration of "outraged moral motherhood," which allowed activists to challenge HUAC "with more courage, candor, and wit than most men had done in a decade of inquisitions, WSP raised women's sense of political power and self-esteem."[90]

Amy Swerdlow described that WSP's "folksy" maternal image illuminated the hearings, but HUAC also proved incapable of red-baiting the group because of the fluidity and informality of its unorganization. It allowed Ruth Meyers to downplay HUAC's charges of communist infiltration by responding that "Women Strike for Peace has no membership."[91] Counsel Alfred Nittle struggled to understand, asking "if a group has no organization and has no members, how in the world does it function?" Iris Freed's reply became renowned. "It is quite remarkable. Sometimes I wonder myself."[92] Accepting that a sketched plan for a WSP Central Coordinating Committee existed on paper, Anna Mackenzie informed Nittle that it was "something that you have given great stature to and made it sound almost as important as a congressional committee. In Connecticut, we don't take it very seriously."[93] Lyla Hoffman similarly attempted to explain that her influence in WSP did not mean that she had an appointed position, nor that policy was directed to women from an executive.[94]

Dagmar Wilson's disarming performance at HUAC was especially effective. Last to the stand, Wilson continued to rebuff all accusations leveled at WSP by calmly explaining the group's unorganizational form. Challenged over comments in which she described herself as "the head" of WSP, Wilson replied that "we are really all leaders." As Counsel Alfred Nittle desperately tried to prove communist infiltration within WSP's ranks, Wilson politely maintained that political affiliations did not matter as "nobody is controlled by anybody in the Women Strike for Peace." Comments toward the end of her testimony proved the subversiveness of unorganization. Counsel Nittle returned to a common tactic deployed by HUAC, in which acceptance of communists was compared to acceptance of Nazis. Nittle challenged Wilson "whether you would knowingly permit or encourage a Communist Party member to occupy a leadership position in Women Strike for Peace." Wilson, predictably, responded that she had "absolutely no way of controlling, do not desire to control, who wishes to join in the demonstrations." Nittle spied his opportunity. "Would you knowingly permit or welcome Nazis or Fascists to occupy leadership positions in Women Strike for Peace?" he asked, hoping that he could illuminate Wilson's hypocrisy, and therefore prove that WSP had communist sympathies. However, to the committee's surprise, Wilson did not budge. She quipped, simply, "if only we could get them on our side." "In fact," Wilson explained, "I would like to say that unless everybody in the whole world joins us in this fight then God help us."[95] Unorganization, and its subsequent requirement for inclusivity, destroyed HUAC's attempts to intimidate WSP.

Despite its celebrated place in WSP lore, the HUAC hearings also forced activists to confront the politics and practicalities of disarmament for the first time. WSP participant and feminist writer Barbara Deming neatly summarized the group's dilemma. Deming often served as a "prod" to WSP's conscious over ideological issues. She expressed her apprehensions over the HUAC encounter in a public "Letter to WISP" six months after the hearings. Deming emphatically determined the heightened strength of WSP, declaring that "a move intended to make us doubt ourselves and each other served in fact to sharpen our sense of why we are acting and to bind us more closely together." However, she expressed concern over "whether or not the stance we take is clear." Deming especially questioned the group's attitude toward unilateral disarmament—whether WSP supported the radical idea that the United States give up its atomic arsenal even if international rivals did not. In an earlier meeting with Arthur Schlesinger, Jr., members of WSP scoffed at the suggestion that they supported such a position. Deming tested this stance: "Suppose an attack upon us by the Soviet Union . . . would we be in favor of retaliation? To spell it out: would we at that point be in favor of slaughtering children? It is hard for me to imagine any woman in our movement . . . giving any answer but 'No.' Yet if that *is* our answer, then we are unilateralists." Deming feared that WSP would struggle to maintain its coherence, or even challenge government officials if the group avoided taking a stance on complex political issues. In the absence of such clarity, Deming asked if a more accurate reflection of WSP was that "we take a resolute stand," but that the government could "count us as temporarily willing, if it just can't be helped."[96]

WSP's reluctance to clarify the specifics of its positions—whether on civil disobedience, pacifism, or the efficacy of arms control treaties—was a problem throughout its existence.[97] Some argued the benefits of such ambiguity about peace work far outweighed the necessity for cohesion. In contrast, Deming suggested that, by failing to define its positions, WSP had become a confused organization. Her article succinctly captured the dilemma facing WSP. The group wished to remain flexible, inclusive, and uncoordinated in order to appeal to as wide a base of support as possible; but doing so meant not deciding official organizational positions on a range of political issues. At the time, key women determined that the solution was to remain committed only to a single-issue—nuclear weapons testing and disarmament.

Accurately gauging the true measure of WSP's constituency remains difficult, because of the group's lack of official membership and lists of its participants. Nevertheless, a 1963 study by sociologist and peace activist Elise Boulding provides insight. Titled "Who Are These Women?," Boulding's report reveals a highly educated and professional group made up of committed activists largely accustomed to life in the peace movement.[98] Sixty-five percent of respondents to Boulding's survey had an undergraduate degree or higher, compared with the contemporary average of six percent among American women. A majority (sixty-two percent) came from families with existing commitments to the peace movement, which Boulding observed "points to the presence of happy non-conformist middle-class families united in their goals in a conformist sector of society." Boulding described WSP participants as "an earnest, thoughtful group of society's favored ones, the educated middle-class professionals and wives of professionals." She also found that WSP did not attract just young and inexperienced activists either, the research "indicating that neither WSP nor older peace groups have any monopoly on either youth or age." An unforeseen consequence of its organizational informality was that it became difficult for those without the time and money to sustain their voluntary participation.

Similar to historian Lisa McGirr's findings about the ascendancy of women's conservative activism in California in the early 1960s, the most influential and sustainable WSP branches emerged in affluent communities in which women could rely on supportive community networks to facilitate their hours of voluntary work.[99] To be sure, not all WSP participants shared the financial heft of philanthropist and New York WSP founder Valerie Delacorte, or Cleveland WSPer Anne Eaton, wife of industrialist Cyrus Eaton, both of whom played instrumental roles in WSP's early operations.

But it was not uncommon for WSPers to hold fundraising get-togethers in the parlors and tennis courts of activists' homes.

On the one hand, WSPers' wealth and social status speaks to an undervalued factor of the group's success—that it was a collective of affluent, well-connected individuals whose societal status provided exclusive opportunities to press their influence on the influential. Women such as Ruth Gage-Colby, Ava Helen Pauling, Anne Eaton, Valerie Delacorte, and Frances Herring brought with them prior relationships and contacts with high-profile journalists, international activists, and political figures. The presence of elite figures among WSP leadership meant that the US government actively communicated with WSP, seeking support during test ban negotiations and asking directly whether the group would back President Kennedy when he wished to resume testing in April 1962.[100] It was through Ruth Gage-Colby that WSP received personal recognition from UN Secretary-General U Thant. However, WSP's key women seemed to willfully disregard matters of wealth and class. While respondents to Elise Boulding's survey felt "that more effort must be made to get working class and uninformed, unaroused people into the group," Amy Swerdlow lamented the "good deal of insensitivity to class differences and to economic inequalities among the White women" of WSP.[101] Unsurprisingly, within WSP's unorganization, leadership and influence required the middle-class privileges of discretionary time and money, and representation at international conferences became an increasingly tense matter as only those who could afford to travel were deemed able to represent WSP publicly.[102]

Key women's disregard of class and wealth divisions manifested in cold detachment and, to a degree, "signs of contempt" toward others.[103] Writing of her experience at the Spring 1962 Geneva Disarmament Conference, Vermont WSP activist Virginia Naeve described WSPers' "aloofness on a very basic level." Asked to accompany WSP because, in her words, "they wanted a rural woman and one of low income," Naeve reflected positively on what the group achieved by confronting international diplomats on the nuclear crisis. But she separately described WSPers who "tried to hurry" overworked waiters and "did not accept the hospitality" they received in Geneva "with any graciousness. They did not sense the importance of these small kindnesses." Furthermore, Naeve believed that the American WSPers did not interact well with their European counterparts. She reported that an English attendee told WSP "with much emotion and finally tears" that "we did not understand what some of them had gone through to get there. She had stood on a crossroads with a small sign and shilling by shilling had waited until she had enough to come. A shilling is about 14 cents. Along with the shillings she took encouragement and insults. A Swedish woman finally told us that all her life she had saved her money for a small house, but when she heard we were coming, she took all that money and paid the fare for five German women to come to Geneva. These declarations came only when the Europeans saw that the doubts of some American women seemed to be overbalancing the whole group's action." "Sadly," wrote Naeve, "it was the American women who could not see that to succeed we must be one and all."[104]

WSP's claimed inclusiveness and single-issue stance briefly eliminated tricky conversations about its politics and priorities. However, the group's unwillingness to consider organizational support for civil rights struggles meant it could not access extensive, vibrant networks of Black women peace activists. Recent scholarship brings this into focus. Jacqueline Castledine illuminates the influence of Eslanda Goode Robeson, Shirley Graham Du Bois, Charlotta Bass, and Thelma Dale Perkins who asserted that "international peace required the successful negotiation of both racial and geopolitical differences." As Castledine observes, "peace did not linger on the margins of their feminist, civil rights, and labor movement work. Rather, it was at the very center of their activism." Dayo F. Gore and Vincent Intondi have similarly highlighted the influence of Black women radicals on international organizations such as the Women's International Democratic Federation, WILPF, and Congress of American Women.[105] Future WSP activists were part of this milieu. Founding activists Jeanne Bagby and Ruth Pinkson both campaigned against segregated housing. Virginia Naeve regularly contributed directly to civil rights organizing and supported Mississippi Freedom Summer.[106] Cora Weiss's extensive efforts deserve note. Weiss organized a speakers' bureau in Wisconsin that brought foreign students to the state to talk about their experiences living overseas. After travelling through West Africa in 1957, she became actively involved with the American Committee of Africa in New York and organized a one-thousand-person dinner for Ghanaian President Kwame Nkrumah in 1958 with sponsorship from the American Committee on Africa and the NAACP. Weiss also coordinated the Africa Freedom Day rally at Carnegie Hall in 1959 and directed the African-American Students Foundation from 1959 to 1963, through which she brought nearly eight-hundred East African students to study at US universities.[107]

By the end of the 1950s, however, white women's progressive organizations began to separate civil rights from other social justice concerns. Castledine explains that the political and financial exigencies of local organizing, especially for progressive groups like the American Labor Party (ALP), "led executive committee members to view peace and civil rights as competing, not complementary, issues." She writes that "when New York's ALP dissolved in 1956, joining such organizations as the Progressive Party and Congress of American Women, it marked the end of many broad interracial alliances among women who had lobbied for significant change in local communities."[108]

WSP maintained the separation of peace and civil rights issues after its formation in 1961. A memorandum issued a month after forming declared that "we subscribe to a single unifying purpose—to develop, as rapidly as possible, support for general and complete disarmament on a multilateral basis under effective international control." Such was the investment in this sole purpose that the group promised to disband when a "disarmament program is so well under way as no longer to need our support."[109] Historian Georgina Denton explains that "despite its universal maternal rhetoric," WSP firmly compartmentalized racism as separate from peace. "While most WSPers claimed to support civil rights in principle," she writes, "many were wary of diluting WSP's anti-nuclear message and alienating potential support."[110]

Black women nevertheless made significant contributions to WSP activities. Coretta Scott King pursued her pacifist concerns by joining WSP on early marches and retained a powerful influence on its activists even when not in attendance.[111] In San Francisco, it was long-time civil rights stalwart Frances Mary Albrier who led the demonstration of Berkeley strikers into the home office of their congressional representative at the first strike for peace.[112] Dora Wilson travelled with WSP's delegation to The Hague in 1964 to protest NATO's plans for a Multilateral Fleet. Virginia Naeve described eighteen-year-old Wilson as perhaps "the most important person to have gone" on the trip because of her dynamism and drive.[113] Clarie Collins Harvey is also consistently overlooked. A leader of Mississippi-based Womanpower

Unlimited, Harvey travelled to Geneva with WSP as a member of its first international delegation before journeying again as part of the group's Vatican Peace Pilgrimage the following year. She frequently extolled the importance of linking peace and civil rights activism, believing that "activism of both races was necessary to improve race relations."[114]

As an organization, Womanpower Unlimited "placed a high priority" on combining antiracism and peace activism. Tiyi M. Morris' illuminating history of the Mississippi organization fills gaps in WSP's history, describing how Womanpower Unlimited encouraged its activists to approach WSP as an additional avenue of peace and civil rights protest.[115] Though "few in number," women of color extended their influence beyond a mere physical presence.[116] As Joyce Blackwell writes in her history of WILPF, Black women brought "concepts not traditionally used by White peace activists."[117] In WSP's case, Clarie Collins Harvey connected the white activists she met to "tangible ways to support civil rights activism" alongside their peace work. Although WSP never became multiracial, it developed a broader, more radical critique of militarism that included racial and economic justice, almost entirely due to the urging of Black women within its ranks.[118]

Black women experienced overt exclusion and racism within WSP. Just two months after the group's formation, a committee meeting highlighted "the absence of Negro, Japanese-American and Mexican-American women" among WSP participants.[119] Attendees made several suggestions to improve, but major problems emerged in Detroit that had ramifications for WSP's entire national body. Since its formation in November 1961, Detroit WFP wrangled over how to appropriately challenge what it saw as two separate "battles": war and racism. Black women joined WFP on every demonstration, with signs reading "End Racism" and "Desegregation, not Disintegration." But Detroit WFP wouldn't let them carry signs that mentioned race and prevented march participants from making statements about civil rights issues on the grounds that they obscured WSP's appeal for nuclear disarmament.[120] Eleanor Garst observed that, "as the initiating group," Detroit WFP "felt that only peace signs should be carried; that to merge the issues created confusion and alienated women (and men) who could see that peace was essential but did not yet see that discrimination is a form of war."[121] In response, Black participants formed the Independent Negro Committee to End Racism and Ban the Bomb, a separate organization that determined war, violence, and racism to be inseparable issues demanding immediate, concurrent challenge. Asserting that their interest in peace and justice was "not a question of civil rights but of human rights," the Independent Negro Committee linked disarmament to the scourge of police violence that reflected immediate dangers of racism in American society.[122]

The Independent Negro Committee was shunned by WSP's national body during planning for the 1962 Geneva disarmament conference. WSP's selection of representatives to serve their delegation was criticized for its exclusivity; first, because the significant financial burden required from anyone making the trip limited its reach to only the most affluent of activists; second, for its lack of Black representation. New York WSPer Edith Ziefert sent out an advertisement stating that "local communities are encouraged to raise funds to send their own representatives." The Independent Negro Committee reached out, wishing to "see the women's peace movement strengthened and broadened" with the inclusion of Black representatives. However, their request was denied. Initially, WSP's coordinators explained that they wished to limit the delegation to fifty women and could not secure more space for their party. However, the Committee alleged that WSP "didn't want to 'overbalance' the group with Negroes." It implored Dagmar Wilson to allow more representatives to attend, even under separate cover. WSP, however, maintained its limit. Claiming they wished to maintain a single-issue protest against nuclear weapons, WSP's leaders were unwilling to "dilute" the campaign by including an appeal to civil rights, even tacitly, by having more women of color among their numbers.[123] Coretta Scott King and Clarie Collins Harvey became the only Black members of the fifty-strong delegation.

The issue did not subside. In June 1962, WSP held its first national conference in Ann Arbor, Michigan, and eighty-two women from twelve states met for the first time. Exchanging stories of the "remarkably good" response they had received for their efforts, the attendees also intended to formalize aspects of their organizational structure. Reporting on the conference for San Francisco WFP, Elsa Knight Thompson explained that the conference allowed WSP to take "the first faltering steps" toward becoming a national organization.[124]

But a matter which had not been on the agenda arose when Kathleen Aberle said that four women from Detroit's Independent Negro Committee, who had applied to attend, were refused on the grounds that they were "a separate organization."[125] Amy Swerdlow observed that "this was strange, indeed, as the premise of the conference was that all women who identified with the WSP movement were welcome." It emerged that white Detroit WFPers had simply refused to allow their Black colleagues to be part of their delegation to Ann Arbor.[126] Aberle, who was herself attending the conference as a member of another organization, the New England Voice of Women, pleaded for the four to be admitted. After "a bitter and painful discussion" and "a period of silence," WSP invited the women of the Independent Negro Committee to join their conference.[127]

Conference reports reflected deep recriminations and a failure to appropriately address WSP's stance.[128] A majority of attendees complacently believed that WSP was already "a living demonstration of integration in action."[129] Gail Eaby, a WSP coordinator from Southern California, wrote in her conference report that "it was decided that we would attract people by the very example of our integrated demonstrations."[130] It was therefore "not necessary, and merely confusing to state explicitly" that it supported civil rights.[131] Dagmar Wilson asserted, "we all realize that civil rights without nuclear disarmament won't do any of us any good" and insisted that WSP therefore prioritize antinuclear campaigns.[132] Elsa Knight Thompson, writing a report for her colleagues in San Francisco WFP, revealed that one white attendee's zeal for inclusivity had them insist WSP accept segregationists if they supported disarmament.[133]

Black participants pushed back, firmly asserting the urgency of the civil rights cause. Grace Boggs told the conference that "if we must continue to live as we have lived—then let the bombs fall! Life just isn't worth it, for the Negro America."[134] Another Black attendee explained that "if the next hundred years are going to be like the last, we don't care whether there is peace or not." Black women challenged WSP's first conference to view peace and racial justice as intertwined, just as progressives in the 1950s had. Instead, Elsa Knight Thompson described these statements hitting her "like a physical blow."[135] Eleanor Garst recalled "shock and disbelief on the faces of good-hearted middle-class white women."[136]

The conference set out to resolve the issue with a vague policy statement that could be interpreted as individual activists and branches saw fit.[137] The Statement of Principles, also known as the Ann Arbor Statement, nevertheless superseded the guidelines local branches had drafted for themselves.[138] It underlined the notion that WSP did not have strict organizational requirements, and instead cherished "the right" and accepted "the responsibility of the individual in a democratic society to influence the course of government."[139] Arguably the most important outcome of the conference was the declaration that WSP was "open to all women." The second line declared, emphatically, that "we are women of all races, creeds and political persuasions." However, the conference simultaneously decided, by consensus that, WSP's disarmament campaign "should not be diluted or obscured by other objectives."[140] Its ambivalent stance on civil rights and its tendency to exclude Black women remained in effect. In lieu of a direct statement of policy, conference attendees published an open letter to Coretta Scott King, herself a regular participant of WSP's early demonstrations. "We identify ourselves with the heroic effort of Negro citizens," it read. Furthermore, although it declared that "our goals are inseparable," it described the movement for civil rights as a "part of the movement for a world of peace, freedom, and justice," to which WSP had dedicated itself.[141]

Local groups were instructed to use this letter in place of a dedicated national policy statement on racial justice, but WSP did not allow its women to represent themselves as WSPers while marching for civil rights. The ambivalence provoked branches to adopt their own, more determined support for civil rights causes. Whittier WSP in Southern California soon wrote to the regional hub in Los Angeles to denounce the "glaring absence" of Black, Latina, and Asian women at the national conference. They railed against the assertion that WSP represented "women of all races, creeds, and political persuasions" while the national group "cannot speak for the women in the United States unless we can show the world that we are in fact composed of women of all races and creeds."[142] Los Angeles women were dissatisfied with this declaration and issued their own, more declarative statement of allyship—"we call upon all women working for peace and freedom to dedicate themselves to the struggle of the Negro people for freedom."[143] Portland WFP offered "a key resolution expressing our 'identification' with the movement for civil rights."[144] San Francisco WFPers Alice Hamburg, Hazel Grossman, Sarah Humes, Betty Winter and a "Mrs. Aaron Chapman" urged WSP to initiate a trip to Mississippi to show solidarity with Freedom Summer campaigns.[145]

Responding to her interactions with Womanpower Unlimited, New York WSP activist Eunice Armstrong wrote that "WSP could learn a lot from your methods and your organization." Several individual WSPers saw the benefits of working more closely with civil rights groups such as Womanpower Unlimited. With no WSP branch in Mississippi, it presented "an excellent opportunity to raise awareness among Jacksonians."[146] Although Dagmar Wilson disagreed with associating WSP with civil rights causes, her fellow Washington WSPers often supported campaigns by organizations such as the Congress of Racial Equality.[147] However, it took until later in the decade for WSP, as a national body, to unequivocally offer its support to Black women.

Attempts to maintain organizational flexibility while maintaining a single-issue stance only partially explains WSP's messy take on civil rights issues. Generally, white WSP activists simply lacked racial awareness. Just after the first national conference, the World Without the Bomb Conference drew 120 people around the world to Accra, Ghana, and extended an invite to WSP. Its staging in the newly independent African state, a symbolic site of global Black liberation led by Kwame Nkrumah, secured the assembly's emphasis on merging the matters of nuclear weapons and colonialism.[148] WSP activist Gail Eaby believed the group had been invited to send a delegation because the conference wanted WSP's message to be "heard by the neutral and emerging nations in person."[149] However, seemingly oblivious to the idea that African American struggles reflected those of African nations, WSP put together an all-white delegation to attend the conference.

As Tiyi M. Morris observes, "there was seemingly no thought of what the perception of WSP might be if they did not include Black women. Such blindness speaks directly to the organization's homogenous orientation and myopic focus."[150] After progressive WSPers expressed consternation, the group re-selected its delegates. Eleanor Garst declined her nomination to attend but expressed ambivalence over whether a white or Black WSPer should take her place. Eventually, Clarie Collins Harvey and Selma Sparks joined Frances Herring and Nancy Mamis on the excursion. Tiyi Morris' analysis of each WSPers' post-conference thoughts further reinforces the shortcomings of WSP's racial consciousness. Harvey and Sparks spoke to the event's location as a site of global anticolonial struggle, underscoring a "comprehensive definition of peace" that drew connections "between disarmament and the dismantling of colonial rule." Mamis and Herring's accounts, in contrast, overlooked the implicit connections between peace, colonialism and freedom. Instead, "they focused solely on the logistics of the conference and issues related to disarmament."[151]

WSP's problematic record mirrors other white women's peace organizations, but its activists' historical narrations mark it as more problematic.[152] For example, Melinda Plastas critiques WILPF's checkered record, probing whether initiatives for greater diversity reflected attempts to improve race relations or simply an unsuccessful effort to "increase Black interest in the peace movement." Nevertheless, Plastas finds that WILPFers understood that their failure to attract women of color was their organization's burden and that, if the peace movement did not represent Black women, it was because their group had made peace seem "so detached from their own suffering."[153] In contrast, WSPers recalled that their inability to welcome women of color was not only a negligible feature of their group's past, but also attributable to those constituencies themselves. Discussing their group's outreach to Latin American women in the community at a 1979 meeting, one San Francisco WFPer claimed that "most Latin-American women are totally absorbed in rearing families and/or augmenting family income."[154]

National Coordinator Ethel Taylor recalled that her difficulties in attracting Black women to the group arose as they were more concerned with tackling violence endemic within their own neighborhoods. "So many groups of people have such immediate problems," she explained, "basic problems like food, housing, jobs, etc. To also join in the struggle against the arms race is almost a luxury they can't afford."[155] Dagmar Wilson similarly appraised the group's problems, stating that "we hardly speak a common language" and acknowledging that Black mothers faced unique hardships that prevented their participation in WSP.[156] "We didn't know what approach to take to bring these women in," recalled Ruth Pinkson, "they were so concerned with their everyday, bread and butter existence—just to get a job, to keep their kids off the streets and so on, that peace was not their immediate concern."[157] Berkeley activist Rose Dellamonica said that "there wasn't a connection" for Black women to join peace movement activities and that "they didn't identify with it."[158] Amy Swerdlow observed that WSP activists "rejected any concept or tactic they thought to be too radical to be understood by the so-called average woman," and believed that "they were not violating their moral principles" by doing so.[159] It follows then, that in rejecting civil rights as a priority issue, WSPers cast the "so-called average woman" as white and seemingly unaffected by racism.

These recollections have had profound repercussions for American women's peace history, leading to white-centric narratives that overlook Black women's contributions. Indeed, antimilitarism was assuredly a Black women's issue. Gerald Gill writes that, throughout the 1960s, public opinion polls "consistently reported that Black women were *the* segment of the populace" most opposed to US militarism overseas. Citing the example of Angela Davis and various Black mothers' antidraft initiatives, Gill argues that scholarship on the antiwar movement and theoretical literature on the feminist politics of peace overlooked this.[160] Writing in 1984, Black women's peace protester Wilmette Brown explained that "Black women have always been giving leadership to the peace movement as a whole by fighting on all the issues of Black women's survival internationally, issues which are still not recognized as 'peace issues.'" She declared that "the biggest ripoffs of the peace movement have been to hide how it has always been Black and White."[161] This distortion of Black peace activism was writ large in a San Francisco WFP historical assessment from 1985. According to WFPers, it was actually the white women in WSP who were "among the first to see the important relationship between the Black liberation movement and the peace movement."[162]

The historically problematic framing of women's peace activism as a white interest is shown in Harriet Alonso's critical but revealing discussion of her own studies. "As I have studied this arm of the peace movement," she wrote, "I have been very aware of its White, middle-class nature, especially in the leadership," a true reflection of groups like WSP and WILPF. Alonso sensitively examines the failure of "these peace women" to "diversify their memberships." However the unintentional framing is still that peace activities were something that only white women had a natural interest in, and that it was the prerogative of white women's organizations to encourage Black women to join them.[163] Race and the women's peace movement is examined through white women's failure to persuade Black women's participation, rather than on recognizing that Black women's interpretation of peace as a radical, interconnected social justice issue was too thorough for WSP to comprehend.

Although scholars highlight the difficulties of white women's peace organizations to attract women of color, they continue to marginalize the Black experience in peace protest. Joyce Blackwell's study of WILPF is especially thorough, explaining that "if Black women were not marginalized by these studies, the conclusions drawn by these historians about racism within WILPF might be different."[164] In a similar vein, WSP activists' recollections of their group's relationship to the Civil Rights Movement does not extend beyond acknowledging that Black women "had pressing concerns" that prevented their involvement in peace activism. Such statements attempt to justify the limited participation of Black women without necessitating an interrogation of WSPers' certainty that theirs was an inclusive group.

Following months of fraught deliberations, the US Congress ratified the Partial Nuclear Test Ban Treaty in September 1963, banning nuclear weapons tests in the atmosphere, outer space, and underwater. WSP activists were entitled to celebrate it as their own achievement. Philadelphia leader Ethel Taylor wrote to the *Philadelphia Inquirer* to exclaim "that self-congratulations are in order for everyone who worked to build up the climate of opinion that helped to make the Nuclear Test Ban possible." She explained that "many senators have, in fact, referred to the influence of the 'Mother's Vote' as a factor in shaping their decision to vote for the treaty." Politically progressive journalist I. F. Stone similarly praised WSP's influence. UN Security-General U Thant, an enduring admirer of WSP's work, received Dagmar Wilson, Helen Frumin, and Lorraine Gordon to thank them for their group's efforts.[165] WSPers were not naive enough to think that their work was done, however. Testing could, after all, continue underground with few impediments. Nuclear weapons production would continue unabated. Wilson was certain that the treaty marked a milestone for the organization, but remained realistic about the agreement itself. Amy Swerdlow and Miriam Kelber, the editors of the *Women Strike for Peace Newsletter*, told readers to remain vigilant. The treaty simply meant "a change of locale for the arms race, rather than a major reversal. It also means a continuing threat of radioactive contamination."[166] Reflecting on the treaty's passage ten years later, Ethel Taylor said it was "less than half what we wanted."[167] Still, activists felt palpable exhilaration over what they had accomplished.

Two years after its founding, WSP could reflect on remarkable success. The vibrant dynamism and inclusive atmosphere of its public demonstrations drew thousands to WSP actions in cities across the country. Furthermore, WSP's unorganization offered a more substantive and influential contribution to the burgeoning social movement landscape than even its own activists wanted to accept. While historians and activists alike place the sphere of women's peace activism into a separate bubble of social movement organizing, WSP made substantive contributions to the student New Left and burgeoning women's liberation movement. Nevertheless, the visible impact of WSP's antinuclear demonstrations was set against its exclusionary attitudes toward women's race and class differences. To cohere its unorganized masses, WSP avoided making declarations supporting the urgency of Black women's civil rights concerns. As such, histories of women's peace activism must reckon with the problematic and ongoing exclusion of poor women and women of color from narratives of the period. In the years to come, WSP's diversion to a long, arduous, and fractious period of protest against American military intervention in Vietnam further complicated attempts to cohere its disparate base.

CHAPTER THREE

Radicalism/Respectability

Alice Herz and Usable Militancy During the Vietnam War

AT AROUND 9 P.M. on the cold, blustery night of March 16, 1965, Alice Herz stood outside Federals Department Store on an unassuming street corner in northwest Detroit. Alone and with few witnesses, the eighty-two-year-old leader of the local Women for Peace branch reached into her purse and took out four cans of Energine cleaning fluid. She emptied the contents over the shoulders of her coat and, striking a match, lit herself on fire. An explosion burst into the street. Passing motorists realized with horror that someone stood consumed in the flames. Leaping from their cars, they rushed toward Herz, covering her with their coats as they attempted to beat out the flames. Their efforts only temporarily spared her life. Ten days later, in Detroit Receiving Hospital, Herz succumbed to her injuries. A note, discovered by ambulance crews shortly after the incident, exclaimed that she had "chosen the flaming death of the Buddhists" in order to "make [herself] heard." She willed the American people to "awake and take action! Before it is too late." With her startling last act, Alice Herz became the first person outside Vietnam to self-immolate in protest of the Vietnam War.[1]

WSP embarked upon an arduous campaign against American military intervention in Southeast Asia. A running joke among WSP activists held that the Vietnam War was "a not-so-funny thing" that "happened on the way to disarmament." The quip, so widespread that it became the working title of Ethel Taylor's memoir, encapsulated the perceived attitude of most in WSP that the war was an unwanted distraction from their antinuclear activities. "We were sidetracked," Taylor declared.[2] Rather than a distraction, WSP's opposition to the Vietnam War between 1963 and 1968 secured its place in history. Individual WSPers had quietly agitated against American military involvement in Southeast Asia since the signing of the Geneva

Accords in 1954, but as the conflict escalated, the peace movement responded with increasing urgency, becoming more militant as the war endured.[3] WSPers similarly grappled with the appropriate response, turning from their customary tactics of marches, letter-writing, and fundraising to embrace increasingly radical acts of civil disobedience. Activists literally banged their high-heeled shoes against the doors of the Pentagon, chained themselves to the White House gates, were beaten bloody by Capitol Police, received death threats from their critics, and arranged trips to meet Vietnamese women who the US government designated "the enemy."[4]

On its face, WSP's militantly antagonistic streak—well-documented publicly and celebrated by its activists—disrupts the idea that maternal peace protest is moderate and staid. However, activists and historians alike follow the stubbornly persistent trend to cast radicalism and respectability as irreconcilably conflicting positions.[5] WSP's public expression of "traditional motherhood" required it to manage its organizational image and portray itself as respectable, rather than radical, which meant downplaying the militant acts of those such as Alice Herz. Such individuals have since been forgotten historically.[6] Recent scholarship has attempted to reconcile WSP's militancy with its respectability and places the group into a "transitional space" between "tradition" and "radicalism"; others apply a sliding scale, aligning the group's history with other stereotypical accounts of the 1960s to observe a gradually increasing radicalism that grew to replace moderate and respectable protests over the course of the Vietnam War.[7] Yet even these accounts mischaracterize how radicalism and respectability, and militancy and moderation blended during WSP's experience of the Vietnam War.

This chapter focuses on two WSP episodes to reveal that maternal women's protest was among the most militant in US social movement history. First, the chapter illuminates Alice Herz's life in unprecedented detail, revealing her as a unique historical actor who, in idea and action, pushed the boundaries of women's political protest.[8] Her self-immolation violated understandings of appropriate action even among the most radical activist circles and still confuses philosophical discourse on nonviolence, with wildly differing perspectives across culture, geography, and gender. Self-immolation remains impossible to place among considerations of nonviolent versus violent protest. For the purpose of this chapter, I describe self-immolation as violent, which is in keeping with studies, such as Louise Brådvik's that distinguish between violent and nonviolent forms of suicide. However, I would nevertheless consider self-immolation as a form of nonviolent protest, in keeping with the beliefs of Buddhist monks such as Thích Nhất Hạnh. Responding to more recent acts of self-immolation in protests for Tibetan independence, the Dalai Lama stated that "self-immolations were acts of non-violence."[9] Nevertheless, Herz's WSP colleagues could not reconcile her life and death with their own sensibilities.

However, this chapter shows that the group was more accepting of other militant acts—so long as they could be curated and exploited to boost the perceived effectiveness of WSP's maternal peace protest. It draws attention to WSP's infamous 1965 Jakarta Meeting with Vietnamese women, which was rightly applauded for bringing together people from warring countries and demonstrating their ability to wage peace. But the meeting nevertheless put WSP in direct conflict with their government. It unnerved many of the group's participants who believed, both at the time and in later recollections, that the meeting pushed both the group and its participants too far. Ultimately, WSP was split on the issue of civil disobedience, and the group was a more nebulous mix of radical militant and staid liberal moderates than often acknowledged. Its record highlights that the most radical, militant, and subversive actions in the history of American dissent was performed by the supposedly staid housewives of the women's peace movement. WSP's anti–Vietnam War experience therefore challenges the radical/respectable dichotomy in women's peace historiography. Militant acts complemented its moderate image, and activists and historians alike pick and choose which actions fit a definition of useful militancy within women's political activism.

WSP's constituents frequently disagreed over the appropriateness of their Test Ban protests. Elise Boulding's 1963 survey of activists found that many did not feel comfortable taking part in any form of public protest, and they were "unable to use the categories of 'enjoyed' or 'not enjoyed' to describe" their experiences of demonstrations. One feared that she looked "like an idiot" by participating in street marches. The majority of participants in early actions took to letter-writing and public education as these were "the least non-conforming" acts open to them.[10] In part, as New York WSPer Cora Weiss explained, this perception of respectability encouraged recruitment and "created entry levels for people into the peace movement."[11] Nevertheless, such beliefs and activities complemented a radicalism and militancy that had served WSP since its founding. Leading figures did not oppose civil disobedience in principle, nor were they afraid to take risks, and the national body generally supported activists who were willing to accept public ire.[12] Their conscious appeal to middle-America forced WSP's leaders to publicly "frown upon unlawful behavior," but WSPers frequently risked jail during their Test Ban protests.[13] A picket of the Nevada nuclear test site in July 1962 led to the arrest and imprisonment of WSP activist Mary Harvey.[14] Definitions of radicalism remain amorphous and arbitrary, and WSP perhaps falls short of the "radical pacifism" embodied by some of its antinuclear peers.[15] But its ideas and actions satisfy more expansive definitions, such as those offered by historians Kathleen Blee and Jo Freeman, that include anyone who envisions "fundamentally new social arrangements" that would "so completely change our society [that] it would be unrecognizable."[16] WSP certainly met this criteria.

With the achievement of the Partial Nuclear Test Ban Treaty, antinuclear groups lost some of their momentum and, as described by historian Paul Boyer, moved from "activism to apathy."[17] WSP pivoted from protesting weapons testing to other arms issues, spending 1964 coordinating an energetic campaign against plans for a nuclear-armed NATO Multilateral Fleet. However, it struggled against declining interest. Dagmar Wilson wrote to her fellow activists late in the year to urge their continued participation, yet even she had scaled back her activities, her secretary explaining in correspondence that she had "temporarily 'retired'" from activism.[18]

With US military intervention in Southeast Asia steadily increasing, it did not take long for WSP to pivot toward a different, looming crisis. WSP's Barbara Bick explained that three years' experience opposing nuclear weapons "has been, in a sense, a training school preparing our women for the present national crisis."[19] Believing that "it was only necessary to bring certain facts to the attention of those making decisions," the initial stage of WSP's campaign against the Vietnam War was characterized by a calm, moral case to the public and elected officials.[20] WSP deployed its tried and tested protest repertoire. An early statement from Peninsula WFP, based in Palo Alto, California, stated that "as American women we are shocked and ashamed that our government is supporting militarily and financially the regime which is perpetrating these atrocities."[21] Toward the end of 1963, San Francisco WFP denounced Madame Nhu, the de facto first lady of South

Vietnam, for her excoriating comments against South Vietnamese peace protesters. They expressed their "shame" that American participation had exacerbated "terrible events" in the region.[22]

Continuing through 1964 and into the following year, WSP participants continued with the protest imagery that had marked their earlier support for a Nuclear Weapons Test Ban. Three hundred WSPers picketed the White House on February 10, 1965, carrying with them petitions gathered from women from thirty-three states who were sympathetic to lobbying for a negotiated peace in Vietnam. While disparaging the cause of their protest, *The Washington Post* nevertheless described the politeness of the marchers, explaining that they "took their picketing positions with practiced aplomb, staying close to the fence and within a given distance between two trees."[23] It took the startling act of an eighty-two-year-old from Detroit to spark more belligerent efforts.

Alice Herz campaigned tirelessly for peace throughout her life. Born in Hamburg in 1882, she worked for the German section of WILPF from 1916 before the rise of Nazism forced her and her daughter, Helga, to flee Europe as Jewish refugees. They spent time in Gurs internment camp before catching one of the last refugee ships to leave occupied France. After time at sea, they spent months languishing in an internment center in Cuba, the experience cementing an already strong commitment to peace and social justice with first-hand exposure to war and the refugee experience. With help from family in the United States and friends in the American Friends Service Committee, Herz and her daughter eventually secured entry visas and settled in Detroit in January 1943.

Alice renewed her involvement in the peace movement shortly after arriving. She re-joined WILPF and, growing concerned with the nuclear arms race during the 1950s, joined SANE. Herz petitioned for naturalization in the United States in 1953 but, even after ten years living and working in the country, her refusal to swear an oath to take up arms in the event of war prevented her from attaining citizenship.[24] She also exerted equal energy toward civil rights, spoke passionately about the plight of Black Americans, and reportedly forced her way into Cobo Hall in 1963 to hear Martin Luther King, Jr., deliver an early version of his "I Have a Dream" speech.[25] Such devotion to social justice causes often aroused suspicion from local authorities. Her incessant campaigning yielded a sizeable file with the Detroit Police Department's "Subversive Squad," a police sergeant describing her as "what I'd call a go-er. I don't think she ever missed a meeting." They knew she was "always out on the march."[26] She worked tirelessly into her eighties, her WILPF colleague Lucy Haessler explaining that "you never saw such energy in anyone—she could travel all night by bus and picket all the next day."[27]

Herz possessed an "enormous thirst for knowledge" and produced a catalogue of writings for German, Swiss, and American publications while developing a status as a radical internationalist and intellectual pacifist leader.[28] Lucy Haessler explained that she was "one of the most universal human beings" she had ever known.[29] A polyglot, Herz taught German at Detroit's Wayne State University and fluently spoke Esperanto, the artificially constructed auxiliary language designed to boost international understanding between different cultures.[30] Her commitment to building a global community of peace and social justice activists saw her maintain affiliations and close friendships with peace groups and pacifists around the world, particularly with Japanese pacifist intellectual Prof. Shingo Shibata, with whom she shared decades of correspondence.[31] One hundred and fifty people attended her eightieth birthday celebrations, although Herz herself claimed to be "too busy for parties."[32] Jewish by heritage, she developed an interest in Quaker teachings and regularly attended the First Unitarian Universalist Church of Detroit. On one occasion, Herz was asked to leave a Quaker meeting for speaking too much.[33] She also read extensively about Muslim, Hindu, and Bahá'í spirituality.[34] Friend and fellow WSP activist Haessler remarked that Alice "never stopped learning—lectures, meetings, study groups, book criticism clubs—any source of enlightenment attracted her."[35] She subscribed to magazines from around the world and kept stacks of past issues around her modest Detroit apartment. Her relative recalled Herz's place as "crammed full of books and magazines" with a "long hallway lined on both sides with mysterious stacks covered in sheets—all publications!"[36]

Testimony from Herz's friends and family speaks to her activist energy, but her radical politics did not stand in opposition to her devotion toward her family. She was the most radical of an extended family who were all drawn to political activism, and Herz adored helping to raise her children, nieces, and nephews with a passion for peace and social justice.[37] After her son, Konrad, became blind, Herz taught herself braille in order to better his education and her communication with him. She became so proficient that, following her son's early death in 1928, Herz decided to teach other children how to read braille. "That was the kind of woman she was," explained a colleague.[38] When her daughter, Helga, secured a place at the University of Grenoble, Herz accompanied her to ensure her safety as Nazism threatened to overtake Europe.[39] Jan Kempe, a surviving relative, recalled that, as a child, she had admired a magazine with a "panda bear on the front cover," and Alice gave it to her as a gift. The magazine subsequently "disappeared from my house." She realized only later in life that her parents had likely discarded it as it had come "straight from Communist China!"[40] The anecdote encapsulates how women like Herz subvert expectations of a radical/respectable binary, showing that radical political actions and values easily coexist with traditional values of maternal respectability. Indeed, despite the militancy of Herz' activism, a Detroit police sergeant affirmed that they never had cause to arrest her.[41]

Herz's tireless public activism ensured her influence within Detroit's social movement scene. A news clipping from December 1961 shows her meeting the Republican mayor of Detroit Louis C. Miriani. Making light of herself, she sent a photograph of the meeting to Shingo Shibata explaining that she was, "on the right side, the smallest person." A member of the First Unitarian Universalist congregation in Detroit, Herz became part of a thriving civil rights activist scene. Indeed, the church counted among its ranks Viola Liuzzo, who was murdered by the Ku Klux Klan while supporting voter registration drives in Mississippi. In an instance of remarkable historical coincidence, Herz and Liuzzo, regular members of the same Detroit church, died for their separate causes on the same weekend.

Herz remained a committed participant in the local WILPF chapter until her death, but the formation of Detroit Women for Peace energized her optimism and hope for disarmament in the early 1960s. She brought her radical politics and a wealth of experience to cofounding Detroit WFP in 1961, writing to Shingo Shibata excitedly about their first activities.[42] She declared that WFP had "cleared the way toward genuine peace. We cannot go back to the old, damaging way."[43] Though juggling commitments with myriad other organizations, Herz emphasized that "no more peace group seems to me more indispensable than WSP."[44] Much admired by her colleagues, she was the branch's national contact point, attended national conferences as Detroit's representative, and was ever-present at regional meetings. She made sure to use her status and influence to connect WSP's national operations to broader global peace networks. Just a year before her death, Herz sent a letter to WSP's Washington, DC, branch to proclaim her excitement for the group's future. "How I regret not to be 28 years old," she wrote, "but 82!"[45]

Toward the end of 1964, the optimism that previously characterized Herz's outlook began to shatter. Although Helga spoke of her mother's "outward-looking attitude" to any concerns, and that she never displayed "a morbid, self-occupied state of mind," Alice began expressing her horror in correspondence with friends. She lamented the "turmoil and dangers of our times" and expressed pity for "this turbulent world."[46] Events in the early months of 1965 led to her final denunciation of American violence. On March 2, 1965, the US Air Force commenced Operation Rolling Thunder, a massive bombing campaign in Vietnam that signaled the beginning of direct American military intervention. Rolling Thunder would continue for the next eight years. The following Sunday, March 7, state troopers and local police forces brutally beat unarmed civil rights activists who took part in a nonviolent march through Selma, Alabama. In an instance of macabre foreshadowing, Helga remembered her mother reacting particularly sensitively to the self-immolations of Buddhist monks in South Vietnam.[47] Lucy Haessler, a Detroit WFP and WILPF colleague and close friend, recalled speaking with Alice in early March, and Herz explained "that this was just the way things had been in Germany. Everything seemed to be closing in."[48] Visiting her friend again on March 15, Haessler found Herz "in a state of great agitation, saying she could not be interrupted, she had a big piece of work to do that she must finish." Haessler assumed it involved a piece of writing and "so was not worried" by her being "preoccupied."[49] The following day, Herz went onto the campus of nearby Wayne State University to make copies of what she was writing—her last testament. She later travelled the five miles from her home to the corner of Oakman and Grand River Boulevard in northwest Detroit. Just before 9 p.m. on March 16, Herz performed her act of self-immolation.[50]

Herz concisely expressed her feelings in terms familiar to WSP supporters in her last testament and final letters to friends and family, posted the night of her self-immolation. She began by addressing "the Nations of the World" and UN Secretary-General U Thant, whom she "trusted more than any other present day leader," before railing against the violence being waged by President Lyndon Johnson, and accusing him of using "his amassed capacity of '400 times OVERKILL' to wipe out, 'if necessary' whole countries of his choosing."

The statement connected the violence in Vietnam to that shown toward civil rights workers in the South in a way few of her contemporaries managed. She explained that she saw the struggle for peace and freedom "as being indivisible." Herz further expressed that she wished "to protest with my whole being against the drift towards total death." Close friend Ruth Gage-Colby described the letter she received "as if you had said: I have no way of stopping the bombing, or preventing use of nuclear weapons, burning by napalm and defoliation by chemicals, or of putting an end to the reign of death and destruction over a beautiful people and their homeland, so for me there is no act of protest extreme enough, but this!"[51] Herz affirmed that ultimate responsibility for militarism lay with the American public and "the colossal lie" of hatred and fear whipped up during the Cold War. Projecting her determined feeling for international solidarity, Herz declared that her self-immolation underlined her solidarity with the Vietnamese people, and that she wished to make herself heard by choosing "the flaming death of the Buddhists."[52] Nevertheless, she stressed that revulsion and horror at the spate of state violence had not overcome her. Explaining the act, Gage-Colby understood that Herz "loved life and revered it as a miracle, fragile and fleeting, yet invincible and eternal, you chose to sacrifice it by fire to illuminate literally your solemn warning."[53] In her final letter to her daughter, Herz explained that she "did this not out of despair, but out of hope for mankind."[54]

Despite its considered ideological underpinning, and the sensitive explanations of friends and family, Herz's death by self-immolation was disregarded by contemporary observers. Unable to fit an appropriately maternal narrative around her shocking protest, journalists devalued Herz's stance by questioning her mental health. Coverage in *Detroit Free Press* consistently depicted Herz as irrational.[55] Hayes Jacobs' *Fact Magazine* article, the only extensive coverage on Herz, limited his readers' interpretation to two choices; "was she senile or was she a saint?" He stated that his friends believed the activist to have been "a nut . . . Senile dementia, undoubtedly." Although a detailed and sympathetic piece, Jacob's article frequently returns to comments made about Herz's mental state that described her as emotionally unbalanced.[56]

Her friends and family earnestly refuted such claims, even when unprompted. Helga Herz, Alice's daughter, spoke to *Detroit Free Press* the day after the incident to explain that her mother was "responsive to reality and completely aware of the policies of this country . . . she didn't do it to satisfy her soul. Or as a kind of solace for depression."[57] Speaking at a remembrance service, fellow peace activist Ruth Gage-Colby maintained that "in an insane society, Alice sought to make a completely sane testimony" and that she "was not a fanatic, nor a propagandist, but a sincere and intelligent lady."[58] The minister of Herz's church avowed that "this is not the work of a crackpot."[59] Herz herself pre-empted the tarnishing of her message. She began her testament with the affirmation that she was "in full possession of [her] physical, mental and spiritual capabilities."[60]

Herz's internationalism also limited her domestic reach. The press highlighted her German nationality, her self-identity as a global citizen presumably undermining her opposition to US policy. Meanwhile, historian Francisca de Haan argues that the perpetuation of Cold War paradigms diminished internationalist activists in historical assessments, as even tentative connections to communism saw international women's organizations such as the Women's International Democratic Federation and the Congress of American Women devalued as fronts. While Herz's anti-imperialism did not suit the popular perception of American housewives and mothers in the 1960s, her transnationalism further stymied historical recognition for her protest.[61]

WSP's complex response represents the negotiation involved in acknowledging acts of self-immolation. As news of her protest broke, Herz's fellow WSPers responded with an outpouring of support. A Detroit WFP press release affirmed that her "courage and love of humanity is engraved in our hearts."[62] A March 20 protest, organized before Herz's act, was turned into a "Walk in Spirit with Alice Herz." The hospital treating Herz received so many flowers that Detroit WFP had to ask WSPers to stop sending gifts.[63] Following her death, the branch organized a large remembrance service at the First Unitarian Universalist Church of Detroit. Attendees included Rev. Henry Hitt Crane, Rosa Parks, and Michigan Representative John Conyers. Senators Wayne Morse and Ernest O. Gruening, vocal allies of the burgeoning antiwar movement, offered their condolences and poignantly described Herz's actions as a "sacrifice."[64] Support for her self-immolation came from a small cohort of figures within WSP who identified with Herz's radical internationalism.[65] Ruth Gage-Colby, a close friend and well-respected peace activist with an enduring commitment to internationalism and Japanese affairs, gave a stirring eulogy at Herz's memorial, venerating her "sublime and selfless deed" as a "testament to life."[66] Los Angeles WSPer Mary Clarke, one of the most forthright proponents of greater ties between American women and Vietnamese anticolonialist groups, also commended Herz's self-immolation.

This initially sympathetic stance soon became complicated by WSP's ambivalence toward radical politics and militant acts of civil disobedience. Herz's self-immolation fell squarely into WSP's existing debates and, ultimately, the group's desire to represent a wider, more moderate constituency meant that it could not use Herz's actions positively. The brief commemoration to Herz that appeared in the March 31 edition of its newsletter was the last time national WSP directly referred to her.[67] Detroit WFP issued a statement emphasizing that it considered the self-immolation to be the act of "an individual." Lillian Lerman reiterated that "Alice had told no one" of her plan.[68] A WSP press release selectively edited Herz's own statement, altering the wording from "I have chosen the *flaming* death" to "I have chosen the *illuminating* death" in an attempt to pacify its tone.[69] Friends and family in possession of Herz's note, the only document that fully explained her rationale for self-immolating, refused to release it to the media.[70]

Some among WSP's ranks seemed unable to process what had taken place. Detroit WFP, the branch she left behind, expressed its unreserved sympathy while accepting that Herz's protest seemed "bizarre."[71] Self-immolation was a foreign act, not just in a cultural sense, but also in the way it challenged WSPers' understood norms of protest. Herz also tested WSP's official take on the growing opposition to the Vietnam War. Even at the onset of mass strategic air bombing, leading WSPers questioned whether "the average American woman" knew enough about Vietnam to justify its prioritization as an antiwar issue.[72] Demonstrations and marches increasingly highlighted the issue in early 1965, as local WSP branches sponsored more anti–Vietnam War activities, but the national body had yet to decide whether to broaden its concerns and tackle the war.[73] Promoting Herz as an exemplar of the group risked undermining its carefully cultivated support base, and activists' calls to make opposition to the war a priority for the organization created rifts among participants.[74]

Herz's protest was overshadowed eight months later by the self-immolation of a male Quaker peace activist, Norman Morrison. In the afternoon of November 2, 1965, Morrison stood outside of the Pentagon holding his one-year-old daughter Emily. Setting her down, Morrison poured a jug of kerosene over his head, and set himself ablaze. He died minutes after being taken away in an ambulance.[75] The press reporting on this instance of self-immolation erased Herz's earlier act, as *The New York Times* declared that Morrison's actions were "unprecedented" in Western society. Historical interest in Morrison's protest similarly ignores Herz's precedent. Paul Hendrickson described Morrison's death as exceptional, while in definitive historical works of 1960s antiwar activism Morrison receives top billing.[76] Herz may receive some mild acknowledgment for her earlier self-immolation, but it commonly follows lengthy discussions of Morrison's November self-immolation before a minor and factually incorrect nod to the fact that "a Detroit Quaker had taken her life" first, some months earlier.[77]

Historian Cheyney Ryan described Herz's "invisibility" as both "perplexing" and "disturbing," particularly because other American self-immolations are highlighted in histories of the 1960s. However, the absence of Herz's life and death in historical accounts of peace protest is, unfortunately, predictably straightforward.[78] The differing timing and location of each protest affected how witnesses, as well as journalists, activists, and politicians, determined their significance, explaining some of the disparity of interest in Herz and Morrison.[79]

Herz acted in March 1965, when public attention was focused on the police beatings of civil rights marchers in Selma and before wider awareness of the conflict in Vietnam had emerged. Morrison's death that November, however, benefitted from a growing antiwar consensus, making his criticism of American militarism easier for the public to comprehend. Similarly, Herz self-immolated outside a department store on a nondescript street in Detroit. Morrison's protest at the seat of the US military carried more overt political symbolism. In fact, he unknowingly set himself afire outside the window of the Secretary of Defense Robert McNamara. These differences in timing and location explain at least some of the disparities of coverage of the death of Alice Herz and Norman Morrison.

But more important is that gender affected how observers received Herz's and Morrison's radical political message. Karin Andriolo identifies the cultural constructions used to distinguish men's suicides as somehow "superior" to those of women. The "analytical vocabulary" that cultural commentators use to describe acts of suicide reinforces a gendered divide: "connotations of dependence, emotionality, and succumbing to internal problems" abound in descriptions of women's suicides, while men's suicides "are described in terms of independence, rationality, and fighting against external forces." Andriola argues that this arises from a "warrior ethos" that Western culture continues to read into men's actions. Therefore, whereas men's suicide is treated as a form of "martyrdom" on behalf of their community—what Andriolo terms a "superior option"—women's suicides are rarely interpreted this way. Analysts of women's suicide therefore strip the "social meaning" of the act.

These gender differences appear starkly in the reporting of each self-immolation. Alice Herz was depicted as unstable, irrational, and isolated. Journalists did not describe her life as one of a loved and loving mother, nor her death as a tragedy. The depth and longevity of political understanding that drove Herz's action was similarly undervalued. Explaining Herz's criticism of Operation Rolling Thunder, a huge development in US military strategy toward Vietnam announced just two weeks earlier, *Detroit Free Press* noted only "an apparent reference" to "bombing raids on Communist supply stations."[80] Instead, they described a perplexing act conducted by an emotionally unstable woman.

In contrast, in the days following his death, Norman Morrison was described as purposeful, deliberate, and effective. Journalists depicted Morrison's death as a family tragedy, the act of a loving father. His young family became the subject of newspaper reports as photos of his wife and children adorned human interest stories that appeared in the immediate aftermath.[81] Meanwhile, the press ruminated on Morrison's life, beliefs, and motivations across in-depth editorials where journalists used his self-immolation as an opportunity to debate the conduct of US action in Vietnam.[82]

Even fellow women peace activists struggled to reconcile Herz's actions with their gendered expectations of protest. Catholic peace and antinuclear activist Dorothy Day denounced self-immolations "in part because they contradicted" Day's belief that women's nonviolent commitment "should be an essentially undramatic affair." As such, Day felt that Herz's visceral act of martyrdom went too far beyond a "respectable" witness against war, which she felt was the desirable way for women to approach the issue.[83] Herz's death continues to be a litmus test for feminist theories of nonviolent civil disobedience. Scholars of suicide and activism remain divided on whether self-immolation is a form of violence; nevertheless, few see it as wholly nonviolent. This is particularly true in feminist conceptions of nonviolence, which holds the desire to deliberately seek suffering as a distinctly masculine venture that contrasts women's nonviolent proclivities.[84] Herz' act clearly transgressed this feminist reading of appropriate nonviolent action. Yet militant and radical acts performed within the feminist and women's liberation movements are accepted as a key feature of their history. A consistent historiographical failure to accept that women could engage in radical protest beyond these movements means that militant acts performed by women's peace protesters, such as Herz, acts are continually overlooked.

Herz's radicalism is only difficult to comprehend in the context of American expectations of gender and activism.[85] Indeed, her intention to convey solidarity with the Vietnamese resonated in exactly the way she hoped. Buddhism, which is central to Vietnamese culture and society, has plenty of precedents for self-immolation. Starting with the 1963 death of Thích Quảng Đức and continuing throughout the next decade, South Vietnam bore witness to countless acts of self-immolation by Buddhist monks protesting the brutality of the American-backed government. The emerging prominence of Thích Nhất Hạnh's teachings reinforced the act as a legitimate form of opposition to the war.[86] The North Vietnamese public in particular recognized the cultural significance of self-immolation. Crowds of people in Hanoi stood "for a moment of silent prayer" upon hearing news of Herz's death.[87] Poets composed songs and recitations celebrating her lifelong commitment to pacifism. Children learned of Herz's solidarity with Vietnam in school. A street in Hanoi was renamed "Rue Herz." Vietnamese Buddhists living in the United States also responded to Herz's actions. Vo-Thanh-Minh, who lived in New York, explained that Herz's heroism "surpasses that of everybody in Vietnam, Buddhist Monks and Nuns included." Minh affirmed that while Christianity "may not permit" self-immolation, in Vietnam "such an act is very encouraging."[88] Reverence extended throughout Asia. An American living in China wrote to a WSPer that Herz was "spoken of with great honor."[89] Women's groups in Japan held a minute's silence to honor her act, with one women's organization declared that Herz was "the conscience of America."[90] The New Japan Women's Association announced their "firm determination" to fulfil her dying wishes.[91] At a memorial held in Tokyo, numerous groups including WILPF and Japan Mother's Congress, "pledged themselves before the photograph of Mrs. Herz to strengthen the movement in Japan in opposition to the war in Viet Nam." Shingo Shibata made significant efforts to commemorate her life. He arranged annual memorial meetings, founded the Alice Herz Peace Fund, and published his correspondence with Herz to ensure her story "became known."[92]

Religious and cultural appreciation certainly affected the reception of Herz's act, but further factors motivated the glowing testimonials of international respondents. Japanese women's status as "victims of atomic bombs" heightened their appreciation for Herz's stance against US militarism.[93] Proximity to the conflict in Vietnam also intensified the sense of gratitude. Keiko Takizawa wrote that Asia had "not been free from war for even a single day" since World War II and extended gratitude that a resident of the United States would oppose their government's conduct in the region.[94] Significantly, Herz's affiliation with international associations and her enduring support for Asian peace initiatives meant activists across the region knew of her.[95] They reciprocated her identification as a global citizen and grieved for the loss of a friend. Cold War political expediency also affected responses to Herz's protest. A number of the Japanese groups who offered public testimonials used Herz's death to campaign against the United States generally. Aside from Shingo Shibata's attempts to have Herz's protest acknowledged, awareness of her exploits spread around the country in the *Akahata Japanese Communist Daily*, which encouraged commemorative services and public condolences throughout the Cold War.[96]

Opportunism also influenced the response of the North Vietnamese government. Herz's outspoken criticism of the United States supplemented North Vietnam's attempts to "strengthen international propaganda, win international sympathy, and exploit contradictions" among its enemies.[97] In a 1965 interview with British journalist Felix Greene, Hồ Chí Minh deftly used Morrison's and Herz's self-immolations to claim that he had the support of the American people. He proclaimed the "high symbolic significance" of such acts and declared that Herz was a hero who represented "the true spirit of America, the America of Washington and Lincoln."[98] The Hồ Chí Minh Revolutionary Museum created a shrine dedicated to Herz.[99] Writing about the phenomenon of Buddhist and Quaker self-immolations during the Vietnam War era, religious scholar Sallie B. King notes that political considerations "obviously" motivated such honors.[100] Herz's protest reinforced the National Liberation Front's narrative that Vietnamese revolutionaries had the support of anti-imperialists around the world. Given the reliance on government messaging to inform the public, the use of Herz's self-immolation as a propaganda tool partly explains why she became so revered by the population.[101]

Herz's radical, violent act—sidestepped and forgotten by some—nevertheless paved the way for further radical, nonviolent opportunities that altered the fortunes of the American peace movement. Two months after Herz's death, the Soviet Women's Committee invited prominent New York WSPer Lorraine Gordon and Southern California WSP Coordinator Mary Clarke to a Moscow celebration marking the twentieth anniversary of the end of World War II.[102] An ulterior motive prompted their acceptance of the invitation. Clarke and Gordon sought out the newly established embassy for the National Liberation Front in Moscow to secure permission to travel to Hanoi. One week later, members of the North Vietnamese Women's Union (VWU), "delighted and excited over the proposal," offered to sponsor their trip. Gordon believed that the WSPers' appearance as "middle-class American women" and "mothers" eventually won over the officials. However it was actually Alice Herz's international influence that raised their credibility.[103] Women from Vietnam revered the "woman in Michigan who had set herself on fire" and were "delighted and excited" to meet with some of Herz's colleagues.[104] As Mary Hershberger writes, the fact that "Herz had belonged to the same organization that these women came from prompted a warm response from the Vietnamese."[105] A dozen women bearing flowers met Clarke and Gordon in Hanoi, and the WSPers received VIP treatment throughout their stay.[106]

Owing to its audacity, no one ever took credit for initiating Clark and Gordon's venture. As an organization, WSP had tried to make contact with women's groups in Vietnam for years; however, Amy Swerdlow portrayed that the pair "decided, on their own initiative" to seek out the Vietnamese representatives. Describing both women as "experts in public relations," Swerdlow claimed that the pair simply did not wish to "implicate WSP in a meeting that it had not endorsed."[107] In contrast, both Clarke and Gordon said that WSP's leadership pushed them to secure a meeting before they left for Moscow.[108] WSPers certainly had conflicting reactions to Clarke and

Gordon's clandestine efforts. Excitement abounded among key women and the Washington, DC, Steering Committee expressed its support, noting that many outside of WSP had "expressed great enthusiasm" for the project.[109]

However, news that two WSPers travelled to North Vietnam without consulting their fellow activists drew stern condemnation within WSP's ranks.[110] Activists knew this was a confrontational act and expressed deep anxiety about the perceived illegality and radicalism that their group would now represent. Meeting with women of other nations was a staple of WSP's activism. As early as 1962, the group met with peace activists from the Soviet Union and travelled to Moscow as part of their antinuclear efforts. However, while those excursions were precarious, they had always been lawful. Travel to Hanoi was not, and Clarke and Gordon's colleagues expressed concern over the legality of the proposed meeting. San Francisco's Hazel Grossman recalled "that there was considerable fear and trepidation about taking the bold step of talking to women of the "other side."[111] These reservations were shared by Francis McNamara, staff director for HUAC, who felt the trip violated the Logan Act. Lyndon Johnson too expressed his alarm to Walt Rostow, his special assistant for national security affairs.[112]

Together with Vietnamese women, Clarke and Gordon planned a subsequent, larger conference for the summer, proposing that a delegation of WSPers meet with women from North and South Vietnam in Jakarta, Indonesia, a neutral location accessible to all involved. Having initially kept their exploits entirely secret, Clarke and Gordon returned to the United States and broke "the most incredible news!"[113] Between July 13 and 18, 1965, WSP sponsored ten American women to discuss war and peace with six women from North Vietnam and three from the National Liberation Front of South Vietnam. The North Vietnamese delegation consisted of a professor, a lawyer, a doctor, a news editor, and two women from the North Vietnam Women's Union. The South Vietnamese delegation had a representative of the South Vietnam Women's Liberation Union, a leader of the Teachers' Patriotic Union, and a member of an organization called Students for Liberation.

Attendees spent sixteen-hour days exchanging views and insight about the history of the conflict, the political climate in the United States, the 1954 Geneva Accords, the physical devastation caused by American intervention in Vietnam, and the "personal tragedies caused by the war."[114] Outside of the formal discussion periods, the American and Vietnamese women shared stories of their families, photos of their children, and comments on "culture and fashion." WSP delegates attended cultural events in the evenings and on one occasion had dinner with Indonesian president, Sukarno.[115] The attendees developed personal bonds and friendships that lasted for years.

The Jakarta Meeting heralded a remarkable new phase of transnational engagement for the American antiwar movement.[116] Indeed, it marked the first of numerous transnational visits and cross-cultural exchange among American and Vietnamese peace campaigners. The scale of WSP's achievement is exemplified by how often others in the peace movement falsely claimed the prize of being the first to Hanoi.[117] As San Francisco WFPer Hazel Grossman observed, WSP's opening exchange "opened the door for all types of US groups to send delegations to the Vietnamese," with groups ranging from Voice of Women and WILPF, religious groups like Clergy and Laymen Concerned About Vietnam, and civil rights leaders and the Black Panther Party following WSP's lead.[118] Following their trip to North Vietnam in 1969, Madeleine Duckles, Cora Weiss, and Ethel Taylor created the Committee of Liaison with Families of Servicemen Detained in North Vietnam (COLIAFAM). This opened lines of communication between American POWs in North Vietnam and their families in the United States and allowed monthly delegations to transport correspondence and packages back and forth.[119] Through COLIAFAM, Cora Weiss, a leader in WSP as well as in the peace movement overall, played arguably the most instrumental role in arranging American delegations to Hanoi during the US war in Vietnam. As Judy Wu writes, "in composing the membership of these monthly delegations, Weiss invited individuals from diverse racial, generational, and gender backgrounds to expand the range of people who otherwise would not have the opportunity to travel to North Vietnam. These journeys invariably reaffirmed and further motivated the travelers' engagement in the antiwar movement."[120]

The Jakarta Meeting moved women from the periphery to prime spokespeople for the antiwar movement.[121] Journalists sought out WSP's expertise on the crisis in Vietnam; its activists undertook speaking tours, relaying their experiences throughout the country; WSPers even addressed the British House of Commons.[122] San Francisco WFPer Frances Herring exclaimed that "the outreach of this Jakarta trip is greater than any previous project."[123] Meetings with Vietnamese counterparts affirmed the ability of American women to work directly for peace, even subverting the position of their own governments. In an extensive report on the meeting published on the

WSPers' return, Mary Clarke wrote, "it's the sons and husbands of ordinary citizens who are doing the dying, and since the statesmen seem unable to stop the mounting death and destruction, the escalating war which threatens the world with annihilation, it becomes the responsibility of ordinary citizens to try to stop it."[124]

Lorraine Gordon explained the significance of the initial 1965 meeting as showing "the world that women are capable of meeting together in spite of their countries killing each other . . . women can do what no governments can do."[125] Though categorically denying that the event represented a conference, WSP members participated in a diplomatic display with their Vietnamese peers. Mary Hershberger argues that WSP made clear that they did not represent "typical" American public opinion, while historian of women's antiwar diplomacy Jessica M. Frazier contends that WSP wanted to act as "liaisons between the US government and North Vietnamese and NLF [National Liberation Front] officials," claiming that they had "access to North Vietnamese and NLF officials whom the US government was ignoring." [126] COLIAFAM's ongoing efforts provided access to North Vietnamese authorities that made WSP the envy of the US government. Having already established contact with North Vietnam Premier Phạm Văn Đồng, WSP members in Jakarta met with Nguyễn Thị Bình, who was a member of the National Liberation Front and later became the foreign minister of the Provisional Revolutionary Government of the Republic of South Vietnam. She became a chief negotiator during the 1973 Paris Peace Accords and maintained friendships with WSPers for many years.[127]

To the extent that it put them "in direct confrontation with the state," activists' trips to Vietnam were the most radical and transgressive acts ever sponsored by WSP. Its participants never quite adopted the language of anticolonial solidarity used by other groups who travelled to Vietnam, such as the Black Panthers, or individuals such as civil rights activist Diane Nash. Nevertheless, WSPers used their trips to assert a unity with the people of Vietnam, at this stage designated enemies of the United States, while declaring their refusal of government authority and legitimacy. "The act of going to Vietnam," Dagmar Wilson said, "is a manifestation of our refusal to recognize the authority of our government to choose for us who our enemies are and who shall be our friends."[128]

Frazier describes WSP's initiatives as "a major victory" and the group's relationship with Vietnamese counterparts allowed it to directly influence government activities.[129] In 1968, WSP representatives again met with Vietnamese women to hold a public peace conference in Paris discussing methods and terms that would end the conflict. The Conference of Concerned Women to End the War drew representatives from the US, Vietnam, Japan, Britain, Australia, New Zealand, West Germany, and Canada. Taking place weeks before formal peace talks began among the governments of those at war, the conference was designed to show that "women from warring nations could meet peaceably to discuss solutions" in a way their governments could not.[130] Madeleine Duckles formed the Committee of Responsibility to bring victims of napalm bombing raids from Vietnam to the United States for medical treatment. Many Vietnamese orphans were subsequently adopted by families in the United States.[131] As the Nixon administration used American POWs and MIAs as pawns to extend the war, WSP's Cora Weiss used COLIAFAM to negotiate with the North Vietnamese to release three POWs as a gesture of goodwill.

In contrast to the cautious rejection of Herz's radical self-immolation, WSPers celebrated their transnational exchanges as unquestioned successes without referring to the initial, radical violent act that made them possible.[132] Writing a history of San Francisco WFP, Hazel Grossman described the Jakarta Meeting's "enormous impact on the peace movement" as "perhaps the most important" contribution the group made throughout its life.[133] The disparity in historical recognition alone reveals how women peace activists deftly navigated the boundaries of radical action. However, WSPers also undertook extensive efforts to tailor the publicity surrounding their meetings with Vietnamese women, illuminated in Jessica Frazier's work on WSP's transnational activism.

Throughout the Jakarta conference, Vietnamese women described their wartime experiences with reference to their resistance efforts and participation in anticolonial struggle. Nguyễn Thị Bình's story was particularly significant. Binh described her anticolonial resistance since 1945. Initially Binh worked as an undercover operative against the French Occupation, during which time she was captured, imprisoned, and tortured. She continued her fight during the period of US intervention against the South Vietnamese regime of Ngô Đình Diệm. Binh frequently depicted Vietnamese women "as fighters," affirming that foreign intervention required them to "defend their nation as combatants." The Vietnamese version of womanhood "included an obligation to take up arms in defense of their homeland." Furthermore,

Binh explained that "wives and mothers who longed for peace fought all the harder." She let the American delegates know that her acts were "consistent with her role as a woman defending her home and her homeland."[134] Binh eventually became an icon. Her determined, feminist poise on the world stage "inspired countless women."[135]

WSP had difficulty reconciling Binh's relatively violent interpretation of maternal responsibility with its own attitude, which was that women had naturally protective and pacifist instincts. The Jakarta delegates therefore modified Binh's story in order to appeal to their desired American audience. As Frazier demonstrates, Mary Clarke downplayed Vietnamese women's agency in the violent anticolonial struggle in their homeland, even describing her new acquaintance Din Thi Huong as "a housewife."[136] In WSP's version of events, Binh was not arrested for her own role in resistance operations, but because of her husband's membership in the NLF. Frazier argues that WSP intended to make Vietnamese women like Binh more relatable to American GI wives and depicted wives and mothers "forced into activism in order to correct the injustices she and her family suffered. She explains that this was done deliberately.[137]

But WSPers did not only wish to make the Vietnamese more sympathetic to a US audience. They also needed to "ignore, overlook, or rewrite Vietnamese women's militia role to maintain their own role as international peacemakers." According to Frazier, "if women were violent, as the version of womanhood put forth by Binh suggested," then WSP's emphasis "on the image of women as maternal pacifists" would lose all credibility.[138]

Excursions to Vietnam reflected a more antagonistic aspect of WSP's antiwar activities. In August 1965, a vast assembly of peace and civil rights activists descended on Washington, DC, to hold four days of demonstrations and workshops on democratic process, Cold War militarism, racial injustice, inequities in labor legislation, and poverty. The Assembly of Unrepresented People drew a number of WSP activists to the capital. Helen Evelev, Ruth Krause, and Ethel Taylor were among three hundred people arrested as participants in the assembly. Reporting on her arrest, Taylor explained that she found "unique and inspiring" the willingness of southern civil rights activists to face jail for their cause. "We felt moved to commit this act of civil disobedience because the demonstrations in which we have been involved for the last few years seem no longer by themselves enough," Taylor declared. "We felt that by allowing ourselves to be arrested, we demonstrated to Americans and to people abroad that there are those who oppose the war so strongly that they are willing to go to jail. There was also that need within ourselves to take this action."[139]

In February 1967, WSP became the first peace group to demonstrate in front of the Pentagon. Thousands of women protested, forcing security guards to hastily close and lock the doors to those outside.[140] Unperturbed by this new development, women at the front of the crowd took off their heels and used them to bang against the closed doors.[141] The scene became renowned, the image burned into the group's history. Nancy Zaroulis and Gerald Sullivan suggested it was "such unladylike behavior, unheard of in 1967 when women were supposed to be seen but not heard."[142]

Fierce scenes also overtook a WSP demonstration outside of the White House in September 1967. Having been refused permission to protest on the site outside, activists were involved in scuffles with police. The press took multiple photographs of angry protesters and women being thrown to the ground; headlines described the "bloody melee."[143] In San Francisco, one hundred women extended a WSP-directed consumer boycott of International Telephone and Telegraph Company to perform a "die-in" outside the company headquarters, identifying as "a dead Vietnamese" or "a dead Cambodian" to highlight the company's complicity in weapons manufacturing.[144] WSP's street theater performances and sit-ins in congressional offices increasingly led to arrests.[145] Amy Swerdlow remembered growing more militant, recalling that "we got involved in civil disobedience, in sitting down in Congress and in front of trains carrying napalm. We chained ourselves to the White House, blocked ships, lay down on the street pretending to be dead Vietnamese."[146]

Actions mirrored a growing fervor among WSPers. In 1967, SWAP leader Anci Koppel extolled the aggressive actions of WSPers who demonstrated at the Pentagon. She wrote to Jo Friedman, "WE HAVE TO THREATEN those that are responsible in the government—practically, physically threaten them. For this reason we here (SWAP) strongly feel that a civil disobedience is badly needed."[147] In a discussion with other activists the following year, grassroots WSPer Judy Sugar voiced her disgust with contemporary political systems, arguing that "Congress represents the establishment. I think the establishment is war-like. So I think to go and ask Congress to do something is a waste of time. I think if you want to deal with Congress it has to be demanding. And I think we can't compromise." Responding to a suggestion that WSP form a women's political party, National Office secretary Sally Bortz scoffed that "if you form a political party, you are acknowledging what I think is a phony belief—that the system works," adding that a party would make "this so-called democratic society legitimate and it is not."[148]

Others advocated strongly for tax resistance, stating that they would feel "guilty of aiding and abetting a genocidal war" through paying her taxes. "I see myself hurling napalm bombs on children, women, and the aged," Koppel wrote, while observing that regular forms of dissent "are met with tear gas, mace, and clubbing."[149] San Francisco WSPer Hazel Grossman adamantly stated that the lesson she drew from Vietnam was to be "more radical."[150] Even Dagmar Wilson appeared to call for revolution.[151] After witnessing US bombing raids during her own visit to Vietnam, she explained to *The Washington Post* that "I felt so passionately angry I wanted to take up a gun and shoot back."[152]

WSP's experience in the anti–Vietnam War movement undermines the most common argument in support of respectable dissent—that it shields protesters from backlash. A respectable, maternal image no longer protected WSP from the worst excesses of violence and harassment wielded by its opponents. It did not prevent the House Un-American Activities Committee from twice investigating Dagmar Wilson: once in 1962 and again after Wilson's refusal to testify in a closed session in 1964. The committee ultimately convicted her of contempt of court and gave her a suspended jail sentence, an episode missing from accounts of WSP's earlier, more famous triumph over HUAC.[153] WSP's "respectable stance did not prevent the FBI from conducting a decade-long counterintelligence investigation into the group. Undercover agents infiltrated the upper echelons of branch leadership; they attended meetings in WSPers' homes, deliberately trying to disrupt its operations. A respectable image did not stop police beating protesters in a "bloody melee" as they sat in front of the White House in 1967, or from WFP in Oakland from having to "run from the batons" during an antidraft demonstration.[154] WSP's respectable stance did not discourage conservative student activists in Young Americans for Freedom from breaking, entering, and trashing WSP's New York office in 1970. They occupied the office for hours, defacing posters, stealing protest literature, and taking lists of names. The police refused to respond to WSP's calls, did nothing to remove intruders from the office, and declined to investigate or charge against those responsible. WSP's respectable stance did not prevent activists receiving death threats. East Bay WFPer Madeleine Duckles received targeted warnings from anticommunist militia organization, the Minutemen, who cordially explained that "the sight of a rifle, the cross-hairs are on the back of your neck."[155]

WSP's use of radical militancy alongside the group's public expressions of moderate, traditional motherhood caused problems for women's peace historians trying to narrativize the group's history. In her authoritative *Peace as a Women's Issue*, Harriet Alonso described that WSP's appeal lay in its identification as "respectable, middle-class, middle-aged peace ladies in white gloves and flowered hats." However, she also explained that WSP held an appeal for "younger, budding feminists" and made other groups, such as WILPF, "seem staid" because of WSP's radical tendencies and use of civil disobedience.[156] These descriptions, while contradictory, are both accurate.

Historian Andrea Estepa offers a similarly compelling narrative. Framing her study around the evocative phrase "taking the white gloves off," Estepa rightly charts an evolution in WSP's political outlook over the course of the Vietnam War. This reflects not only a willingness to more directly confront government authority, but also an increasingly radical ideological critique of war. Pointing to the 1967 White House demonstration as the turning point, Estepa writes that "WSP grew increasingly concerned with questions of economic and racial justice," and "began to understand peace as a domestic as well as a foreign policy issue."[157] Similarly, Petra Goedde notes WSP's transition and shows how it served as a bridge for women to more comfortably acquiesce to radical acts of protest.[158]

Estepa's rendering is accurate. WSP did evolve over the course of the war. A clique of radical, militant, politically energetic leadership influenced WSP from its founding, but activists were only more willing to publicly take part in militant civil disobedience later. Nevertheless, the depiction of a gradual radicalization reinforces a stubbornly persistent feature of women's peace history depicting an irreconcilable dichotomy between respectability and radicalism.

Scholars of the women's movement increasingly highlight the analytical fallacy. Stephanie Gilmore argues that activists embrace "dynamic and multiple ideologies along with accompanying strategies, tactics, and goals."[159] Laura E. Nym Mayhall asserts, "historians have long questioned the existence of a simple dichotomy," but the distinction between militancy and respectability "remains a powerful, if sometimes unarticulated, organizing principle for understanding differences" across women's activist groups.[160] A respectable/radical framework continues to inform descriptions of women's peace activism as a gentle and moderate strand of social movement organizing, in opposition to the more "authentic" radicalism of the feminist and women's liberation movements. Indeed, the problems radicalism caused for women's peace initiatives is depicted by scholars such as Wesley Phelps and Louise Krasniewicz, who both show the counterproductive rifts and clashes between rival groups over appropriate forms of activism.[161]

A radical/respectable dichotomy must be challenged because it supports prejudicial discourse about authenticity and legitimacy within movement groups. David Snow and Remy Cross find that "many professed radicals claim to have a more 'authentic' or 'true' sense of how to best achieve social change" as they feel closer to "the grassroots" of issues.[162] Militancy in the suffrage movement provided authority in dominant narratives, as Mayhall observes that "the image of the tortured suffragette figures prominently in canonical histories."[163] In the women's peace movement, the respectability of activists determined their status as legitimate spokespersons. WSP's selection of Dagmar Wilson as leader and figurehead exemplifies this. But this respectable disposition found WSP excluded and shunned by elements of the peace movement who chastised WSPers as inauthentic and illegitimate activists. A WSP drive to collect 73,000 voter pledges for presidential candidates with peaceful intentions seemed "too mild a broth by far" to movement members who saw "moderates as seduced by the system." Meanwhile, elements of the draft resistance movement felt "abandoned" by WSP's reluctance to support their more radical acts.[164]

Equally, some scholars and activists suggest the radicalism, militancy, and civil disobedience of maternal peace activists is somehow inauthentic. Kyle Harvey, for example, writes that where they engaged in civil disobedience or militant acts, women peace activists in WILPF adopted the "tactical toolbox of the radicals" in their choice of protest, rather than believing in such methods in an ideological sense. Instead, it was for "collectives of more radical feminists" to legitimately utilize "expressive protest" and "a rejection of the oppression of hierarchy."[165] The radical/respectable dichotomy, then, suggests that housewives and mothers cannot be radical, and that radicals cannot be housewives and mothers.[166] The forgotten life and death of Alice Herz is only one example of the erasure of radical maternal peace activism caused by this kind of historiography.

The gradual radicalism depiction also downplays that, even during the group's most radical period, a sizable number of WSP activists continued to balk at militant acts expressly because it did not fit their organizational identity. The Jakarta Meeting split WSP's participants: historian Mary Hershberger explained that "it went far, perhaps too far," and she listed a mixture of cultural and political taboos that included treason."[167] Shortly after the meeting, Lyla Hoffman reaffirmed to WSP's national conference that "the role of WSP must be aimed at leading the millions of worried women and mothers," explaining that "they will not follow us into demonstrations with students, nor into police vans. They will not join us in lying across railroad tracks. It is therefore our responsibility to devise new actions for suitable, ordinary, apolitical, ladylike, worried mothers."[168]

Months after WSPers banged their shoes against the doors of the Pentagon, WSP's steering committees continued to receive complaints about and criticisms of the "negative" and "unorderly" demonstration.[169] WSP activists who did not participate asserted that "if the aim was to draw in more women, that kind of behavior would not do it," and that "it had alienated their neighbors."[170] The WSPers' complaints was prescient as newspapers recorded a loss of support for the marchers as a result of their "conduct."[171] Seemingly minor and innocuous acts of dissent rankled with some. At a DC WSP meeting at Chevy Chase Library, Folly Fodor was disturbed that "someone there early had turned the [American] flag upside down. The librarian was much upset and we must see that nothing else is done wrong, or we could not use the library again."[172] Even indirect association with activists who burned their draft cards proved too much.[173] In her analysis of the group, Amy Schneidhorst explains that "even in supportive families, traditional gender roles that prescribed women care for the children and home ensured that these women must limit their activities to lawful dissent." Lillian Hayward explained that her husband "would not have been able to handle the family without me," while Cora Weiss also expressed reluctance to engage in acts that could lead her to serving jail time.[174] Even in instances that WSP provided babysitters and caregivers for mothers who found themselves in jail, many WSPers remained opposed to acts of civil disobedience.[175]

WSP's antidraft work nevertheless demonstrates that it productively balanced competing ideas through its maternal peace praxis. Throughout the country the group encouraged its women to support young men at risk of selective service. Activists in the New York, Boston, and Chicago areas found themselves in fortuitous locations given the groundswell of draft resisters there. On the West Coast, branches from Los Angeles to Seattle attempted to create "cross-fertilization" of their campaigns to create nationally coordinated actions.[176] When Palo Alto mother Evelyn Whitehorn made a high-profile legal challenge against the draft, Aubrey Grossman, the husband of San Francisco WFPer Hazel Grossman, represented her.[177] But counseling provided the main source of work. The purpose of WSP's counselors was not to politicize or encourage resistance, only to inform men of their rights under draft law.[178] WSP volunteers counseled as many as "100,000 men across class and race lines" as they took over responsibility "for the leg work, secretarial work and fund raising that is involved."[179] Such work seemed a perfect fit for WSPers wishing to emphasis their maternalism. Amy Swerdlow wrote that it exemplified "women's age-old ability to carve out political space and power for themselves in a man's world by acting in the service of others."[180] In essence, many WSPers chose to provide support for draft resisters, but reconciled the potential marginalization of this work by framing the issue through a maternal lens: protecting and supporting those taking more oppositional stands to selective service.[181]

WSP proclaimed its opposition to the draft in its "Women's Declaration of Conscience." Developed "at the same time and in the same political context" as a similar resolution by SDS, Swerdlow contended that "WSP avoided anything that smacked of left ideology" and contrasted with the SDS resolution that was "at least five times as long . . . more ideological, radical, and combative." WSP spoke morally, rather than politically, and tried to bring mothers together against the war. The statement proclaimed, that "as Americans," WSPers' children had been "taught respect for the rights of others and to stand up for their belief in justice. They now refuse to violate these principles." Expressing their outrage "as mothers, sisters, sweethearts, wives," WSP affirmed its "moral responsibility to assist these brave young men," fully aware of any legal risks involved in such a stance. WSP's support was "typically parental" and was framed differently than the aid offered by other activists.[182] WSP's experience supports Michael Foley and Ellen DuBois who suggest that women found space for themselves within some aspects of antidraft work when abiding by traditional, maternal roles.

Such impressions of WSP's draft work reinforce its moderation and respectability; however, this element coalesced with a keenly radical analysis of the selective service system, and direct, radical interventions to support draft resistance. In a striking contrast to their previous disregard, WSPers exhibited clear understanding of the racial and class overtones of the draft.

LA WSP's Valerie Sissons observed that those who escaped service "would be replaced by a poor or minority youth," while Berkeley and Oakland WFP published a pamphlet explaining that "the draftee for Vietnam is 'young, often working-class, often Black.'"[183]

Amy Schneidhorst illuminates a "symbiotic" relationship wherein the supportive community that WSP provided encouraged younger, radical activists to take more risks.[184] But WSP's complicity with draft resistance went further than just community support. Detroit WFP activist Lucy Haessler posed as a resisters' relative and secretly ferried those fleeing to Canada.[185] The FBI and the US Federal Attorney in Philadelphia considered bringing Ethel Taylor before a grand jury for sedition because of her activities in draft resistance.[186] WSPers understood the acute risks involved. Hazel Grossman exclaimed that they "risked imprisonment themselves (after all Benjamin Spock, MD, outstanding writer on infancy, was put on trial for simply urging the youth to resist)." She further compared WSP's activities to "American predecessors" that "offered sanctuary for fugitive slaves in the 19th century."[187]

WSP became more visibly radical through the years of its anti–Vietnam War campaign, but its ongoing maintenance of respectable image presents a stubborn challenge. Alice Herz proves singularly difficult to write into histories of women's activism, but the most radically militant acts of protest ever performed by American social movements emerged from the perceptibly staid forum of maternal women's peace activism. The Jakarta Meeting demonstrates WSP's penchant for radical acts of dissent, but this retains a prominent place in WSP's story because it was an act that could be curated into a usable form for its activists. Andrea Estepa's depiction of the group "taking the white gloves off" is an evocative summation that nevertheless reaffirms a dichotomy between radicalism and respectability that cannot sufficiently account for WSP's activism. Ultimately, WSP was split on the issue of civil disobedience. While some women took "the white gloves off," many others kept them on.[188] What can be said for sure is that the group was a more nebulous mix of radical militant and staid liberal moderates than often acknowledged. WSP's major success in the period was maintaining a cohesion between all its participants as the Vietnam War tested the boundaries of appropriate action. However, as the war continued, divisions between branches in different parts of the country began to widen.

CHAPTER FOUR

San Francisco Women for Peace and Local Histories of the Women's Peace Movement

FORTY PARTICIPANTS OF WASHINGTON, DC, WSP met on Saturday October 5, 1968, to discuss assorted tensions afflicting their beleaguered group. Held in founding member Folly Fodor's house, the Washington Retreat Meeting went over arguments and disputes that plagued DC WSPers in the previous year. Attendees debated their group's character, arguing over whether they should remain a single-issue campaign group focused on nuclear weapons or should broaden to tackle "poverty, racism, war." They noted declining participation and a lagging enthusiasm. Some felt their antiwar work was ineffectual; others observed a monetary crisis worsened by what they felt was WSP's unnecessary commitments to the antiwar efforts of other organizations. Still others gave the practical reason of not having "gobs of time" to devote to their activism. Such introspection caused high-profile figures to consider winding down WSP entirely. Fodor observed that "it would be a shame to close shop. But I don't think that because we have a mimeograph and a few reams of paper and an office that that's a reason to continue either." A month later, citing her dispiriting exhaustion, Dagmar Wilson quietly retired WSP.[1]

In stark contrast, across the country in the San Francisco Bay Area, activists had cause to celebrate. East Bay WFP attracted three hundred people for a meeting in which they related the Vietnam War to social, political, and economic conditions in the city of Oakland. The November/December issue of WSP's national newsletter *Memo* provided a "great article" about San Francisco WFP's role in the draft resistance movement. Bay Area groups' No More War Toys campaign resulted in Macy's removing violent playthings from their stores. Fresh off a successful lobbying campaign in coalition with Coretta Scott King and the Poor People's Campaign, San Francisco WFP cemented the influential role of the women's peace movement in the city by opening a shared Women's Peace Office with their WILPF counterparts. Founded with the intention of better coordinating both group's activities, the Peace Office signaled a visible confidence among Bay Area WFP activists as their antiwar activities grew.[2]

WSP's famed unorganization encouraged branches to develop autonomy from one another, but the resulting specificities and variations of local activism remain overlooked in national narratives of WSP history that depict a harmonious, cohesive body. As historian Stephanie Gilmore succinctly puts it, "sweeping nationally based narratives of a movement cannot possibly capture completely the nuance and texture" of mass activism.[3] While an analysis of activist geography is important for determining the "variable causes of social movement success and failure," it offers more significance when used to explore local activist identity and experience.[4] This chapter responds to these new, localized interpretations of women's activist history by illuminating WSP efforts in places other than the East Coast. It highlights the group's Bay Area operations to explore variations in activist identity, politics, and memory, in order to demonstrate that women peace activists were not confined by organizational boundaries and, in fact, frequently transcended important markers of WSP's collective identity.

Activists in the Bay Area told a founding story that placed the emergence of San Francisco and East Bay WFP in the context of ongoing regional activist initiatives, notably departing from WSP's national narrative that foregrounded efforts in Washington, DC. Activists were informed by distinct cultural contexts, prioritized different campaigns, celebrated their own leaders, used distinctive branding, and developed separate strategies and rhetoric rooted in the regional politics from which they emerged. This chapter documents Bay Area activists' commitment to a range of inter-organizational social justice activities in the region. San Francisco WFP developed a heightened presence in Bay Area activist initiatives during the Vietnam War, supporting causes beyond the traditional WSP plank and collaborating effectively with other organizations. Charting this story illustrates the tensions that grew between East and West Coast WSP, the divisions between national leaders and local organizers, and the evident stress of ongoing activism. This chapter therefore not only provides a more intricate history of WSP; it also asserts the meaningful collaborative contributions of women's peace activism during the 1960s. Nowhere is this clearer than in the experiences of WFP activists in the San Francisco Bay Area.[5]

The West Coast provided fertile ground for the development of the most active and effective WSP branches in the country, rooted in distinct cultural contexts that allowed the branches to develop regional autonomy distinct from the more nationally influential hubs on the East Coast. As Lisa McGirr's and Michelle Nickerson's separate investigations of women's conservative organizing find, "Southern Californians, in particular, had a higher interest and concern in foreign affairs than in other sections of the country," in part due to the "defense-oriented business climate."[6] The region benefitted from an upsurge in grassroots liberal and middle-class leftist political activism during the 1950s and "mirrored the growth of New Left activism in universities."[7] WSP efforts in Southern California coalesced these existing networks and ongoing local initiatives under the stewardship of Mary Clarke.[8] A former Communist Party member, Clarke ensured that WSP operations in Los Angeles and beyond carried the region's legacy of radical left activism.[9]

Farther north in Seattle, an antimilitarist activist community stretching back to World War II mingled with the progressive political hub centered on the campus of the University of Washington. In large part due to the work of the "senator from Boeing" Henry M. "Scoop" Jackson, Seattle became home to countless defense industries, with nuclear-equipped Trident submarines stationed around Puget Sound and the nearby Hanford nuclear reactor bringing the nuclear age physically close to home.[10] Prominent businessperson and peace movement luminaire Anci Koppel led Seattle Women Act for Peace (SWAP) from its formation in 1961 through the 1990s.[11] Thorun Robel joined her, having first lent her particular talents to the peace movement at a demonstration against fascism before World War II, intervening in a struggle between a police officer and a fellow student. "On impulse," Robel "whacked the policeman with her purse and was immediately arrested."[12]

Even amid the energetic activism scene on the West Coast, San Francisco Bay Area branches had privileged circumstances. Historians of activism frequently describe an exceptionalism to the region. Katherine Turk's absorbing history of the National Organization for Women depicts San Francisco as a "wide open town" that was a "thriving center of radical politics and cultural nonconformity. Rich with bohemian subcultures and a vital refuge for gay and lesbian people, San Francisco hummed with Beat-inspired bookstores, coffee shops, and jazz clubs."[13] Similarly, Stephanie Gilmore describes San Francisco as "home to a thriving gay and lesbian community, a student population protesting the war and advocating for free speech, and diverse racial and ethnic populations." Historian Anthony Ashbolt remarks that "radicalism in the San Francisco Bay Area had a quality, character, and intensity lacking from other parts of California and, while it never became central, it was always ready to take center stage."[14] San Francisco's legacy of longshoremen strikes encouraged a robust labor movement, while it claimed a reputation as the site of the northern civil rights movement.[15] Geographically small but culturally thriving, communities and causes frequently overlapped and its long history of interwoven social movement activism distinguished San Francisco from the rest of the country. Local activists regularly found common cause within one another's campaigns, asserting the exceptional strength of San Francisco as a site of progressive activism.[16]

The region benefitted from the robust presence of peace organizations, notably WILPF, whose local branch regularly advertised educational talks and meetings that were open for all in the Bay Area to attend. Such was the local WILPF's status that the national organization opted to hold its 1955 annual convention in downtown San Francisco, an auspicious occasion that also marked WILPF's fortieth anniversary. The 1962 international conference, only the second WILPF congress to be held in the United States since the organization's founding in 1915, also took place in San Francisco.[17] During their first action on November 1, 1961, San Francisco WFP spokesperson Lenore Peters explained to San Francisco's Mayor George Christopher that "our city is no ordinary metropolis. The birthplace of the United Nations, it is a world city, and what it does can carry weight and influenced throughout the United States and in the tribunal of the world. These are unusual times. This is an unusual city."[18]

Bay Area WFP initiatives began through Dr. Frances Herring. A gifted intellectual and professor of government at University of California, Berkeley, Herring was a stalwart member of WILPF in the Bay Area and drew considerable respect from her colleagues. After she completed a PhD in philosophy and economics at Berkeley she worked as a researcher for the city of Davis's Bureau of Public Administration, developing an interest in California's "nuclear activity" which, she believed, was a subject about which "nobody seemed to know much about." She undertook an investigative assignment, educating herself in physics and engineering from "ground zero" before authoring a 250-page book, *The Development and Control of the Nuclear Industry in California*. Herring's work brought the glaring dangers of California's nuclear power industry to the attention of the California State Legislature for the first time.[19]

The report led Herring to become more active in the peace movement, and as her status in WILPF grew, she developed a close friendship with Nobel Prize–winning chemist Linus Pauling and his wife, Ava, a human rights activist committed to women's rights, racial equality, and international peace. Herring and Ava Pauling's tireless campaigning for peace and disarmament put them among some of the most significant, and often unheralded, women antinuclear figures of the era. Together they organized the Conference of Sixty Scientists Against the Spread of Nuclear Weapons in Oslo, Norway, in May 1961, at which the assembled group of international scientists demanded the end of nuclear weapons testing.[20] As nuclear crises built over the summer of 1961, Herring wrote to friends, expressing her hope that the "good nucleus of peace activists" already operating in the Bay Area would soon coalesce into a formidable campaign group. Upon receiving Dagmar Wilson's appeal to strike, Herring recalled that "it was my Berkeley-East Bay and other progressive friends who rallied."[21]

While Herring contributed her elite intellectual heft, credit for Bay Area WFP's organizing efforts is also owed to the efforts of close friends Alice Hamburg, Hazel Grossman, and Madeleine Duckles. Hamburg, born to poor Russian Jewish immigrants on a North Dakota homestead, moved to Berkeley to study and became a teacher. She immediately asserted her commitment to racial justice by campaigning for integration in Bay Area schools. She joined San Francisco WILPF in 1950 to further her already persistent efforts toward peace and civil rights. Hamburg's longstanding public support for W. E. B. DuBois and Paul Robeson brought her to the FBI's attention, and in 1951 she appeared before the State Un-American Activities Committee. Presaging WSP's later encounter with HUAC, Hamburg refused to fold and instead attacked the "flagrant violation of the democratic principles which are the very foundation of our great American heritage."[22] She continued to rail against HUAC, participating in the fracas between activists and police that took place on the steps of San Francisco City Hall on May 13, 1960, which came to be known as Black Friday. Police used fire hoses to remove anti-HUAC campaigners from the grounds of City Hall, which lead to sixty-four arrests and twelve hospitalizations.[23]

According to Anthony Ashbolt, events such as Black Friday "birthed the New Left" in San Francisco. But Black Friday was also personally important to Hamburg, because that was when she first worked with close ally and fellow WILPF member Hazel Grossman.[24] Known for "her generosity, elegant dress and manners, and her love of Ireland," Grossman shared a lifelong commitment to peace and social justice with her husband, Aubrey. For four decades she worked with various local and international peace groups, notably campaigning for nuclear disarmament and to end the wars in Vietnam and Central America. Grossman attended the World Peace Council meeting in New Delhi in 1961 where, foreshadowing later WSP initiatives, she met with Vietnamese men and women and learned about their struggle against US intervention.[25]

Across the bay in Berkeley, Madeline Duckles, a long-time member of the American Friends Service Committee and another influential contributor to the local WILPF, carried her years of experience into forming East Bay Women for Peace.[26] Duckles' political education began through a combination of her studies at University of California, Berkeley, in 1933 and the great San Francisco longshoremen's strike the following year. Her rising awareness of race relations, anti-imperial struggles, and labor issues merged with a "natural and right and proper" concern for peace and justice. Duckles joined WILPF in the 1940s but expanded her peace work with the World Council of Peace, for whom she gave antiwar speeches throughout Europe. She remained active until her death in 2013.[27]

Herring, Grossman, Hamburg, and Duckles formed two separate, but interconnected groups: San Francisco Women for Peace located in the city itself, and East Bay Women for Peace, based across the water in Berkeley. They flourished under the structure of unorganization and declared the importance of being "an independent group" as an example for other branches to follow.[28] Every WSP branch in the country developed individual reputations, with distinctive characters, strengths, weaknesses, and idiosyncrasies publicly acknowledged by activists.[29] The Bay Area WFP branches quickly developed a reputation as the best organized among WSP peers nationally. Such differences often sprung from leaders' personalities and the prevailing community scene.[30] As Melinda Plastas argues, WSP was influenced as much "by local personalities, politics, and interests of women who took up the challenge as they were by the wishes of national leaders."[31] Bay Area WFP branches' were influenced by the determined enterprise, positive experience, and confident organizational skill of its leading participants.

From the outset, WSP's leaders on the East Coast emphasized that WSP, "at all times," be thought of "in terms of a national movement."[32] However, WSP participants outside of the East Coast came to identify themselves more with their locality and region than with the national organization of which they were ostensibly a part. Some participants felt alienated from their peers in other parts of the country, especially from the national body and WSP's decision-making hub on the East Coast. Northwest Suburban Women for Peace referred to the main regional branch in Chicago as its "parent organization," with this branch in turn considering itself an "affiliate" of national WSP.[33] Seattle WSPers expressed a sense of belonging to the national organization and were, in turn, valued and admired for their dedication to national operations by their colleagues elsewhere. Nevertheless, SWAP emphasized its responsibility to peace efforts in the Pacific Northwest over national efforts.[34] Indeed, perhaps owing to geography, members of SWAP appeared to feel more loyalty toward their counterparts on the West Coast in general.[35] They lamented that "we are living far away" from fellow WSPers on the East Coast.[36]

Nowhere was regional separation demonstrated more clearly than in narrativizations of Bay Area branches' founding.[37] Departing from the national founding story affirming that WSP "emerged from nowhere," Bay Area WFPers explicitly rooted their groups in the region's well-known efforts toward nuclear disarmament, both in organizational accounts and individuals' autobiographies. Hazel Grossman's personal version of San Francisco WFP's formation began with her experiences dating back before World War II. She recalled her involvement in "peace strikes in the thirties" before she joined WILPF in the 1950s. Contextualizing WSP's birth in 1961, she affirmed links between the group and her attendances at the World Peace Council meetings, "where [she] met Vietnamese for the first time and learned about their struggle against US intervention."[38] East Bay WFP activist Rose Dellamonica, recounting how her group formed, expressed an affiliation to her region first before explaining that she belonged to a national organization. Making clear that she identified with the region, she explained that she was a part of East Bay Women for Peace, which was simply "affiliated with WSP."[39]

Activists described particularly strong links between WFP's formation and the area's WILPF branch. Grossman declared that San Francisco WFP "was born in 1961 as a sister organization to the Women's International

League for Peace & Freedom."[40] San Francisco WFP's Dr. Leona Bayer described her group as "the spiritual daughter" of WILPF, whereas the area's journalists and public knew of WSP as "a sister organization."[41] Even the official archive records at the University of California, Berkeley, reflect this narrativization. The bibliographic introduction states that, in 1961, "the women's peace movement coalesced in the Bay Area around the founding of the San Francisco Women for Peace." But when drawing links to the national body of Women Strike for Peace, the archive states only that this "national 'parent' organization" was established "at the same time."[42]

West Coast activists' sense of autonomy extended into decisions over the branding of their local branches. Although there was an emblem identifying the national organization, branches across the country chose to create and display their own designs. The logos employed by local branches showed no connection to each other or to the national organization and, when taken together, produced a somewhat confused public image. Further distinction arose over the naming of local groups, especially as it related to use of the term "strike." Branches in the east followed the example set by the Washington, DC, founders and referred to themselves as Women Strike for Peace. However, away from the East Coast, most branches dropped "strike" from their name and branding, referring to themselves as Women for Peace. The Seattle branch stood out among its peers, choosing the name Seattle Women Act for Peace, or SWAP. The national organization itself flirted with a name change in 1962. Out of a desire to become an internationally recognized organization, key women attempted to enter Women's International Strike for Peace into the group's lexicon. Dagmar Wilson felt that acronym WISP "is a beautiful word, much better than WSP."[43] After deliberating over the name Women Act for Peace, Los Angeles opted instead to continue using WISP and refer its members as WISPers, but the name never achieved national use and faded shortly after 1962.[44]

The differences in branch names created practical difficulties in coordination and, in the absence of a national effort united under a common name, public confusion sometimes arose. SWAP, for example, needed to constantly remind its public that "Seattle Women Act for Peace is a branch of Women Strike for Peace."[45] Their business cards and policy statements also made clear that they were affiliated organizations. The experience of San Francisco women perhaps best exemplifies internal debate about naming. While publicizing their November 1, 1961, march, participants opted to call themselves "San Francisco Women Act Together for Peace." This name adorned letterheads and press releases in the weeks that followed. Various adaptations appeared over the next few years before the branch settled on "Women for Peace." The name remained from 1963.[46]

Philadelphia founder and WSP National Coordinator Ethel Taylor subsequently downplayed any tensions over the group's title, asking, "What's in a name? We were all dedicated to the same cause."[47] However, as Wendy B. Sharer's examination of WILPF's naming process illuminates, the title of an organization entails a deeper rumination on individual and group identity. Sharer highlights that "the processes of organizational self-naming can elucidate the rhetorical strategies and struggles involved in achieving collective identification."[48] This was particularly important in WSP and, for those who had previous activist experience, "strike" took on huge significance. Ruth Gage-Colby, a well-respected pacifist leader prior to her involvement with WSP, recalled the appeal of WSP's name. She recalled, "when I saw Dagmar Wilson's ad saying, 'Women Strike for Peace' I said to myself, 'This is different.' If the ad had said Women for Peace, I'd have said, 'God bless the ladies,' and paid no further attention. But the word 'strike' struck a chord with me."[49] Yet the majority of branches declined to use "strike" in their name. Those working in communities renowned for class struggle and labor activism felt allusions to a strike "too militant" for the image they wanted to convey.[50] In California, Alice Hamburg recalled that "when we decided to form an ongoing organization in the Bay Area, the term 'Women's Strike,' seemed a bit too militant to some, and we settled on 'Women for Peace.'"[51]

In the 1960s, WSP's leaders understood the obligation to acknowledge their group's diverse names, and national conference literature accommodated different monikers, referring to "Women Strike for Peace and Women for Peace."[52] The San Francisco Bay Area branches appeared particularly sensitive to these differences, recognizing that other names applied to their colleagues around the country. When advertising a 1962 documentary focusing on WFP efforts in the Bay Area, an illustrated advertisement featured the various names and logos used by branches throughout the country.[53] Alternately they would hedge on how they called the national body in newsletters and mailers using, for example, "Women/Strike/For Peace."[54] While no overt animosity toward the name ever arose, regular attempts to change the national organization's title from "Women Strike for Peace" to

"Women for Peace" continued through the mid-1980s.[55] Historically, given the ideologically charged reasons that some branches chose not to call themselves Strike for Peace, using this term to refer to the organization paints the whole with a stance that many activists rejected. In the same way that using "organization" and "members" contradicts activists' own terminology, referring to the whole group as Women *Strike* for Peace suited national depictions weighted toward branches on the East Coast.[56]

Bay Area WFPers made significant contributions to WSP's activities and asserted a notable influence within the national body. In December 1961, Frances Herring announced to WSP contacts that she and New York activist Ruth Gage-Colby had taken it upon themselves to begin coordinating international activities. Swerdlow wrote that "this announcement, coming from California, raised no suspicions or objections among WSP women," partly because of WSPers' independence generally but also because Herring had "great influence on Wilson and the other Washington founders."[57] Herring was instrumental in coordinating WSP's first exchange with peace women from the Soviet Union in 1962. Meanwhile, Bay Area WFPers continued to marshal local activists to continual protests, pickets, and demonstrations. In February, 200 WFP activists from San Francisco crowded into the office of California Governor Edmund G. Brown and demanded a plan "for a 'peace-oriented' economy for California."[58] The branch organized a series of demonstrations to commemorate Hiroshima Day. It compiled and distributed a video of WSP activities throughout 1962 to celebrate the region's achievements.[59]

As countercultural activist Jerry Rubin once explained, California lacked significant federal governmental sites that could serve as "props" for the attention of protests, such as the Pentagon and White House in Washington, DC, or the New York Stock Exchange. Bay Area WFPers therefore directed their attention to more proximate sites, highlighting the local injustices of global military nuclear policies. They attacked what they perceived as California's increasing dependency on military contracts and war-related industry; they directed their protests against levels of Strontium 90 in dairy supplies at Berkeley's Public Health Department; and they used the proximity of the Livermore nuclear weapons facility to grow their group.[60] Both San Francisco WFP and East Bay WFP were involved with the Save Angel

Island Campaign, which opposed military and commercialized activities in San Francisco Bay while urging the preservation of Angel Island's "primitively attractive environment."[61] In March 1964, San Francisco WFP appealed for the redistribution of rations and medical kits from Oakland Naval Base to "people who are starving now," drawing links between the local financial drain of disaster planning and the absurdity of civil defense initiatives broadly.[62] Such local priorities shaped methods and tactics for Bay Area WFPers specifically, but national WSP also depended on these community actions to maintain its visibility. The dynamism and mystique of local branch activism, such as occurred in and around San Francisco, created interest in WSP's first few months as newcomers "clamored" to join the spontaneous upsurge of community activism.[63]

It was also WFP activists in the San Francisco Bay Area who commenced WSP's protests against the Vietnam War. East Bay activist Madeleine Duckles recalled that her group was "concerned with Vietnam" in late 1962, joining with their WILPF and AFSC colleagues to discuss how to limit creeping US intervention in Southeast Asia.[64] By March 1963, as a test ban treaty continued to dictate WSP's attention nationally, California groups held a statewide conference warning that tensions in Vietnam were at an "extremely critical phase," urging members "now is the time to mobilize."[65] The following October, Palo Alto's Peninsula Women for Peace took to the streets in protest against the Vietnam War. They declared that "as American women we are shocked and ashamed that our government is supporting militarily and financially the regime which is perpetrating these atrocities."[66] San Francisco WFP denounced Madame Nhu, the de facto first lady of South Vietnam, for her criticism of peace protesters in South Vietnam and called for the "withdrawal of all US aid to the Diem Government." They expressed their "shame" that American participation had exacerbated "terrible events" in Southeast Asia.[67] On October 18, 1963, a group of nineteen San Francisco WFPers led by Joan Robbins "marched in a body" to the State Department office of the city's Federal Office Building. They demanded that "the United States withdraw military aid from Vietnam, support an international commission to enforce the decisions of the Geneva Conference, and give debate on the Vietnamese conflict first priority in the United States."[68] The following year, San Francisco WFPers were "thrown out" of the Federal Office Building for protesting the growing conflict.[69]

Despite a "chilly" public reaction and little support from news media, Bay Area women persisted, granting themselves the reputation as the first to make concerted efforts against American intervention in Southeast Asia, before the antiwar movement coalesced.[70] Their concerns were so prompt and assertive that they drew concern from colleagues on the other side of the country. New Jersey WSPer Esther Newill explained that her peers seemed stubbornly reluctant to broach opposition to the Vietnam War. She claimed that a "culture of silence" pervaded discussion in New York and that she felt "almost gagged" from voicing her opposition in the city. Newill directly accused key women of colluding to shut down WSP's early opposition to the war.[71] Others similarly "dissented strongly" from proposals to make the Vietnam War a priority, feeling both that it would show WSP as a partisan organization and that further discussion needed to take place before the group decided on its policy.[72] WSP's leaders exercised caution. They would not commit to protesting the war until they felt the "typical American housewife" cared about it.[73]

WSP's national leadership actively resisted offers to join their California affiliates, but in their later historical assessments the actions of activists in the Bay Area allowed the group as a whole to claim a legacy as one of the first critics of the war. WSPers appropriated what were at the time unpopular efforts of their West Coast peers, discounting the substantial resistance that emerged from key women opposed to making such a decision so early. Dagmar Wilson later took pride in these actions, asserting that her group's members "were the first people to take to the streets protesting the Vietnam War."[74] Later historical assessments, such as those by Charles DeBenedetti and Mitchel K. Hall, also assert that WSP was the first opponent of the war.[75] Local collectives challenged military interventionism early, but WSP's first national policy statement outlining its opposition to the Vietnam War was issued in October 1965, six months after Alice Herz's self-immolation, seven months after the start of Operation Rolling Thunder, over a year following the Gulf of Tonkin incident, and at least two full years after California WSP activists first expressed their unpopular opposition to American intervention.[76]

It is unclear how and why Bay Area women came to recognize the urgency of tackling the conflict before others, though it reflected the region's general propensity for antiwar initiatives. San Francisco, after all, became the first major American city to force a vote on ending the conflict in Southeast Asia.[77] WFP's efforts also grew out of appreciation for expansive considerations of peace and social justice developed in concert with regional partners. Local WSP branches regularly cooperated and cosponsored actions with other organizations in their area; key women lent their indefatigable support to SANE, SDS, and the National Mobilization Committee to End the War in Vietnam.[78] Amy Swerdlow recalled that other groups "always wanted the bodies that WSP could produce. We could send 2,000 people to New York on a train to any of the demonstrations."[79] But commitment and willingness to support efforts beyond WSP's boundaries distinguished West Coast women from their peers elsewhere. In Oakland, East Bay WFP regularly cosponsored community initiatives with the Black Panther Party, whereas New York WSPers seemed "very prissy and too peaceful and uninteresting" to engage with such militant organizations.[80] Southern California WSP was willing to form an alliance with SDS in 1965, whereas Washington WSPers felt reluctant to associate with a group so willing to engage in civil disobedience.[81]

Coalition work did not just mean involvement in causes removed from the organization's founding purpose, but collaboration with groups of people not typically representative of national WSP's desired image. Some warned that WSP would be "engulfed" by other groups and campaigns unrepresentative of the group's values and beliefs. Swerdlow noted that she harbored more cynicism toward the antiwar movement than she had toward the test ban movement. "Those young men in SDS," she explained, were not like "that wonderful group of people" she encountered in previous campaigns.[82] Though satisfying the individual concerns of various WSPers, extensive involvement in the work of other groups caused activists to devote less time to WSP and ultimately scattered the group's energies. WSP's National Office cautioned its activists that coalition work dissipated energies, distracted attention, sucked funds, and generally led to branches not "playing a role as Women Strike for Peace" while they were "just supporting—running to this group, that group."[83]

Over the course of the war, Bay Area WFP expanded their anti–Vietnam War efforts to account for the multiple violent consequences of the conflict. An ongoing boycott of Dow Chemical connected women's purchasing power to support of American militarism. East Bay's Madeline Duckles was instrumental in the creation of the Committee of Responsibility, a voluntary collective of medical professionals, religious figures, and private citizens who evacuated war-injured children from Vietnam to the United States for treatment.[84] Duckles, the Northern California chair of the committee, "met every one of those children" off the plane at Travis Air Force Base.[85]

Throughout the conflict, Bay Area WFP groups committed themselves to supporting the efforts of national WSP and were wholehearted supporters of excursions to Vietnam. Draft resistance became a priority concern as the war continued. The San Francisco Bay Area developed a reputation as "a haven for draft resisters" and, while Boston had more of a reputation as a locus of resistance initiatives, San Francisco was the originator of mass national efforts against the Selective Service Act.[86] Demonstrations and street protests took place against the war and the draft through the late 1960s, often provoking violence. In October 1967, a large demonstration of 4,000 before the Oakland Induction Center was attacked by police. WFP women supporting the march reportedly "had to run from the batons."[87]

San Francisco WFP made important contributions to wider efforts through its Draft Resistance Committee, a joint effort with the local branch of WILPF. Support took many forms: financial help, sanctuary for resistors sought by the army or federal marshals, legal assistance, talking with parents, locating counselors or religious advisors, or simply an offer to join a community of similar-minded people. Both WFP and WILPF participants became draft counselors.[88] Bay Area WFPers also provided instrumental support for Evelyn Whitehorn's ultimately unsuccessful effort to use "parental authority" to stop the US Army from drafting her eighteen-year-old son for service in Vietnam. Whitehorn, from Palo Alto, just south of San Francisco, received legal representation during the case from Hazel Grossman's husband, Aubrey. San Francisco WFP, however, struggled to cajole other branches into supporting Whitehorn's fight. In a letter to Amy Swerdlow in 1981, Hazel Grossman wrote that "our women at the time were not ready to get involved in urging, or rather encouraging 18-year-olds not to register."[89] The case is an example of how WFPers in San Francisco were typically firmer in their support for draft resistance efforts than their peers in other regions, who often deliberated on the extent to which WSP should support and encourage noncompliance.

Avowedly declaring that in "unity there is strength," Bay Area WFP concentrated on building effective partnerships with peace groups; labor organizations; student protesters; racial justice campaigns; and other neighborhood concerns.[90] This partly demonstrated Bay Area WFP's separation from the national body. East Bay WFP reflected their "spiritual" alienation from the rest of the group, confessing that "we are distant" from national WSP "in feeling as well as fact."[91] Mixing with more proximate campaigns and organizations was one way to maintain connected to a larger whole. It also reflected an approach to organizing unique to San Francisco, where social movement activism was often "rooted in coalitions with other groups" and more collaborative than efforts elsewhere.[92]

The sheer vitality and concentration of activity in the Bay Area proved impossible to avoid. As San Francisco and Berkeley became a global hub for student activism in the early 1960s, WFPers consistently lent their support.[93] Draft resistance and boycotts of Dow Chemical aside, the Bay Area WFPers aligned with the student counterculture in visible displays of support. Alice Hamburg threw her backing behind the Free Speech Movement that grew out of University of California, Berkeley, in the fall of 1964 and became the first mass act of civil disobedience on American college campuses in the 1960s.[94] As students in the Bay Area turned their attention to the Vietnam War in 1965, WFPers increasingly found common cause and joined campus activists as partners. The student-led Vietnam Moratorium Committee, a coordinated national effort involving three-thousand campus organizers, had its University of California, San Francisco, affiliate work closely with San Francisco WFP, to the extent that some of its protest ephemera could only be "purchased directly" from WFP's local office.[95] East Bay WFP, headquartered on the campus of University of California, Berkeley, joined students in denouncing the institution's complicity in military research.

Support for the Civil Rights Movement was another example of how Bay Area WFP went beyond the cautious position of branches elsewhere. Having campaigned for integration in schools while a teacher in the 1940s and 1950s, Alice Hamburg continued to apply herself to racial justice causes in concert with her peace work. She travelled to the South to participate in civil rights campaigns, including the Mississippi Freedom Summer in 1964.[96] Hamburg also urged the antiwar effort to add a racial perspective to its agenda. Her influence was such that, after the debacle over civil rights at WSP's 1962 national conference, Bay Area groups avowed their opposition to national policy and enacted their own statements.

Their own historical accounts showed that "the most important action of Women for Peace" was its calling of the First International Day of Protest on March 20, 1965, which united "the demand for 'Peace in Vietnam' with the demand for 'Justice in Selma.'"[97] East Bay and Oakland WFP regularly co-sponsored community initiatives with the Black Panther Party.[98] East Bay Women for Peace were particularly enthusiastic about engaging in activities with "the new women's coalition to fight poverty, war, and repression."[99] WFP in San Francisco worked closely with Coretta Scott King and the Southern Christian Leadership Conference "to effectively support the Poor People's Campaign."[100] Meanwhile WILPF and WFP both initiated the Bay Area campaign for the Congressional Black Caucus' Transfer Amendment to move funds from the Pentagon to jobs and social programs.[101] While it is correct to say the white women's peace movement struggled with civil rights, San Francisco Bay Area initiatives clearly departed from the example of colleagues elsewhere.

Bay Area WFP's lack of clear dedication toward women's issues is particular striking, given their penchant for collaboration and partnership beyond peacework and because feminist efforts in the region relied on just the type of coalition building and partnership WFP frequently joined. Stephanie Gilmore's illuminating dive into NOW's San Francisco branch affirms that "as one might expect in San Francisco, feminism was rarely seen in opposition or contradiction to other movements for social justice." Instead, it was integral to the "world-wide revolution of human rights." Indeed, Gilmore argues that examining coalitions "is the only meaningful way to comprehend NOW's feminist history in San Francisco." The "left coast" feminism emerging in California in the mid-1960s found a natural home in San Francisco, which was, as Gilmore describes, a "logical place for feminism to emerge."[102] The general public proved more sympathetic of campaigns for gender equality and support for women's issues. *San Francisco Examiner* journalist Russ Cone, supporting the formation of the National Organization for Women in 1966, explained that the city "is bound to be a prime target" for the group's activism given the poor record of equal employment in San Francisco City Hall, which was something the *Examiner* had frequently attacked.[103] Although NOW was criticized from within for its narrow focus on "political change," its San Francisco branch helped build the thirty-group Bay Area Women's Coalition.[104]

This vibrant scene is more notable in its absence among the archival records and testimonies of WFP activists, who commonly foregrounded their work for peace and social justice in other areas, such as civil rights. WFP did occasionally support and sponsor joint initiatives on women's issues. In September 1969, San Francisco WFP was one of over thirty organizations to send representatives to the first women's coalition meeting at the initiative of San Francisco NOW. Among other things, the meeting planned to work toward an expansion of childcare centers, the end to the criminalization of abortion, enforcement of Title VII, and passage of ERA. WFP also supported the nonprofit organization San Francisco Women's Centers, which planned to "facilitate a woman's center in San Francisco" that would "coordinate particular needs of women such as health, law, education, creative arts, research, childcare, and emergency housing facilities." Along with several local groups including WILPF, WFP put its name to a Women's Center ad appearing in the November 1973 newsletter for the lesbian organization Daughters of Bilitis, also demonstrating at least tacit support for the thriving lesbian community in San Francisco. [105]

Bay Area WFP's close relationship with WILPF provided the area with an especially strong women's peace movement presence and distinguished San Francisco from the rest of the country. The two organizations shared membership nationwide. WSP activists were, nevertheless, especially brusque when describing their organizational relationship. In Los Angeles, Mary Clarke "was very anti-WILPF." Ava Pauling similarly believed that Los Angeles WILPF was "quite reactionary" and did "not believe that they will help very much."[106] Amy Swerdlow revealed that, in March 1962, WILPF National Executive Committee advised local WILPF branches to "remain officially separate," even if allowing activists to "cooperate with WSP as individuals, not as an organization."[107]

However, San Francisco WILPF and WFP commonly appeared cooperative and collaborative, cosponsoring talks and educational drives while also sharing the coordination of demonstrations and lobbying initiatives.[108] Individual leaders often represented WFP and WILPF at the same time, even signing mailers and letters by affirming their affiliation with both organizations.[109] Alice Hamburg, Hazel Grossman, Frances Herring, and Vivian Hallinan were all, at one time or another, board members and presidents of the San Francisco WILPF branch, alongside their participation in the San Francisco WFP branch. In her autobiography, Hamburg recalled that "over the years, the lines between WSP and WILPF have blurred. In the Bay Area we worked closely together and a number of women, including myself, are active members of both."[110] In their historical depictions, San Francisco WILPF and WFP activists made efforts to credit one another, together, for what they had achieved. A 1984 Women for Peace Newsletter declared that "we in Women for Peace and Women's International League for Peace and Freedom on both sides of the Bay, in conjunction with others, were instrumental in initiating and assisting with almost every major antiwar march and demonstration which took place."[111]

The most significant joint WFP-WILPF initiative emerged in 1965 when San Francisco branches created the Women's Peace Office, a shared headquarters located on the fifth floor of the city's International Center. Hamburg recorded that, by this time, WFP and WILPF "were cooperating in all our activities" and the shared office became an "outgrowth of work already being conducted."[112] WILPF and WFP ran the office jointly, initially using the space to share administrative costs with an all-volunteer staff, but regularly declared annual budgets of just over $10,000 (close to $80,000 in 2025), with funds contributed by both WFP and WILPF individuals. The office received enough to start a General Peace Fund, funded on a continuing basis to support the office's efforts for "international peace, universal disarmament and an end to poverty, racism, and repression at home."[113] With the shared space, WFP and WILPF used the Women's Peace Office to distribute joint mailers, sponsored by both the local WFP and WILPF branches but printed on Women's Peace Office letterhead. The office reached the combined local membership of both organization in this way.[114] Mailers drafted and distributed from the office often described individual initiatives sponsored by the separate organizations, but made it clear that both groups supported and encouraged one another's events and encouraged women to become involved without regard for official membership or affiliation. Although always signed by several key women, commonly Grossman and Hamburg, they were not distinguished as being a representative of either WILPF or WFP.

The office quickly merged the local organizations' ongoing activities to the extent that the Peace Office became the working base for both organizations and an "information and action center" for the entire Bay Area from the mid-1960s.[115] Most of WFP's work in San Francisco after 1965 occurred in the shared space of the Women's Peace Office. There, women researched and distributed literature; organized weekly vigils held at Union Square on Saturday afternoons; leafletted supermarkets and other locations on current issues; lobbied officials in San Francisco, Sacramento, and nationally; collaborated with community oriented groups such as the National Welfare Rights Organization, United Farm Workers, anti-imperialist women of color and women's liberation groups, and the People's Coalition for Peace and Justice; and hosted a Correspondence Committee that exchanged volumes of communication with national, state, and local representatives. San Francisco's Peace Office also extended invitations to women's groups throughout Northern California for combined visits to San Francisco's congressional offices and the Soviet consulate, eventually forming a new coalition named Women for a Meaningful Summit to push for more dialogue between nuclear powers. The office at 50 Oak Street became the active headquarters of the Coalition for SALT II in the seventies, and joint WFP–WILPF endeavors continued to support the nuclear freeze, a comprehensive nuclear test ban, and opposition to US military interventions in Central America during the 1980s.[116] Activists involved with the office recognized their influential contributions to the social movement landscape, with Hazel Grossman declaring in 1985 that a "record of the Women's Peace Office will provide dramatic testimony on how a relatively small number of women made a definite mark on history" to become a "necessary part of the history of the San Francisco Bay Region's peace movement."[117] Indeed, the San Francisco Women's Peace Office lasted longer than the National Office of Women Strike for Peace.[118]

The significance of the Women's Peace Office lay not only in the reach of its activities, but in its forging of a distinct women's peace activist identity that transcended the boundaries of affiliation to WFP and WILPF. San Francisco WFP activists acknowledged that, at the very least, the office reinforced their distinctive presence among their peers in other WSP branches, contrasting the national body's estrangement from other women's peace initiatives to reveal that WFP and WILPF in San Francisco publicly maintained a formal, official partnership for nearly fifteen years. The area's activists' themselves declared that "San Francisco is the only area in the country where WILPF and WFP have been able to work together in a shared office." But activists involved in the Peace Office also avowed that it had "established a separate identity" entirely, combining area WFP and WILPF participants while allowing those organizations to function separately.[119] Such was the merged identity offered by the Women's Peace Office that newcomers to the women's peace movement in San Francisco had to be told that WSP "considers itself a separate and distinct organization."[120]

Activists reinforced the unique identity of the Women's Peace Office through their joint protest activities, but revealed its extent in their historical accounts. In November 1986, WSP branches across the country held celebrations marking the twenty-fifth anniversary of the group's founding, honoring "all who have participated over the years." San Francisco activists paired their observance by also commemorating "25 years of united action of Bay Area Women's International League for Peace & Freedom and Bay Area Women for Peace," recognizing that WFP in the area should also celebrate "years of working together with WILPF out of our joint San Francisco office."[121] Planners affirmed that the 25th birthday event in San Francisco "will not only commemorate the 1961 birthday of the Women Strike for Peace movement, but it will celebrate the unity of Women for Peace and the Women's International League for Peace and Freedom in the struggle for peace over the years."[122]

Throughout the 1980s, San Francisco WFPers and WILPFers compiled joint archive materials and initiated an oral history project.[123] Hazel Grossman explained that the project would "attempt to gather together and organize all our old papers, WILPF, Women for Peace on both sides of the Bay, and Coalitions we participated in" in order to "tell the story of the San Francisco Bay Area branches of the Women's International League for Peace and Freedom and Women for Peace."[124] This cohesive, shared vision of an intertwined women's peace history also led to the combined storage of the activists' archival materials. The Bancroft Library at University of California, Berkeley, houses the official records for San Francisco and East Bay branches of WFP and WILPF together, titling them "Women for Peace." Each organization's files are compiled separately, but within this larger collection.[125]

As historian Georgina Denton notes, "scholars tend to study activists and organizations in the context of distinct social movements and rarely pay much attention to alliances across difference."[126] Acknowledging the extent to which women's peace activists worked beyond organizational boundaries in local communities complicates the WSP story, especially when histories of the women's peace movement divide individuals and events into separate groups. In Miami, for example, WSP branch founder Thalia Stern was "at the center of the action" for most peace groups in the area. Historian Raymond Mohl writes that Stern applied inimitable commitment to social justice concerns and used her status in multiple organizations to cosponsor various campaigns.[127] Mohl approaches the subject from a geographic perspective rather than an organizational one, accounting for all activities in Miami rather than concentrating on only WSP in the area. While a testament to Stern's efforts to support peace initiatives in Miami, this approach also reveals the stifling effect of national, organizational women's peace histories. Referring to Stern as a "WSP leader" limits recognition of her impact, as does differentiating Stern's WSP campaigns from her joint initiatives with other groups. They were all part of one cause.

The correct story of the women's peace movement in San Francisco is, instead, a shared tale of WFP and WILPF, as the Women's Peace Office activists show in the history they recorded and produced. The intertwined context of the San Francisco's women's peace movement disrupts national organizational accounts that intentionally separate WSP and WILPF, requiring that past actions be credited to one or the other organization.

The planning and coordination for the 1968 Jeannette Rankin Brigade protest provides a telling example of the problems arising from national, organizational approaches to history. The Brigade brought thousands of protesters to Washington, DC, on January 15, 1968, for an all-women demonstration against the Vietnam War. Headed by Jeannette Rankin, the first woman to serve in Congress and the only congressional member to vote against entry into both World War I and World War II, the demonstration drew a broad coalition of women's groups to the capital, including peace organizations, liberal societies, church groups, radical feminists, and racial justice campaigners.

After marching on the White House and Congress, the Brigade convened an assembly of women to discuss the brutality of war, the neglect of domestic human needs, and future plans for the mobilization of women for peace efforts. The demonstration made headlines throughout the country, the *Miami Herald* reporting that the "several thousand protesters" brought to the opening of Congress "the specters that haunt it the most: the Vietnam war and the race problem."[128] But the demonstration became infamous for a confrontation between peace activists and radical feminists from the New York Radical Women, an emerging force in the women's liberation movement. Disdaining the maternal identity adopted by WSP, New York Radical Women used the occasion to stage a mock funeral during which they "buried traditional motherhood."

For WSPers, the Jeannette Rankin Brigade represented a provocative watershed in the story of their relationship to feminism, absorbed into the group's organizational history as a distinctly WSP affair. In *Women Strike for Peace*, Amy Swerdlow described the Brigade as a WSP-led initiative that drew coalitional support under activist Vivian Hallinan. This impression is reflected in general histories of the American women's movement. In *Tidal Wave*, Sara Evans described the demonstration as a WSP-directed event operating under a different "banner."[129] Ruth Rosen similarly explains that WSP single-handedly organized the all-women antiwar protest against the Vietnam War, naming themselves the Jeannette Rankin Brigade "in honor of the congresswoman" rather than recognizing Rankin's own involvement. In this description the demonstration was assuredly a WSP affair.[130]

WILPF's organizational histories propose an entirely different story. Catherine Foster, a former associate legislative director of WILPF who wrote a history of the organization, explained that the Brigade was the brainchild of Jeannette Rankin, someone Foster affirms was a "longtime WILPF member."[131] In *Peace as a Women's Issue*, which was written as a general overview of women's peace activism but is essentially a history of WILPF, Harriet Alonso similarly claims that Rankin initiated the Brigade. Alonso uses as evidence Rankin's prior assertion that "if 10,000 women would be willing to risk imprisonment to end the war, then the fighting would cease." Thousands of women responded to Rankin's suggestion, which resulted in "a WILPF member's proposal that Rankin lead a march on Washington."[132] In both Foster's and Alonso's histories of WILPF, the Brigade was a WILPF initiative. Alonso describes "a coalition of women's organizations, including WILPF and WSP," that spearheaded the subsequent organizing, but Foster more emphatically asserts WILPF's sole credit. She writes that "WILPF was instrumental in the coalition that brought together a medley of women from all parts of the United States," and describes activists who had joint affiliation with WILPF and WSP, such as Frances Herring and Lucy Haessler, as if they exclusively acted on behalf of WILPF when participating with the Brigade.[133]

Neither WSP's or WILPF's versions of the Brigade's history are false, nor even especially inaccurate. They simply highlight that national organizational accounts of women's peace activism often conflict by attempting to claim sole ownership of shared individuals and events. Reading the Jeannette Rankin Brigade from a local perspective of activism in San Francisco instead produces a more interconnected story. First, it reveals that WSP did not endorse the Brigade nationally. In November 1967, New York WSP's Coordinating Committee met to discuss planning for the Brigade demonstration and recommended that WSP "not participate as an organization in the formation of the 'Jeannette Rankin Brigade' since it is a parallel organization to WSP with a similar program," suggesting instead that WSP concentrate on its own specific program. New York's Coordinating Committee refused to allow its WSPers to act as "spokesmen for WSP."[134]

Second, the Bay Area's specific activist context produces a further complication. Indeed, it was area activist Vivian Hallinan who initially contacted Jeannette Rankin to raise the prospect of a "Brigade" named after the congresswoman. Hallinan was, for a time, president of San Francisco WILPF, but she is perhaps better described as a mainstay of progressive and anti–Cold War activism in the Bay Area generally.[135] Described by Jacqueline Castledine as a "former Wallace supporter" and Progressive Party activist, rather than either a WSPer or a WILPFer, Hallinan promoted an idea of positive peace throughout her peace work and "linked inner-city poverty, the Vietnam War, and the oppression of women to the theory of structural violence."[136] In her post-demonstration reporting, Carolyn Lewis of *The Washington Post* referred to Vivian Hallinan as the "Brigade founder" and identified her as "a West Coast leader of the Women's International League for Peace and Freedom."[137] Recognizing WSP's instrumental role through the influence of Sylvia Lichtenstein, Cora Weiss, and Mary Clarke, the *Post* story emphasized the coalitional leadership guiding the Brigade. Distinct organizational accounts that try to demarcate WSP's actions from others do not adequately capture the dynamism of women's peace coalitions.

Bay Area WFP branches continued to embark on successful local coalitions against the Vietnam War, but its relationship with other WSP branches and the national body became strained toward the end of the 1960s. Unorganization, key to WSP's earlier success, left the national group ill-suited to facilitate the sustained cohesion required to maintain a long-term attack on the war. The urgency of protest during the Vietnam War exacerbated the fundamental paradox between decision-by-consensus and WSP's trademark spontaneous action. National conferences frequently disagreed over what goals to prioritize in coming years. Central coordinators seemed unable to verify how many members, or even branches, operated under their auspices.[138] Recruitment suffered as spontaneous protests prevented the advertising of future events.[139] When interested parties wished to join WSP branches in their area, National Office staff could not be sure if any existed.[140]

Lack of formal membership allowed WSP participants to feel little responsibility for financial upkeep. With no membership dues and no obligation for branches to pay retainers, WSP could not rely on a guaranteed influx of money to keep itself afloat. Instead, it remained "totally dependent upon contributions from individuals and groups."[141] Printing costs, postage, and mailing proved a burden, particularly for regular issues of *Memo*, while office space and staff also increased operating costs.[142] The National Office consistently recorded debts, issuing emergency appeals for cash with alarming frequency toward the latter half of the 1960s. It often claimed to be "within weeks" of closing if it failed to receive quick funds.[143]

Individual differences became more visible as the shared understanding of WSP's organizational identity frayed. As Jo Reger writes, identifying sites of discord among social movement groups actually highlights the rich ideological disputes occurring among activists.[144] This is certainly the case in WSP, with ranging clashes over methods of protest and prioritization of issues. Geographic differences emerged clearly as early as the 1962 HUAC hearings. Although the hearings were celebrated as a famous victory within WSP circles, Leandra Zarnow writes that the HUAC affair also put to record Dagmar Wilson's irritation with New York WSP, whose organizing style and enthusiasm for political lobbying was at odds with other WSP branches of the time and encouraged HUAC's suspicions in the first place.[145] WSP's unorganzation presaged women's liberation, and suffered similar problems, notably what Jo Freeman termed the "tyranny of structurelessness," a dynamic that plagued nonhierarchical organizations of the women's liberation movement. "Contrary to what we would like to believe," she wrote, "there is no such thing as a structureless group. Any group of people of whatever nature that comes together for any length of time for any purpose will inevitably structure itself in some fashion."[146] WSP's unorganization similarly fostered the growth of an "entrenched leadership clique" that, by the end of the 1960s, tended to act without consulting the broader membership.[147]

Decentralization ensured that, according to San Francisco WFP, "less active groups, who consequently have more time to write are leaving too much of an imprint on the national memos."[148] These circumstances led to a leadership cadre almost exclusively populated by figures who could fund their own travel to WSP meetings, especially annual national conferences. East Bay WFPer Vivian Raineri observed that "those who can afford to go are the ones who go, which leaves out new voices, new opinions, new strength. And it is essentially the same women who go year after year."[149] National Secretary Barbara Bick criticized the lack of national representation.[150] She suggested that WSPers share the financial burden of conference attendance, with every attendee paying the same amount to build up a travel fund for "other women, i.e. from the South." But such a system met with resistance from those "larger, more affluent urban groups" who had convenient access to meetings.[151] Many grassroots members voiced disgust with what they perceived to be a failure in the group's decision-making process. The rushed planning of the 1965 Jakarta Meeting set a concerning precedent for future national actions.[152] An open letter from a Queens, NY, WSPer concisely depicted the mood. "It is too bad that out of so momentous an opportunity . . . a breakdown of communication has come about. In the short but proud history of WSP no previous project has demanded more careful examination, more objective questioning among ourselves . . . immediately there was an act of short-sighted expediency which denigrated one of WSP aims and thus sapped our strength."[153] Detroit WFP concurred, writing to the National Consultative Committee in 1965 that the Jakarta Meeting "tore a big hole" in the group.[154]

A growing divide emerged between the East and West Coasts over the course of the 1960s. Activists in the Northeast and Washington, DC, certainly enjoyed more national influence than those elsewhere. Former Riverdale WSPer Esther Newill suggested that leaders in New York attempted to sabotage debates involving large groups of grassroots WSPers in favor of their own proposals.[155] Washington, DC, women exercised significant authority over the rest of the organization and implemented projects without consulting the rest of the group's members.[156] It was an accepted fact that Washington WSP used privileges that other branches could not exercise. Regional figures recognized that "D.C. women are in effect national leaders as well as local activists." In November 1968, Aline Berman expressed her fears that members working in the Washington local office could "wield considerable influence" over national decisions, while the year prior, National Office Secretary Lynda Barrett faced questions over blurred lines of authority and the local branch's significance. "We wonder just what the special significance of the Washington Steering Committee is," asked Maryland WSPer Daryl Stewart. "Is it also a national steering committee? Where does the Washington Steering Committee end and the national structure of WSP begin?"[157] Amy Swerdlow acknowledged that WSP's structure fostered regional tensions, observing that those in the Midwest "who thought of themselves as 'more grass roots'" resented coastal power blocks, while California WSPers felt that the "Northeast was favored in decision-making."[158]

For their part, WSP's branches expressed a lack of enthusiasm toward the national body.[159] East Bay WFP spoke of their alienation from the national body, confessing that "we are distant in feeling as well as fact."[160] San Francisco WFP "felt for the longest time that they did not need" a national office. Branches competed for status. While San Francisco WFP believed itself to be "one of the most active sections of Women for Peace," New York WSPers believed that "in terms of their leadership and capability," their branches were "entitled to more" representatives than other areas.[161] Lack of communication from East to West Coast branches provoked further clashes. Since the first strike in November 1961, branches consistently found that "local people haven't been kept informed enough as to memos and proposals for national action."[162] The trend worsened throughout the decade. Although a member of WSP's National Coordinating Committee, Anci Koppel often felt left out of the decision-making process due to a lack of timely and appropriate updates from her East Coast counterparts.[163] On this she shared a rare point of accord with Mabel Proctor, the leader of neighboring Tacoma WFP. Proctor and Koppel's clashing personalities sometimes escalated into public quarrels, with SWAP's leader once accusing her Tacoma counterpart of being jealous of her own branch's stature. However, the Washington State leaders both agreed that "communication from the National to its branches or groups has been woefully neglected, especially with the groups outside of the east coast."[164] In fact, seven years after WSP's formation, many women in small branches throughout the United States did not even know what Dagmar Wilson looked like, nor had they met other key eastern women who they felt ran the organization.[165]

By the late sixties, WSP no longer drew national representation for its actions. The famed 1967 Pentagon protest, at which WSPers banged their shoes on the building's closed doors, comprised women "mostly from Philadelphia and New York." So did the White House confrontation later that year.[166] On hearing of WSP's plans for the 1968 Jeannette Rankin Brigade demonstration, Seattle Women Act for Peace wrote to coordinators informing them that "we cannot mobilize thousands or hundreds to go to D.C."[167] With most national conferences, consultative committees, and planning meetings taking place away from the West Coast, Seattle's Anci Koppel lamented the prohibitive costs of travel. "If our next National is held in Chicago," she reasoned, "the [West Coast] women will have to spend approximately $300 for air transportation."[168] Nowhere did regional divides appear more than in the planning for national conferences. Key women intended to rotate host cities in order to achieve "broad national representation," and most conferences took place in Midwestern cities to share the burden of travel for women throughout the country.[169] Nevertheless, New York WSPers frequently vocalized their preference for conference locations in neighboring areas and northeastern cities.[170] WSP branches in California, Oregon, and Washington State boasted large followings, but only two of the fourteen national conferences held between 1962 and 1975 took place on the West Coast: San Francisco in 1965 and Santa Barbara in 1975.[171] Even these instances provoked complaints from eastern women.

Planning for the 1965 national conference resulted in debacle.[172] At the previous year's conference, attendees agreed that San Francisco would host the next annual meeting. However, key women in the east began voicing their opposition as soon as the 1964 conference adjourned. In national meetings eastern leaders kept "expressing the wish that the conference" would be held somewhere other than "all the way out west." San Francisco WFP received no formal indication of any misgivings and worked feverishly throughout the year to confirm arrangements, book venues, and drum up interest "throughout the state." However, on September 22, 1965, just a month before the start of the planned conference, Washington, DC, New York, and Philadelphia representatives held a regional conference. Attendees resolved that a San Francisco conference was "undesirable" and again voiced concern over their own travel costs for the upcoming national, realizing that "not more than one or two people from each area were willing to put up the money for the trip." Although they had been unresponsive to the same pleas previously made by their West Coast counterparts, East Coast WSPers worried that "important policy and action commitments" would arise with "inadequate representation from areas that give a great deal of strength to the movement." They worried that conference proposals would therefore lack legitimacy and raised "concern that groups would not feel a commitment to policies and actions so arrived at." Without conferring with any other WSP activists, the eastern regional conference contacted Chicago WFP and asked them to host the national conference instead. After Chicago agreed, San Francisco finally received word that they had been stripped of their hosting responsibilities, in time for a planned Bay Area meeting that gathered to continue plans for the conference.

Bay Area women were incredulous over the actions of their East Coast colleagues. Holding an urgent meeting that evening, East Bay and San Francisco WFP activists agreed that they "could not accept such a summary decision by just 3 groups, affecting months of anticipation and just approximately 5 weeks before the planned date." They issued an "emergency" poll to determine the attitudes of WSPers from across the country. West Coast activists maintained that they had paid substantial costs to travel "to three previous national conferences," and countered eastern concerns of inadequate attendance with their own reservations about national representation at the potential Chicago conference. Sensing that eastern women undervalued their input, they argued that they "also have contributions to make to the movement even if they do not represent as many people as the states east of the Mississippi." Bay Area activists harbored "resentment" at both the time and "manner" of the proposed change. Writing to support the Californian point of view, Mabel Proctor argued that the proposed change "would cause any group to hesitate about taking on a future National Conference job, lest the same thing happen again." She further observed that actions of those in the Northeast would "reduce the unity we have gained nationally."[173] After much chagrin, San Francisco hosted the 1965 conference after all, at which WSP formally adopted its national position paper in opposition to the Vietnam War.

Problems of conference planning did not improve and subsequent organizing for the 1968 national conference again saw easterners refusing to travel great distances. In August that year, Barbara Bick began liaising with members of WSP's National Coordinating Committee (NCC) to plan. The committee expressed its intentions to focus on national representation, due to their observation that previous conferences had lacked such attendance. "We must not let fragmentation develop," it affirmed. "This would be a negative contrast to our previous cohesion which did make an impact and did attract women to our movement."[174] Kay Johnson offered to plan the event in Denver, which had, in previous years, been "frequently suggested as a good middle of the country location." NCC members responded with "complete agreement" in favor of Denver. Eight prominent women from across the country concurred, among them Ethel Taylor from Philadelphia, Mary Clarke in Los Angeles, Anci Koppel in Seattle, and Jean Shulman from New York. However, while clarifying the consensus, Bick "heard via the grapevine that there was some negative feeling about Denver from some New York women."[175] Cora Weiss said "it's too far and too soon and too expensive" to attend, while others in New York felt that "they won't be able to get many to Denver" either.[176] Favor for the conference suddenly cooled. Two weeks after selecting Denver as the host city, Bick confirmed the NCC's reversal of the "complete agreement" it had previously established, explaining that "the WSP national conference will have to be postponed due to the inability of the NCC to achieve consensus."[177] Delegates from Washington, DC, Philadelphia, and New York met again to discuss the "political situation" that surrounded the arrangements. They collectively arranged for Chicago and North Shore Women for Peace to once again host the conference in Illinois.

A closer examination of WSP's fatigue reveals the toll that antiwar work took on the organization's participants. In discussing the challenge women faced in juggling "activism with expected gender roles in their families and communities," Amy Schneidhorst recognizes that this was not strictly "a woman's problem." She notes the affirmations provided by David Dellinger as he discussed the difficulties, he faced in trying to limit his "activist duties" for the sake of his family.[178] Nevertheless, WSP women's familial duties applied unique pressure to their activist lives. Responding to a mailer in April 1968, Olga Penn of Detroit Women for Peace gave an honest assessment of her branch's situation. "We have more or less fallen apart," she wrote, "Naomi is in a hospital with angina and I am rather shackled to a guy who has had 3 coronaries and has to be driven to and fro. My time is limited."[179]

Regional disagreements exacerbated this toll and revealed themselves powerfully in 1970 during the tenure of Trudi Young, WSP's first official national coordinator.[180] At twenty-eight, Young was much younger than many of the WSP leadership, but she was respected throughout the antiwar movement for her talents and dynamism.[181] She directed the High School Regional Project for the AFSC, held acclaim as the first women draft counselor and trainer to work for the Central Committee of Conscientious Objectors, and worked as national coordinator for the mass antiwar coalition—New Mobilization Committee to End the War in Vietnam (New Mobe) in Washington, DC. Young "was one of the prime movers" behind the March Against Death, a November 1969 parade down Pennsylvania Avenue in Washington, DC, carrying signs with the names of dead US soldiers and destroyed Vietnamese towns. She also served on the board of COLIAFAM alongside Madeline Duckles, Ethel Taylor, and Cora Weiss.[182]

Despite her credentials and experience, Young did not last long as WSP's national coordinator. She began with enthusiasm, specifying her priorities as re-establishing the sense of "community" that many WSPers felt had long since vanished.[183] This, Young hoped, would once again unify the organization and foster stronger "national/chapter relationships."[184] To demonstrate her affinity for the organization, the new national coordinator visited often neglected West Coast activists and travelled to North Vietnam as a representative of WSP. Such displays endeared her to leading West Coast figures who threw their support behind Young's initiatives.[185] Yet Young received hostility from other branches. She confided in her West Coast allies, explaining how she endured "shitty-difficult days of dilemma" in the face of "a basic lack of trust and a basic breakdown in group process."[186] Young said she received "daily calls about my immaturity, lack of organization, political misjudgment. I get long analyses about so and so's background and emotional instability and therefore 'don't take her seriously.'" Less than a year after assuming the leadership of WSP, Trudi Young resigned. She forwarded her announcement directly to seventy WSP branches, offering a damning indictment of "the inter-personal harassment" she experienced. But the source of Young's "disillusion" rested squarely in the growing distrust that festered between WSP branches in different parts of the country. She lamented the weight of "emotional hassles necessary to work in WSP" caused by "lack of trust, personal ego involvement, failure to organize the many new women."[187] Young left to join Clergy and Laymen Concerned about Vietnam as co-director and remained an active contributor to antiwar campaigns for the duration of the Vietnam War.[188] Seattle's Anci Koppel, a reliable supporter of Young's, wrote to her to admit that "the women in the East have let you down."[189]

Narrowing the geographical focus of WSP to a local level expands the story of the women's peace movement, revealing its vibrancy and unheralded contributions to American social movement history. WSP formed an effective and visible part of the anti–Vietnam War movement, receiving plaudits from many of its coalition partners, praise from historians of the period, and positive reflections from its former activists. But focus on San Francisco goes some way to correcting an East Coast–heavy narrative of WSP's history. Women on the East Coast described an organization in decline. However, viewing the story of WSP's anti–Vietnam War activism from the perspective of San Francisco Bay Area WFP reveals a much more energetic, collaborative, and influential role for women's peace activism within the antiwar movement generally. Examining geographical differences shows how these varied contributions and "local personalities" of branch-level work proved more influential to WSP's life than "the wishes of national leaders."[190] WFPers working in the Bay Area did not simply experience "a local variant of a national story," but forged their own unique histories.[191] Although WSP lauded its localized operations, this local lore is entirely absent from its history.

A focus on local distinctions also reveals the fractious environment in which much of this work took place. WSP's campaigns during the Vietnam War were an invigorating experience, but took their toll on branch accord.[192] Where once cohesion could be relied on, cracks emerged within and between branches as fatigue and factionalism grew.[193] Acknowledging the differences, fissures, and fractures among branches explains the previously difficult-to-understand decline that WSP experienced toward the end of the 1960s. It also presaged the difficulties WSP would face as it experienced the transformations and social dislocations associated with the rise of the women's liberation movement.

CHAPTER FIVE

Remapping a Feminist Peace History in the 1970s

IN 1973, AMID HER ongoing academic research, Amy Swerdlow wrote a progress report. The former New York WSP leader was among the first entering class of master's students in women's history at Sarah Lawrence College. For her thesis, Swerdlow examined the ideological compulsion guiding her own women's activist group. She described WSP's founding as a "spontaneous expression of motherly concern," noting the essentialist attitudes of leading figures who described themselves as "housewives and mothers." However, she asserted that WSP's attempts to "liberate" women by drawing them into the political arena and its organizing "separately as a woman's peace group" made a "permanent contribution to the political aspect of the women's movement." Describing it as a "forerunner" to women's liberation, Swerdlow ultimately affirmed that WSP was "basically a feminist movement."[1]

The assertion would have surprised both witnesses to and participants of WSP demonstrations in 1961. The group's support for women's rights politics was uneven, reflecting contradictory influences. One was a public nonfeminism that was both a reaction to anticommunist suspicion and a true reflection of some participants' sentiments. Another was pride in maternal identity that, for many, rightly justified their involvement in radical politics, while for others was exaggerated for tactical reasons. And then there was the less visible but still instrumental influence of feminist thinkers and campaigners, which was often resisted by their more cautious, inexperienced peers.

Its experiences over the next decade altered WSP.[2] Internal fractures and seemingly endless campaigning changed the tone of leadership as Dagmar Wilson withdrew to be replaced by popular Philadelphia founder Ethel Taylor. Meanwhile, having encountered a new generation of feminists who attacked WSP's "misplaced priorities," activists reconsidered the maternal assumptions that guided their peacework.[3] Their underlying principles did not change—they still believed that women were different from and more nurturing than men and should therefore exert their political power to ensure peace. But WSPers started to embrace new links and collaborations with feminist campaigns to showcase the urgency with which women should embrace their peacework.[4] For the first time they began directly connecting their peace work to broader campaigns for women's freedom, declaring that "peace is a woman's issue."[5]

In this sense, the WSP described by Amy Swerdlow had only just emerged in the early 1970s. But the rapidly changing social, cultural, and political circumstances required a historical reassessment in order to justify WSP's ongoing influence amidst a resurgence of feminist campaigning. As this chapter reveals, WSP's leaders reacted to their new circumstances by projecting an enduring commitment to women's rights and equality, "remapping" a feminist agenda onto earlier activities.[6] Reflected in Swerdlow's academic work and the publicly consumable histories promoted by leaders, WSPers now placed themselves within the story of the women's movement's reemergence and invoked their status as "harbingers of the women's liberation movement."[7] The nonfeminist peace activism of the 1960s became feminist as WSP reappraised the more overtly political participants among its ranks, in particular Bella Abzug. However, this chapter also explains that, despite this notable change in language and rhetoric, WSP's own feminist politics remained vague and ambiguous. Therefore, perspectives on WSP's history varied as maternal activism was periodically valued and devalued in feminist literature. Navigating different circumstances, founders and leaders offered contested memories with conflicting interpretations of their group's feminist priorities. In this sense, authoritative histories of WSP responded to the "protest afterlives" and "remediation" of the value of activist motherhood.[8]

Historian Andrea Estepa reflects that, "over the course of the 1960s, WSP had achieved something remarkable: it had survived."[9] But just barely. Its fractures took a particularly heavy toll on the group's leader, Dagmar Wilson. Her status as the figurehead of such a decisive national antiwar organization thrust Wilson, reluctantly, into the national spotlight. She serves well as a profile in social movement leadership: her humility, dislike of attention, and reluctance to lead were powerful qualities that made her the perfect leader. However, they were also the traits that exacerbated the toll of relentless publicity and endless responsibility that such leadership required.[10] Faced with endless commitments on her time, Wilson often struggled to sustain her zeal. She recalled that her closest coworkers "saw that I could not handle the 'office' work of WSP."[11] Her household served as an unofficial clearing house. Many who wanted to contact WSP but could not find an address opted to write to Wilson personally.[12] Wilson had severe anxiety about public speaking and she later wrote that leading at events "takes a tremendous lot out of me. I can't do as many as I would like, because I can't be sure of being good that many times."[13] Even in later life Wilson reflected that she felt "quite unqualified for the work" she performed.[14]

Wilson temporarily "retired" in 1964, but she remained WSP's most high-profile figure and continued to travel, write, march, and speak as the group's leader.[15] In 1966, she gave a revealing interview to in the magazine section of *The Washington Post*, in which she regretted the toll her position had taken on the lives of her family.[16] Wilson reflected on the calm of her pre-WSP days. "We used to have a very smoothly running household," she said. "It was very relaxed. Now it's hit or miss all the time. Our standard of living has gone down."[17] She recalled that her role in WSP was "hard on the family, no question about it." Though her children had reacted to their mother's activism with "initial excitement," her various commitments ultimately proved "very disruptive" and took her "out of the family."[18]

Having successfully faced down a HUAC investigation in 1962, Wilson was again subpoenaed by the committee in 1964 for having requested an entry permit to the United States for Japanese peace leader Professor Yasui Kaoru. Although part of a 150-person welcoming committee, both Wilson and her WSP colleague Donna Allen were among just three people targeted by HUAC. They were found in contempt of the court in 1964 for refusing to testify to the committee unless it dropped its insistence on holding closed hearings. Wilson received a suspended jail sentence.[19] WSP mounted a campaign as Defenders of "Three Against HUAC," but the second HUAC investigation in two years interrupted Wilson's attempts to revive a professional career.[20] She felt that she had been forced to assume responsibility for WSP as no one else seemed willing to "afford the risk" of "jail, loss of income, and ostracism."[21] Wilson explained that "any satisfaction of martyrdom has been far outweighed by inconvenience, wasted time and personal outrage."[22] She worried particularly deeply about the impact and embarrassment her status as a vocal critique of the American government had on her husband's work for the British Embassy.

The burden of leadership came to a head in 1968. In April, Wilson embarked on a rewarding and highly acclaimed trip to Hanoi with other WSP participants, but on her return, she began raising the prospect of a rotating, elected leadership to share the weight of responsibility that she felt rested unfairly on her. At the Washington, DC, retreat meeting held at Folly Fodor's house in October 1968, Wilson again sought support for ideas that would reshape the group's leadership structure. She acknowledged that others in WSP valued her advice, direction, and ideas, elevating her to a status as "the mythical Dagmar Wilson." This, unfortunately, required that Wilson be frequently nominated as WSP's representative for myriad campaigns, causes, and events, when she really had hoped to just take her place "in the ranks" of the organization since it formed in1961.[23] Throughout the Washington retreat meeting, Wilson's ideas elicited enthusiasm from the other attendees, but proposals that would have reduced the demands on her time drew a less favorable response.[24]

One month later, in her keynote address to WSP's 1968 national conference, Wilson disclosed being plagued by stress. She told her audience that "I'm using SO damned much of my energy—and I've GOT to see more resulting from that expenditure of my energy, otherwise I simply cannot go on this kind of way."[25] Indicating that she would withdraw from activism altogether, Wilson emphasized "the kind of tension and anxiety" she faced on a daily basis and declared that "I can't keep this up for another twenty years if that's as long as I'm going to live." Wilson used her speech to level an ultimatum at those in attendance. "I really have to make a confession here today," she said, "the way we've been doing things, which has been so marvelous, and such a relief, is now to me becoming exactly the opposite—and it's a terrible drain, and I know that I'm not going to be able to go on in this way."[26] The speech amounted to a letter of resignation. The following month Wilson asked others to replace her for prearranged engagements.[27] Citing undisclosed personal reasons, the "mother" of the group quietly withdrew from active participation.[28]

WSP limped into the 1970s, lacking harmony among its participants, lacking influence among the social movement landscape, and more importantly, lacking a sense of coherent identity. After Trudi Young's stint as

WSP's national coordinator ended, local leaders found it "terribly difficult" to maintain their enthusiasm.[29] Participants bemoaned Dagmar Wilson's absence. Though never formally designated as a national leader, her presence offered a "cohesive force."[30] Without her leadership, WSP's fractures worsened. With branches "on the brink of breaking up," activists travelled to the 1972 national conference "looking for a saving program," but returned disappointed when they did not find one.[31]

Recognizing the need for decisive change, key women among WSP's national leadership turned to the skills and dependable presence of Philadelphia leader Ethel Taylor. Respected and well-liked by WSPers across the country, Taylor commanded substantial influence. Founder of Philadelphia WSP, she guided the branch to having a sizeable national presence with protests and educational outreach held on the streets and shopping malls of the greater Philadelphia area. Such was her national standing, Taylor travelled to Vietnam as part of a WSP delegation in 1969 with East Bay's Madeline Duckles and Cora Weiss from New York. As WSP drifted at the turn of the decade, Taylor served as an acting national figurehead, and her peers quickly campaigned for her to take on the position formally. Following a brief consultation period among branch leaders, she officially became WSP's national spokeswomen and coordinator in 1974.[32] New York WSPer Jean Shulman dryly congratulated her, recommending "a good, well-deserved rest" before she tackled "the 'battle' ahead. Lots of luck!"[33] Taylor immediately embarked on a trip to meet activists throughout the West Coast, hoping to restore accord out of concern that "we were becoming two separate groups."[34] Taylor saw "women I had been writing to but never met" and spent time with some "whom I hadn't seen for years." Cohesion quickly returned. The visit ended so positively that Seattle women offered to host WSP's next national conference.[35] Publishing a report of her trip, Taylor expressed that her "love affair" with WSP had grown deeper. "Flying across the country I was very conscious of the tremendous distance which separates us," she wrote. But, after meeting "with all of our sisters," she declared that "it is only physical distance which separates us—we are as close together as if we lived next door."[36]

The renewed profile of the American feminist movement was a far more consequential development for WSP activists. Recent scholarship rightly corrects the impression that American feminism was "in the doldrums" during the postwar era, but there nevertheless existed a period of abeyance from which women's activism on gender equality needed to re-emerge.[37] The 1963 publication of Betty Friedan's *The Feminine Mystique* remains a milestone for its exposition of the widespread, private disillusion of American women who felt severely unfulfilled in their proscribed roles as wife and mother.[38] Governmental recognition of sexism, and the pursuit of legal frameworks to address workplace discrimination, yielded the Presidential Commission on the Status of Women and its final report, *American Women*, alongside the creation of the Equal Employment Opportunity Commission, which arose from the 1964 Civil Rights Act.[39] Enforcement of laws remained inadequate and young women stirred to activism in the Civil Rights Movement and the New Left recognized that existing campaigns for justice ignored discrimination on account of sex and gender. In 1965, the National Organization for Women (NOW) was formed by feminist luminaries such as Aileen Hernandez, Shirley Chisholm, and Pauli Murray to lobby for further change within the political system.[40] Meanwhile, radical feminism and women's liberation emerged as new ideological concepts rooted in group-consciousness-raising sessions that identified sources of women's oppression.

Groups such as WSP ensured the continuation of women's organizing throughout this period, and the group should be categorized as a key influence in shifting American culture toward gender equity politics over the course of the 1960s. However, appeals for equal pay, reproductive rights, and women's liberation moved the theater of women's activism away from WSP's antiwar concerns—not least as increasing numbers of women began to challenge the traditional social expectation that women serve primarily as mothers.

WSP's organizational interest in gender equality remains difficult to determine. The group's formation and initial rise to prominence needed the influence of its leftist/feminist leadership group represented by figures such as Shirley Lens, Mary Clarke, Amy Swerdlow, and Bella Abzug. Their assessment of gender politics was often more advanced, but less visible than that of celebrated feminist public figures of the time, such as Betty Friedan.[41] WSP activists took a keen interest in the history of women's rights activism, some expressing their belief that through their peace activities they were linked to previous social justice initiatives led by women abolitionists and suffragists.[42] Furthermore, as historian Rhodri Jeffreys-Jones argues, many women in the antiwar movement "abhorred the stridency of feminism but wanted political equality," and that "their preference for political and legislative means of opposing the war went hand in hand with legitimization of women in politics."[43] In this sense WSP's women's rights credentials need not have required a thorough expression of feminist politics.

Nevertheless, WSP's archives show little deliberate organizational engagement with contemporary women's rights issues, and the image, political rhetoric, and even publicly avowed nonfeminism exhibited by WSP activists throughout the 1960s contradicted the surreptitious influence of the group's feminist key women. This is particularly clear through statements made by founder and figurehead Dagmar Wilson, who affirmed WSP's distance from feminism and frequently referred to their maternal identity as an important contrast to women's liberation. Wilson explained to the press that WSP was not "striking against our husbands" and that "our organization has no resemblance to the Lysistrata theme, or even the suffragettes."[44] In December 1961, she addressed a gathering of a hundred WSP participants to explain that "as women we must get our 'naughty, naughty boys' to sit down to 'supper' and talk it over. The United Nations is the 'supper' table of the world." She added that "we must not get involved in political issues, then we cannot go astray."[45] In this sense, determining WSP's feminism depends greatly on which activists are produced in evidence—those like Abzug, or those like Wilson.

The point is not that maternal activism cannot be feminist—it can.[46] However, WSP's peacework in early-to mid-1960s did not include a robust demand for gender equity or women's full political participation. Although they criticized male leaders, ridiculed the masculinist thinking guiding nuclear weapons policy, and inserted women's maternal influence into policy debate, many WSPers did not challenge the presumption that the figures in government tasked with changing anything would be men. Describing the beliefs of the "new woman striker" associated with WSP in the mid-1960s, Washington, DC, founding participant Eleanor Garst wrote that they were "pointing out that in this age, the truest patriot *is the man* who promoted peace." She continued by suggesting that politicians "aren't selling the women" on nuclear war because women "aren't hampered by political considerations." WSP, therefore, were "letting *him* know how they feel."[47] Los Angeles WSP's *Peace de Resistance* cookbook, conceived of and written by Southern California coordinator Mary Clarke for distribution among peace activists, similarly depicted the unchallenging femininity of WSP participants. "We'll have peace too," Clarke wrote, "we women, with one foot in the kitchen and one foot in the world."[48] As historian of radical pacifism Marian Mollin describes, among contemporary women's antinuclear activism represented by WSP, "gender equality was still a long way off."[49]

WSPers also did not challenge those who depoliticized their radical stance on the nuclear status quo. Efforts to project "a ladylike, ordinary image" found favor with journalists who, suggested Amy Swerdlow, were "intrigued with the contradiction between domesticity and political activism."[50] A 1962 *New York Times* article nevertheless offered a problematic depiction of the WSP activists it covered. Although reflecting positively on the demonstration, journalist Jeanne Molli described WSPers as presenting the "formidable appearance of mothers-in-law" and identified such political heavyweights as Ruth Gage-Colby as a "Bronx housewife" while identifying Mary Ann Porcher solely by her husband's occupation as a pediatrician. The *Times* article reflected the type of coverage WSP received throughout the 1960s, offering a positive appraisal of the group's antinuclear campaign but demonstrating a belittling condescension for activists themselves.[51] Nevertheless, WSPers enjoyed the coverage and sought to repeat this image for the press. Of the *Times* article, Swerdlow wrote that "the WSP women were delighted to be described as amateurs." In the aftermath of the Test Ban Treaty's passage in 1963, Philadelphia coordinator Ethel Taylor wrote to the *Philadelphia Inquirer* to make a promise "that the women would continue to march in the name of motherhood."[52]

In this way, WSP followed the example of all other maternal peace groups who firmly set themselves and their actions aside from women's rights campaigns, exclaiming instead that their antinuclear campaign represented "the most important issue women ever faced—the preservation of life in the nuclear age."[53] In her study of peace campaigns during the Cold War, Petra Goedde writes that "neither WILPF nor WSP members would have identified themselves as feminist organizations."[54] WILPF historian Catherine Foster writes that the "feminist identity" of her group "waned and by 1965 it saw itself primarily as a peace organization, rather than an organization for women's advancement."[55] The sentiment remained consistent throughout the decade. In a 1965 Christmas Card Campaign leaflet, WSP directly rebuffed associations with feminist goals and stated its campaigns were directed toward the "average woman" who, it believed, did not lobby or picket but "does worry."[56] Certainly much of this rhetoric was forced on

WSP by a political environment that would shun all efforts toward peace if it also upset other aspects of Cold War orthodoxy. Nevertheless, some WSPers' comments revealed a virulent dislike for the women's liberation movement. In June 1970, Anne Eaton, who had so effectively organized WSP efforts in its first few years, denounced the "militants of the Women's Lib" in a commencement address for Hathaway Brown School. Eaton declared that the women's liberation movement had "done for true feminism what the Boston Strangler did for door-to-door salesmen. We must be kind to these people—they all need mothering—but do not take them seriously." Eaton believed instead that, for personal and political empowerment, the women of America needed to look to the example set by Women Strike for Peace, who were "just women who acted like real women."[57]

Antiwar protests became more militant and confrontational toward the end of the 1960s, but maternal peace activists did not experience a comparable radicalization of their gender politics. Comments to the press revealed little change in the public face of WSP from the first strike in November 1961. After a march in Sacramento in 1967, California WFPers explained to the *Sacramento Bee* that the women participants had "all made casseroles for dinner" for their families to eat while they left to protest.[58] The emergence of other peace organizations, such as Another Mother for Peace, demonstrated the ongoing popularity of peace protest grounded in the identity of motherhood.[59] Maternal peace activists did not offer a conception of antiwar thought that critically promoted peace "as a woman's issue" beyond declaring the cessation of violence as a mother's responsibility. As historian Judy Wu explains, "maternalist peace activists who subscribed to 'traditional' gender roles and justified their political interventions as part of their responsibilities as mothers and housewives" found the most unpalatable impact of the Vietnam War to be "the destructive impact of war on heteronormative family life."[60] Cora Weiss, having returned from North Vietnam, reported on her trip that "not a family in North Vietnam has been left intact by the war."[61] Such statements suggest, in peace historian Harriet Alonso's determination, that WSP had not yet addressed "the main theme" that defines a feminist peace movement, which is "linkage between institutionalized violence and violence against women."[62]

Some WSP activists' rejection of women's equality campaigns directly inspired the rise of the radical feminist movement. In 1967, the National Conference for New Politics brought influential New Left figures to Chicago to build a third-party presidential ticket for the forthcoming presidential election. Separating into groups to compose potential resolutions for a policy plank, a "woman's workshop" comprising burgeoning women's liberation figures such as Jo Freeman and Shulamith Firestone developed proposals that presidential candidates could use to spearhead the campaign for women's equality. However, when reporting back to the chair of the conference, the woman's workshop was flatly rejected. The chair explained that he had already accepted a resolution on "women's issues" and would not accept an additional one. This resolution, Freeman recalled, had come from WSP activists who had not even attended the woman's workshop. Their resolution asked only that women work to secure peace, excluding the gender-specific grievances addressed by workshop attendees. Despite attempts to unify the two resolutions and include statements on women's inequality, the WSPers resisted. Freeman and Firestone felt betrayed. WSP's dependence on an image of staid domesticity further "fueled antagonism," and the group's presumption that it represented American women was "the last straw" for Firestone and Freeman.[63] They pointed to their experience at the conference as their moment of political awakening and "the genesis" for the radical feminist movement.[64]

Firestone subsequently orchestrated opposition to WSP at the January 1968 Jeannette Rankin Brigade demonstration. The Brigade drew a coalition of women's activist groups to Washington, DC, to petition Congress for an immediate end to the Vietnam War while also calling for Congress to "use its power to meet the poverty and freedom crisis at home." San Francisco peace activist Alice Hamburg, a key organizer of the demonstration for WILPF and WSP groups, recalled that the Brigade "consciously united the issues of war and poverty, reaching across race and class issues" and that it tried to "insert feminist demands into the struggle for peace."[65] Lawyer, radical feminist, and civil rights advocate Florynce Kennedy similarly urged Black women to participate, saying that they should "feel particularly offended by the posture of their government in neglecting the needs of non-white people at home and killing non-white people abroad."[66] But the convergence of older liberal women, peace organizations, and church groups along with younger radicals and militants from the women's liberation movement produced divisive antagonism from within the Brigade's own ranks. Alice Echols writes that "the women planning the protest wanted to ensure that the demonstration would be peaceful, while the younger, leftist women felt that nonviolent protest had long since outlived its usefulness." During months of planning, activists criticized the milquetoast demands of the Brigade's initial demands while asserting that petitioning Congress at all no longer constituted a politically useful act.[67] Radical feminists took particular umbrage with the implication that women bore special responsibility for ending war.

After five-thousand women descended on the Capitol as part of the Brigade, a group met to discuss the brutality of war, the neglect of domestic human needs, and future plans for mobilization toward peace efforts. It was there that activists from the radical feminist group New York Radical Women confronted Brigade participants.[68] Taking issue with the Brigade's perceived reliance on maternal identity, they declared that women's peace activists "condoned and even enforced the gender hierarchy in which men made war and women wept." They staged a mock burial of "traditional womanhood" in Arlington National Cemetery using a dummy "complete with feminine getup," with a "blank face" and "blonde curls."[69] Firestone publicly rebuked the women's peace movement, excoriating the antiwar protesters for coming as "tearful and passive reactors," rather than as political agents.[70] Although making a broader attack on "the cultural icon of the stay-at-home mom," WSP was, as key organizer of the march, the specific focus of this ire.[71] WSPers described "an incoherent rant" against their group that seemed "bizarre, insulting, threatening, and strangely unsettling."[72]

That WSP's maternal domesticity had been attacked in equal measure by both radical feminists of the women's liberation movement and liberal feminists such as Betty Friedan speaks to the group's vulnerability to criticism from diverse elements of the contemporary women's movement. This vulnerability aggravated a crisis over purpose and identity, steadily building since WSP's formation, that overcome the group in 1968 and continued into the early 1970s. WSPers who previously considered themselves radical found that they had been rejected by a younger generation that condemned their "misplaced priorities" as the embodiment of women's oppression.[73]

WSPers also found that they did not have a monopoly on women's peace activism. In 1971, WSP participated in an exceptional meeting in Toronto between North American women's peace activists and delegates from Vietnam. The Indochinese Women's Conferences grew from a similar 1969 initiative sponsored by WSP and the Canada Voice of Women, during which Vietnamese women met with numerous North American audiences while traveling through Canada. The Vietnamese Women's Union subsequently requested a follow-up visit and reached out to participants of the women's liberation movement and anti-imperialist women of color from the Third World Women's Alliance. Around one thousand women from across North America gathered to attend the conferences in 1971, hoping to reinforce the "global sisterhood" of antiwar activists and work out solutions to end the conflict in Southeast Asia. The conferences demonstrated the multiplicity of politics and identity among women anti-imperialists in the United States and the complex process of negotiation that occurred to foster an international peace movement. Judy Wu writes that WSP and Voice of Women "had to expand beyond their traditional membership base of middle-aged, middle-class, white maternalist women" in order to involve the more diverse constituency.[74]

The gathering ended in acrimony.[75] By calling their part of the event a "women's liberation conference," WSP drew scorn from attendees who disparaged the perceived attempt to "turn the independent women's movement into an adjunct to the antiwar and anti-imperialist movements," and charged that "women's liberation was barely addressed."[76] For their part, WSPers lamented their group's handling of the conference. Former National Coordinator Trudi Young noted WSP's "failure to organize the many new women who came turned on and left turned off to WSP."[77] Amy Swerdlow recalled that, in developing an agenda for the conferences, WSP only pushed "to develop empathy and understanding of the Vietnamese predicament," in contrast to others who insisted "that there be a thorough discussion of the relationship of patriarchy to militarism and an investigation of the role and status of women in Vietnam, including their attitude towards lesbianism." She candidly reflected that "some of us in WSP were, after ten years of militant antiwar struggles, just beginning to make a connection between war and male violence against women. I was one of those."

The Indochinese Women's Conferences revealed the differences between WSP's representations of maternalist solidarity and the more critical feminist analyses that connected militarism, violence, and the oppression of women. Indeed, Swerdlow wrote that "a number of the WSPers considered the question on lesbianism frivolous and diversionary, but others were beginning to recognize that issues such as sexual choice are as essential to the self-determination of women as national independence is to the self-determination of all the people of Vietnam."[78] An article subsequently published in the radical feminist journal *Notes from the Third Year: Women's Liberation*, expanded the critique to claim that "women who remained committed to antiwar activism could be interpreted as having false consciousness."[79] Judy Wu explains that the piece, titled "the Fourth World Manifesto," charged that any women neglecting women's liberation in favor of antiwar appeals as "'dupes' and 'tools' of the male Left."[80]

The Jeannette Rankin Brigade demonstration and Indochinese Women's Conferences accelerated WSP's search for purpose, spurring its activists to reconsider their personal and collective relationship with the rejuvenated women's movement and new developments in feminist thought. Conflicts with radical feminists "were provoking, frustrating, and even confusing," Amy Swerdlow recalled, "but for some WSP women they were also a transformative experience, one that changed our lives."[81] For many WSPers it was the first exposure to any form of feminist thought, and the experience forced them to confront their assumptions regarding gender roles. WSPer Evelyn Alloy explained that the ire of other women had extended "the boundaries of my thinking and understanding."[82]

The challenge to WSP did not just come from negative encounters. WSP's exhilarating Vietnamese excursions provided similar encouragement. Some WSPers' comments reflected an unfortunate elitism and continued reference to family roles, as they described Vietnam as "a formerly colonial backward country" while revealing that their understanding of women's oppression in the region was based on Vietnam's having abolished polygamy "only as recently as 1960."[83] But following her trip to Hanoi in 1971, Amy Swerdlow reported that "Vietnam is a nation filled with extraordinary women" who had "made great strides in achieving power and decision-making positions." She declared that "women's lib was in a very advanced stage there."[84] California coordinator Mary Clarke glowingly recorded Hồ Chí Minh's encouragement that Vietnamese women "should not wait for government or party decree to liberate her; she must struggle for her own liberation" while explaining that she was "convinced that they have advanced in their equality to the point of no return."[85] New York WSPer Cora Weiss similarly observed that "women are very much up front in Vietnamese life today."[86] The combination of radical feminist confrontations and positive encounters with women in Vietnam had a transformative influence on WSPers' developing feminist consciousness.

In the "watershed year" of 1970, WSPers took their first steps toward engaging more meaningfully with the movement for women's equality. On August 26, they joined Betty Friedan and the National Organization of Women to organize the Women's Strike for Equality.[87] Protest events and political activities drew half a million participants across the country to challenge gender inequality. Meanwhile, Bella Abzug, a divisive but vigorous activist for New York WSP, successfully ran for the House of Representatives. Her campaign, framed by the refrain "This Woman's Place is in the House . . . the House of Representatives!" prioritized women's equality in government and politics. Abzug secured resolute support from a coalition of women's liberation groups, young women, neighborhood and community Black groups, Jewish women, Puerto Rican voters, and celebrities such as Barbara Streisand. But she credited WSP victory to the "major role" played by rank-and-file New York WSPers, who had consistently rallied support to Abzug's electoral campaigns throughout the 1960s. This time, however, Abzug declared it "a triumph for all of us," while WSPers took her victory as "an affirmation of the WSP program."[88]

WSP organizers tried to attract new members from the resurgent women's movement, advertising their 1970 national conference as "a women's conference" instead of a "strictly WSP conference."[89] The following year, at the 1971 National Conference in Evanston, IL, WSP made passage of the Equal Rights Amendment a campaign goal.[90] Dagmar Wilson's departure left a hole of influence that was filled by women who disliked using "housewife and mother" as a political identity.[91] These leaders started to urge supporters to act as "women" rather than as "mothers."[92] Pam Block, a WSP intern during the 1980s, noted this transformation in her article "Motherhood in WSP 1961–1973." She wrote that, as American women started to see themselves as more than just mothers, the group dropped their maternal emphasis.[93]

WSPers never definitively articulated their feminist outlook. While placing more emphasis on the importance of peace and disarmament as an aspect of women's freedom, WSPers did not entirely move away from their earlier avowals of the inherent peacefulness of women. Instead, they responded to the rise of cultural feminism by repositioning their maternal peace politics in different language. Cultural feminist ideas—proclaiming that differences did indeed exist between men and women and that patriarchal culture had undervalued "women's experiential history of preserving, rather than destroying the race"—were in keeping with WSP's existing projection of maternal identity.[94] Jane Alpert's *Mother Right* supported WSPers' confidence that mothers had a responsibility to campaign for peace an affirmed that the "resumption of matriarchy" could save the planet.[95] Barbara Deming, who frequently encouraged ideological debate within WSP, argued that radical feminists undervalued "the capacity to bear and nurture children," as it gave women a "spiritual advantage."[96] Cultural feminism offered an alternative understanding of gender and femininity with which many WSP activists could more comfortably align their own identities. WSP activists became more confident and comfortable with finding a role for themselves within cultural feminism than the radical feminism that originally confronted them.

Likewise, WSP never formalized its relationship with the women's movement and the group's presence at women's rights events often reflected the initiative of particular individuals, rather than organizational endorsement.[97] In the absence of formal statements clarifying the group's stance on campaigns and issues relating to women's liberation and sexual equality, WSP's official attitude remained unclear. Several individuals did offer their own personal views on specific subjects while representing WSP. Dagmar Wilson, for example, hailed the development of birth control.[98] Nadine Vesel wrote that Chicago WFP "certainly" supported the ERA.[99] Bella Abzug's crusade for abortion rights, gay rights, and economic equality were well known.[100] However, formal statements offering guidance on key issues did not emerge from either local branches or the National Office. Considering the visibility of grassroots social justice campaigns and their proximity to WSP branches—for example, the lesbian rights movement in San Francisco in the 1970s—it is notable that branch staff did not refer to them.[101] Little evidence emerges to suggest that members discussed the aims of the women's liberation movement in committee meetings or at national conferences. Other women's peace groups offered wavering support for the ERA, and it was not certain that all WSP activists would have held sympathetic views either. [102]

WSP did demonstrate more sensitivity toward women's issues and gender equality, but more commonly encouraged participants in the American women's movement to add peace activism to *their* concerns, rather than integrate a more radical, feminist conception of peace and antiviolence into WSP initiatives. As National Coordinator Ethel Taylor affirmed, WSP wanted to encourage women's movement participants to recognize that "peace is a woman's issue." WSPers wanted to reach "many new women" with an agenda centered on new directions for peace activism.[103] Amy Swerdlow, for example, noted that WSP's primary motive in joining the Women's Strike for Equality in 1970 "was to add to the women's rights agenda a call for the immediate withdrawal of all US forces from Southeast Asia."[104] Adopting the language of women's liberation, WSP issued the Women's Declaration of Liberation from Military Domination. The fliers declared that "we women will no longer tolerate the domination of our lives and the lives of our families by the war-makers in the Pentagon," but remained focused on ending the conflict in Southeast Asia and repealing the military draft.[105]

The group composed a fuller articulation of this appeal in 1974 with the Women's Plea for Survival, an attempt to raise "the consciousness of women to the disarmament issue."[106] Press releases declared "women must liberate themselves from military domination," tying the suffrage movement to antiwar campaigns by declaring that "when women got the vote they thought it would mean an end to war. But in fact, wars, weapons, and destructive technology have increased." While the Women Strike for Peace and Survival campaign reflected a more expansive vision for peace and women's rights, WSP nevertheless continued to urge American women to use their political power exclusively for peace initiatives.[107] As Taylor wrote in a letter to the editor of the *Philadelphia Inquirer* in May 1975,

> Women are barred from the policy making positions in government, and with a few exceptions have always been barred. Our equality must be total. The self-perpetuation of men in positions of power and determinants of our future and the future of our children is not carved in stone. It happens by default—our default. We once said that if women got the vote that enfranchisement would end wars. But we sat back and allowed wars, weapons and destructive technology to happen as we furnished the military juggernaut with our sons. There can be no force more powerful than sisterhood determined to end the arms race, not the human race.[108]

WSPers carried this energy into their contributions toward International Women's Year (IWY) in 1975 and the subsequent 1977 National Women's

Conference. The UN hosted a conference in Mexico City to promote global gender equality as part of its 1975 IWY activities, with delegates attending from all over the world. In the United States, a National Commission on the Observance of International Women's Year, set up by President Gerald Ford, produced a 400-page document with 115 recommended government initiatives arising from the conference. While the commission drafted its report, WSP activist and now-congresswoman Bella Abzug sponsored a bill to expand the responsibility of the National Commission to include a series of state conventions culminating in a National Women's Conference. Succeeding Ford, President Jimmy Carter reconstituted the National Commission in early 1977 with tutelage from Assistant for Public Liaison Midge Costanza, an outspoken feminist. The new commission adopted a more feminist approach, and Abzug assumed the leadership as presiding officer, with commissioners including Gloria Steinem, Ruth Abram, and Jean O'Leary.

WSP achieved significant representation in IWY events. Bella Abzug became a globally revered feminist icon following a well-received speech to the conference in Mexico City.[109] Hazel Grossman travelled to East Berlin in August 1975 and contributed to the World Congress for IWY as a representative of San Francisco WFP. She managed to persuade the US Preparatory Committee to accept Women for Peace as a formal part of the committee.[110] Amy Swerdlow also served among the US delegation.[111] National Coordinator Ethel Taylor was appointed as a commissioner and, with Mary Clarke, Martha Baker, and Edith Villastrigo adding to the contingent, WSP had a noteworthy presence at the 1977 National Women's Conference.[112] Other peace activists also provided valuable contributions to the conference, but WSP activists felt the involvement of their representatives validated their work specifically.[113] Much was made of Jimmy Carter's appointment of Taylor in particular. San Francisco WFP told its followers that President Carter "recognized us" with his appointment of WSP's national coordinator.[114]

The 1977 Houston conference took place over four days in November 1977, with twenty-thousand women descending on the city. Speeches, roundtables, and consultations resulted in *The Spirit of Houston*, a 26-plank national plan of action.[115] Precious little federal legislation actually resulted from the conference's recommendations. Doreen J. Mattingly and Jessica L. Nare claim that "perhaps the most significant impact" of the occasion was "in consciousness raising and networking."[116] Nevertheless, the conference endorsed broad initiatives toward women's equality in American society. It opened with the arrival of runners carrying a torch from Seneca Falls to Houston in order to link the 1977 conference to the historic 1848 convention on women's rights. Betty Friedan's announcement that she supported the Sexual Preference resolution—"the civil-rights-for lesbians plank"—threw aside her famous opposition "to aligning feminism with 'the lavender menace.'"[117] The ERA also emerged as a top priority for the National Commission.[118] The conference adopted a resolution supporting the amendment's ratification with a huge majority, and Lindsy Van Gelder later described the carnival atmosphere, recalling "we conga-danced in the aisles" for the issue.[119] Many other feminist concerns were also addressed by the conference, including abortion rights, domestic abuse, poverty, and national healthcare.[120] Historians Dominic Sandbrook and Bruce Shulman both argue that the 1977 women's conference marked "the crest of the feminist wave."[121]

Attendance at the National Women's Conference suggests WSP's tacit approval for a particular and identifiable stance on women's rights. The conference, for example, advanced a concept of women's equality that directly contrasted the particular brand of conservative, antifeminist maternalism advanced by Phyllis Schlafly. Schlafly had opposed the ERA since the early 1970, founding the conservative interest group Eagle Forum in 1972 to stage a national campaign against the amendment. Gaining a reputation as the "sweetheart of the silent majority," Schlafly felt that women enjoyed a privileged position in American society and that the feminist movement would destroy gender-specific protective legislation and exemptions upon which many women relied. She publicly disparaged the National Women's Conference Commission as "a front for radicals and lesbians." When the IWY received a $5 million federal appropriation for its series of conferences, Schlafly felt that the government had directly funded the campaign for the ERA. She encouraged conservatives and anti-ERA activists to disrupt state conventions that were drafting resolutions and electing delegates for the 1977 national conference. Schlafly also organized a counter-rally to be held in direct opposition to the National Women's Conference, using it to denounce the "lesbianism" and the "misfits and perverts" of the IWY meeting on the other side of the city.[122] With its involvement in IWY initiatives and the National Women's Conference, WSP positioned itself in opposition to Schlafly's vision of maternal antifeminism. Ethel Taylor's position as a commissioner for the conference made WSP's connection to the conference's endorsement of abortion, same-sex relationships, and the ERA even more explicit.[123] Contrary to Schlafly's criticisms, the conference also did not become an antifamily rally, passing many resolutions that sought more government assistance for homemakers and widows.[124]

WSP activists involved in IWY nevertheless devoted their energies toward advocating the minor resolutions on peace and disarmament. In her 1998 memoir, Ethel Taylor recalled that she "had not actually been involved, except peripherally, in the women's movement" prior to working for the National Women's Conference. But her belief that peace should occupy a prominent place in the International Women's Year program encouraged her to participate. She kicked off her involvement with a letter to the *Philadelphia Inquirer*, stating her belief that "International Women's Year 1975 can be meaningful only if it signals the beginning of the total involvement of women in the liberation of our country and the world from military domination and expansion which can destroy us all."[125] In a 1975 op-ed to *The New York Times* co-written with Sandy Kravitz, Taylor further emphasized that "it is exciting to see women emerging as a force" in the United States. But, if International Women's Year was to be successful, "it must signal the beginning of the total involvement of women" in the campaign for peace and disarmament.[126] The International Decade of Women was "the time to start" protesting.[127] Despite their significant representation, WSPers could not make concerns over nuclear disarmament and issues related to war and peace a significant priority for the 1977 conference, despite the theme of peace being endorsed by the 1975 Mexico City Conference.[128] A session on peace and disarmament involving Congresswomen Pat Schroeder and disarmament activist Randall Forsberg only took place in an ad hoc format.[129] Its resolution in the National Plan of Action appeared within a broader section discussing women in foreign policy, international development, and human rights.[130] Some doubted whether the resolution "indicated a pledge of continued support for peace," noting the fact that, out of a delegation of over twenty thousand, only twenty-five hundred signed an anti–neutron bomb petition.[131]

The most profound impact of this period appears in WSP activists' burgeoning historicism of their past activities and support for women's rights endeavors. Historical descriptions written during the 1960s reflected the group's pervasive maternalism, reinforcing WSP's distance from the feminist movement. During WSP's early years, Washington, DC, founder Eleanor Garst drafted an unpublished history with a version of events that spoke clearly to the group's maternal public image. She referred to activists' traditionally feminine appearance, affirming participants' childcare responsibilities, and foregrounding the familial priorities of the group's activists.[132] Garst used contemporary statements and meeting minutes taken herself in the early 1960s to reinforce her depiction. She recalled colleagues dictating that WSP "must not get involved in political issues."[133] Had WSP folded toward the end of the 1960s, Garst's chronicle may have remained the only attempt at historicizing the organization from an activists' point of view. WSP would be remembered as a maternal group comprised of self-described nonfeminists.

WSP's nostalgia grew during the 1970s amid a cultural reclamation of women's history. Gerda Lerner's work in particular drew attention to the way histories of the United States neglected women.[134] Lara Leigh Kelland shows that the women's liberation movement reclaimed "past narratives of women who had realized personal success, resisted patriarchal limitations, and worked for women's equality." This produced an "identity-based history" that could strengthen and unify the American women's movement around a shared memory.[135] Nourished by this environment, WSPers staged reunions with former colleagues to reminisce and reflect on their own story.[136] In 1970, a commemorative issue of the group's newsletter, *Memo*, looked "back on the 60s" with testimonials from WSP activists.[137] The compilation set a precedent for future plenary speeches, meetings, and conferences to ruminate on WSP's past. Mary Clarke's address to the 1972 national conference in Santa Barbara offered her history of WSP, highlighting "its policies and achievements." Enamored with the speech's content, attendees duplicated and distributed a transcript so that non-attendees could read it.[138] Whereas keynote addresses of previous conferences dealt with contemporary issues, plenaries honoring the group's past became a key feature of national conferences.[139]

Depictions of WSP in the 1970s contributed to a vivid and robust lore that not only reinforced perceptions of the past but allowed contemporary activists to develop their own sense of purpose from shared memories of the group.[140] Social movement theorists increasingly recognize this important practice of remembering as vital to sustaining an activist group's identity.[141] As social movement scholar Timothy Gongaware writes, "common understanding of the past" influences decisions "in the present."[142] Mary Clarke acknowledged these intentions directly in her 1972 national conference plenary, explaining to her audience that "the reason I've gone into our past is: How can we know who we are until we know who we've been."[143] Ethel Taylor's address the following year suggested that current activists use past experience to inform their efforts.[144] Nostalgia, lore, and collective memory practices are also important to instill continuity as transformations in collective identity take place. Movement leaders create a "useable past" by carefully emphasizing certain historical aspects and events that can produce "a sense of permanence." This is vital to retain the connection and commitment of participants.[145] As newcomers to the group had little knowledge of WSP's history prior to their joining, their perception of the organization's past relied on the impressions that long-term activists provided.[146]

Rather than just seeking an intragroup memory that could bring their own organization together, WSPers altered how they saw their past relationship with the women's movement to legitimize their ongoing work. In WSP's case, becoming involved in the women's movement required a simultaneous revision of its memory. Activists started to permeate their history with allusions to a longstanding commitment to contemporary feminist issues, making subtle changes to their narrative to place themselves among the popular rise of women's movement activism. Clarke's "moving and revealing history of WSP" at the 1972 National Conference affirmed that "we started as a one day phenomena, but the answer came back loud and clear: we want to be a women's movement, where we make the decisions and not continue as the stamp lickers and office workers with nothing to say."[147] Invoking the past in this way, Clarke proclaimed that WSP had always been a leading proponent of the vision for women's equality feminists were expressing in the 1970s. Following WSP's contributions to IWY, Sarah Diamondstein of Westchester WFP wrote to *The New York Times* that WSP did not "have to turn our energies to the women's movement," because "we were already in the women's movement."[148] By 1979, WSP had codified this story and the eighteenth anniversary journal declared that a "fiercely" feminist rhetoric and outlook had always pervaded WSP.[149] Lacking a legacy of public commitment to feminist causes, WSP repositioned their past espousals of gender politics and centered what were previously considered radical fringe elements of their organization.

The rehabilitation of Bella Abzug's role in WSP shows the tangible impact of changing historical perspective. Abzug was a fervent political actor throughout her life. Her mother once said that her daughter was a feminist from the day she was born; Abzug once jested that her "parents had the foresight to give birth to me in the year women got the vote."[150] As a child, she gave speeches on social justice and women's rights in front of her father's butcher shop.[151] After her father's death, she was not allowed to recite the Kaddish, the Jewish mourning prayer, because she was a girl. But she defiantly attended her synagogue every day for a year to recite the prayer anyway.[152] After graduating from Columbia Law School, Abzug noticed that union officials ignored her on account of her gender, so she began wearing her trademark wide-brimmed hats to ensure she would attract attention.[153] As a young attorney she defended Willie McGee, a Black man from Mississippi accused of raping a white woman with whom he had a consensual relationship. The case became a cause célèbre. Although McGee was ultimately executed, Abzug's defense raised a considerable challenge to conventional understandings of Jim Crow sexual politics.[154] In the illuminating *Battling Bella*, Leandra Ruth Zarnow explains that "what is so striking about Abzug's journey is how consistent she was, stubbornly so." Abzug "drew her energy from being part of causes and movements bigger than herself, but she was always driven to challenge injustices as she saw them."[155]

Abzug enthusiastically joined WSP shortly after its formation, joining a circle of her former Hunter College alumni in Judy Lerner, Amy Swerdlow, and Mim Kelber, but expanding her friendship network to include Barbara Bick, Eleanor Garst, Mary Clarke, Claire Reed, Shirley Margolin, and Lorraine Gordon. Zarnow explains that Abzug "saw WSP as a politically diverse group." Her friends provided Abzug with stimulating late-night talks about peace and politics, but she was nevertheless impatient with WSP's organizational commitment to what she called a "moralistic performance of respectable motherhood."[156] Many of her new colleagues disliked Abzug's demeanor, personally and politically. Norman Mailer once said that Abzug's voice could "boil the fat off a taxicab driver's neck," and her brash tones and caustic putdowns fundamentally contrasted with her generally staid and quiet WSP colleagues.[157] Although Abzug established a "web of influence" within New York WSP, Alan Levy's history of Abzug's political life notes WSPers' "fatigued shakes of the head," largely because they felt that Abzug did not embody the "correct" image the organization wished to project.[158] She was aware of this criticism, reflecting that "they often said, 'Don't let her speak, because she represents something different than what we're trying to portray.'"[159]

Much of the dislike for Abzug emerged in response to her outspoken demands for more rigorous legislative action. Abzug anticipated that WSP's otherwise disarming "moralistic performance" of motherhood would "make it harder for peace women to cultivate a reputation as adept political operators."[160] She lamented her colleagues' dependence on moral appeals for peace, while WSPers, in turn, disliked Abzug's willingness to become involved in the "dirty" world of mainstream politics. Although Abzug felt her peace activism expressed "motherly love," some disgruntled WSP colleagues claimed that Abzug "wasn't motherly enough."[161] New York WSP colleague and historian Amy Swerdlow recalled that other women in her group "couldn't stand" Abzug. "She was always yelling at us," Swerdlow explained, "and no one paid attention."[162]

Abzug's political fervor reflected a separate, more feminist faction from the majority of women who had joined WSP out of "moralistic persuasions."[163] Abzug pleaded for WSPers to recognize their voice. She wanted women to "know what you're talking about. You have to learn what it is." She advised that "it's okay to show your emotion and come in as a mother and as a woman to say this is going to hurt my children, but it's not good enough." This attitude did not sit well with WSP's founder Dagmar Wilson, who was "always a little leery" of Abzug.[164] Abzug recalled having difficulties because "I was a feminist. They were not."[165] The fact that Abzug had come to WSP "accustomed to the concept of billable hours" exacerbated her frustrations, a point expounded by Andrea Estepa who observes that Abzug "felt her time was more valuable" than that of other WSPers.[166] "I made inroads into my earning capacity," Abzug recalled, "I spent all my extracurricular time as a volunteer like anybody else, but for me it was a sacrifice." She remained critical 20 years later.[167] Gloria Steinem revealingly commented that WSP's disdain for Abzug actually "encouraged her feminism."[168]

Abzug rarely featured in stories about WSP in the early to mid-1960s, but her presence and influence grew over the course of the decade.[169] Her political action panel at New York WSP's 1967 conference declared that "The Women's Vote is the Peace Vote," and encouraged WSPers to "approach all women's interest groups and organizations in each community—women in churches, Negro communities, labor, PTA's, the professions and arts, with particular emphasis on women in public life and in elected offices, to spread the campaign to their constituencies."[170] Outside of WSP, she was more commonly known as a women's rights advocate than as a peace or antinuclear campaigner.[171]

Abzug retained a public reputation as a forceful proponent of women's participation in politics, and a dependable and successful asset for Democratic politicians hoping to mobilize voters for an election. Her own run for office in 1970 received broad public support from women, people of color, and the gay community in New York.[172] On her first day in office Abzug tabled a resolution calling for the end of the Vietnam War. She was the first to call for President Nixon's impeachment in 1972.[173] She introduced the first gay rights bill to Congress in May 1974.[174] *US News and World Report* polled congressional representatives in 1972 and found Abzug to be the third most influential member.[175] Throughout her time in Congress she prioritized women's rights issues and demonstrated her flair for pointed remarks about gender hierarchies, once deriding Congress for its "impotence" while remarking that "it's always a shock, I'm sure, to wake up one day and find out you're impotent."[176]

As the presiding officer for the National Commission on the Observance of International Women's Year, Abzug garnered a warm and enthusiastic reception from women around the world.[177] Journalist Myra Macpherson claimed that Bella Abzug's work for the women's movement would prove to be her "major legacy."[178] Former vice-presidential candidate Geraldine Ferraro explained that Abzug "didn't knock lightly on the door. She didn't even push it open or batter it down. She took it off the hinges forever!"[179]

WSPers' altered attitude toward feminism and women's movement activism caused them to reconsider Abzug's historic role in their own organization. The 1970 commemorative memo favorably highlighted Abzug's role as national legislative chairwoman of WSP and her ten-year service as political action director, overlooking the intense disapproval some participants felt toward her feminist politicking.[180] On her election to Congress, WSP celebrated that, finally, it had "our own woman on the Hill." The group clutched Abzug and took her victory as a validation for its own activities and "an affirmation of the WSP program."[181] Swerdlow wrote that the group's "most extraordinary achievement in the political arena was electing its own legislative and political chairperson, Bella Abzug, to the US House of Representatives. This accomplishment was duplicated by no other peace or women's group of the 1960s."[182] For her part, Abzug continued her unrelenting support for WSP activities. Having previously struggled to get the organization to listen to her, Abzug started delivering plenary speeches to WSP national conferences and, on the occasions she could not attend meetings, delegates read statements she sent in absentia.[183] She directed her congressional staffers to help WSPers meet Speaker of the House Carl Albert and arrange bail when participants spent the night in jail.[184] In 1974, WSP made Abzug their Woman of the Year.[185] Decades later, WSP activists continued to point to Abzug's personal achievements as evidence of their whole group's success.[186]

The public record similarly changed to suit Abzug's new position at the forefront of the group's history. Abzug barely featured in news reporting and public stories of WSP during the 1960s, at the height of the group's activism.[187] But later testimonials heralded Abzug as a vital force that drove the group throughout the decade, granting her credit for founding WSP and equating her influence to that of Dagmar Wilson. Despite the stark differences in personality, politics, and performance, Abzug and Wilson are referenced together as joint founders of WSP. Historian Leandra Zarnow writes that Abzug "rarely corrected those who assumed she had been there from the start."[188] After her death, *The Washington Post*, *The New York Times*, and *Los Angeles Times* all declared her "a founder of Women Strike for Peace."[189] Some archival collections now describe the group's success with reference to Abzug's influence. An introductory note to the Seattle Women Act for Peace Archives at the University of Washington states that "WSP was founded by Bella Abzug and Dagmar Wilson," while the online Jewish Women's Archive frames its entry on WSP almost entirely around Abzug.[190] Academic histories also list the group's founding among Abzug's achievements and describe her involvement in the 1960s without reference to the strained relationship she had with both leaders and grassroots activists.[191]

WSP's reappraisal of Abzug was certainly not cynical. To accept Nancy F. Cott's suggestion that historians should pay more attention to "self-naming" among women activists, WSP's activities in the 1960s should not be defined as feminist.[192] But withholding such a classification does not fully account for the context in which WSP acted. Claire Goldberg Moses' compelling examination of the ebb and flow of feminist identity throughout history shows how widespread use of the term "feminist" in the late nineteenth century narrowed in subsequent decades, largely as socialist organizations folded demands for sex equality into broader campaigns for social revolution and transformation of economic structures.[193] The term did not exist in an appropriate form for WSP to identify with during its formative years in the early 1960s. However, as Goldberg Moses writes, by the early 1970s the Women's Liberation Movement "reclaimed the term 'feminist' for their politics" in order to distinguish themselves from other radical liberatory causes of the era. The emerging wave of women's studies scholarship further "recovered women's earlier struggles and had named these struggles 'feminism,'" sparking what Goldberg Moses describes as a "recuperation" of the term itself.[194] In this new political environment, WSP's women peace activists could reframe their past endeavors and "connect to a historical tradition" that was now "widely acceptable."[195] That WSP altered its standpoint in light of the changing social environment is therefore not surprising.

Nevertheless, Abzug's changing status provides a useful measurement for determining the significance of "remapping" women's peace history. WSPers' contemporary activities and statements in both public and private show that, throughout the 1960s, they wanted to keep their maternal peace activism separate from campaigns for gender equality and forthright appeals for women's political leadership. But the later reassessment of Abzug's status exemplifies how WSP's altered perspective on feminism caused a reconsideration of its organizational history and memory. Swerdlow acknowledged that reassessments of Abzug arose from the influence of later social, cultural, and political contexts. Recognizing that Abzug "did not fit the WSP 'mother and housewife' image," Swerdlow wrote, "it was not until the second-wave of feminism legitimized self-assertive professional women" that she became "recognized and admired" by WSP activists.[196]

The value and relevance of motherhood continued to provoke debate among feminist theorists, scholars, and activists into the 1980s. *The Politics of Housework*, a collection published in 1980, opened with Ellen Malos's emphatic assertion that "there will be no true liberation of women until we get rid of the assumption that it will always be women who do housework and look after children."[197] A widely influential article published in 1970 by Redstockings member Pat Mainardi, also titled "The Politics of Housework," subsequently re-emerged and provoked further debate over power dynamics between men and women within relationships.[198] Maternal peace activism became a locus for such debates. Despite her earlier expressions of solidarity with WSP, Simone de Beauvoir offered new criticisms of the group in 1983, declaring that "women should desire peace as human beings, not as women."[199] Micaela di Leonardo's cogent evaluation of maternal protest in

1985 argued that the "Moral Mother" figure prevents critical discussion of the relationship between gender and militarism.[200] Di Leonardo's ranging critique of maternal peace protest argued that it stops women from having to "become feminists," privileges a specifically heterosexual image of womanhood, and serves as a poor organizing tool for continued activism that is particularly vulnerable to "empirically based counterarguments."[201] Others came to maternalism's defense. Sara Ruddick constructed a general account of "maternal practice" based on her own experiences as a mother, defending the connection between maternalism and peaceful beliefs by arguing that the goals and practices of motherhood informed political attitudes.[202] Alice Echols argues that the idea of women's inherently peaceful nature "became almost commonplace in the women's movement by the 1980s."[203]

Yet peace activists themselves continued to wrangle over expressions of maternal identity in their work. In 1981, organizers of the Women's Pentagon Action clashed with the more moderate Women's Party for Survival, an organization specifically formed to cater to women who "objected to the significant visibility of lesbian feminists" in alternative groups.[204] Similar disagreements thereafter "plagued" the Women's Pentagon Action and created rifts "over race, class, sexuality, and notions of womanhood" in much the same way that they had frustrated groups such as WSP in the late 1960s. Such debates were not limited to individual organizations. In 1983, the Women's Peace Presence to Stop Project E.L.F. in rural Clam Lake, WI, loosely affiliated with the Seneca Women's Encampment for a Future of Peace and Justice and the Greenham Common Women's Peace camp, argued about whether to include women who expressed "non-traditional" gender identities alongside "mainstream women (who are more 'straight')." Some attendees believed that "too strong an emphasis on women's issues might be counterproductive" to their campaign against militarism, while lesbian feminists who attended the camp "expressed great discomfort" at having to "hide who they are" and "modifying [their] own behavior (whether sexual, religious, spiritual, etc.)" while staying in northern Wisconsin.[205] WILPF, while providing indispensable support for the Seneca Women's Encampment for a Future of Peace and Justice in 1983, asked to carefully consider "how much feminism" the camp could enact to suit the rural, conservative area of Romulus, NY.[206]

This variable context informed Amy Swerdlow's "official" histories of WSP. She became interested in the new women's movement at the turn of the 1970s, convincing WSP to support the 1970 Women's Strike for Equality and first raised the prospect of the group's involvement in International Women's Year. Re-entering academia, Swerdlow completed both her master's and her Ph.D. with theses examining WSP's maternal politics and the group's successful campaign for the 1963 Partial Test Ban Treaty. In her role as associate director of women's studies at Sarah Lawrence, she introduced a resolution for women's studies at the National Women's Conference and became instrumental in founding Women's History Month.[207]

Swerdlow recognized the power that contextual debates had on informing women's peace history. In her conclusion to 1993's *Women Strike for Peace*, written throughout the previous two decades, she situated her evaluation of WSP "in current debates among feminist scholars and activists regarding the relationship of traditional female culture to radical social change and to feminism." It was "in the spirit of WSP as it was transformed in the early 1970s." Swerdlow believed that WSPers challenged "the gendered division of labor and power in the political culture of the Left as well as the Right." The surrounding debates of motherhood, feminism, and peace activism compelled her robust defense of WSP's maternal rhetoric.[208] "Ladies Day at the Capitol," first published in *Feminist Studies* in 1982, directly engaged with Sara Evans' *Personal Politics* by celebrating the display of WSP's maternal identity at the 1962 HUAC hearings. Swerdlow argued that, by not stepping "outside the traditional sex role assumptions" while critiquing "man's world," WSP activists "began the transformation of woman's consciousness and woman's role."[209] The acclaimed article recreated WSP's creative and dramatic efforts at a time when "most progressive movements, including feminism, were at a low ebb."[210]

However, Swerdlow's opinion changed over time, and she may have conflated WSP's journey to the 1970s feminist context with her own. Her initial research report in 1973 contended that WSP "was basically a feminist movement, though many of its present day leaders would deny this."[211] She provided a more emphatic opinion for WSP's eighteenth anniversary commemorative journal six years later, claiming that "WSP policy throughout" the 1960s was "fiercely autonomist and feminist."[212] But she moderated later expressions. In a 1989 chapter, "'Pure Milk, Not Poison,'" she explained that WSP had "accepted for itself a secondary, supportive, helping, and enabling role" among antiwar protesters, rather than engaging with attitudes toward women's liberation.[213] After the publication of *Women Strike for Peace* in

1993, Swerdlow again defended the political identity of "traditional" motherhood. "We were middle-class housewives working from Christmas card lists and church rosters," she explained. "We were the lady next door, we were concerned about our children, not political power."[214] This reflects the continued challenge of justifying maternal women's peace activism while American feminist discourse continually debated the value of motherhood. It also shows the difficulty of reconciling WSP's ambivalent stance toward women's liberation with some activists' perceptions that they were, and always had been, feminist agitators. If, as Swerdlow argued, activists "were not aware in their early years that they were fighting a battle of the sexes," then feminism was not a feature of WSP's original identity.[215]

WSP activists supported and contradicted Swerdlow's findings in equal measure, with contested memories and confusion over the group's feminist priorities a consistent feature in recollections, reminiscences, and autobiographies. Former participant Naomi Goodman recalled how WSP inspired the politicization of her friends and colleagues. "There was a song at one of the later WSP gatherings," she said, "which included words to the effect that we joined to help peace and found ourselves in the process. This has certainly been true."[216] Nevertheless, many leading figures took steps to continue putting space between WSP and the feminist movement. East Bay Women for Peace firmly separated itself from the new, more radical phase of feminist antinuclear activism embodied by the Women's Pentagon Action of 1980.[217] Alice Hamburg's absorbing history of the San Francisco Women's Peace Office clearly demarcated WSP's antinuclear priorities from "the lure of feminist" political action groups attracting other potential recruits. Hamburg furthermore responded to questions about her experience of sexism in the peace movement by explaining that "gender roles had not been a concern of mine." She had, however, "noticed ageism" both within and outside of WSP."[218] Hamburg's obituary described her activism as "a precursor to feminism."[219]

Meanwhile, in 1998, former National Coordinator Ethel Taylor published an "anecdotal" history of her own experiences in WSP and wrote that "in retrospect we were the harbingers of the women's liberation movement. Our discussions were certainly consciousness-raising." Yet, in the same book, Taylor also recalled that she "had not actually been involved, except peripherally, in the women's movement" prior to working for the National Women's Conference.[220] Eleanor Garst continued to refer to WSPers as "housewives" acting "quite out of character in those lady-like times."[221] Cora Weiss did not consider herself a women's liberationist having never "thought of any issue in terms of male and, much less male vs. female."[222] In a 1989 oral history interview, Dagmar Wilson proudly identified herself as a feminist and evoked her family's close ties to suffrage activism. She declared that she would have taken part in the first-wave of women's rights activism. But she also explained that WSP was "not a women's movement," but a "peace movement activated by women" emphasizing that "there's a difference in that." Adding that WSP emerged out of ideas linked to women's liberation, she underlined her belief that "we were not a feminist movement. We were simply women working for the good of humanity."[223]

Such assessments complicate the idea that maternal peace protests were guided by feminism. In *Peace as a Women's Issue*, Harriet Alonso notes that WSP's early appeal came from its "respectable, middle-class, middle-aged peace ladies in white gloves and flowered hats." She recognizes that this image subsequently "put off" younger members of the women's liberation movement. However, Alonso also argues that WSP held an appeal for "younger, budding feminists" and made other groups, such as WILPF, "seem staid" in comparison.[224] Given the change in WSP's collective identity, and the contestations that leading figures express in their memory, both evaluations of WSP are accurate, dependent on the period in which WSP is being referred and the activists providing the story. WSP's fluid organizational history therefore shows how the fortunes of maternal peace protest are beholden to changing evaluations of motherhood made in feminist circles, and the influence gender identity and feminist beliefs exert on the protest memories of the women's peace movement.[225]

Examining Swerdlow's authoritative histories of WSP in the context of these ongoing debates highlights the difficulty of historicizing WSP's feminist politics. Amy Swerdlow's description of WSP as "basically a feminist organization" mischaracterizes its contemporary approach and transposes an understanding of gender and activism onto an era in which it did not appear. However, it does potently reflect how activists in the 1970s understood their history. Evidently, women's peace activism proclaimed as nonfeminist in the 1960s subsequently became feminist as activists began their involvement in a more public phase of women's equality activism. WSP's organizational history, particularly as understood and expressed by participants in the 1970s and 1980s, "remapped" a feminist agenda onto earlier activities that did not accurately reflect contemporary beliefs and attitudes.[226] As social movement scholars pay more attention to collective memory practices when trying to understanding organizational identities, charting changes to gender identity is a vital part of considering the context of memory creation within activist groups, especially for histories of the women's peace movement.[227]

Historical depictions of WSP have been skewed by a lack of examination of its activities beyond the 1960s. As its experience in the 1970s reveals, activists transformed their understanding and identity to become involved in a more public phase of women's movement activity. As evaluations of WSP depend on the perspectives of its former participants, acknowledging the fluidity of activist identity and the change to organizational memory is important for historicizing the group's activities. It is the context of these changes throughout the 1970s and 1980s that informed Amy Swerdlow's authoritative histories.[228] This aids interpretations of the women's peace movement generally, demonstrating that its activists express differing interpretations of gender and feminism at different periods in their history and frequently needed to defend their legitimacy within the women's movement. Ironically, while the group is celebrated for the success it achieved by campaigning in the name of "traditional motherhood," it was the move away from a maternal position toward a more nuanced and pragmatic argument that allowed WSP to maintain historical credibility.[229]

Yet WSP could not quite make peace a women's issue. That required a resurgence of feminist antimilitarism that moved to the forefront of the American peace movement in response to the bellicose presidency of Ronald Reagan. Feminist peace activists connected war to violence against women in a more pronounced way, some declaring that "challenging militarism is essential for a feminist revolution."[230] WSP continued to write its history with the latest developments in mind, applying another layer of contemporary context onto its remapping of the past. However, continuing doubts over the value of maternal peace protest, and a creeping sense of the WSP's irrelevance, saw its fortunes decline over the next decade. By 1990, WSP's existing leadership were forced to confront the end of their organization.

CHAPTER SIX

Finding Success at the End of Women Strike for Peace

IN A 1987 INTERVIEW for the Women's Peace Oral History Project, Judith Porter Adams asked New York WSPer Ruth Pinkson to comment on the campaigns to which she had devoted her life. Pinkson had been present in WSP since its founding in 1961, joining after decades of work as a union organizer and antisegregation activist. She appeared downhearted. "Having been involved for so many years, all my life, since being a kid and seeing so many things happen," Pinkson reflected, "I don't think we'll see that much change."[1] In the previous decade, WSP tackled numerous campaigns, replacing its anti–Vietnam War activism with resurgent interest in environmentalism, poverty, and women's equality. It also necessarily returned to the antinuclear campaign that motivated its founding. Heightened militarism from the governments of the US and Soviet Union ended the period of détente and brought back the specter of nuclear destruction. The 1980 election of Ronald Reagan catalyzed nuclear fears, only for the American electorate to reward the president's militarism with a landslide reelection in 1984. WSP's antinuclear advocates were weary. Deliberately informal operations, which previously drew newcomers into WSP, now made the group appear disorganized and ineffective to a younger generation seeking more professional, structured opportunities to influence the political system. Reliant on the initiative of their aging leadership, WSPers acknowledged that they needed to wind down their group's operations and leave the "unfinished business" of nuclear disarmament incomplete. In 1990, after nearly thirty years of effort, WSP closed its National Office.[2]

Yet Ruth Pinkson was not entirely pessimistic. WSP, she said, could draw many positives from the general public's attitude toward war and nuclear weapons. The 1980s radically transformed the landscape of American antiwar opinion. The brash posturing of the Reagan administration, which shamelessly announced both that nuclear war was survivable simply if the public had "enough shovels" to dig trenches, but also that twenty-million American dead were an "acceptable" loss from such a conflict, was now frequently challenged.[3] Public commentators ridiculed decades of political consensus around nuclear arms, dispelling the myths of survivability and the absurd bravado of military planners. Hypothetical scientific studies modeled the catastrophic effects of a nuclear conflict, while real medical studies publicized the scandalous rates of cancer suffered by soldiers forced to participate in 1950s atmospheric nuclear tests.[4] Meanwhile, WSP's reemerging nuclear fear mirrored unprecedented public popularity for antinuclear activism, now led primarily by women such as Randall Forsberg and Dr. Helen Caldicott and the global phenomenon of women's peace encampments made famous by activists at Greenham Common in the UK and the Seneca Women's Encampment for a Future of Peace and Justice in upstate New York. Ruth Pinkson saw the ideas she so vigorously advanced and for which WSP had been attacked in earlier decades were now accepted as common sense. She felt that it was "tremendous progress." Looking toward the future, she observed that, "it will be a better world for my grandchildren than I had inherited." Pinkson concluded that, although things moved slowly, "so many things are heartening."[5]

This chapter documents the final decade of WSP's national operations, exploring the juxtaposition of the group's declining organizational influence amid growing antinuclear public opinion. WSP failed to draw new participants into its fold during an era marked by an unprecedented surge in women's peace protest. With bold new actions and modern organizations, a new generation of feminist peace activists overtook WSP at the forefront of the women's peace movement, making its aging leadership appear out of step with the tone and style of 1980s activism. These developments, however, vindicated WSP's long struggle and its activists seemed in little doubt of their historical relevance. As its three-decade-long campaign against nuclear weapons came to an end, WSPers eagerly supported initiatives to record the history of their group, hoping that future generations would learn of their contributions to the peace movement. Much as the cultural upheavals of the 1970s provided a context with which activists understood their own feminist identities, the overwhelming public support for disarmament in the 1980s informed how WSPers interpreted their success. As this chapter reveals, the fortunes of the antinuclear movement, and the weight of the ongoing nuclear emergency, led to varying accounts of WSP's past that were informed by individuals' own levels of ongoing commitment. Emboldened by the current mood, they positively reflected on their past and, even as their organization declined, remained confident that they had "made a difference."[6]

After the 1973 Paris Peace Accords WSPers celebrated the end of US military operations in Vietnam, but their group faced an uncertain future. Journalists reported on dwindling turnouts and a lack of interest in marches and protests, heralding "the decline of the demonstration."[7] Further antiwar protests drew only "puzzled" looks from ambivalent bystanders who appeared "willing to believe" that peace was emerging in Vietnam.[8] Ron Young of the AFSC recalled his members asking at the close of the war, "OK, now what do we do?"[9] WSP's National Coordinator Ethel Taylor understood that "we cannot keep chanting 'Out Now' when as far as the American people are concerned we are out now."[10] She wrote to activists to suggest that "WSP involvement in the war from the early years took us away from what we had organized for—an END TO THE ARMS RACE—NOT THE HUMAN RACE. Now we must get back to it."[11] Acknowledging that the arms race had accelerated without their resistance, disarmament once again became WSP's "chief priority."[12]

The once vibrant antinuclear movement dissipated in the late 1960s. Formerly imposing organizations such as SANE had "dwindled into tiny, marginal groups" while the Canadian Voice of Women, a group that grew in tandem with WSP, dropped the subject of nuclear arms from its agenda altogether.[13] WSP acknowledged that "disarmament" had become "an impersonal concept," an old word that "doesn't register with the impact it used to" compared to more pressing crises.[14] But antinuclear groups were brought back to life by burgeoning public awareness for environmentalism. Pollution was the zeitgeist of the early 1970s, following the Santa Barbara channel oil spill, a fire on the polluted Cuyahoga River in Cleveland, frequent smog reports out of Los Angeles, and observances of the slow "death" of the Great Lakes.[15] Earth Day, celebrated on April 22, 1970, brought together millions of concerned Americans as governmental figures from both parties voiced their support. President Richard Nixon, though personally unmoved by any environmental issues unrelated to the conservation of national parks, capitalized on the public mood. His 1970 State of the Union address mentioned no less than thirty-six separate environmental initiatives, including the creation of the Environmental Protection Agency.[16]

For many new environmentalists, scrutiny of radioactive pollution led them naturally to a distrust of nuclear weapons. Disarmament activist Prof. Frank von Hippel recalled that he did not become a disarmament activist until he "became involved" in opposing nuclear energy.[17] In 1973, controversy over the environmental damage caused by nuclear weapons testing on the Alaskan island of Amchitka led to the formation of Greenpeace. Southern California WSP coordinator Mary Clarke warned against becoming preoccupied with the "popular bandwagon" of environmentalism, advising that WSP use and coordinate "other movements" while reminding her colleagues that peace was "our thing."[18] However, others were attuned to the public interest, affirming the links between nuclear power, ecological hazards, and the militarism that grounded their own interests. WSP asserted that its own historic efforts against nuclear weapons testing put it "in the forefront of the ecological fight."[19] Some WSPers even began criticizing peer groups that did not include an environmental critique in their protests.[20]

A return to the unfinished business of nuclear disarmament renewed WSP's status and influence on the American social movement landscape. In 1977, Mary Clarke excitedly wrote to Dagmar Wilson to inform her that WSP had experienced "a revival" in fortunes.[21] They found a supporter in President Jimmy Carter, who personally endorsed WSP's efforts toward disarmament and asked for their support for his future arms limitation initiatives.[22] Although they did not consider Carter a "hero," they appreciated that "at least he's scared." WSPers therefore felt that his views were "very close to [their] own.[23] They were encouraged by the president's start. Carter scrapped the development of the B-1 bomber and the neutron bomb in his first two years. He also brokered the momentous Camp David Accords peace agreement between Egypt and Israel and energetically pursued another round of Strategic Arms Limitation Talks (SALT II) with the Soviet Union.[24] Following years of unsuccessful attempts to meet with policymakers, a delegation of WSP members finally had the opportunity to enter the Oval Office and convene with defense representatives face to face. Carter's courting of WSP confirmed their renewed influence as spokespeople for the disarmament movement.[25]

Antinuclear activism surged in this period, but its success was mitigated. A rising conservative consensus grew amid the political and social upheavals of the 1970s, gaining ground as Carter seemed to mishandle foreign and domestic crises. While "stagflation" debilitated the domestic economy, hawkish interest groups such as the Committee on Present Danger, the Heritage Foundation, and Phyllis Schlafly's Eagle Forum capitalized on Carter's perceived weaknesses to exert a growing influence on foreign policy discourse.[26] Meanwhile, the government's sustained admonishment of the Soviet Union's human rights record rekindled Cold War tensions. Soviet Premier Brezhnev deployed the next generation of intermediate range nuclear missiles, referred to as SS-20 by NATO, capable of striking any target in Western Europe. Carter responded with a more combative foreign policy stance. The president sanctioned the full development of the MX missile, pledged to raise the military budget, and signed the Presidential Decision Directive 59 that proposed preparations for extended nuclear war. The fragile détente between the US and the Soviet Union dissipated and nuclear tensions rose once more.

WSPers felt betrayed. The group criticized the Carter administration's increased defense spending and reduced domestic budget.[27] SWAP's Anci Koppel denounced the president's motivations as "downright immoral."[28] Others accused him of "nuclear insanity," while the National Office released a statement in late 1979 declaring that he should not be re-elected.[29] WSP even remained divided over whether it should approve SALT II, an agreement for arms limitations that nevertheless allowed weapons production to continue for several years. Though some saw it as a "first step" toward disarmament, others, including National Coordinator Ethel Taylor, felt that SALT II endorsed and codified the arms race.[30] Dissatisfied with the candidate choices in the 1980 presidential election, WSP withheld support for the president and refused to endorse any alternative candidate.

Having exploited social and cultural alienation, economic dislocations, and "anger over the decline of US global power," the New Right's ascendency culminated in the landslide election of their presidential candidate, Ronald Reagan.[31] Previously dispirited, WSP immediately assumed a sense of urgency. Two days after Carter's defeat, WSP put aside its reservations over SALT II. Ethel Taylor sent a telegram to the outgoing president urging him to "act now" to pass the treaty while he still could. Others implored defeated senators to "use the remaining months of their term to achieve ratification" of the agreement. WSP admonished the openly militaristic attitudes of the new administration, foreseeing a "dangerous confrontational period" with the Soviet Union that threatened nuclear holocaust. "Frankly," declared Taylor, "we are scared."[32] So began a prolonged period of agitation against the Reagan administration.

With nuclear war appearing less "unthinkable," disparate antiwar initiatives reformed.[33] The AFSC organized an urgent meeting of disarmament advocates to discuss arms control in late 1979. Mobilization for Survival, Clergy and Laity Concerned, and the Fellowship of Reconciliation endorsed a nuclear moratorium.[34] Meanwhile Randall Forsberg, a defense and disarmament researcher, grew convinced that the peace movement should unify around a single, achievable aim—a bilateral agreement between the US and the Soviet Union to halt the testing, production, and deployment of nuclear weapons.[35] She stressed that "no major disarmament effort can succeed without the support of the majority of middle class, middle-of-the-road citizens." In 1979, she drafted a Call to Halt the Nuclear Arms Race, stressing previous arms limitation campaigns were either circumvented, or "too technical for the patience of the average person." She made an uncomplicated, single-issue demand—that both the US and the Soviet Union freeze nuclear stockpiles at their current levels.[36] "The Call" became widely popular and rallied peace activists into a Freeze Movement.[37]

The values that had underpinned WSP's nuclear criticism for two decades now appeared common sense.[38] In February 1982, *The New Yorker* published a series of articles by journalist Jonathan Schell depicting the implications and consequences of a nuclear war. The serialization and later publication of *The Fate of the Earth* drew praise and horror in equal measure for its depiction, not only of "the extinction of mankind," but of "the death of the earth."[39] Film and television provided their own visual interpretations of a post-nuclear world. In November 1983, ABC aired *The Day After*, a television movie following the residents of Lawrence, Kansas, as they attempted, in vain, to survive a nuclear exchange between the US and the Soviet Union. A wave of controversy followed the film because of harrowing images of victims unable to escape the attack and left facing certain death amid the rubble of their idyllic community.[40] The movie encouraged high school teachers to include antinuclear discussion as a lesson topic in their classrooms, leading students at Calhoun High in New York to write letters of support to women peace protesters at Greenham Common in the UK.[41]

Meanwhile, new medical research vindicated WSP's historic stance against atmospheric nuclear testing, showing that communities subjected to fallout from 1950s weapons tests developed cancer in higher numbers than those in other parts of the country.[42] A lawsuit brought by soldiers whose health was affected by their involvement in weapons tests embroiled the US government in scandal, while mounting evidence proved that former administrations consistently misled the public and knowingly subjected them to harmful doses of nuclear radiation.[43] Scientifics models of "nuclear winter" confirmed the environmental devastation that would follow a nuclear war.[44] Assurances that the United States could recover from a war within "just two to four years" seemed recklessly naïve in light of these new understandings.[45] On June 12, 1982, a million people marched through New York City to protest the nuclear arms race in the largest demonstration in American history.[46] One participant encapsulated sentiments by declaring that "there's no way the leaders can ignore this now . . . it's not just hippies and crazies anymore. It's everybody."[47]

The mobilization of women was the most significant development for the American antinuclear movement. On November 17, 1980, the Women's Pentagon Action drew thousands of women to a series of demonstrations at the Pentagon. With street theater performances, Women's Pentagon Action declared "we are in the hands of men whose power and wealth have separated them from the reality of daily life and from the imagination. We are right to be afraid."[48] Historian Wesley D. Phelps explains that the Women's Pentagon Action "expressed a distinctly feminist critique of the Cold War nuclear arms race" which offered "a bridge between Reagan-era American feminism and the major antinuclear movement of the early 1980s."[49]

The Women's Pentagon Action inspired a spreading phenomenon of women's peace encampments, which formed permanent presences at military sites around the world. Beginning in 1981, women staged a years-long presence at RAF Greenham Common in the UK to protest the proposed stationing of American cruise missiles in Europe. Historically considered in isolation, Greenham was one of a multitude of other, localized peace camps that were connected in what activists described as a "web." Participants created prefigurative communities, experimenting with alternative lifestyles while integrating educational and consciousness-raising initiatives with peace protest. Embracing a diverse constituency of liberals, radicals, lesbians, environmentalists, antinuclear activists, and self-identified "ordinary women," encampments were crucibles of feminist identity formation that transformed the lives of participants. There were at least forty locations of ongoing communities defined as peace encampments, though there were likely many more when factoring in other contemporary iterations such as ecofeminist camps. The majority formed in the United States from 1983 until 1986, with notable initiatives at Seneca, NY, Kent, WA, and Minneapolis, MN. There was a significant cluster in the UK and throughout Europe, with at least two more in Australia. Peace camps attracted hundreds of thousands of women participants during the 1980s, with lasting legacies for those who attended and the communities in which they were located.[50]

The significance of this new phase of women's peace activism rests not just in sheer numbers, but in its ideological analysis of the intersections of feminism and pacifism. Historian Gerard De Groot derisively called peace camp protesters "lunatics," writing that they thought "that the way to get rid of Cruise was to knit a long scarf around the missile base and hang tampons on the fence."[51] This misses the community organizing, education, lobbying, and consciousness-raising initiatives performed by the camps. Peace camps were intense sites of feminist/pacifist theorizing that drew support and contributions from luminaries such as Barbara Deming and Grace Paley. Encampments identified structural patriarchal violence of the nuclear arms race manifesting, physically, in weapons facilities, but also socially in domestic violence and murder. Alongside its antinuclear challenge, the Puget Sound Women's Peace Camp in Seattle campaigned against pornography, demanded better police protection for women, and led initiatives to find the Green River Killer—the most prolific serial killer in America history who operated in the Seattle-Tacoma area of Washington State in the mid-1980s.

Alongside radical feminist antimilitarism, rising numbers of liberal and maternal peace activists also rejuvenated the women's peace movement. Following her successful revival of Physicians for Social Responsibility, Australian physician and antinuclear activist Dr. Helen Caldicott formed the Women's Party for Survival in 1980 as a counterpoint to the radical lesbian feminism of groups like the Women's Pentagon Action.[52] Initially gathering around a kitchen table in Cambridge, MA, the Women's Party for Survival promoted itself exclusively to women using maternal identity as its frame for understanding nuclear arms. Caldicott argued, repeatedly, that preventing nuclear war was "the ultimate parenting issue."[53] Caldicott rolled Women's Party for Survival into a new, more professional, and bureaucratic outfit, Women's Action for Nuclear Disarmament (WAND). The group listed as its most important legislative priority the passage of bills "that can lead to a bilateral testing moratorium and eventual negotiation of a comprehensive test ban treaty."[54]

The women's peace movement of the 1980s bore striking similarity to earlier periods of activity. Through Caldicott, WAND used the same rhetoric to inform its peace work that informed WSP in the early 1960s. It justified its work by declaring that "as mothers we must make sure the world is safe for our babies."[55] WAND's founding statement argued that "as women, we have traditionally been assigned the responsibility of caring for and raising children" and, "accustomed to managing a home, a family, and a job, [women] can organize the United States for survival."[56] The value of maternal identity and traditional expectations that women protesters act "respectably" continued to provoke heated analysis between different sections of the women's peace movement. Feminist theorists such as Simone de Beauvoir remained critical of women organizing around maternal identity, but WAND's soaring membership showed the latent power of such a stance.[57]

Despite the unprecedented size and energy of the women's peace movement, WSP notably lacked visibility amid the new surge in activity. WSP leaders were initially unconvinced of the prospects of Randall Forsberg's Freeze Movement and limited their support for the campaign. National Coordinator Ethel Taylor wrote to her group that the initiative was "a marvelous tool," but doubted its effectiveness as it was not legally binding.[58] In turn, the public viewed WSP as peripheral and ineffectual compared to newer groups. Judy Mann, a journalist who wrote about the politics of the women's movement, lamented that British peace activists visiting the United States chose to base their operations in WSP's headquarters, "which is hardly the political arm of the League of Women Voters."[59] WSP activists supported the organizing and maintenance of women's peace camps in the UK and the US, but kept themselves apart from the radical feminists driving the new upsurge in women's peace protest.[60] East Bay WFP offered advice to the organizers of the 1981 Women's Pentagon Action but affirmed the ideological distance they felt from its organizers.[61] Reflecting WSP's irrelevance, radical feminists attacking the value of maternal peace protest directed their ire toward newer groups, rather than the elder stateswomen of WSP.

WSP nevertheless sought to capitalize on the new climate of protest with a recruitment drive.[62] Veteran activists began to publicize WSP, exhorting that its open, moderate stance fit perfectly with the Freeze Movement.[63] In addition to marches and demonstrations, WSPers made effective use of flyers, ads, and billboard signs. SWAP paid for two hundred signs in Seattle's buses urging the public to "Elect Candidates Who Will Work for Peace," while New York WSP had a Spectacolor sign on a Times Square Building. Los Angeles WSP bought their own billboard and, in Philadelphia, ten billboards in strategic locations linked nuclear war to the city's tricentennial celebrations. They read "Philadelphia—300 Years to Build—30 Seconds to Destroy." East Bay WFP arranged newspaper interviews and talk shows while helping to organize Berkeley Students for Peace. Dagmar Wilson worked locally in Loudon County, VA, to organize groups. Meanwhile, in Chicago, Shirley Lens reveled in her reputation as a gadfly having encourage the formation of two area groups. On April 10, 1982, some 50,000 people attended a demonstration on disarmament initiated by Chicago WFP.[64]

WSP made particular efforts to highlight the absurdity of strategists who saw nuclear war as a winnable event. A 1980 article co-authored by Colin S. Gray, an advisory member to the Arms Control and Disarmament Agency proved useful to WSP's endeavors. Gray expressed the view, shared by several defense planners, that the estimated deaths of twenty million American citizens should not dissuade the government from launching a nuclear war.[65] WSP exploited the comment, intimating that the government considered millions of American lives expendable. Asserting that Reagan considered there to be an "acceptable" level of civilian deaths, Ethel Taylor designed an advertisement for nationwide dissemination. It declared "I Refuse to be One of 20 Million 'Acceptable' Dead," and urged members of the public to become "one of twenty million" to state "I am not a statistic. I and my family refuse to be part of the 20 million acceptable dead."[66] The campaign's simplicity, both in highlighting government attitudes and personalizing the effects of nuclear war, brought substantial support from members of the public.[67] Thousands of people responded to the project. Though participation did not require communication with WSP, many sent notes of support to branch staff.[68] The campaign certainly raised interest in WSP and proved highly popular among other peace organizations. *Bulletin of the Atomic Scientists* reproduced the ad as a full-page item in their February 1983 edition and the particular phrasing used by the campaign also brought acclaim.[69] Gender and security scholar Carol Cohn juxtaposes the slogan with the abstract language often employed when discussing nuclear war. She notes that the "very act of putting phrases like '20 million acceptable dead' into human consciousness cracks our conceptions" and highlights the reality that exists behind the "theoretical plans of defense intellectuals."[70]

Reagan's determined confidence in his "dream" of a Strategic Defense Initiative (SDI) offered another avenue to ridicule American nuclear militarism.[71] SDI's plan to use futuristic lasers to blast missiles out of the sky was derogatively labeled "Star Wars" by its opponents, including members of the scientific community who rebuffed the president's unrealistic expectations of "current technology."[72] With public opinion on SDI remaining mixed, WSP sought to galvanize opposition, predicting that "Star Wars will fall on the facts of it—when enough people have the facts."[73] Noting public confusion and lack of knowledge about SDI, Ethel Taylor drafted *A Basic Primer on Star Wars for the Legitimately Confused*. A central part of WSP's Stop Star Wars campaign, the booklet addressed "all those Americans who are legitimately confused by and scared of this escalation of the nuclear arms race into space." Taylor concisely described the impossibilities of SDI's planned function and spelled out the farcical nature of research into the program. WSP ridiculed Reagan's vision by pointing out the similarities between SDI and a futuristic weapon featured in *Murder in the Air*, a 1940 movie starring the president. *A Basic Primer* mockingly remarked that he "is now starring in another science fiction production."[74] Referencing the criticisms of renowned scientists, the booklet argued that the public were correct to be confused about the program, as officials had systematically "swindled" them through a concerted program of "disinformation and the selling of Star Wars."[75]

A Basic Primer was distributed with an "educational kit" designed to help others teach the intricacies of SDI to the public.[76] The inclusion of a detailed slide show and accompanying script encouraged WSPers to lead study groups and public meetings on the issue. "A Short Course for the Legitimately Confused" covered the origins and history of the nuclear arms race before discussing SDI and the 1968 Anti-Ballistic Missile treaty. It then explained, in simple terms, how missile defense was expected to function and the problems involved, and it encouraged people to "start the process of change where they live."[77] By combining *A Basic Primer* with an appealing educational show, WSP's Stop Star Wars campaign proved highly popular. Fellow peace activists called it an "excellent tool . . . both informative and readable."[78] The group distributed 45,000 copies of the booklet in 1986. By the following year Taylor reported it had gone into its "eighth 10,000 printing."[79]

The widespread public distribution of WSP materials masked poor attendance at its events. Only twenty-two women attended the 1982 Philadelphia national conference, while twenty-nine travelled to Berkeley the following year, substantially lower than the near 100 participants who reliably attended such meetings in previous decades.[80] Ultimately WSP was unable to cultivate sustained commitment from anyone but the stoic leaders that had served since the early 1960s. Ethel Taylor initiated most of WSP's projects during the 1980s as she felt solely responsible for the instigation of national campaigns.[81] The burden on WSP's leaders to keep the organization going became clear in the aftermath of Shirley Lens' withdrawal from Chicago WFP. Lens had influenced activities in the Chicago area since the branch's foundation. On announcing her decision to retire in 1986, the branch felt it would struggle "to keep Women for Peace as a viable group." Lens's colleagues exhorted that "we will have to pitch in to help fill the gap."[82] An unsigned letter written to former figurehead Dagmar Wilson recorded it as a "sad fact" that "we have [fewer] branches than when we started and the same people are in positions of leadership."[83]

WSP could not entice younger peace activists to join them. Addressing the 1984 national conference, WSP activist Pat Gross voiced her exasperation, exclaiming "although WSP has not lost ground, it is barely holding its own . . . now is an ideal time to increase our membership, but HOW?!"[84] WSPers worried that "we are not developing a replaceable leadership," and unease grew over the group's ageing character.[85] Ethel Taylor remarked at the 1986 national conference that "25 years ago, our feet didn't hurt, our eyesight was keener, and we had more of a waistline."[86] She saw the recruitment of younger activists as an urgent necessity if WSP was to secure the future of the organization. Los Angeles WSPer Mary Clarke observed that "our natural allies in our work are our sons and daughters, a generation that has inherited our mistakes and problems, but a generation that has taken heart from our challenge."[87] However, older activists began to recognize their inability to entice their children to join. Ethel Taylor's daughter, while proud of her mother's efforts, did not herself "take time for activism."[88]

WSP's problems were exacerbated by its activists' reluctance to update its approach and processes to meet contemporary social protest attitudes. In the early 1980s, many peace organizations recognized the need for more professionalized operations than had been required previously. Writing later in the decade, John Trinkl addressed the disarmament movement specifically to note that "too many progressive grassroots organizations are wedded to old-fashioned notions about citizen participation." In the 1980s, he added, building a mass movement had less utility than "motivating grassroots activists to execute a simple financial transaction—writing a small but substantial check."[89] WAND confronted this necessity, conducting a nine-month research initiative into organizational strategy. It accepted that "tremendous social and technological change," including the development of telecommunications and the "complexity of everyday life," necessitated a reassessment in how it communicated with the public.[90] WAND acknowledged that most people now "would prefer to write a check and delegate management responsibility to a trained professional staff."[91] The majority of the public now understood the dangers and consequences of nuclear war and did not need further convincing. Instead, it set out to tackle policy at a governmental level. Professional lobbyists, complemented by donor networks and financial contributions, appeared the most effective way to achieve this. The Freeze movement also engaged with political processes and formed political action committees to "manipulate the technology and organization of contemporary campaigning."[92] Bradford Martin suggests that, while heavily influenced by their 1960s predecessors, the majority of 1980s activists started to develop "new tactical innovations . . . to supplement 1960s-style direct action."[93]

At WSP's 1982 national conference, influential activists from the New York branch asserted the need to modernize. They suggested that WSP's operations needed formal structure, which would require abandoning the unorganization that had come to define the group's collective identity. Trying to cope with the array of new antinuclear initiatives open to them, New York WSPers recommended a larger, more financially stable national office and the installation of official leadership positions, including an administrator, legislative director, and secretary-treasurer. More consequential was the proposal to institute official, paid membership with a $25 annual fee. Since its formation WSP had resisted any proposal that required participants to sign up for formal membership and pay regular fees.[94] The changes proposed at the 1982 conference therefore represented a radical shift in WSP's operations and in its sense of self. Following a detailed proposal, the conference agreed to create a foundation for research and education, professionalizing the informal research committees that were vital to WSP's early success. The foundation granted tax-exempt status to WSP for the first time, making it comparable to its contemporaries, such as WILPF, while yielding more financial benefits. WSP would offer an easier method of fundraising and the prospect of receiving income from new donors exclusively offered grants to tax-deductible organizations.[95] The appearance of the foundation's label on WSP campaign documents made the group appear more professional.[96]

Those accustomed to the traditional methods were openly uncomfortable with attempts to change WSP and expressed their discontent. Dagmar Wilson, at this stage more involved with local organizing as a part of Loudoun County Citizens for Disarmament, wrote of her unhappiness at proposed modifications to WSP. Edith Villastrigo, the national legislative director, also voiced concerns.[97] New processes caused "quite a bit of confusion," obliging Secretary Ruth Tabak to distribute a step-by-step guide of the organization's latest procedures.[98] While some urged WSP to revert to its previous setup, those wishing to modernize grew exasperated with what they saw as stubborn unwillingness to adapt to contemporary circumstances.[99]

The reluctance to alter WSP's operations arose from more than just uncertainty over new processes. Opponents were far more concerned that changes to the group's methods would profoundly alter its very identity. WSP had always publicized that the structureless format of the group was an outgrowth of their attitudes toward activism and community organizing generally. Making WSP into a more professional unit therefore troubled its activists on a deeper level. Couching their opposition to the new membership policy in practical terms, Washington, DC, WSPers opined that making WSP "a membership organization and an activist women's movement" deeply affected them personally.[100]

Edith Laub, who continued to support the modernization of WSP, acknowledged that "our women were terrified of losing their identity, their privacy, their 'differentness'" should WSP try to change its method of organizing.[101] Even aesthetic updates made to WSP's newsletters led to criticism. Following some redesigns, an unsigned letter sent to WSP's leaders complained that their group no longer held its former appeal. That the organization now owned a word processor meant it had "enough money," and therefore should no longer need to request funds from its supporters. WSP appeared able and willing to "hire editors" and "pay for printing," signaling a departure from its previously unsophisticated methods. "Hurrah for your becoming more affluent," the complaint continued, "but you attract me less." The author of the letter ruminated nostalgically on the amateur qualities of past mailings, "mimeographed, stapled together. It gave me the impression that here were women really working for peace, an inexpensive voice crying in the wilderness that touched my heart and made me contribute." By updating the newsletter to a "modern format," the complainant felt that WSP had betrayed its very identity.[102]

Many long-standing groups experienced similar problems in this period. Assessing WSP's recruitment of new, young activists, Libby Frank asserted that Church Women United and WILPF also wrestled with membership issues. She noted that, at one meeting, she "sat next to" the 65-year-old William Sloane Coffin, President of SANE/Freeze and a veteran of the peace movement. "He spoke at a WILPF luncheon in NYC and he thinks he was the youngest person there!"[103] But these more robust organizations absorbed such challenges and actually expanded their membership in this period. By early 1985 SANE boasted over a hundred-thousand members. WAND's professional approach appealed to young female activists who swelled its ranks to twenty-five thousand. Meanwhile, its certain organizational structure and historic prestige ensured that WILPF progressed throughout the decade.[104] In contrast, WSP's persistence in its loose organizational structure saw it ill-equipped to deal with the issue. Discussions at its 1983 national conferences conceded that WSP could not compete with its rivals. Its "sister group WILPF" appealed to WSP's constituency, but was in a better position to do so, while "many women have already joined" SANE or WAND.[105]

Aversion to modernization was particularly debilitating for WSP as it failed to respond to new motivations guiding women's activism. In its 1960s heyday the organization depended on people to volunteer administrative and organizational help. The ascent of women's liberation, however, empowered women to demand payment for these sorts of tasks. The National Organization for Women took the position that volunteering was akin to unpaid housework and extended women's domestic subordination into the public sphere. NOW observed that modern middle-class women felt that such work conferred "little status" and reinforced women's low self-image.[106] WSP acknowledged these sentiments. Leaders stated that "these are different times than 25 years ago. Women need to work for money." They observed that "the full-time volunteers who used to be available are not available anymore" and accepted that "two of our most active, loyal younger

Philadelphia members" would look for part-time paying jobs and limit their contributions to WSP. But it still struggled to adapt to this climate and chose not to install more paid positions. Rather than it being "a reflection on the worth of the organization," WSP's leaders felt these circumstances were "a reflection of reality" they could do little to change.[107]

The peace movement's surge of optimism and confidence shattered after President Reagan's landslide 1984 re-election.[108] Many voters agreed with the Democratic platform, but vice-presidential candidate Geraldine Ferraro explained that Reagan's "style had been more appealing to the voters than his substance . . . his politics of optimism, of never being the bearer of bad news, had catapulted him into popularity—and victory."[109] Having campaigned for Walter Mondale, WSPers seethed with frustration. Amy Swerdlow recalled wanting to "tear my hair out and say 'for heaven's sake, what's going on in this country?!' "[110] The huge Republican victory came as a blow to Freeze activists who had hoped to influence the election. Frances B. McCrea and Gerald E. Markle noted that the movement itself "began to fall apart" in 1985.[111] Randy Kehler, one of the leaders of the Freeze campaign, explained that "the movement suffered from having a support based that was 'a mile wide and an inch deep.' "[112]

Some still working with WSP had a more positive attitude, staying confident and refusing to dwell on the apparent setbacks they faced. A rumor circulating around San Francisco in 1984 claimed that Women for Peace was "dead."[113] However, WSPers dug in for "four more years of Reagan." Some voiced determined optimism on his re-election. At the 1984 national conference, Pat Gross declared that "now is an ideal time to increase our membership."[114] Ethel Taylor supported such an attitude, believing that "the Reagan victory will be the prod to goose millions of Americans into the peace force because of fear."[115] East Bay WFP activist Rose Dellamonica asserted that, while nuclear weapons continued to exist, "the job doesn't end and the responsibility doesn't end—I will probably have this sense of responsibility until the end of my life."[116] Underlying this tenacity was an understanding that WSP had to tie up loose ends. The group had "unresolved business," chiefly the fulfilment of their founding purpose and, in May 1985, WSP publicly endorsed Joint Resolution 3 legislation that urged President Reagan "to resume talks with the Soviets for a comprehensive nuclear test-ban treaty."[117] In their statement, the organization invoked their own historical legacy, tying the Comprehensive Test Ban Treaty to their earlier campaign for the Partial Test Ban Treaty. It declared that "President Kennedy's Limited Test Ban Treaty pledged signers 'to achieve the discontinuance of all test explosions of nuclear weapons for all time and to continue negotiations to this end.' This commitment is yet to be fulfilled." Emphasizing their determination, WSPers declared "a ban on all nuclear explosions is the unfinished goal of Women Strike for Peace."[118]

Progressives also faced a battle over history. Believing that the public's pessimistic attitudes toward the recent past harmed the United States, Reagan relitigated the battles of the previous decade and called for the public to "recapture our dreams, our pride in ourselves and our country" and "bring about a spiritual revival in America."[119] The president thought that attitudes toward the 1960s inhibited such a revival and resolved to dispel any lingering doubts over the period's legacy. In August 1980, as a presidential candidate, he had controversially declared that the Vietnam War represented "in truth, a noble cause" at the Chicago Veterans of Foreign Wars convention.[120] Although this rhetorical flourish delighted the veterans present, it received a mixed reaction elsewhere. In *The Boston Globe*, Mary McGrory attacked Reagan for his choice of words, claiming that it revived the "poisonous enmity" of the war years. She claimed that he wanted to "rehabilitate" the legacy of the war in order to fight another one.[121] Responses to the proposed design for the Vietnam Veterans Memorial further symbolized public division over the appropriate legacy of the Vietnam War.[122] Described by historian John Bodnar as "more an expression of grief and sorrow than a celebration of national unity," many felt the memorial represented the "political war waged here at home" rather than the sacrifice of Vietnam veterans who deserved a more fitting tribute to their patriotism.[123]

Yet Reagan's attempts to re-evaluate America's 1960s experience reflected the public mood and journalists observed that the president's view of the period was widely shared.[124] Historian Phillip Jenkins writes that, for many, conditions in the 1980s "were bad, it seemed, because sixties values had let them get so bad."[125] While some accounts cite the decade as a period of "Great Reconciliation" between 1960s liberalism and rising conservative attitudes, divisions remained throughout the 1980s, especially among past social movement activists.[126] Todd Gitlin and Tom Hayden, former presidents of SDS, eulogized the 1960s for having opened up political and cultural space.[127] In contrast, Peter Collier and David Horowitz, former co-editors of the radical magazine *Ramparts*, rejected the New Left and "shouted good riddance to *The Destructive Generation*."[128]

A surge in publications addressing the social movements of the 1960s spurred increased concern in how WSP would be represented historically. Amy Swerdlow highlighted critical pieces by Mary McGrory and Dave Dellinger as particularly troublesome.[129] Adding to her consternation was the fear that these types of work "will shape the memory and the consciousness of the next generations." New activists were eager to learn about the history of the women's peace movement, but lacked the content to do so. Jill Liddington, an organizer of the women's peace camp at Greenham Common in the UK, explained that the upsurge in women's peace activities stoked "curiosity about precedents." She remarked that "it provoked the question: did women do anything for peace *before* Greenham?"[130]

Women peace activists responded in kind. Attempting to create a forum for integration, information sharing, dialogue, and action, the Seneca Women's Peace Encampment offered a summer program of workshops to raise awareness about issues relating to women and peace.[131] Chief among them was a workshop celebrating "herstory" that placed the recent upsurge in protest within a long history of women's activism.[132] The story of WSP was disseminated to a new generation. A pamphlet explaining the peace camp phenomenon stated that "seeds for believing the effectiveness of such actions" came from previously successful instances of feminist organizing, such as the "women's peace strike of 1961." The piece continued by equating the impact of WSP with the historic 1848 Seneca Falls Women's Rights Convention.[133] Workshops taught the history of women in the peace movement by describing centuries of women's efforts before reciting the "herstory of WSP."[134] WSP could not, Swerdlow wrote, afford to be forgotten, nor have its activities "distorted" by historians. She made her purpose clear. "There is no doubt that we, in WSP, made history . . . now I think we must write it."[135]

In this climate, WSP sought to increase its history-making efforts. Having previously limited themselves to intraorganizational initiatives like commemorative journals and anniversary celebrations, WSP activists now had cause to expand their horizons. Dagmar Wilson provided guest lectures for community groups and peace campaigns that wished to hear her expertise on the "roots of the women's peace movement."[136] Bay Area branches in particular emphasized that "it is a good thing to remember and treasure our past."[137] Having developed a close relationship with WSP following the 1965 Jakarta meeting, the Vietnamese Women's Association requested information to supplement a book and museum exhibition about the Vietnam War. WSPers set out to compile "posters, articles, photos" and various other materials.[138] Requests also came from "historical societies, universities and people engaged in Peace and Conflict Studies." Such requests raised concerns that no written record of the organization's activities existed. Acknowledging that their archival materials were in a "terrible disorder," WSPers resolved to arrange their records and build an accurate and concise history of their experiences.[139]

Meanwhile, the Palo Alto branch of WILPF developed a project that sought to record the personal testimonies from women's peace activists. Under the leadership of branch member and Stanford University instructor Judith Porter Adams, the Women's Peace Oral History Project conducted oral interviews with WILPF and WSP activists in the San Francisco Bay Area. The initiative expanded into a ten-year-long nationwide venture, involving 256 recordings of over 90 members of the women's peace movement.[140] Eager to have their stories put on record, a number of WSP activists begin their own historical projects.[141] Hazel Grossman and Alice Hamburg, having led the San Francisco Women's Peace Office for many years, set about writing a history of women's peace activities in the city.[142] Hamburg also interviewed activists for the Women's Peace Oral History Project. National Coordinator Ethel Taylor began drafting her own anecdotal account of WSP. In Seattle, branch leader Anci Koppel enrolled in an oral history course at her local college, hoping to record interviews dedicated to SWAP's history.[143]

Understanding that capturing their history required materials from an array of past and present activists, leaders reached out to their colleagues. A 1984 newsletter implored "if you have flyers, newsletters or other mementos of the sixties and early seventies, please contact our office. We will need lots of help!" Participants of the Women's Peace Oral History Project often recommended other people for interviewers to speak with.[144] Swerdlow made a conscious effort to "recognize the contributions of as many women as possible."[145] She asked WSPers to complete questionnaires to inform her research, making clear her belief that "the WSP story is not mine, but ours. Just as we worked together to make our history, I think we have to work together to write it."[146] After requesting help gathering materials, San Francisco WFP gleefully reported that "not only are we the recipients of numerous cartons of historical documents and offers of additional materials. But close to one hundred members and friends of Women for Peace and WILPF have sent generous donations. We are receiving offers of help to do interviewing and office work. We also need professional help in transcribing interviews of our 'peace veterans.'"[147]

Nevertheless, projects encountered limitations as past and present leaders assumed responsibility for their output. Amy Swerdlow often asked key figures to revise her work prior to its publication.[148] She sent every chapter and other large extracts of her work to Dagmar Wilson for her "frank and honest" feedback.[149] Wilson obliged, offering significant comments and edits to Swerdlow's writing. Wilson's centrality to key events in WSP's past provided many insights. Nevertheless, Swerdlow's work often ceded to Wilson's personal judgment. On one occasion, she apologized for a piece of writing that had not "given proper weight to the vulnerable position" Wilson was in. She further sought to reassure the former leader that she had a final say on her work. "Don't worry," Swerdlow wrote Wilson, "nothing will be published without you seeing it."[150]

Most efforts had to run under the initiative of contemporary leaders who were points of contact. However, they often struggled to get responses from grassroots figures. Cora Weiss appealed for archival material to build a history of anti–Vietnam War activism, but her efforts largely involved correspondence with key women.[151] Hazel Grossman similarly argued that in order to compile an accurate history of WFP's activities in San Francisco, "we will have to depend at least in part on former chairs and officers."[152] Key women recognized that they had simply lost touch with former grassroots figures and were, therefore, unable to solicit their stories. Some branches, for various administrative reasons, did not send their materials to be recorded, meaning their own unique accounts were lost. SWAP in particular was unrepresented in the histories, not being involved with nationwide oral history projects or the compiling of national records.[153] Accordingly, few grassroots participants, either past or present, gave their own perspective to the rapidly building story of WSP.

The contemporary social movement landscape informed WSPers' historical outlook and influenced how the group framed its past. The Reagan administration's failed attempts to expand US military intervention in Central America allowed WSPers to foreground the legacy of their anti–Vietnam War campaigns. With revolutions and counterrevolutions occurring across

Central America, the president saw in the region "an opportunity to resume the anticommunist struggle abandoned in Vietnam."[154] He even invoked the notion of falling dominoes to justify intervention.[155] WSP took solace from the difficulties the president faced in achieving support for his policies.[156] Amy Swerdlow argued that the "United States can't invade Nicaragua as easily as it could have" if anti–Vietnam War activism had not occurred.[157] Ruth Pinkson found "tremendous support" for non-interventionist policies to have come from the group's earlier activism, while Donna Allen proudly declared that "we stopped the thing in Central America. You know we did."[158] Todd Gitlin supported these sentiments, suggesting that Reagan's continuing inability to whip the public to support his desired military interventions owed much to the work of previous antiwar campaigns.[159] Historian Bradford Martin states that "it is a notable outcome of this era . . . that Americans do not speak of the 'Nicaragua War.'"[160]

The fluctuating organizational fortunes of WSP added further texture to WSPers' determinations of their successes and failures. San Francisco WFP clearly outlined this influence on their historical perspective, writing that "A review of our accomplishments is a very difficult task in the face of the present very reactionary Reagan administration. The road behind us has been very long, and not easy, but the road ahead seems much rockier, if it is not to end in nuclear holocaust."[161] Aware that history-writing served to inform and encourage ongoing efforts, the branch explained that "this look backwards will, we think, uncover some historical strengths and weaknesses and aid us in the work ahead."[162]

The Women's Peace Oral History Project interviewed New York WSPer Esther Newill in 1980, just prior to Reagan's election and in the midst of Carter's rising militarism. In this context, Newill offered a sobering reflection of her time with WSP. She condemned the group's early reluctance to oppose the Vietnam War, referred to frequent divisions within groups, and suggested that leading figures stymied grassroots voices. Reflecting on the contemporary peace movement, she chastised WSP's Jobs for Peace campaign that intended to lobby Congress and call for the diversion of military funds toward work programs. Newill declared, "so far as I'm concerned this is just a lot of bullshit. Memorialize Congress? Why, these bastards are the same ones that have been approving more money for the war machine than any president has asked for!" Newill's diatribe offered a pointedly pessimistic reflection of the contemporary disarmament movement as she bemoaned her own inability to become enthused by its efforts. "I'm old and tired now, I want results! I'm not interested in any kind of an effort that does not have, well, I want a 75% chance of success!"[163]

Just three years later, Newill appeared transformed. She became involved with direct action protests at the Livermore weapons development facility in California in 1983 that resulted in the mass arrest of hundreds of protesters and their detention in the Santa Rita Women's Jail. The protesters decided to call the prison the "Santa Rita Peace Camp" for the duration of their stay. They remade the prison in the image of the Greenham Common and Seneca Peace Camps, offering educational workshops, nightly entertainment shows, and art classes. The protesters' jovial attitude won over several guards. The whole experience refreshed Newill. She recounted with humor her involvement with the Livermore protests and the Santa Rita Peace Camp. Departing from the sentiments expressed in her earlier interview, she praised WSP, remarking that its idea that "everyone is a leader and no one is a leader" created "a long and painful process, but my gosh it works!" Her faith in the peace movement refreshed, she encouraged others to join the cause, claiming that "we're unbeatable." Newill continued by stating her belief that "in the course of winning this struggle, and I know we're going to win, we're going to change society!" The transformation in tone, from pessimism to unbridled positivity, reflected the persuasive influence of contemporary circumstances on Newill's memory. As the fortunes of the movement improved and instances of activism increased, WSPers adopted a more positive outlook on their past efforts. They saw their actions as "part of an ongoing process" that, they believed, would result in the attainment of their goals. While providing WSPers with relevant contemporary issues to inform their histories, the rising fortunes of the women's peace movement allowed WSPers to reflect positively on their past achievements.[164]

A particularly important influence on WSP's historical record was the variable commitment to activism of those offering their reflections, and notable differences emerged between those who remained active and those who had withdrawn. Amy Swerdlow, active in WSP only in a peripheral sense by the late 1980s, did not think it remained a relevant organization. She acknowledged "I'm not that faithful in Women Strike for Peace . . . I don't see myself as one of those women who kept marching." This attitude toward activism appeared to influence her appraisal of WSP. Asked whether she had any advice to "a young person" wishing to get involved, she answered, "I would not send them to Women Strike for Peace" over other organizations. Based on Swerdlow's attitude, it is perhaps unsurprising that her history of WSP placed the organization in the context of the 1960s and early 1970s. Its later activities did not seem relevant to the story Amy Swerdlow wished to tell. Throughout her 1987 oral interview she referred to the group in the past tense, despite its ongoing activities. She exclaimed that she would "hit the streets" again in the cause of peace, but her reduced interest in activism affected the way in which she discussed WSP.[165]

In contrast, current participants exhibited a more positive reflection of the group's continuing efforts than those no longer involved. Attitudes toward the group were not necessarily informed by the fortunes of the organization as it declined toward the end of the 1980s, but by the ongoing belief that efforts toward disarmament had to continue. Ethel Taylor in particular felt the upkeep of WSP's status as her personal burden. While Swerdlow could arguably take a more objective view of WSP, Taylor's position as national coordinator meant she defended the organization's work.[166] In their interviews for the Women's Peace Oral History Project in 1987, both she and Edith Villastrigo, the organization's national legislative director and essentially Taylor's second-in-command, made deliberate efforts to praise WSP's current activities. They spoke of the One in Twenty Million Campaign and ongoing efforts to cut funding for the Strategic Defense Initiative.[167] While Swerdlow consigned WSP to history, Taylor considered the group's late 1980s work "our most successful campaign."[168]

Additionally, the current WSPers proclaimed their enduring affinity with the group. Taylor spoke of WSP as "the most important entity" in her life. The organization took on abstract qualities for the national coordinator, becoming "more than an organization; it's a state of mind." In glowing terms, both Taylor and Villastrigo emphasized the transformative experience of working for peace and the harmonious community they encountered after becoming involved.[169] The reflections offered by remaining WSP activists represented what William Howarth and Martha Solomon call "oratorical autobiography," in that their motivations for recording the past determined what they recalled and how they recalled it.[170] In discussing their life stories current WSPers wished to create "a tool for recruiting new members" and provide an "inspirational model for followers"[171] Activists still involved in peace work did not offer reflections of the past from a teleological position but in the midst of their campaigning. As such, they tied the history of

WSP to the belief that their work was ongoing, offering an appraisal of the past that entailed a defense of the group's continuing relevance. WSPers promoted an idealized vision of their peace work as a vocation that others should become involved in, whether or not WSP survived.[172]

This perception explains the emphasis that activists placed on the personal fulfilment they gained from WSP's campaigns. The transformative impact of working for the peace movement appeared through Taylor's descriptions of the group's past. She described herself as a housewife following her marriage in 1937. "I cleaned a lot," she wrote in her memoir, to the extent that she was "polishing the polish."[173] As a result of working in WSP, Taylor's life changed. She proudly recalled her work as national coordinator of an internationally recognized peace group. Recounting her trip to Hanoi in December 1969, she gauged the progress she had made in her life from childhood. "It blew my mind that little Ethel Barol, child of the Depression, formerly of Longstreth School, was standing with a baby in her arms in Hanoi, North Vietnam, as an emissary of the US women's peace movement." Other narratives also revealed stories of women's political transformation. Dagmar Wilson is frequently referred to as a "political novice," someone with "no political experience" who managed to organize a nationally supported political movement that received recognition from around the world.[174] Amy Swerdlow believed that WSP created an environment for American women to become empowered. She explained that "thousands of women who had identified themselves only as housewives found to their surprise that they could do serious research."[175] In this sense, the depiction of WSP is altered from that of a group strictly concerned with peace to one that intended to change the lives of its activists. This fits the notion that activists offered oratorical autobiographies with their recollections. It was through gauging their own transformation, as participants in WSP activities, that activists shared their life stories.

Nevertheless, WSPers in the 1980s rarely foregrounded the group's contributions to the women's movement. In response to continuing debates about the value and contribution of maternal identity within women's peace circles, Amy Swerdlow used her histories of WSP as a defense of traditional motherhood. The publication Swerdlow's first historical article on WSP, the celebrated "Ladies' Day at the Capitol," was praised by the *Feminist Studies* journal for its contextual relevance to women's activism of the 1980s.[176] However, activists' continued interest in nuclear concerns led them to frame

WSP's past in relation to the fortunes of antinuclear activism. Ethel Taylor used a number of approaches to demonstrate WSP's continuing relevance, but one technique in particular involved distancing WSP from any notion that it had achieved its aims. One anecdote in particular served to emphasize the perception that the organization remained an irreverent and outspoken critic of the establishment. Following the National Women's Conference in 1977, President Jimmy Carter personally invited Taylor to attend a reception at the White House. On arriving she was stopped by a security guard for additional checks. Taylor asked why she alone had been subject to such scrutiny. The guard replied, "there's a bad Ethel Taylor out there and we had to make sure it wasn't you."[177] Taylor reveled in the story and retold it on many occasions. "If only he knew!" she later quipped. "I silently cackled and went on to join my colleagues."[178]

The retelling of Taylor's anecdote provides two useful insights. First, it demonstrates the leader's perception of her ideal role—a subversive, rebellious figure who displayed irreverence toward authority. The anecdote became a source of pride for the peace activist, who gleefully assumed the identity of "Bad Ethel Taylor," a constant check on the government's rampant militarism. Taylor closely tied her own identity to the image of WSP through her role as national coordinator. By referring to her own conduct, she argued that WSP remained important critics of government policy. Second, by foregrounding WSP's work in the late 1970s with reference to this brief incident, the national coordinator attempted to distance WSP from establishment figures who had actually supported the group's work. Indeed, during President Carter's term in office, WSP activists generally boasted that the administration tacitly endorsed the group's work. Taylor herself worked closely with the IWY Committee having received the personal approval of President Carter. Midge Costanza, Carter's liaison with nongovernmental organizations, was a WSP supporter who managed to set up a meeting between activists and representatives of the Defense Department, the ACDA, and the National Security Council.[179] However, Taylor felt that being considered "bad" by the security services better served WSP's image than that of its activists being welcomed into government circles as valid spokespeople for the peace movement.

Given her strong affinity for WSP, other reflections on the group's successes made by Taylor seem oddly pessimistic. She reflected that "to work for something or to have a job and rarely have a real success, never see the light, you can really go nuts."[180] She almost entirely dismissed the impact WSP had on nuclear disarmament and regretted that the passage of the Partial Test Ban Treaty, previously an emblem of WSP's historical victories, did not yield further gains. Taylor remarked that on her entry into peace activism "there were two bombs, and they were both ours. Now there are 50,000 in the world."[181] This candid assessment was not unique within the antinuclear movement. Activists realized that, while the Partial Test Ban Treaty made progress, nuclear weapons testing had not completely ceased.[182] Measuring the success of a peace activist group entails certain caveats, such as understanding that even small steps can count as achievements, especially if the goal is as difficult to obtain as general world disarmament.[183]

In one poignant refrain, Taylor downplayed WSP's success and highlighted a failure. As if to cement the perception that her fortunes were tied to those of WSP, she took the inability to secure general nuclear disarmament as a personal defeat, calling it something that would "look lousy on your resume." However, Taylor offered this perspective in the midst of her activism. She remained energetically committed to peace work and looked to future goals. Because nuclear disarmament had not been achieved, she determined that women needed to continue mobilizing and acting for peace.[184] The tone of her recollections mirrored the pronouncements made by Taylor during her tenure as WSP's national coordinator. She wrote off the Partial Test Ban Treaty in 1973 as "less than half of what we wanted," quashing the potential for activists to feel that their work was complete.[185] Though referring to myriad small successes achieved during the Vietnam War and the widespread acceptance of antinuclear sentiments by the general public, Taylor discredited the notion that WSP had achieved what it had set out to achieve in 1961 out of a belief that, by highlighting the work still to be done, she could spur potential activists to join the peace movement.[186] Her later memoir built upon stories shared in oral interviews that continued to communicate this message. Taylor argued that "the reason for WSP's existence since 1961 was the eradication of these weapons as a step toward universal disarmament. It still is."[187]

WSP leaders were unable to stymie the organization's inexorable decline. Faced with "galloping attrition in membership all over the country" and diminishing public influence, WSP began a two-year initiative in November

1988, tasked with "building, growing, and maintaining" WSP "as a national organization."[188] A notice to branch leaders in March 1989 urged WSPers to resolve the group's "unfinished business," the securing of a Comprehensive Test Ban Treaty, within the next decade.[189] But the attempt to rally was in vain. Taylor acknowledged that, although WSP had made a "real national contribution in grassroots education" in the last few years, the National Office only survived thanks to the "continuous painful struggle on the part of a few of us to maintain it" and the "financial generosity" of several others.[190] By the end of the decade WSPers accepted "we are no longer visible and viable as a national movement. Although our cause is vital and connected to other causes, it is for the other causes that women are marching."[191] In February 1990, a national board of representatives made the decision to close the National Office. "With a heavy heart," leaders broke the sad news to their branches and Ethel Taylor wrote "a difficult letter" to WSP activists explaining the reasons for the closure.[192] She offered her resignation and, without a National Office, felt her plans for future involvement "in abeyance."[193] Key women attempted to calm WSPers by intimating that the absence of a National Office would not end the organization. Nevertheless, the news brought considerable upset.[194] On March 15, 1990, Women Strike for Peace closed the doors to its National Office.

In announcing the decision to close the National Office, Ethel Taylor offered her thoughts. "I think we should feel good about ourselves and nothing lasts forever. We have done fantastic things and broken ground in the forefront of other groups. But that's not now."[195] The statement encapsulated the attitudes of WSP activists in the 1980s. In a practical sense, the organization faded without much struggle, despite some campaigns exhibiting the group's ability to engage with public concerns. Yet the state of the organization did not diminish the resolve of activists who felt optimism toward the future and vindication of their past efforts. They felt their campaign had been successful in the sense that the public's stance on nuclear weapons and American military intervention generally reflected WSP's historic concerns. Although spent as an organizational force by 1990, the positive reflections offered by activists in this period would forever inform perspectives on WSP's history.

Any sense that WSPers' lifelong commitment to peace activism had come to an end soon evaporated. Individuals resolved to continue their campaigns locally under their existing WSP monikers. A Transitional Coordinating

Committee, set up in April 1990, heard that Seattle activists felt it "unanimous for WSP to continue," while across the country in New York, WSPer Celia Fink reported that the branch had "got 82 renewals recently."[196] Similar local WSP operations continued in Los Angeles, East Bay, Philadelphia, and Washington, DC. Though the Cold War drew to a close, President George H. W. Bush's hesitation toward arms control and brewing conflict in the Persian Gulf saw activists pursue further avenues of protest. WSPers vowed to maintain pressure on the government. Meanwhile, as a Comprehensive Nuclear Weapons Test Ban Treaty continued to elude negotiators, WSP's remaining participants maintained their focus on the cause that sparked their group into life thirty years earlier.[197] Although the WSP organization had diminished significantly, their individual commitment allowed them to take comfort in past achievements and look to the future with optimism and determination.

CONCLUSION

"We Made a Difference"

THE UNIVERSITY OF CHICAGO Press published Amy Swerdlow's definitive history of WSP in 1993. *Women Strike for Peace: Traditional Motherhood and Radical Politics in the 1960s* concluded over two decades of Swerdlow's effort to correct the "historical amnesia" afforded the group. During this time, she collated WSP's organizational archive, designed and delivered graduate courses on women's peace studies, and published widely on the history and legacy of WSP. A former New York WSP leader who become professor of women's history at Sarah Lawrence College, Swerdlow presented her organization as "ignored or misrepresented" by "male movement leaders and historians of the social movements of the 1960s." In her book's introduction, she made her aims clear, explaining that "my purpose was not only to add the story of WSP to the historical record, but also to make certain that the middle-aged women of WSP are recognized as significant actors."[1]

Women Strike for Peace offered a glowing testimonial of the group's first decade from Swerdlow's participant-observer perspective, while nevertheless yielding an academic and clear-eyed critique of WSP's complexity. With its subtitle, *Traditional Motherhood and Radical Politics in the 1960s*, Swerdlow's work acknowledged both the "maternal feminine roles" that informed WSP's public rhetoric and image during the 1960s and the unashamed militancy of many WSP activists. Swerdlow firmly asserted that "any evaluation of WSP as a women's movement must acknowledge that without setting out to do so, WSP's militant struggle against militarism in the 1960s helped give dignity to the denigrated term *housewife* and to change the image of the good mother from passive to militant, from silent to eloquent, from private to public."

Women Strike for Peace received significant praise after its publication, and peace historians continue to draw extensively—almost exclusively—from Swerdlow's work to inform examinations of women's participation in Cold War peace activism. Her historicism did indeed add their group back to historical record, contributing to an upsurge of interest in women's historic peace activities in the early 1990s.[2] Journalist Noreen O'Donnell reported on the power of Swerdlow's *Women Strike for Peace* in an article documenting the increased popularity of peace studies courses that were "sweeping campuses" in the immediate aftermath of the Cold War.[3] Yet Swerdlow was not alone in her historical exploits. Many other former and current WSP colleagues similarly worked on maintaining their group's legacy. They bequeathed vast resources to local and national archives, the subsequent collections of organizational documents, letters and correspondence, diaries, protest literature, and autobiographical texts meaning that WSP has one of the largest archival footprints of any Cold War–era social protest organization. By the time WSP closed the National Office in 1990, its activists had developed and articulated lore that covered the group's formation, its activities, successes, and values. They described WSP as the "most important entity" in their lives beyond their immediate families, something that stuck with them even after their direct involvement ended.[4]

Vivid and captivating accounts revealed that WSPers wished their group to be remembered for its courage, humor, and maternal authority. When former National Coordinator Ethel Taylor retold a comical story of being arrested in 1973, she added the quip that "only in WSP" could such a series of events occur.[5] These anecdotes are now woven throughout scholarship of the antiwar movement, frequently used as set-pieces to introduce readers to the subject with warm, personal, experiential flourishes characteristic of the group's historical accounts.[6] WSPers continually declared their significant contributions to the major moments in peace and social justice history. Taylor reflected this sentiment in her autobiography, published in 1998. An "anecdotal" account of her life in activism, she framed the book around one emphatic assertion; *We Made a Difference.*[7]

However, contemporary reviews show how WSP's radical militancy disappeared from common knowledge. Journalists frequently got caught up in WSP's founding story, uncritically repeating the eye-catching narrative of housewives and mothers challenging Cold War militarism. Reviewing *Women Strike for Peace* for the *Philadelphia Inquirer*, journalist Ann

Davidon explained that "on November 1, 1961, about 50,000 women across the country 'took off their aprons,' to demonstrate against nuclear testing." Describing WSPers as "conventional women," Davidon continued, "they were still largely women in gloves and hats, women to whom jail would be unthinkable in ordinary times, but who were willing to be arrested to end the killing. The act of going into the streets and even going to jail 'radicalized' thousands when they realized that their courage and visibility could influence public policy."[8] Ethel Taylor's autobiography further solidified this impression. *Philadelphia Daily News*'s Rose DeWolf summarized *We Made a Difference* as "a mother's book." She told her readers that, in 1961, Taylor was "a housewife, a community volunteer, and the mother of a 20-year-old daughter and a 14-year-old son." Recounting the group's formation, Davidon simply explained that "a friend in Washington, D.C., wrote to say she was organizing a one-day mothers' protest." In this rendering, WSP "started very simply. Ethel Taylor, a suburban Philadelphia mother joined a group of other moms concerned about a hazard to their children's health. Next thing you know, she was spending the next four decades picketing, protesting, getting arrested, and being investigated by the CIA, the FBI, the Army, the Navy, and the State Department. Hey, it's not always easy being a mother."[9]

WSP's initial articulation of quiescent, white American, middle-class ideals of maternalism continues to prevail, with adverse consequences for histories of the women's peace movement. Its activists decontextualized from the movements of which they were a part, homogenizing and flattening the history of their group and overlooking the intricacies of individual activists and local branch experiences. Meanwhile, historians' and activists' ideas of what constitutes "appropriate feminine" identity shaped their descriptions of the past. Maintaining the emphasis on WSP's "traditional motherhood" prevented instrumental activists from securing a legacy of involvement with the group if they did not abide by these descriptions. Alice Herz's death did not suit an image of respectable protest sought by her colleagues, nor did Bella Abzug's "new politics" suit an image of maternalism her colleagues wished to convey. Sedate evaluations of women's peace activism have allowed this particular arena of organizing to become detached from an ever-expanding body of work on the women's movement. WSP's status within historical narratives of the women's movement and, by extension, evaluations of whether peace is considered "a woman's issue," therefore depend on how narratives consider maternal identity.

An accurate depiction of WSP's history needs to balance its range of participants. The group was not strictly demure or respectable, and this book challenges assumptions about maternal peace protest. WSP had a fluctuating, but engaged and ever-evolving relationship with the women's movement and was responsive to changes in established understandings of feminist protest. Neither was WSP an entirely militant outfit, nor a hub of submerged feminism. Activists expressed uneven support for civil disobedience, women's rights, and gender equity campaigns. The statements of participants throughout the 1960s speak for themselves. This book urges consideration in describing maternal peace protest so as not to oversimplify differences, nor put too much distance between the two positions of "traditional motherhood" and "radical politics" that Swerdlow intended to bring together in 1993.

This book illuminates these historiographical challenges in order to assert the need for further recognition of the women's peace movement and historical exploration of groups like WSP. Its size and achievements alone demand greater recognition, as WSP mobilized thousands to push for disarmament and the end to conflict around the world. It made groundbreaking contributions to the social movement landscape of Cold War America, and its rhetoric, political analysis, and organizational style influenced the development of student and feminist movements that are often considered completely separate from maternal activism. The group was also significant because it effectively promoted peace as a women's issue during a period of profound social, cultural, and political change. By advancing the story of WSP's activities beyond the 1960s, this book illuminates how Cold War–era social movement activists developed and evolved the political identity of motherhood over the tumultuous final decades of the twentieth century. While its maternal protest reflected past efforts, *Not Just a Housewife* reveals the unique, overlooked analytical importance WSP provides as a result of its longevity.

Acknowledging WSP's full history shows the thriving lineage of women's peace protest while recognizing the group's unique role in connecting disparate women's activist initiatives. While WSP's direct relationship to feminist movements was indeed complicated, it was not static and underwent radical change over the course of the Cold War. But of greater importance is the corrective of women's peace history that is required if historians are to accurately depict WSP. An interrogation of WSP necessitates mapping the contours of women's peace history, revealing how simple renderings of women's peace groups distort the otherwise vibrant history of women's peace activism. Instances of radical militancy force a reconsideration of WSP groups specifically, and the maternalism of the women's peace movement generally. Narrow analytical paradigms that depict women's peace groups through a maternal lens stymie efforts to fully comprehend the nature, meaning, and contributions of peace activism to the broader women's movement throughout American history, in addition to overlooking the complexity of groups such as WSP.

WSP's story is not just a WSP story, and it is not enough to simply recapture the variety of that group's past; the historical consciousness of its activists must be recognized. WSP's historicism, and Amy Swerdlow's academic histories in particular, assumed a foundational place in histories of women's peace activism. Tackling the contextual motivations that influenced WSP's memories adds texture to these histories but, looking more broadly, WSP was only one maternalist forum within a much more varied, diverse, and thriving environment of women's peace protest encompassing radical feminists, church and club groups, women in mixed-gender groups, Black women's anti-imperialism, ecofeminists, and environmentalists, among many others. Determining WSP's place in histories of peace and women's organizing takes on renewed importance given the broader boundaries that now mark women's twentieth-century organizing, and this book argues that women's activism for peace, even if considered maternal and respectable, is an overlooked but significant contributor to the broader context of the Cold War–era social movements.

As Judy Wu writes about the Indochinese Women's Conference at the turn of the 1970s, "there were three North American sponsors of the IWCs: 'old friends' or more 'traditional' women's peace organizations; 'new friends' or women's liberation activists; and 'Third World' women or women of color in North America." They reflected "the political multiplicity of North American women and the complex process of negotiation that occurred to foster an international peace movement."[10] Whereas narratives of the women's movement now reveal coalitions across organizations and beyond distinct movements, women's peace history remains limited. Lara Track's recent history of WSP illuminates its connections to other organizations, offering an enlightening response to this historiographical challenge.[11] Histories of the more radical feminist antimilitarism of the 1980s are slowly beginning to emerge but have much catching up to do.

The closure of its National Office in 1990 is a useful marker for closing this version of WSP's story, but it by no means signified the end. Dispersed across the country, WSPers continued to rail against militarism, lamenting conflict in the Balkans and the Persian Gulf while setting their sights on a Comprehensive Test Ban Treaty. They celebrated that particular goal in September 1996. Yet without skipping a beat, they announced that "work goes on. ABOLITION by the year 2000 of all nuclear weapons."[12] WSPers supported the formation of new women's peace organizations, such as Women in Black and CodePink, who replicated WSP's historical example to bring their own critiques of militarism to a new generation of activists.[13] This is, perhaps, the most important takeaway from an expanded history of women's peace activism—the necessity to correct ruptures in historicism of women's organizing. As WSP's former National Coordinator Ethel Taylor declared in the final line of her autobiography, "we made a difference . . . and the beat goes on."[14]

NOTES

Introduction

1 Leandra Ruth Zarnow, *Battling Bella: The Protest Politics of Bella Abzug* (Harvard University Press, 2019), 43; Amy Swerdlow, "The Politics of Motherhood: The Case of Women Strike for Peace and the Test Ban Treaty," (PhD diss., Rutgers University, 1984), 2.

2 Amy Swerdlow, *Women Strike for Peace: Traditional Motherhood and Radical Politics in the 1960s* (University of Chicago Press, 1993), 23, 54.

3 Zarnow, *Battling Bella*, 39–63.

4 Dagmar Wilson interview, April 15, 1989, Women's International League for Peace and Freedom Collection ARS.0056, Stanford University Archive of Recorded Sound; Sidney Lens, *Unrepentant Radical: An American Activist's Account of Five Turbulent Decades* (Beacon Press, 1980), 292.

5 Zarnow, *Battling Bella*, 42–43; Suzanne Braun Levine and Mary Thom, eds., *Bella Abzug: How One Tough Broad from the Bronx Fought Jim Crow and Joe McCarthy, Pissed Off Jimmy Carter, Battled for the Rights of Women and Workers, Rallied Against War and for the Planet, and Shook Up Politics Along the Way* (Farrar, Strauss and Giroux, 2007), 63.

6 Amy Swerdlow cast WSP's stance as a projection of "traditional motherhood" in the subtitle of her definitive historical account. See *Women Strike for Peace*, 138.

7 "WSP Played a Major Role," Swarthmore College Peace Collection, WSP Records SCPC-DG-115 (hereafter SCPC WSP Records), C1:3, WSP Related Material About-By Bella Abzug, Swarthmore College.

8 For its first decade WSP did not have an official national leader; however, the group's founder Dagmar Wilson adopted the mantle as its de facto figurehead. In 1968, she quipped that her WSP colleagues and the general public held her in such esteem as to be a "mythical" figure. "Washington WSP 'Retreat' Meeting at Folly Fodor's, Saturday, October 5, 1968," SCPC WSP Records, A1:2, Washington WSP Retreat October 5, 1968, 4.

9 For example, Harriet Hyman Alonso, *Peace As a Women's Issue: A History of the U.S. Movement for World Peace and Women's Rights* (Syracuse University Press, 1993), 11.

10 Swerdlow, *Women Strike for Peace*.

11 Betty Friedan, *The Feminine Mystique* (Penguin Classics, 2010), 307. Originally published in 1963 by W.W. Norton.

12 For example, Dorothy Sue Cobble, Linda Gordon, and Astrid Henry, *Feminism Unfinished: A Short, Surprising History of American Women's Movements* (Liveright Publishing Corporation, 2014); Victoria Hesford, *Feeling Women's Liberation* (Duke University Press, 2013); Melissa Estes Blair, *Revolutionizing Expectations: Women's Organizations, Feminism, and American Politics, 1965–1980* (University of Georgia Press, 2014); Alison Dahl Crossley, *Finding Feminism: Millennial Activists and the Unfinished Gender Revolution* (New York University Press, 2017).

13 "Draft of Letter (for individual salvation and signature and note if desired) to Accompany Leaflet, September 22, 1961," SCPC WSP Records, A1:2, Documents Describing WSP History.

14 Ruth Rosen, "Next Time, Listen to Mother," *Los Angeles Times*, August 7, 1997.

15 Petra Goedde, *The Politics of Peace: A Global Cold War History* (Oxford University Press, 2019), 1–11; Swerdlow, *Women Strike for Peace*, 23; "Keynote Address by Ethel Taylor at WSP National Conference, Chicago, Illinois, October 1973," SCPC WSP Records, A1:3, National Conference—1973, Chicago IL, 1.

16 Emily E. LB. Twarog, *The Politics of the Pantry: Housewives, Food, and Consumer Protest in Twentieth-Century America* (Oxford University Press, 2017), 2–5; Isaac Barnes May, "The Great Fight For Democracy, Religion, and the Home: The Committee to Oppose the Conscription of Women and the Secularization Process, 1942–1944," *Peace & Change* 42, no. 1 (2017): 69; Melissa R. Klapper, *Ballots, Babies, and Banners of Peace: American Jewish Women's Activism, 1890–1940* (New York University Press, 2013).

17 Michelle Nickerson, *Mothers of Conservatism: Women and the Postwar Right* (Princeton University Press, 2012), xii.

18 Sylvie Murray, *The Progressive Housewife: Community Activism in Suburban Queens, 1945–1965* (University of Pennsylvania Press, 2003).

19 Amy C. Schneidhorst, *Building a Just and Secure World: Popular Front Women's Struggle for Peace and Justice in Chicago during the 1960s* (Bloomsbury Publishing, 2011); Ian McKay, "Margaret Ells Russell, Women Strike for Peace, and the Global Politics of 'Intelligent Compassion,' 1961–1965," in *Worth Fighting For: Canada's Tradition of War Resistance from 1812 to the War on Terror*, eds. Lara Campbell et al. (Between the Lines, 2015), 119–34; "Issues for Discussion No. 5, 22 October 1963," Wisconsin Historical Society WSP Records (hereafter WHS WSP Records), MSS 433, 2:10, Ephemera, Wisconsin Historical Society, Madison, WI.

20 Schneidhorst, *Building a Just and Secure World*; Amy C. Schneidhorst, "'Little Old Ladies and Dangerous Women': Women's Peace Activism and Social Justice in Chicago, 1960–1975," *Peace & Change* 26, no. 3 (2001): 374–90; Harriet Hyman Alonso, "Mayhem and Moderation: Women Peace Activists during the McCarthy Era," in *Not June Cleaver: Women and Gender in Postwar America, 1945–1960*, ed. Joanne Meyerowitz (Temple University Press, 1994), 128–50.

21 Cynthia Stavrianos, *The Political Uses of Motherhood in America* (Routledge, 2015), 53. See also JaneMaree Maher, "Thematic Review: Motherhood and Contemporary US Politics," *Politics & Gender* 12 (2016), e12, 1–10.

22 See, for example, Gerard J. De Groot, *The Bomb: A Life* (Harvard University Press, 2004); Milton S. Katz, *Ban the Bomb: A History of SANE, The Committee for a SANE Nuclear Policy, 1957–1985* (Greenwood Press, 1986); Lawrence S. Wittner, *Resisting the Bomb: A History of the World Nuclear Disarmament Movement, 1954–1970 (Vol. 2 of The Struggle Against the Bomb)* (Stanford University Press, 1997), 252.

23 Swerdlow, *Women Strike for Peace*, 12; Amy Swerdlow, "Ladies' Day at the Capitol: Women Strike for Peace Versus HUAC," *Feminist Studies* 8 no. 3 (1982): 493; "'Pure Milk, Not Poison': Women Strike for Peace and the Test Ban Treaty of 1963," in *Rocking the Ship of State: Toward a Feminist Peace Politics*, eds. Adrienne Harris and Ynestra King (Westview Press, 1989), 225–37; "'Not My Son, Not Your Son, Not Their Sons': Mothers Against the Vietnam Draft," in *Give Peace a Chance: Exploring the*

Vietnam Antiwar Movement, eds. Melvin Small and William D. Hoover (Syracuse University Press, 1992), 159–70.

24 Marian Mollin, "Women's Struggles within the American Radical Pacifist Movement," *History Compass* 7, no. 3 (2009): 1064–90.

25 Jill S. Greenlee, *The Political Consequences of Motherhood* (University of Michigan Press, 2014), 156.

26 Peace scholar Harriet Hyman Alonso determined that "the motherhood theme" permeated "almost every one" of the women's organizations that she wrote about. Alonso, *Peace As a Women's Issue*, 11.

27 Laura McEnaney, "Atomic Age Motherhood: Maternalism and Militarism in the 1950s," in *Women's America: Refocusing the Past*, eds. Linda K. Kerber and Jane Sherrow de Hart (Oxford University Press, 2000), 452; Dee Garrison, *Bracing for Armageddon: Why Civil Defense Never Worked* (Oxford University Press, 2006) 94–116.

28 Jacqueline Castledine, *Cold War Progressives: Women's Interracial Organizing for Peace and Freedom* (University of Illinois Press, 2012), 126–29.

29 WSP's Feed the Cities campaign and initiatives to tackle drug abuse are just two examples of this, see SCPC WSP Records, ACC 97A-061:1, Feed the Cities; University of California, Berkely, San Francisco Women for Peace Records BANC MSS 89/132 c (hereafter UCB WFP Records), 11:24, Women Organized for a Sane Approach to Drug Abuse, 1990. See also Georgina Denton, "'Neither Guns Nor Bombs—Neither the State Nor God—Will Stop Us From Fighting for Our Children': Motherhood and Protest in 1960s and 1970s America," *The Sixties* 5, no. 2 (2012): 205–28.

30 Blair, *Revolutionizing Expectations*, 147.

31 Cobble et al., *Feminism Unfinished*, xiv.

32 For example, Goedde, *The Politics of Peace*, 128–61.

33 For example, Track *Frieden und Frauenrechte im Kalten Krieg*; Schneidhorst, *Building a Just and Secure World*; Jessica M. Frazier, *Women's Antiwar Diplomacy During the Vietnam War Era* (University of North Carolina Press, 2017); Andrea Estepa, "Taking the White Gloves Off: Women Strike for Peace and 'the Movement,' 1967–73," in *Feminist Coalitions: Historical Perspectives on Second-Wave Feminism in the United States*, ed. Stephanie Gilmore (University of Illinois Press, 2008), 84–112. Other studies examine WSP within broader studies of women's organizing, such as Castledine, *Cold War Progressives*; Mary Hershberger, *Traveling to Vietnam: American Peace Activists and the War* (Syracuse University Press, 1998); Judy Tzu-Chun Wu, *Radicals On the Road: Internationalism, Orientalism, and Feminism During the Vietnam Era* (Cornell University Press, 2013).

34 Andrew J. Ross, "Preemptive Strikes: Women Strike for Peace, Antinuclear Pacifism, and the Movement for Biological Democracy, 1961–1963," *Peace and Change*, 46 (2021): 178; McKay, "Margaret Ells Russell," 119–20.

35 Estepa, "Taking the White Gloves Off," *Feminist Coalitions*, 104.

36 Melissa Estes Blair insightfully expands considerations of women's movement activism but concludes that "by the end of the 1980s, much of the forward momentum of the women's movement had stalled" throughout the United States. *Revolutionizing Expectations*, 147. This discounts the global resurgence of radical feminism found in antinuclear campaigns such as the Women's Peace Encampment movement.

37 Estepa, "Taking the White Gloves Off," *Feminist Coalitions*, 104.

38 "My Personal Impressions of the Ann Arbor Conference—Elsa Knight Thompson," UCB WFP Records, 3:28, First National Conference, Ann Arbor, MI, 1962, 2.

39 Although Amy Swerdlow referred to this as "nonorganization" in *Women Strike for Peace*, (70–96), the archival record suggests that "unorganization" had more widespread use. For example, "Elise Boulding, 'Who Are These Women?: A Progress Report on a Study of the Women Strike for Peace,' 1963," SCPC WSP Records, A1:2, Documents Describing WSP History, 11; "Issues for Discussion No. 5, October 22, 1963," WHS WSP Records, MSS 433, 2:10, Ephemera; "East Regional Meeting (plus L.A.) of WSP—Philadelphia, Nov 8–9, 1964," SCPC WSP Records, A1:3, Regional Conferences.

40 Tom Hayden, "Crafting the Port Huron Statement: Measuring Its Impact in the 1960s and After," in *The Port Huron Statement: Sources and Legacies of the New Left's Founding Manifesto, ed.* Richard Flacks and Nelson Lichtenstein (University of Pennsylvania Press, 2015), 21; Francesca Polletta, *Freedom is an Endless Meeting: Democracy in American Social Movements* (Chicago University Press, 2002), 149–50.

41 Though not the first—Lara Track beat me to the punch by exploring WSP from 1961 to 1990. Lara Track, *Frieden und Frauenrechte im Kalten Krieg: Women Strike for Peace und die amerikanische Frauenrechtsbewegung im Spiegel transnationaler Kooperationen, 1961–1990* (Transcript Publishing, 2024).

42 Swerdlow, "Ladies' Day at the Capitol," 494; Wittner, *Resisting the Bomb*, 252.

43 See, for example, Murray, *The Progressive Housewife*, 124.

44 Say Burgin, "Understanding Antiwar Activism as a Gendering Activity: A Look at the U.S.'s Anti-Vietnam War Movement," *Journal of International Women's Studies* 13, no. 6 (2012): 18–31.

45 Andrea Estepa illuminates WSP's move toward a more radical stance but confines her study to the group's anti–Vietnam War experience. Estepa, "Taking the White Gloves Off," *Feminist Coalitions*, 84–112.

46 Jon Coburn, "Basically Feminist: Women Strike for Peace, Maternal Peace Activism, and Memory of the Women's Peace Movement," *Journal of Women's History* 33, no. 2 (2021): 136–62.

47 "Progress Report on WSP Research," SCPC WSP Records, C1:3, Research on WSP by Amy Swerdlow.

48 Jo Reger, *Everywhere and Nowhere: Contemporary Feminism in the United States* (Oxford University Press, 2012), 34, emphasis in the original; Crossley, *Finding Feminism*, 17–20. See also Suzanne Staggenborg and Verta Taylor, "Whatever Happened to the Women's Movement?" *Mobilization: An International Quarterly* 10, no. 1 (2005): 41.

49 Jon Coburn, "'I Have Chosen the Flaming Death': The Forgotten Self-Immolation of Alice Herz." *Peace & Change* 43, no. 1 (2018): 32–60.

50 Amy Swerdlow quipped that this action was WSP meeting "the enemy." *Women Strike for Peace*, 167–232.

51 For example, Barbara Ryan, "Ideological Purity and Feminism: The U.S. Women's Movement from 1966 to 1975," *Gender and Society* 3, no. 2 (1989): 239–57; Laura E. Nym Mayhall, "Defining Militancy: Radical Protest, the Constitutional Idiom, and Women's Suffrage in Britain, 1908–1909," *Journal of British Studies* 39, no. 3 (2000): 340–71; Marian Quartly and Judith Smart, *Respectable Radicals: A History of the National Council of Women of Australia 1896–2006* (Monash University Publishing, 2015).

52 Alice Echols, "'Women Power' and Women's Liberation: Exploring the Relationship Between the Antiwar Movement and the Women's Liberation Movement," in *Give Peace a Chance: Exploring the Vietnam Antiwar Movement (Essays from the Charles DeBenedetti Memorial Conference)*, ed. Melvin Small and William D. Hoover (Syracuse University Press, 1992), 173–74; David A. Snow and Remy Cross, "Radicalism within the Context of Social Movements: Processes and Type," *Journal of Strategic Security* 4, no. 4 (2011): 118–19; Wesley G. Phelps, "Women's Pentagon Action: The Persistence of Radicalism and Direct-Action Civil Disobedience in the Age of Reagan," *Peace and Change* 39, no. 3 (2014): 339–65; Louise Krasniewicz, *Nuclear Summer: The Clash of Communities at the Seneca Women's Peace Encampment* (Cornell University Press, 1994).

53 Stephanie Gilmore, *Groundswell: Grassroots Feminist Activism in Postwar America* (Routledge, 2013), 4. Gilmore draws upon Vicki Ruiz "Shaping Public Space/Enunciating Gender A Multiracial Historiography of the Women's West, 1995–2000," *Frontiers: A Journal of Women Studies* 22, no. 3 (2001): 22–25.

54 Susan K. Freeman, "From the Lesbian Nation to the Cincinnati Lesbian Community: Moving Toward a Politics of Location," *Journal of the History of Sexuality* 9, nos. 1 and 2 (2000), 137–74; Byron A. Miller, *Geography and Social Movements: Comparing Antinuclear Activism in the Boston Area* (University of Minnesota Press, 2000), 4.

55 Garst's records are now at the Wisconsin Historical Society. WHS WSP Records, M83–327.

56 "Memo: Special Commemorative Issue, 1970," University of Washington, Seattle, Seattle Women Act for Peace Records, 4073 (hereafter UWS SWAP), 3:13, Women Strike for Peace, 1962–2000; "Journal of Women Strike for Peace Commemorating Eighteen Years of Conscientious Concern for the Future of the World's Children," SCPC WSP Records, A1:2, Documents Describing WSP History.

57 Judith Porter Adams, ed., *Peacework: Oral Histories of Women Peace Activists* (Twayne, 1991); "Women's Peace Oral History Project," Women's International League for Peace and Freedom Collection ARS.0056, Stanford University Archive of Recorded Sound; "Missoula Women for Peace Oral History Project," OH 389, Archives & Special Collections, Maureen and Mike Mansfield Library, University of Montana.

58 Alice Sachs Hamburg, *Grass Roots: From Prairie to Politics: The Autobiography of Alice Sachs Hamburg* (Creative Arts Books Company, 2001); Lorraine Gordon, *Alive at the Village Vanguard: My Life In and Out of Jazz Time* (Hal Leonard, 2006); Ethel Barol Taylor, *We Made a Difference: My Personal Journey with Women Strike for Peace* (Camino Books, 1998); Dagmar Wilson, "Tainting the Antinuclear Movement: HUAC and the Irrepressible Women Strike for Peace," in *The Price of Dissent: Testimonies to Political Repression in America*, ed. Bud Schultz and Ruth Schultz (University of California Press, 2001), 278–88; Pat Cody and Fred Cody, *Cody's Books: The Life and Times of a Berkeley Bookstore, 1956–1977* (Chronicle Books, 1992); miscellaneous examples in Judy Kaplan and Linn Shapiro, eds., *Red Diapers: Growing Up in the Communist Left* (University of Illinois Press, 1998); James W. Clinton, ed., *The Loyal Opposition: Americans in North Vietnam, 1965–1972* (University of Colorado Press, 1995).

59 Lara Leigh Kelland, *Clio's Foot Soldiers: Twentieth-Century U.S. Social Movements and Collective Memory* (University of Massachusetts Press, 2018), 6, 71.

60 Catherine Fosl and Lara Kelland, "'Bring Your Whole Self to the Work': Identity and Intersectional Politics in the Louisville LGBTQ Movement," *The Oral History Review* 43, no. 1 (2016) 138–52.

Chapter One

1 Wilson interview, April 15, 1989, ARS.0056; "11/1/1961 Original Call for WISP," Swarthmore College Peace Collection, WSP Records SCPC-DG-115 (hereafter SCPC WSP Records), A2:1, Documents Describing WSP History; Amy Swerdlow, *Women Strike for Peace: Traditional Motherhood and Radical Politics in the 1960s* (University of Chicago Press, 1993), 15–26; Rose DeWolf, "A Mother's Book Recalls Four Decades of Activism," *Philadelphia Daily News*, November 3, 1998.

2 Robert D. Benford, "Controlling Narratives and Narratives as Control within Social Movements," in *Stories of Change: Narrative and Social Movements*, ed Joseph E. Davis (State University Press of New York, 2002), 57.

3 Lisa Tetrault, *The Myth of Seneca Falls: Memory and the Women's Suffrage Movement, 1848–1898* (University of North Carolina Press, 2014), 5.

4 "Memo—Special Commemorative Issue, 1970," WHS WSP Records, 3:13, WSP, 1962–2000, 1.

5 "Journal of WSP Commemorating Eighteen Years of Conscientious Concern for the Future of the World's Children," SCPC WSP Records, A1:2, Documents Describing WSP History.

6 Verta Taylor, "Social Movement Continuity: The Women's Movement in Abeyance," *American Sociological Review* 54 (1989), 761.

7 For example, see Toshihiro Higuchi, *Political Fallout: Nuclear Weapons Testing and the Making of a Global Environmental Crisis* (Stanford University Press, 2020), 127–28.

8 Benford, "Controlling Narratives," 57–62.

9 For comparison, recent historians of the Civil Rights Movement have challenged the apparent spontaneity of the Montgomery bus boycott and Greensboro lunch counter sit-ins, not to lessen the impact of those initiatives but to recognize the painstaking women-led organizational work and decades-long precursors that ensured the success of these initiatives. Danielle L. McGuire's *At the Dark End of the Street: Black Women, Rape, and Resistance—A New History of the Civil Rights Movement from Rosa Parks to the Rise of Black Power* (Alfred A. Knopf, 2010), and Polletta's *It Was Like a Fever: Storytelling in Protest and Politics (Chicago University Press, 2006)*, demonstrate the analytical significance of this approach.

10 Madeleine Duckles interview, November 22, 1985, ARS.0056; Ruth Pinkson interview, October 1987 ARS.0056, Stanford University Archive of Recorded Sound.

11 Amy Swerdlow, "A Child of the Old, Old Left," in *Red Diapers: Growing Up in the Communist Left*, ed. Judy Kaplan and Linn Shapiro (University of Illinois Press, 1998); 249–56.

12 Ethel Barol Taylor, *We Made a Difference: My Personal Journey with Women Strike for Peace* (Camino Books, 1998), 5.

13 Duckles interview, November 22, 1985, ARS.0056; Swerdlow, "A Child of the Old, Old Left," 249–56.

14 Ruth Pinkson, "The Life and Times of an Elderly Red Diaper Baby," in *Red Diapers: Growing Up in the Communist Left*, 231–36; "Cora Weiss," in *Peacework: Oral Histories of Women Peace Activists, ed.* Judith Porter Adams (Twayne, 1991), 37–46; "Elise Boulding," in *Peacework*, 185–92; "Madeline Duckles," in *Peacework*, 159–66; Edith

Villastrigo interview, October 1987, ARS.0056; Ethel Taylor interview, October 5, 1987, ARS.0056; Frances Herring interview, June 1, 1985, ARS.0056.

15 Harriet Hyman Alonso, "Mayhem and Moderation: Women Peace Activists during the McCarthy Era," in *Not June Cleaver: Women and Gender in Postwar America, 1945–1960*, ed. Joanne Meyerowitz (Temple University Press, 1994), 128–50.

16 Jonathan Bell, "Social Democracy and the Rise of the Democratic Party in California, 1950–1964," *The Historical Journal* 49, no. 2 (2006): 524.

17 Amy C. Schneidhorst, *Building a Just and Secure World: Popular Front Women's Struggle for Peace and Justice in Chicago during the 1960s* (Bloomsbury Publishing, 2011), 6–20; "Women Join Today in Plea Against War," *Chicago Daily Tribune*, November 1, 1961, 3; Sidney Lens, *Unrepentant Radical: An American Activist's Account of Five Turbulent Decades* (Beacon Press, 1980), 292–93.

18 Susan Paynter, "SWAP: Seeking Peace Decade after Decade," *Seattle Times*, January 26, 1998.

19 "A Fond Farewell: Thorun Robel," University of Washington, Seattle, Seattle Women Act for Peace Records, 4073 (hereafter UWS SWAP), 2:34, Robel, Thorun, 1988–1998.

20 "Biographical Notes, August 31, 1981," UWS SWAP Records, 1:36, Speeches and Writings, 1955–Feb 1982; Pinkson, "The Life and Times of an Elderly Red Diaper Baby," in *Red Diapers*, 235.

21 Myrna Oliver, "Alice Hamburg, 96; Activist Began Women's Peace Group," *Los Angeles Times*, November 19, 2001; Judith Scherr, "Local Activist, Alice Hamburg, Dies at 95," *Berkeley Daily Planet*, November 14, 2001.

22 "Hazel's 70th Birthday Celebration, 6/23/83," University of California, Berkely, San Francisco Women for Peace Records BANC MSS 89/132 c (hereafter UCB WFP Records), 17:22, Grossman, Hazel, and Grossman, Aubrey, 1967–2000; "Fire Hoses Douse 200 S.F. Rioters," *Los Angeles Times*, May 14, 1960.

23 James Paddison, "San Franciscans for Academic Freedom and Education and the Bay Area Opposition to HUAC, 1959–1960," *California History* 78, no. 3 (1999): 188–201.

24 Alonso, "Mayhem and Moderation, 128–50.

25 Robert A. Divine, *Blowing on the Wind: The Nuclear Test Ban Debate, 1954–1960* (Oxford University Press, 1978), 3; David Tal, *The American Nuclear Disarmament Dilemma: 1945–1963* (Syracuse University Press, 2008), 64.

26 Lawrence Wittner, *One World or None: A History of the World Nuclear Disarmament Movement Through 1953. Volume One of The Struggle Against the Bomb* (Stanford University Press, 1993), 40–42.

27 Harriet Hyman Alonso, *Peace as a Women's Issue: A History of the U.S. Movement for World Peace and Women's Rights* (Syracuse University Press, 1993), 156.

28 Harriet Hyman Alonso, "Dissension in the Ranks: The New York Branch of WILPF vs. the National Board, 1914–1955," *Peace Review* 8, no. 3, (1996): 337–42; Catherine Foster, *Women for All Seasons: The Story of the Women's International League for Peace and Freedom* (University of Georgia Press, 1989), 23.

29 Foster, *Women for All Seasons*, 27.

30 Dario Fazzi, *Eleanor Roosevelt and the Anti-Nuclear Movement: The Voice of Conscience* (Palgrave Macmillan, 2016).

31 Mina Carson, *Ava Helen Pauling: Partner, Activist, Visionary* (Oregon University Press, 2013).

32 Letter from Frances Herring to Philip Noel-Howard, July 17, 1961, UCB WFP Records, 18:35, Oslo Conference on Nuclear Weapons, 1961 May.

33 Marcus Gleisser, *The World of Cyrus Eaton* (Black Squirrel Books, 2005), 112–33.

34 McGuire, *At the Dark End of the Street.*

35 Lori A. Flores, "An Unladylike Strike Fashionably Clothed: Mexicana and Anglo Women Garment Workers Against Tex-Son, 1959–1963," *Pacific Historical Review* 78, no. 3 (2009): 367–402.

36 Jacqueline Castledine, *Cold War Progressives: Women's Interracial Organizing for Peace and Freedom* (University of Illinois Press, 2012), 92.

37 Castledine, *Cold War Progressives*, 102.

38 Gerald Gill, "From Maternal Pacifism to Revolutionary Solidarity: African-American Women's Opposition to the Vietnam War," in *Sights on the Sixties*, ed. Barbara Tischler (Rutgers University Press, 1992): 178–79.

39 Dayo F. Gore, *Radicalism at the Crossroads: African American Women Activists in the Cold War* (New York University Press, 2011), 60.

40 Elaine Tyler May, *Homeward Bound: American Families in the Cold War Era* (Basic Books, 2008), 91–102; Dee Garrison, *Bracing for Armageddon: Why Civil Defense Never Worked* (Oxford University Press, 2006) 94–95; Laura McEnaney, "Atomic Age Motherhood: Maternalism and Militarism in the 1950s," in *Women's America: Refocusing the Past*, ed. Linda K. Kerber and Jane Sherrow de Hart (Oxford University Press, 2000).

41 Robert A. Jacobs, *The Dragon's Tail: Americans Face the Atomic Age* (University of Massachusetts Press, 2010), 64–65; Winzola McLendon, "Nuclear War Is but an Error or Whim Away," *The Washington Post*, September 27, 1960, B3.

42 McEnaney, "Atomic Age Motherhood," 449.

43 Dee Garrison, "'Our Skirts Gave Them Courage': The Civil Defense Protest Movement in New York City, 1955–1961," in *Not June Cleaver: Women and Gender in Postwar America, 1945–1960*, ed. Joanne Meyerowitz (Temple University Press, 1994), 206.

44 McEnaney, "Atomic Age Motherhood," 453.

45 Marian Mollin, *Radical Pacifism in Modern America: Egalitarianism and Protest* (University of Pennsylvania Press, 2006), 73–96.

46 "Your Family's Stake in Disarmament: A Women's Conference, April 23 1960," SCPC WSP Records, B1:9, Local Peace Work 1960.

47 Emily E. LB. Twarog, *The Politics of the Pantry: Housewives, Food, and Consumer Protest in Twentieth-Century America* (Oxford University Press, 2017), 3; Annelise Orleck, *Rethinking American Women's Activism* (Routledge, 2015).

48 John Wicklein, "Quakers in Times Sq. Easter Vigil Pray for Peace," *The New York Times*, April 1, 1961, 1.

49 David Hostetter, "House Guest of the AEC: Dorothy Hutchinson, the 1958 Fast at the Atomic Energy Commission, and the Domestication of Protest," *Peace & Change* 34, no. 2 (2009): 134.

50 Scott H. Bennett, *Radical Pacifism: The War Resisters League and Gandhian Nonviolence in America, 1915–1963* (Syracuse University Press, 2003), 207–16.

51 Newsletter of Queen's Women Strike for Peace, 1(2) May 10, 1962, Wisconsin Historical Society WSP Records (hereafter WHS WSP Records), M83–327, Ch 4 Working Papers on High Altitude Testing, Clippings, April 1962, 2.

52 Jon Coburn, "Making a Difference: The History and Memory of Women Strike for Peace, 1961–1990" (PhD diss., Northumbria University, 2015), 39–40. Based

on "Mary Sharmat's Statement Regarding Her Civil Defense Protest," *PBS: American Experience: The Race for the Superbomb.* http://www.pbs.org/wgbh/amex/bomb/filmmore/reference/primary/sharmat.html. Accessed November 4, 2015.

53 Garrison, *Bracing for Armageddon*, 100–15.

54 Schneidhorst, *Building a Just and Secure World*, 6.

55 "Pacifists March 87 Blocks Here," *The New York Times*, April 3, 1961, 23.

56 "Your Family's Stake in Disarmament: A Women's Conference, April 23, 1960," SCPC WSP Records, B1:9, Local Peace Work 1960.

57 Marie Hammond-Callaghan, "Bridging and Breaching Cold War Divides: Transnational Peace Building, State Surveillance, and the Voice of Women," in *Worth Fighting For: Canada's Tradition of War Resistance from 1812 to the War on Terror*, ed. Lara Campbell et al. (Between the Lines, 2015), 135; Frances Herring interview, May 2, 1985/Unspecified Dates in 1985, ARS.0056.

58 "Eleanor Garst: Chapter 1, Who Are These Women?" WHS WSP Records, M83–327, Working Papers for Ch 1, 2, WSP Formation, Test Ban Efforts, 2, 4; "Summary of Meeting of Portland Women Deeply Concerned about the Current and Continuing Threat of Nuclear War, September 21, 1961", UCB WFP Records, 1:19, WSP National and Other Cities Beginnings; Coburn, "Making a Difference," 50, based on Kathy Robinson, "Alliance for Nuclear Accountability Award to Carol Urner on April 5, 2011," Women's Action for New Directions. Accessed November 3, 2015. www.wand.org.

59 Schneidhorst, *Building a Just and Secure World*, 6.

60 Letter from Frances Herring to Philip Noel-Howard, July 17, 1961, UCB WSP Records, 18:35, Oslo Conference on Nuclear Weapons, 1961 May.

61 Richard Dudman, "Dagmar Wilson: Striking for Peace," *The Washington Post Potomac*, April 13, 1966, WHS WSP Records, MSS 433, 2:11, Biographical Data on Dagmar Wilson; McKay, "Margaret Ells Russell," 121.

62 Wilson interview, April 15, 1989, ARS.0056.

63 Cesar Searchinger, *The Way Out of War* (Macmillan, 1940).

64 Dudman, "Dagmar Wilson: Striking for Peace."

65 Wilson interview, April 15, 1989, ARS.0056.

66 "Dagmar Wilson, Biographical Summary," WHS WSP Records, MSS 433, 2:11, Biographical Data on Dagmar Wilson; Wilson interview, April 15, 1989, ARS.0056.

67 Wilson interview, April 15, 1989, ARS.0056.

68 Dagmar Wilson, "Tainting the Antinuclear Movement: HUAC and the Irrepressible Women Strike for Peace," in *The Price of Dissent: Testimonies to Political Repression in America*, ed. Bud Schultz and Ruth Schultz (University of California Press, 2001), 284.

69 Villastrigo interview, October 1987, ARS.0056.

70 Dagmar Wilson, "Radiation Exposure," *The Washington Post*, May 16, 1959, 10.

71 "Eleanor Garst: Chapter 1: Who Are These Women?" WHS WSP Records, M83–327, Working Papers for Ch 1, 2, WSP Formation, Test Ban Efforts, 29.

72 Wilson interview, April 15, 1989, ARS.0056.

73 Donna Allen interview, April 26, 1989, ARS.0056.

74 Wilson interview, April 15, 1989, ARS.0056.

75 "Dagmar Wilson's corrections for Amy Swerdlow's Draft Dissertation," SCPC WSP Records, ACC 2013–050:17, Draft Chapters 1–5, Amy Swerdlow's Dissertation with Dagmar's Biographical Corrections 1981.

76 Wilson interview, April 15, 1989, ARS.0056.
77 "Dagmar Wilson's corrections for Amy Swerdlow's Draft Dissertation," SCPC WSP Records, ACC 2013–050:17, Draft Chapters 1–5, Amy Swerdlow's Dissertation with Dagmar's Biographical Corrections 1981.
78 Mollin, *Radical Pacifism in Modern America*: 73–96.
79 Letter from Folly Fodor to Loraine Flox, December 27, 1961, WHS WSP Records, M83–327, Nov 1, 1961 Strike, Media Coverage, Aftermath, Org Corr; "Women for Peace Exploratory Meeting, September 21, 1961," WHS WSP Records, M83–327, Working Papers for Ch 1, 2, WSP Formation, Test Ban Treaty.
80 "Women for Peace Exploratory Meeting, September 21, 1961," WHS WSP Records, M83–327, Working Papers for Ch 1, 2, WSP Formation, Test Ban Treaty.
81 "Janet N. Neuman: Peace Activist," *The Washington Post*, March 26, 1992, C4; Swerdlow, *Women Strike for Peace*, 5, 189.
82 Allen interview, April 26, 1989, ARS.0056.
83 Dagmar Wilson, Margaret Russell, Eleanor Garst, Jeanne Bagby, Mary Chandler, and Folly Fodor. See for example Swerdlow, *Women Strike for Peace*, 19; "Eleanor Garst: Chapter 1: Who Are These Women?" WHS WSP Records, M83–327, Working Papers for Ch 1, 2, WSP Formation, Test Ban Efforts; "RE: Janice Holland Peace Awards, September 21, 1962, at the Presidential Arms Hotel," SCPC WSP Records, A2:1, Literature—1962, 1822 Mass Ave NW Wash DC.
84 "Women's Strike for Peace (WSFP)," American University DC Office of the Women Strike for Peace Records (hereafter AU WSP Records), 19, FOIA—FBI Files: 100-39566, Vol. 1, 3; "2,000 In L.A. Join Women's Peace Strike," *Los Angeles Times*, November 2, 1961, B1.
85 Allen interview, April 26, 1989, ARS.0056.
86 "Elise Boulding, 'Who Are These Women?: A Progress Report on a Study of the Women Strike for Peace,' 1963," SCPC WSP Records, A1:2, Documents Describing WSP History, 12.
87 Swerdlow, *Women Strike for Peace*, 63–65; Letter from Folly Fodor to Loraine Flox, December 27, 1961, WHS WSP Records, M83–327, Nov 1, 1961 Strike, Media Coverage, Aftermath, Org Corr.
88 "Eleanor Garst: Chapter 1: Who Are These Women?" WHS WSP Records, M83–327, Working Papers for Ch 1, 2, WSP Formation, Test Ban Efforts.
89 "4/29/67, New Orleans, Louisiana," AU WSP Records, Box 19, FOIA—FBI Files: 100-39566, Vol. 18, 3; "Eleanor Garst: Chapter 1: Who Are These Women?" WHS WSP Records, M83–327, Working Papers for Ch 1, 2, WSP Formation, Test Ban Efforts.
90 "Eleanor Garst: Chapter 1: Who Are These Women?" WHS WSP Records, M83–327, Working Papers for Ch 1, 2, WSP Formation, Test Ban Efforts; Andrea Estepa, "Taking the White Gloves Off: Women Strike for Peace and the Transformation of Women's Activist Identities in the United States, 1961–1980," (PhD diss., Rutgers University, May 2012), 65.
91 McKay, "Margaret Ells Russell," 119–34; "Issues for Discussion No. 5, October 22, 1963," WHS WSP Records, MSS 433, 2:10, Ephemera; "Information: Women's March for Peace, Nov 1. 1961," SCPC WSP Records, A2:1, Literature—1961, 1413 29th St NW & 7616 14th St NE Wash DC; Swerdlow, *Women Strike for Peace*, 65.
92 Barnes May, "The Great Fight for Democracy, Religion, and the Home," 64–92
93 Letter from Lewis Strauss to Eleanor Garst, June 19, 1958, WHS WSP Records, MSS 433, 1:1, General Correspondence, 1958–1962.

94 Swerdlow, *Women Strike for Peace*, 59–63.
95 "Eleanor Garst," AU WSP Records, Box 2, Leadership, 1975, 1979, 1982–1987, 1990–1998, N.D.
96 "Eleanor Garst: Chapter 1: Who Are These Women?" WHS WSP Records, M83-327, Working Papers for Ch 1, 2, WSP Formation, Test Ban Efforts, 6.
97 Leila Rupp and Verta Taylor, *Survival in the Doldrums: The American Women's Rights Movement, 1945 to the 1960s* (Oxford University Press, 1987), 22.
98 "Eleanor Garst: Chapter 1: Who Are These Women?" WHS WSP Records, M83-327, Working Papers for Ch 1, 2, WSP Formation, Test Ban Efforts; Swerdlow, *Women Strike for Peace*, 17.
99 "Eleanor Garst," AU WSP Records, Box 2, Leadership, 1975, 1979, 1982–1987, 1990–1998, N.D.; "Eleanor Garst: Chapter 1: Who Are These Women?" WHS WSP Records, M83-327, Working Papers for Ch 1, 2, WSP Formation, Test Ban Efforts.
100 Mollin, *Radical Pacifism in Modern America*, 77–81.
101 "Eleanor Garst: Chapter 1: Who Are These Women?" WHS WSP Records, M83-327, Working Papers for Ch 1, 2, WSP Formation, Test Ban Efforts, 6; Mollin, *Radical Pacifism in Modern America*, 77–81.
102 Swerdlow, *Women Strike for Peace*, 43.
103 "History of WSP by Barbara Drageaux, Portland WILPF Newsletter, 1994," AU WSP Records, Box 2, History 1961–1994.
104 "Washington WSP 'Retreat' Meeting at Folly Fodor's, Saturday, October 5, 1968," SCPC WSP Records, A1:2, Washington WSP Retreat—October 5 1968.
105 "Eleanor Garst: Chapter 1, Who Are These Women?" WHS WSP Records, M83-327, Working Papers for Ch 1, 2, WSP Formation, Test Ban Efforts, 11–13.
106 Estepa, "Taking the White Gloves Off" (PhD diss.), 65.
107 "Eleanor Garst: Chapter 1, Who Are These Women?" WHS WSP Records, M83-327, Working Papers for Ch 1, 2, WSP Formation, Test Ban Efforts, 11–13.
108 "Eleanor Garst—Draft of Letter to Accompany Leaflet, September 22, 1961," SCPC WSP Records, A1:2, Documents Describing WSP History.
109 Gore, *Radicalism at the Crossroads*, 60.
110 Lens, *Unrepentant Radical*, 292.
111 "Draft of Letter (for individual salvation and signature and note if desired) to Accompany Leaflet, September 22, 1961," SCPC WSP Records, A1:2, Documents Describing WSP History.
112 Boulding, "Who Are These Women?" 9.
113 Ellen Lentz, "Mood Is Tense Along the Berlin Wall," *The New York Times*, October 29, 1961, E5; "Soviet Tanks Quit Berlin Wall; U.S. Follows Suit, Tension Eases," *The Boston Globe*, October 29, 1961, 61.
114 William Fulton, "Ridicules Reds as Show-Offs in U.N. Debate," *Chicago Daily Tribune*, November 1, 1961, 3; Sam Pope Brewer, "Britain Urges Firm Test Ban," *The New York Times*, November 1, 1961, 16; Julius Duscha, "West Denounces Soviet Blast; Protest Rallies Held in Europe," *The Washington Post*, October 31, 1961, A8; "Russian Fall-Out Drifting Over U.S.," *The New York Times*, October 29, 1961, 16.
115 "Protests Against Super-Bomb Staged in Several Countries," *The Washington Post*, November 1, 1961, A12.
116 "Brick Marked '50 MG' Strikes Soviet Mission," *The New York Times*, November 1, 1961, 16.

117 "100 Picket Red Embassy to Protest Bomb Tests," *The Washington Post*, November 1, 1961, A12.
118 "Arrests Near Embassy: Demonstration Against Bomb," *The Guardian*, October 31, 1961, 2.
119 Marie Smith, "500 Women Picket for Peace," *The Washington Post*, November 2, 1961, D1; "2,000 in L.A. Join Women's Peace Strike," *Los Angeles Times*, November 2, 1961, B1; "Women Stage Peace Strike Throughout U.S." *Chicago Daily Tribune*, November 2, 1961, 4; "300 Women Protest Here Against Nuclear Testing," *The New York Times*, November 2, 1961, 5.
120 Robbie Lieberman, *The Strangest Dream: Communism; Anticommunism, and the U.S. Peace Movement, 1945–1963* (Syracuse University Press, 2000),166.
121 "Women Stage Peace Strike Throughout U.S." *Chicago Daily Tribune*, November 2, 1961, 4.
122 Taylor, *We Made a Difference*, 3.
123 "Thousands of Women Join in Plea for Peace," *Los Angeles Times*, November 2, 1961, B3.
124 Sidney Tarrow, "Mentalities, Political Cultures, and Collective Action Frames: Constructing Meanings through Action," in *Frontiers in Social Movement Theory*, ed. Aldon. D. Morris and Carol. M. Mueller (Yale University Press, 1992), 177.
125 Schneidhorst, *Building a Just and Secure World*, 7.
126 Swerdlow, *Women Strike for Peace*, 18; Sophia Wyatt, "One Day Strike for Peace," *The Guardian*, December 4, 1961, 6; Letter from Joyce Eggington to Dagmar Wilson, November 9, 1961, SCPC WSP Records, A3:6, 1961; Alice Sachs Hamburg, *Grass Roots: From Prairie to Politics: The Autobiography of Alice Sachs Hamburg* (Creative Arts Books Company, 2001), 172.
127 "Ruth Gage-Colby Address to United Nations, New York City, December 12, 1961," SCPC WSP Records, A3:6, 1961.
128 Herring interview, June 1, 1965, ARS.0056.
129 "We can congratulate ourselves on a beginning," SCPC WSP Records, A2:1, Literature—1961.
130 "Women for Survival," SCPC WSP Records, A2:1, Literature—1961.
131 "Report to Women Around the United States of America, on the Women's Strike for Peace, November 1961," SCPC WSP Records, A2:1, Literature—1961.
132 Eugene Rosi, "Mass and Attentive Opinion on Nuclear Weapons Tests and Fallout, 1954–1963," *Public Opinion Quarterly* 29, no, 2 (1965): 280.
133 Telegram from Governor Edmund G. Brown to Wallace Thomson, October 30, 1961, SCPC WSP Records, B1:1 Beginnings of LA WSP (1961).
134 "From Bruce to Secretary of State, August 31, 1961," Papers of John F. Kennedy, Presidential Papers, National Security Files, JKNSF-302-001-p0002, John F. Kennedy Presidential Library and Museum, Boston, MA.
135 "Women Join Today in Plea Against War," *Chicago Daily Tribune*, November 1, 1961, 3.
136 "Protests Against Super-Bomb Staged in Several Countries," *The Washington Post*, November 1, 1961, A12.
137 Marie Smith, "Takes Peace Plea to the Soviets," *The Washington Post*, November 1, 1961, D1.
138 "Parents Bring Children to Peace March," *Chicago Daily Tribune*, November 6, 1961, 18.

139 "Resume of Two Decades of Women Strike for Peace Actions," AU WSP Records, Box 2, History 1961–1994.
140 Swerdlow, *Women Strike for Peace*, ix.
141 Amy Swerdlow, "Ladies' Day at the Capitol: Women Strike for Peace Versus HUAC," *Feminist Studies* 8 no. 3 (1982): 494.
142 Taylor, *We Made a Difference*, cover page.
143 "Eleanor Garst to Ruth Pinkson RE: History of WSP for 20th Anniversary," AU WSP Records, Box 2, History 1961–1994.
144 Duckles interview, November 22, 1985, ARS.0056.
145 "Bay Women Made Dupes by Reds," *San Francisco Examiner*, May 21, 1962, 10.
146 Alonso, "Mayhem and Moderation," 147; Joanne Meyerowitz, "Beyond the Feminine Mystique: A Reassessment of Postwar Mass Culture, 1946–1958," *The Journal of American History* 79, no. 4 (1993): 1455–82; Daniel Horowitz, *Betty Friedan and the Making of the Feminine Mystique* (University of Massachusetts Press, 1998), 205.
147 Swerdlow, *Women Strike for Peace*, 72–73.
148 Stephanie Coontz, *The Way We Never Were: American Families and the Nostalgia Trap*. (Basic Books, 2000), 33.
149 Francisca de Haan, "Continuing Cold War Paradigms in Western Historiography of Transnational Women's Organizations: The Case of the Women's International Democratic Federation (WIDF)," *Women's History Review* 19, no. 4 (2010): 547–73.
150 See for example, Catherine Fosl and Lara Kelland, "'Bring Your Whole Self to the Work': Identity and Intersectional Politics in the Louisville LGBTQ Movement," *The Oral History Review* 43, no. 1 (2016): 138–52.
151 "LA WSP Thoughts Regarding the 'Statement of Purpose' to be Discussed at Champaign-Urbana," SCPC WSP Records, A1:3, National Conference—1963, Champaign IL; Ruth Gage-Colby, "WSP," *New World Review* (June 1963), 5.
152 Letter from Dagmar Wilson to Mrs. L. John Collins, December 14, 1961, SCPC WSP Records, A3:6, 1961.
153 "Report to Women Around the United States of America, on the Women's Strike for Peace, November 1961," UCB WFP Records, 18:1, East Bay WFP Berkeley Office Records, Oct-Dec 1961; "Women for Peace, Chicago Area," UCB WFP Records, 1:19, WSP National and Other Cities Beginnings; Wilson interview, April 15, 1989, ARS.0056.
154 Swerdlow, *Women Strike for Peace*, 15; Swerdlow, "Ladies' Day at the Capitol," 493; "WSP KPFK Commentary, May 1969," SCPC WSP Records, A2:2, Literature—1969, 2140 P St NW, Washington, DC.
155 "Speech for Kay Johnson's Luncheon, 1-4-65," WHS WSP Records, MSS 433, 2:12, Dagmar Wilson Speech Notes.
156 "Highlights of WSP History," AU WSP Records, Box 2, History 1961–1994; "Women for Peace Welcome You to a Special Lunch Banquet," Chicago History Museum Women for Peace (Chicago, IL) Records (hereafter CHM WFP Records), 10:9, Lens, S, Women for Peace.
157 "Celebrate Celebrate Celebrate," UCB WFP Records, 15:10, Women's Peace Office—Activities and Campaigns, 1980–1989.
158 "Jan 1997 Anci's Words at the Occasion of SWAP's 36th," WHS WSP Records, MSS 433, 1:39, Speeches and Writing—Misc., April 1990–1998, n.d.; "Report to Women Around the United States of America, on the Women's Strike for Peace, November 1961," UCB WFP Records, 18:1, East Bay WFP Berkeley Office Records, Oct—Dec 1961.

159 Swerdlow, *Women Strike for Peace*, 247n1.
160 Most recently the reference to 50,000 participants on WSP's first strike can be found in Elizabeth Eaves, "Can Women Save the World?" *Bulletin of the Atomic Scientists*, June 15, 2017; also Ross, "Preemptive Strikes," 161–182; and Toshihiro Higuchi, *Political Fallout*, 127–128.
161 Foster, *Women for All Seasons*, 28.
162 Swerdlow, *Women Strike for Peace*, 27.
163 For example, Role of San Francisco Women for Peace in the US War Against Vietnam—Hazel Grossman's response to letter from Vietnamese Women's Union, UCB WFP Records, 1:8, Historical Information for Vietnam Women's Association, 1984.
164 Taylor, *We Made a Difference*, xvi; Wilson, "Tainting the Antinuclear Movement, 284.

Chapter Two

1 Nat Dickinson, "Frannie: A Profile of Francis W. Herring," University of California, Berkely, San Francisco Women for Peace Records BANC MSS 89/132 c (hereafter UCB WFP Records), 17:27, 46–47.
2 James Schurz, "Women Mass by Hundreds," *San Francisco Examiner*, November 2, 1961, 1.
3 James Schurz, "Bay Women Protest the Bomb," *San Francisco Examiner*, November 2, 1961, 14.
4 Letter from Councilman Robert V. McKeen to President Kennedy, November 24, 1961, UCB WFP Records, 18:1, East Bay WFP Berkeley Office Records, Oct—Dec 1961; Letter from Councilman John J. Dunn to President Kennedy, November 6, 1961, UCB WFP Records, 18:1, East Bay WFP Berkeley Office Records, Oct–Dec 1961; Letter from Alvin R. Leonard, M.D., Director of Public Health to President Kennedy, November 1, 1961, UCB WFP Records, 18:1, East Bay WFP Berkeley Office Records, Oct–Dec 1961.
5 Nat Dickinson, "Frannie: A Profile of Francis W. Herring," UCB WFP Records, 17:27, 46–47.
6 "Circular from Ad Hoc Committee of Women Members of East Bay Peace Groups, November 8, 1961," Swarthmore College Peace Collection, WSP Records SCPC-DG-115 (hereafter SCPC WSP Records), B2:1 East Bay.
7 Taylor, *We Made a Difference*, x; Amy Swerdlow, *Women Strike for Peace: Traditional Motherhood and Radical Politics in the 1960s* (University of Chicago Press, 1993), 4–5.
8 Timothy B. Gongaware, "Subcultural Identity Work in Social Movements: Barriers to Collective Identity Changes and Overcoming Them," *Symbolic Interaction* 35, no. 1 (2012): 8.
9 "Eleanor Garst: Chapter 1: Who Are These Women?" Wisconsin Historical Society WSP Records (hereafter WHS WSP Records), M83–327, Working Papers for Ch 1, 2, WSP Formation, Test Ban Efforts, 18.
10 Amy Swerdlow, "Ladies' Day at the Capitol: Women Strike for Peace Versus HUAC," *Feminist Studies* 8 no. 3 (1982): 495.
11 Milton S. Katz, *Ban the Bomb: A History of SANE, The Committee for a SANE Nuclear Policy, 1957–1985* (Greenwood Press, 1986), 54–55.

12 Letter from Lucy Adelman to Margaret Russell, November 12, 1961, SCPC WSP Records, B1:1, Beginnings LA WISP 1961.
13 "WISP Conference, Impressions & Reporting by Gail Eaby," SCPC WSP Records, B1:1, Minutes, Conference Reports 1961 and 1962. Emphasis in the original.
14 "Los Angeles WSP Statement at Ann Arbor Conference, June 9–10, 1962," SCPC WSP Records, A1:3, National Conference—1962, Ann Arbor MI.
15 "Women Strike for Peace, Minutes December 2, 1961," WHS WSP Records, M83–327, Working Papers for Ch 1, 2, WSP Formation, Test Ban Efforts.
16 This was initially done through something called the *Women's Peace Movement Bulletin*, a national information pamphlet edited by social scientist, peace activist, and volunteer Elise Boulding especially for WSP. As the group grew and consolidated, branches had less of an obligation to share details of their campaigns nationally, though they remained in constant communication with one another through other channels. Letter from Lucy Adelman to Margaret Russell, November 12. 1961, SCPC WSP Records, B1:1, Beginnings LA WISP 1961; Elise Boulding, "Who Are These Women?: A Progress Report on a Study of the Women Strike for Peace, 1963," SCPC WSP Records, A1:2, Documents Describing WSP History, 2.
17 Dagmar Wilson interview, April 15, 1989, ARS.0056, Stanford University Archive of Recorded Sound; Amy Swerdlow, "'Pure Milk, Not Poison': Women Strike for Peace and the Test Ban Treaty of 1963," in *Rocking the Ship of State: Toward a Feminist Peace Politics*, ed. Adrienne Harris and Ynestra King (Westview Press, 1989), 227.
18 Rhodri Jeffreys-Jones, *Peace Now! American Society and the Ending of the Vietnam War* (Yale University Press, 1999), 157.
19 Lisa McGirr, *Suburban Warriors: The Origins of the New American Right* (Princeton University Press, 2015), 66.
20 For example, works on the Student Nonviolent Coordinating Committee, such as Wesley Hogan, *Many Minds, One Heart: SNCC's Dream for a New America* (University of North Carolina Press, 2009); Barbara Ransby, *Ella Baker & The Black Freedom Movement: A Radical Democratic Vision* (University of North Carolina Press, 2003), 239–272; Ted Dientsfrey, "A Conference on the Sit-Ins," *Commentary*, June 1960.
21 Richard Flacks and Nelson Lichtenstein, "Introduction," in *The Port Huron Statement: Sources and Legacies of the New Left's Founding Manifesto*, ed. Richard Flacks and Nelson Lichtenstein (University of Pennsylvania Press, 2015), 2.
22 Swerdlow, *Women Strike for Peace*, 10.
23 Temma Kaplan, "Community and Resistance in Women's Political Cultures," *Dialectical Anthropology* 15, nos. 2 and 3 (1990): 259–67; Laure Bereni and Anne Revillard, "A Paradigmatic Social Movement? Women's Movements and the Definition of Contentious Politics," *Sociétés contemporaines* 85 (2012), 17–41.
24 Jacqueline Castledine, *Cold War Progressives: Women's Interracial Organizing for Peace and Freedom* (University of Illinois Press, 2012), 144–46.
25 Catherine Foster, *Women for All Seasons: The Story of the Women's International League for Peace and Freedom* (University of Georgia Press, 1989), 28.
26 Michelle Nickerson, *Mothers of Conservatism: Women and the Postwar Right* (Princeton University Press, 2012), 139–40.
27 The term "key women" frequently appears in descriptions of the group as a terminological substitute for "leader," with Amy Swerdlow justifying its use by stating that it was "a WSP term." Swerdlow, *Women Strike for Peace*, 52, 71; "1973 Progress

Report on Women Strike for Peace Research," SCPC WSP Records, C1:3, Research on WSP by Amy Swerdlow.

28 Swerdlow, *Women Strike for Peace*, 52; "Memo to West Coast Women for Peace, December 4, 1962," UCB WFP Records 3:30, WSP and the House Un-American Activities Committee.

29 Swerdlow, *Women Strike for Peace*, 75.

30 "American Women Report on Meeting with Vietnamese," SCPC WSP Records, B1:3, Trip to Djakarta 1965.

31 Dorothy Holland, Gretchen Fox, and Vinci Daro, "Social Movements and Collective Identity: A Decentered, Dialogic View," *Anthropological Quarterly* 81, no. 1 (2008): 96.

32 Jeffreys-Jones, *Peace Now!* 157; Swerdlow, *Women Strike for Peace*, 70–96.

33 Timothy B. Gongaware's work is particularly insightful. See, for example, "Subcultural Identity Work in Social Movements: Barriers to Collective Identity Changes and Overcoming Them," *Symbolic Interaction* 35, no. 1 (2012): 8.

34 Maryann Barakso, *Governing Now: Grassroots Activism in the National Organization for Women* (Cornell University Press, 2004).

35 Swerdlow, "Ladies' Day in the Capitol," 495.

36 Letter from Kay Hardman to Homer Jack, January 6, 1963, SCPC WSP Records, ACC 92A-118:1, British Peace Groups.

37 Andrew J. Ross, "Preemptive Strikes: Women Strike for Peace, Antinuclear Pacifism, and the Movement for Biological Democracy, 1961–1963," *Peace and Change*, 46 (2021): 161–82.

38 "Middle-Class Masses," by Eleanor Garst, from *Magazine of the Fellowship of Reconciliation*, September 1962, SCPC WSP Records, B1:7, Working Documents 1961–1964.

39 *Communist Activities in the Peace Movement*, 2148; "Journal of Women Strike for Peace Commemorating Eighteen Years of Conscientious Concern for the Future of the World's Children," SCPC WSP Records, A1:2, Documents Describing WSP History; Dagmar Wilson interview, April 15, 1989, ARS.0056. Emphasis mine.

40 "Middle-Class Masses," by Eleanor Garst, from *Magazine of the Fellowship of Reconciliation*, September 1962, SCPC WSP Records, B1:7, Working Documents 1961–1964. My emphasis.

41 Wherein a social "movement" is defined as a broad "set of opinions and beliefs in a population," and a social movement "organization" is a smaller, focused group "which identifies its goals with the preferences of a social movement," John D. McCarthy and Mayer N. Zald, "Resource Mobilization and Social Movements: A Partial Theory," *American Journal of Sociology* 82, no. 6 (1977): 1217–18. Melvin F. Hall wrote that "the peace movement is composed of many segments of the population that want, work for, and promote peace. Nonetheless there are numerous peace movement organizations," Melvin F. Hall, *Poor People's Social Movement Organizations: The Goal is to Win* (Praeger Publishers, 2005), 6–8. Subsequent waves of women's activism better suit the description of WSP's operations. For example, Kaplan, "Community and Resistance," 259–267; Bereni and Revillard, "A Paradigmatic Social Movement?," 17–41. Verta Taylor and Nancy Whittier's work on lesbian feminist activism deployed the alternative term "social movement community" in an attempt to capture the range of activism that occurs beyond an institutional base, "Collective Identity in Social Movement Communities: Lesbian

Feminist Mobilization," in *Frontiers in Social Movement Theory*, ed. Aldon. D. Morris and Carol. M. Mueller (Yale University Press, 1992), 104–129. See also Suzanne Staggenborg, "Social Movement Communities and Cycles of Protest: The Emergence and Maintenance of a Local Women's Movement," *Social Problems* 45, no. 2 (1998): 180–204.

42 Harriet Hyman Alonso, "Review," review of *Women Strike for Peace: Traditional Motherhood and Radical Politics in the 1960s*, by Amy Swerdlow, *The American Historical Review* 99, no. 5 (1994): 1773–74. For examples of historians describing WSP as a movement, see Ross, "Preemptive Strikes," 161–182; Foster, *Women for All Seasons*, 27; Ruth Rosen, *The World Split Open: How the Modern Women's Movement Changed America* (Penguin Books, 2001), 59.

43 Swerdlow, *Women Strike for Peace*, 9.

44 Swerdlow interview, September 25, 1987, ARS.0056.

45 Swerdlow interview, September 25, 1987, ARS.0056.

46 Swerdlow, *Women Strike for Peace*, 237.

47 Amy C. Schneidhorst, *Building a Just and Secure World: Popular Front Women's Struggle for Peace and Justice in Chicago during the 1960s* (Bloomsbury Publishing, 2011).

48 Whereas social movement historian Van Gosse describes the New Left as a "movement of movements" encompassing everything that happened in the 1960s, Michael S. Foley takes WSP's older participants to mean it was as an outlier compared to the New Left's apparently younger communities of student peace activists, Van Gosse, *Rethinking the New Left*; Richard Flacks and Nelson Lichtenstein eds. *The Port Huron Statement*. Historians of WSP similarly disagree. Jacqueline Castledine implies that WSP was tangential to the New Left rather than a constituent part of it, Castledine, *Cold War Progressives*, 149.

49 "Southern California WSP RE: International Conferences and Visits," SCPC WSP Records A1:3, 1963 National Conference.

50 Ross, "Preemptive Strikes," 170.

51 Marianne DeKoven, *Utopia Limited: The Sixties and the Emergence of the Postmodern* (Duke University Press, 2004), 123.

52 Arthur Marwick, quoted in DeKoven, *Utopia Limited*, 123. See also Flacks and Lichtenstein eds. *The Port Huron Statement*.

53 Andrea Estepa, "Taking the White Gloves Off: Women Strike for Peace and the Transformation of Women's Activist Identities in the United States, 1961–1980," (PhD diss., Rutgers University, May 2012), 6. There is an opportunity here to delve into the intellectual foundations and legacies of the Call to Strike, but I'll leave it to someone with more stamina than I have to take up the challenge.

54 Sylvie Murray, *The Progressive Housewife: Community Activism in Suburban Queens, 1945–1965* (University of Pennsylvania Press, 2003), 3. See also Judith N. Shklar, *American Citizenship: The Quest for Inclusion* (Harvard University Press, 1991).

55 Polletta, *Freedom is an Endless Meeting*, 128; see also Francesca Polletta, "Strategy and Democracy in the New Left," in *The New Left Revisited*, ed. John McMillian and Paul Buhle (Temple University Press, 2003), 177, n39.

56 Swerdlow, *Women Strike for Peace*, 52.

57 "Circular from Ad Hoc Committee of Women Members of East Bay Peace Groups, November 8 1961," SCPC WSP Records, B2:1 East Bay.

58 From WSP-WFP Sacramento Clearing House, June, 15 1963, UCB WFP Records, 3:1 Other CA Area Offices Literature
59 Mary Ann Holser for Peace Education Clearing House Southern California Women Strike for Peace, UCB WFP Records, 4:3 Peace Education in Schools. Emphasis in the original.
60 James J. Farrell, *The Spirit of the Sixties: Making Postwar Radicalism* (Routledge, 1997), 130; Swerdlow, *Women Strike for Peace*, 81; Wilson interview, April 15, 1989, ARS.0056.
61 Ross, "Preemptive Strike," 164–82.
62 Swerdlow, *Women Strike for Peace*, 22.
63 Estepa, "Taking the White Gloves Off" (PhD diss.), 65.
64 Petra Goedde, *The Politics of Peace: A Global Cold War History* (Oxford University Press, 2019), 134–36.
65 "Message from Simone de Beauvoir, 1964," SCPC WSP Records, ACC 01A-005:9, National WSP Statements About.
66 Betty Friedan, *The Feminine Mystique* (Penguin Classics, 2010), 307.
67 Daniel Horowitz, *Betty Friedan and the Making of the Feminine Mystique* (University of Massachusetts Press, 1998).
68 Leandra Ruth Zarnow, *Battling Bella: The Protest Politics of Bella Abzug* (Harvard University Press, 2019), 151–2.
69 Polletta, *Freedom is an Endless Meeting*, 150.
70 Kelsy Kretschmer, *Fighting for NOW* (University of Minnesota Press, 2019), 4.
71 Swerdlow, *Women Strike for Peace*, 241.
72 "2D A-Test 'Strike' Staged by Women," *The New York Times*, December 2, 1961, 3.
73 "Ask Disarmament, Nuclear Test Ban in Demonstrations," *Palladium-Item* (Richmond, Indiana), December 31, 1961, 2.
74 Charles Portis, "2 Men—1,700 Women, Peace Train to Capital, January 16, 1962," in *Escape Velocity: A Charles Portis Miscellany* ed. Jay Jennings (Butler Center Books, 2012), 21–24; "'Peace Train' Off to D.C.," *The World-News*, January 15, 1962, 1; "Area Women Join in 'Peace Train," *The Herald News*, January 15, 1962, 50.
75 Marjorie Hunter, "President Responds to Pickets for Peace," *The New York Times*, January 16, 1962, 1.
76 Swerdlow, *Women Strike for Peace*, 193–195.
77 "Eleanor Garst Draft Chapter Four," WHS WSP Records, M83–327, Ch 4 Working Papers on High Altitude Testing, Clippings, April 1962, 6.
78 *Women Strike for Peace*. 1962. Alice Richards, Harvey Richards, with narration from Frances Herring; "Women Strike for Peace Script," SCPC WSP Records, ACC 90A-028:4, West Coast Film Script.
79 Andrew E. Wessel, "The American Peace Movement: A Study of its Themes and Political Potential," *RAND Corporation*, December 1962, iii.
80 "Cora Weiss," in *Peacework: Oral Histories of Women Peace Activists, ed.* Judith Porter Adams (Twayne, 1991), 42.
81 Regarding Policy Paper #7 on International Conferences and Visits (5/15/63), SCPC WSP Records, B1;7, Working Documents 1961–1964.
82 "Middle-Class Masses," by Eleanor Garst, from *Magazine of the Fellowship of Reconciliation*, September 1962, SCPC WSP Records, B1:7, Working Documents 1961–1964.
83 Ross, "Preemptive Strike," 178.

84 AU WSP Records, Box 19–22, FOIA FBI Files—100-39566.
85 Taylor, *We Made a Difference*, 30, 67; "Eleanor Garst Draft Chapter Four," WHS WSP Records, M83-327, Ch 4 Working Papers on High Altitude Testing, Clippings, April 1962. Comparison of FBI files and WSP's Steering Committee meeting minutes confirms the presence of an informant at a February 22, 1967, gathering of core activists, out of Alice Alt, Betty North, Edith Villastrigo, Martha Hersh, Ginny Freeman, Folly Fodor, Lynda Stein, Martha Dudley, Ella Tulin, Thelma DuVinage, Donna Allen, Helen Corning, Richi Orchin, and Ana Reyler. "Steering Committee Meeting, February 22, 1967," SCPC WSP Records, A1:1, Minutes of Steering Committee 1965–1970; "The Spring Mobilization for Peace: Information Concerning, March 21, 1967," AU WSP Records, Box 19, FOIA FBI Files—100-39566 Vol. 17 (1).
86 Edith Villastrigo interview, October 1987, ARS.0056; Ethel Taylor interview, October 5, 1987, ARS.0056; Esther Newill interview, February 23, 1980, ARS.0056.
87 Swerdlow, "Ladies' Day at the Capitol," 502.
88 Mary McGrory, "Nobody Controls Anybody," *Washington Evening Star*, December 14, 1962, 1; Russell Baker, "Observer," *The New York Times*, December 15, 1965, 6; Wilson interview, April 15, 1989, ARS.0056.
89 Swerdlow, *Women Strike for Peace*, 112; Swerdlow, "Ladies' Day at the Capitol," 507.
90 Swerdlow, "Ladies' Day at the Capitol," 515.
91 "United States Congress House Committee on Un-American Activities," *Communist Activities in the Peace Movement (Women Strike for Peace and Certain Other Groups): Hearings Before the Committee on Un-American Activities, House of Representatives, Eighty-Seventh Congress, Second Session. December 11–13 1962, Including Index* (Government Printing Office, 1963), 2095–96.
92 *Communist Activities in the Peace Movement*, 2132.
93 *Communist Activities in the Peace Movement*, 2140.
94 *Communist Activities in the Peace Movement*, 2104.
95 *Communist Activities in the Peace Movement*, 2200.
96 Barbara Deming, "Letter to WISP," *Liberation*, April 1963.
97 "Ethel Taylor, January 18," SCPC WSP Records, ACC 01A-040:2, National Conference 1978 SALT I; "Results of Two Discussion on Policy and Agenda for Second National WSP Conference at Urbana, Reconstructed from Notes Take by G. Blum and A. Swerdlow," SCPC WSP Records, A1:3, National Conference—1963, Champaign-Urbana IL.
98 Boulding, "Who Are These Women?" 6–12.
99 Lisa McGirr, *Suburban Warriors*.
100 "Eleanor Garst Draft Chapter Four," WHS WSP Records, M83-327, Ch 4 Working Papers on High Altitude Testing, Clippings, April 1962, 2.
101 Swerdlow, *Women Strike for Peace*, 76; Boulding, "Who Are These Women?" 12.
102 "WISP Coordinating Council Meeting," SCPC WSP Records, B1:1, Minutes Conference Reports 1961 and 1962.
103 Estepa, "Taking the White Gloves Off" (PhD diss.), 71.
104 Virginia Naeve, "Frontiers: Geneva Journey," *Manas* XV, no. 20 (1962): 12–13. See also Estepa, "Taking the White Gloves Off" (PhD diss.), 71–73.
105 Vincent J. Intondi, *African Americans Against the Bomb* (Stanford University Press, 2015), 68; Gore, *Radicalism at the Crossroads*, 46–59.
106 Ruth Pinkson interview, October 1987, ARS.0056; Tiyi M. Morris, *Womanpower*

Unlimited and the Black Freedom Struggle in Mississippi (University of Georgia Press, 2015), 74.

107 Gail Hovey, "Peter and Cora Weiss: The Atmosphere of African Liberation," in *No Easy Victories: African Liberation and American Activists over a Half Century, 1950–2000*, ed. William Minter et al. (Africa World Press, 2008), 79–82.

108 Castledine, *Cold War Progressives*, 126–129.

109 "Women Strike for Peace Memorandum, December 5, 1961," SCPC WSP Records B2:1, East Bay.

110 Georgina Denton, "Mothers Joining Together in Sisterhood: Women Strike for Peace and the National Welfare Rights Organization in the 1960s and 1970s," *Journal of the Motherhood Initiative* 3, no. 2 (2012): 123.

111 Swerdlow, *Women Strike for Peace*, 91–92.

112 Gerald Gill, "From Maternal Pacifism to Revolutionary Solidarity: African-American Women's Opposition to the Vietnam War," in *Sights on the Sixties*, ed. Barbara Tischler (Rutgers University Press, 1992): 179.

113 Morris, *Womanpower Unlimited*, 105–107.

114 Morris, *Womanpower Unlimited*, 49–50, 85–90.

115 Morris, *Womanpower Unlimited*, 90.

116 Estepa, "Taking the White Gloves Off" (PhD diss.), 22.

117 Joyce Blackwell, *No Peace Without Freedom: Race and the Women's International League for Peace and Freedom, 1915–1975* (Southern Illinois Press, 2004), 178.

118 Morris, *Womanpower Unlimited*, 103–104.

119 SCPC WSP Records, B1:1, Minutes, Conference Reports 1961 and 1962, Minutes of Women's International Strike for Peace Continuations Meeting, January 6 1962, 9.

120 Swerdlow, *Women Strike for Peace*, 90; "Expanded Version of the Talk Given November 16, 1986 at the WSP and WILPF 25th Anniversary Celebration, by Frances Herring," UCB WFP Records, 17:26, Herring, Frances, 1991–1993.

121 Eleanor Garst History of WSP Chap. LV, WHS WSP Records, M83–327, Ch 4 Working Papers on High Altitude Testing, Clippings, April 1962, 10.

122 Matthew D. Lassiter and the Policing and Social Justice HistoryLab, "Commissioner Edwards: Liberal Reform," *Detroit Under Fire: Police Violence, Crime Politics, and the Struggle for Racial Justice in the Civil Rights Era* (University of Michigan Carceral State Project, 2021), https://policing.umhistorylabs.lsa.umich.edu/s/detroitunderfire/page/george-edwards. Last accessed February 11, 2025; Letter from Gwendolyn Mallet to Bertrand Russell December 28, 1962, McMaster University Bertrand Russell Records, RA2: 184128.

123 Letter from Representatives of the Independent Negro Committee to End Racism and Ban the Bomb, Detroit, to Dagmar Wilson, March 24, 1962, WHS WSP Records, MSS 433, 2:7, Correspondence of Dagmar Wilson 1961–1964.

124 "Eleanor Garst Draft Chapter Four," WHS WSP Records, M83–327, Ch 4 Working Papers on High Altitude Testing, Clippings, April 1962, 8.

125 "Report on the National Conference, June 8–10," SCPC WSP Records, A1:3, National Conference—1962, Ann Arbor MI.

126 Swerdlow, *Women Strike for Peace*, 90.

127 Report on the National Conference, June 8–10, WHS WSP Records, M83–327, Ch 4 Working Papers on High Altitude Testing, Clippings, April 1962.

128 Swerdlow, *Women Strike for Peace*, 90.

129 "Report on the National Conference, June 8–10," WHS WSP Records, M83–327, Ch 4 Working Papers on High Altitude Testing, Clippings, April 1962.
130 "WISP Conference, Impressions & Reporting by Gail Eaby," SCPC WSP Records, B1:1, Minutes, Conference Reports 1961 and 1962.
131 "Report on the National Conference, June 8–10," WHS WSP Records, M83–327, Ch 4 Working Papers on High Altitude Testing, Clippings, April 1962.
132 Swerdlow, *Women Strike for Peace*, 91–92.
133 "My Personal Impressions of the Ann Arbor Conference—Elsa Knight Thompson," UCB WFP Records, 3:28, First National Conference, Ann Arbor, MI, 1962, 3–4.
134 "Eleanor Garst History of WSP Chap. LV," WHS WSP Records, M83–327, Ch 4 Working Papers on High Altitude Testing, Clippings, April 1962, 10.
135 "My Personal Impressions of the Ann Arbor Conference—Elsa Knight Thompson," UCB WFP Records, 3:28, First National Conference, Ann Arbor, MI, 1962, 3–4.
136 "Eleanor Garst History of WSP Chap. LV," WHS WSP Records, M83–327, Ch 4 Working Papers on High Altitude Testing, Clippings, April 1962, 10.
137 "Expanded Version of the Talk Given November 16, 1986 at the WSP and WILPF 25th Anniversary Celebration, by Frances Herring," UCB WFP Records, 17:26, Herring, Frances, 1991–1993.
138 "San Francisco Women Acting for Peace, Statement of Precedents, Draft," SCPC WSP Records, B2:2, 1962 San Francisco and East Bay WFP Memos, Minutes, Finances.
139 "Ann Arbor Statement, First National Conference, June 1962," SCPC WSP Records, A1:3, National Conference—1962, Ann Arbor MI.
140 "My Personal Impressions of the Ann Arbor Conference—Elsa Knight Thompson," UCB WFP Records, 3:28, First National Conference, Ann Arbor, MI, 1962, 3.
141 Swerdlow, *Women Strike for Peace*, 91–92.
142 "To Los Angeles WISP from Whittier Area WISP, July 2 1962," SCPC WSP Records, B1;7, Working Documents 1961–1964.
143 Swerdlow, *Women Strike for Peace*, 92.
144 Portland Women for Peace Steering Committee Meeting, July 9, 1963, SCPC Records, D3:1, Oregon.
145 Morris, *Womanpower Unlimited*, 119.
146 Morris, *Womanpower Unlimited*, 95.
147 Swerdlow, *Women Strike for Peace*, 92; "From Women Strike for Peace an Appeal to Negro Women," SCPC WSP Records, B1:1, 1961–1963.
148 Wayland Young, "Mosquitoes in Accra," *The Bulletin of the Atomic Scientists* (September 1962): 45–47.
149 SCPC WSP Records, B1:1, Minutes, Conference Reports 1961 and 1962, WISP Conference, Impressions & Reporting by Gail Eaby.
150 Morris, *Womanpower Unlimited*, 97.
151 Morris, *Womanpower Unlimited*, 97–101; Frances W. Herring, "The World Without the Bomb: Story of the Accra Assembly," July 1962, UCB WFP Records, 15:18, SF WILPF—Activities and Campaigns, 1961–1969.
152 Blackwell, *No Peace Without Freedom*, 189–91; Intondi, *African Americans Against the Bomb*, 70; Stephanie Gilmore, *Groundswell: Grassroots Feminist Activism in Postwar America* (Routledge, 2013), 133.
153 Melinda Plastas, *A Band of Noble Women: Racial Politics in the Women's Peace Movement* (Syracuse University Press, 2011), 146, 220.

154 "Notes on WILPF-WF Meeting, September 27, 1979," UCB WFP Records, 1;10, SF WFP-SF WILPF, Members Meeting Concerning Relationship.
155 Taylor interview, October 5, 1987, ARS.0056.
156 "Keynote address given by Dagmar Wilson to the National Conference of Women Strike for Peace in Chicago (Evanston) Illinois, November 9, 1968," SCPC WSP Records, A1:3, National Conference—1968, Winnetka, IL.
157 Pinkson interview, October 1987, ARS.0056.
158 Rose Dellamonica interview, September 10, 1985, ARS.0056.
159 Swerdlow, *Women Strike for Peace*, 121–22.
160 Gill, "From Maternal Pacifism to Revolutionary Solidarity,"178, 185–92
161 Wilmette Brown, *Black Women and the Peace Movement* (Falling Wall Press, 1984), 25–28
162 "Why Listen to What Women for Peace Has to Say," UCB WFP Records 1:9, Historical Sketches by Members, 1982, 1985.
163 Harriet Hyman Alonso, *Peace as a Women's Issue: A History of the U.S. Movement for World Peace and Women's Rights* (Syracuse University Press, 1993), 7.
164 Blackwell, *No Peace Without Freedom*, 192.
165 Swerdlow, *Women Strike for Peace*, 12, 81, 94.
166 Kathleen L. Endres, "NY Peaceletter," in *Women's Periodicals in the United States*, ed. Kathleen L. Endres and Therese L. Lueck (Greenwood Press, 1996), 259.
167 "Keynote Address by Ethel Taylor at WSP National Conference, Chicago, Illinois, October 1973," SCPC WSP Records, A1:3.

Chapter Three

1 Jon Coburn, "'I Have Chosen the Flaming Death': The Forgotten Self-Immolation of Alice Herz." *Peace & Change* 43, no. 1 (2018); "To Alice Herz—In Memory, by Ruth Gage-Colby," WILPF News Bulletin, March, 1968, Swarthmore College Peace Collection, WSP Records SCPC-DG-115 (hereafter SCPC WSP Records), Ruth Gage-Colby acc. 86-A-151; Hayes B. Jacobs, "The Martyrdom of Alice Herz," *Fact Magazine* (July–August 1965), 11–17.
2 Amy Swerdlow, *Women Strike for Peace: Traditional Motherhood and Radical Politics in the 1960s* (The University of Chicago Press, 1993), 125–142.
3 Letter from Senator James H. Duff to Ethel Taylor, May 24, 1954, SCPC WSP Records, A1:3, Ethel Taylor—Congressional Correspondence (1951–1972).
4 Swerdlow, *Women Strike for Peace*, 187–232.
5 Kathleen M. Blee observes a consistent historiographical failure to accept that women could engage in radical protest beyond the boundaries of the feminist and women's liberation movements. Kathleen M. Blee, "Introduction: Women on the Left/Women on the Right," in *No Middle Ground: Women and Radical Protest*, ed. Kathleen M. Blee (New York University Press, 1998), 2. For an example of this in scholarship on women in the peace movement, see Kyle Harvey, *American Anti-Nuclear Activism, 1975–1990: The Challenge of Peace* (Palgrave Macmillan, 2014), 68–92. These distinctions have been challenged, for example, by Stephanie Gilmore, "The Dynamics of Second-Wave Feminist Activism in Memphis, 1971–1982: Rethinking the Liberal/Radical Divide," in *NWSA Journal* 15, no. 1 (2003): 94–117; Barbara Ryan, "Ideological Purity and Feminism: The U.S. Women's Movement from 1966 to 1975," *Gender and Society* 3, no. 2 (1989).

6 Coburn, "'I Have Chosen."

7 Petra Goedde, *The Politics of Peace: A Global Cold War History* (Oxford University Press, 2019), 149; Andrea Estepa, "Taking the White Gloves Off: Women Strike for Peace and the Transformation of Women's Activist Identities in the United States, 1961–1980," (PhD diss., Rutgers University, May 2012).

8 Penelope Adams Moon, "'We Aren't Playing That Passive Role Any Longer': American Women's Protest of the Vietnam War," in *Restaging War in the Western World: Noncombatant Experiences, 1890–Today*, ed. Marrtje Abbenhuis and Sara Buttsworth (Palgrave Macmillan, 2009), 151–52.

9 Louise Brådvik, "Violent and Nonviolent Methods of Suicide: Different Patterns May Be Found in Men and Women with Severe Depression," *Archives of Suicide Research* 11, no. 3 (2007); Thích Nhất Hạnh, *Vietnam: Lotus in a Sea of Fire* (Hill & Wang, 1967), 106;Véronique Laloë, "Review: Patterns of Deliberate Self-Burning in Various Parts of the World," *Burns* 30 (2004), 207–15; Karin R. Andriolo, "Gender and the Cultural Construction of Good and Bad Suicides," *Suicide and Life-Threatening Behavior* 28, no. 1 (1998): 37–49; Thomas Kauffman, *The Agendas of Tibetan Refugees: Survival Strategies of a Government-in-Exile in a World of International Organizations* (Bergahn Books, 2015), 70.

10 Boulding, "Who Are These Women?" 9–10.

11 "Cora Weiss," in *Peacework: Oral Histories of Women Peace Activists, ed.* Judith Porter Adams (Twayne, 1991), 42.

12 Amy Swerdlow, "Ladies' Day at the Capitol: Women Strike for Peace Versus HUAC," *Feminist Studies* 8 no. 3 (1982).

13 Amy C. Schneidhorst, *Building a Just and Secure World: Popular Front Women's Struggle for Peace and Justice in Chicago during the 1960s* (Bloomsbury Publishing, 2011), 118–19.

14 "Nevada A-Site March; Calif. Woman Jailed," *San Francisco Examiner*, July 16, 1962, 9.

15 Marian Mollin, *Radical Pacifism in Modern America: Egalitarianism and Protest* (University of Pennsylvania Press, 2006), 1, 142.

16 Blee, "Introduction: Women on the Left/Women on the Right," 2; Jo Freeman, *The Politics of Women's Liberation* (Longman, 1975), 50–1; Ryan, "Ideological Purity and Feminism."

17 Paul Boyer, "From Activism to Apathy: The American People and Nuclear Weapons, 1963–1980," *The Journal of American History* 70, no. 4 (1984): 821–44.

18 Letter from Dagmar Wilson to WSPs, November 1, 1964, Wisconsin Historical Society WSP Records (hereafter WHS WSP Records), M83–327, Working Papers for Ch 1, 2, WSP Formation, Test Ban Efforts; Reply to Mrs. Harold J. Stein from Dorothy Maund, Secretary to Dagmar Wilson, February 6, 1964, SCPC WSP Records, A3:1, D. Wilson Files—Invitations to Speak, etc. (1964).

19 "Issues for Discussion—Pre-Conference, Scheduled for 21–24 October 1965," SCPC WSP Records, A1:3, National Conference—1965, San Francisco CA, 4.

20 "To SAC, WFO (100–39566) from SA Joseph A. Connors Jr., 11/9/66," AU WSP Records, Box 19, FOIA FBI Files—100–39566 Vol. 15 (1).

21 "Statement from Peninsula Women for Peace, 31 October 1963," UCB WFP Records, B3:1, Other CA Area Offices Literature.

22 "S.F. Women for Peace to Confront Madame Nhu, 28 October 1963," SCPC WSP Records, B2:2, 1963, Early WFP Activity Against Vietnam War.

23 Elizabeth Shelton, "Mothers' Lobby Pickets for Viet-Nam Pullout," *The Washington Post*, February 12, 1965, B3.
24 Spencer C. Tucker, *The Encyclopedia of the Vietnam War: A Political, Social and Military History* (2nd ed.) (ABC-Clio, 2011), 483–84.
25 Taylor Branch, *At Canaan's Edge: America in the King Years, 1965–68* (Simon & Schuster, 2007), 120.
26 Jacobs, "The Martyrdom of Alice Herz," 12.
27 Jacobs, "The Martyrdom of Alice Herz," 15; Coburn, "I Have Chosen."
28 "From Detroit Women for Peace," SCPC WSP Records, ACC 92A-118:1.
29 Jacobs, "The Martyrdom of Alice Herz," 15.
30 Shingo Shibata, ed., *Phoenix: Letters and Documents of Alice Herz*, (B. R. Grüner, 1976), 171–73.
31 Jacobs, "The Martyrdom of Alice Herz," 15; "Letter from Alice Herz to Prof Kaoru Yasui, November 30, 1963," in *Phoenix*, 135.
32 Letter from Lucy Haessler to Amy Swerdlow, March 25, 1973, SCPC WSP Records, ACC 94A-051:6, Alice Herz.
33 Jan Kempe interview with author, January 8, 2018.
34 SCPC Alice Herz Papers, Reference Material: Religion (Bahá'í, Christianity, Islam); Coburn, "'I Have Chosen."
35 Jacobs, "The Martyrdom of Alice Herz," 15.
36 Kempe interview with author, January 8, 2018.
37 Kempe interview with author, January 8, 2018.
38 "Letter to Daughter Explains Why Woman Set Self Afire," *The Detroit News*, March 18, 1965.
39 Jacobs, "The Martyrdom of Alice Herz"; Tucker, *The Encyclopedia of the Vietnam War*, 483–84.
40 Kempe interview, January 8, 2018.
41 Jacobs, "The Martyrdom of Alice Herz," 12; Coburn, "I Have Chosen."
42 Letter from Alice Herz to Mr. and Mrs. Shingo Shibata, December 12, 1961, SCPC WSP Records, ACC 92A-119:1, Alice Herz.
43 Letter from Alice Herz to Belle Schulz, February 5, 1963, SCPC WSP Records, ACC 92A-118:1, Alice Herz.
44 Letter from Alice Herz to Washington, DC, WSP, February 4, 1964, SCPC WSP Records, A3:4, Michigan 1964–1966.
45 Letter from Alice Herz to Washington DC, WSP, February 19, 1964, SCPC WSP Records, A3:5, Comments on MEMO (1963–1969).
46 "Letter from Alice Herz to Prof Kaoru Yasui, November 30, 1963," in *Phoenix*, 135; "Letter from Alice Herz to Prof Shingo Shibata, December 28, 1964," in *Phoenix*, 138.
47 Letter from Lucy Haessler to Amy Swerdlow, March 25, 1973, SCPC WSP Records, ACC 94A-051:6, Alice Herz; Jean Sharley, "Pacifism Sparked Her Fiery Sacrifice," *Detroit Free Press*, March 18, 1965, 1.
48 Jacobs, "The Martyrdom of Alice Herz," 15.
49 Letter from Lucy Haessler to Amy Swerdlow, March 25, 1973, SCPC WSP Records, ACC 94A-051:6, Alice Herz.
50 Although it is uncertain why Herz acted when she did, it has been suggested that she intended to self-immolate on Wayne State University campus on March 18 to

coincide with a planned student protest. However, after making copies of her last testament in the university library, she realized she had accidentally left the original on the copier. Fearing her plans would be reported to authorities, she acted that day. The location is similarly curious. The corner of Oakman and Grand River—the site of Herz's self-immolation—is five miles northwest of Wayne State University's campus and is an innocuous site to make such a visceral political protest against war and violence. Coburn, "I Have Chosen"; Branch, *At Canaan's Edge*, 120.

51 "To Alice Herz—In Memory, by Ruth Gage-Colby," WILPF News Bulletin, March, 1968, SCPC Ruth Gage-Colby acc. 86-A-151.

52 Jacobs, "The Martyrdom of Alice Herz," 15.

53 "To Alice Herz—In Memory, by Ruth Gage-Colby," WILPF News Bulletin, March, 1968, SCPC Ruth Gage-Colby acc. 86-A-151.

54 Coburn, "I Have Chosen."

55 Robert DeWolfe, "Sets Herself Afire in Vietnam Protest," *Detroit Free Press*, March 17, 1965, 1.

56 Jacobs, "The Martyrdom of Alice Herz," 11–12.

57 Sharley, "Pacifism Sparked Her Fiery Sacrifice," 1.

58 "Tribute by Ruth Gage-Colby to Alice Herz at the Memorial, April 4, 1965, Detroit," SCPC WSP Records, ACC 94A-051:6, Alice Herz.

59 "Detroit Widow Sets Self Afire In Viet Protest," *The Washington Post*, March 18, 1965, A18.

60 Shibata, *Phoenix*, 3–4.

61 Francisca de Haan, "Continuing Cold War Paradigms in Western Historiography of Transnational Women's Organizations: The Case of the Women's International Democratic Federation (WIDF)," *Women's History Review* 19, no. 4 (2010): 547–73; Coburn, "I Have Chosen."

62 "Press Release for Immediate Use," SCPC WSP Records, ACC 92A-118:1, Alice Herz.

63 "From Detroit Women for Peace," SCPC WSP Records, ACC 94A-051:6, Alice Herz.

64 "In Memoriam—Alice Herz, 1882–1965," SCPC Alice Herz Papers, Alice: Biographical Information.

65 Coburn, "I Have Chosen."

66 "Tribute by Ruth Gage-Colby to Alice Herz at the Memorial, April 4, 1965, Detroit," SCPC WSP Records, ACC 94A-051:6, Alice Herz.

67 *Memo*, 3(16) (March 31, 1965), WHS WSP Records, MSS 433, 1–19, Memo October 1964–August 1966, 5.

68 "From Detroit Women for Peace," SCPC WSP Records, ACC 94A-051:6, Alice Herz.

69 "March 18, 1965 Press Release, Lucy Haessler," SCPC WSP Records, ACC 92A-118:1, Alice Herz.

70 Jacobs, "The Martyrdom of Alice Herz," 17.

71 "We Walk in Spirit with Alice Herz," SCPC Alice Herz Papers, Alice: Biographical Papers.

72 Swerdlow, *Women Strike for Peace*, 129; see also Schneidhorst, *Building a Just and Secure World*, 76.

73 "Issues for Discussion No.5, 22 October 1963," WHS WSP Records, MSS 433, 2:10, Ephemera; Coburn, "I Have Chosen."

74 Esther Newill interview, February 23, 1980, ARS.0056, Stanford University Archive of Recorded Sound.

75 Paul Hendrickson, *The Living and the Dead: Robert McNamara and Five Lives of a Lost War* (Vintage Books, 1996), 190–235; Charles DeBenedetti and Charles Chatfield, *An American Ordeal: The Antiwar Movement of the Vietnam Era* (Syracuse University Press, 1990), 129–130; Nancy Zaroulis and Gerald Sullivan, *Who Spoke Up?: American Protest Against the War in Vietnam, 1963–1975* (Holt, Rinehart, and Winston, 1985), 1–4, 61–62, 132–33.

76 Hendrickson, *The Living and the Dead*, 197.

77 Mitchell K. Hall, *Because of Their Faith: CALCAV and Religious Opposition to the Vietnam War* (Columbia University Press, 1990), 4.

78 Cheyney Ryan, "The One Who Burns Herself for Peace," *Hypatia* 9, no. 2 (1994): 21–39.

79 For a full accounting of the differences between Herz's and Morrisons' historical legacies, and the gendered dynamics motivating the "forgetting" of Herz, see Coburn, "I Have Chosen."

80 DeWolfe, "Sets Herself Afire," 1.

81 "War Critic Burns Himself to Death Outside the Pentagon," *The New York Times*, November 3, 1965, 1; "Pacifist, Tot in Arms, Dies by Fire Outside Pentagon," *The Boston Globe*, November 3, 1965, 1; Bremner, "His Life Was One Long Protest Against Killing," *The Boston Globe*, November 7, 1965, 49; "Colleagues Stunned by Quaker's Self-Immolation," *The New York Times*, November 4, 1965, 5; "Hate of War Led to Fiery Death," *The Boston Globe*, November 4, 1965, 12.

82 "War Critic Burns Himself to Death Outside the Pentagon," *The New York Times*, November 3, 1965, 1; "Colleagues Stunned by Quaker's Self-Immolation," *The New York Times*, November 4, 1965, 5; Donald Bremner, "His Life Was One Long Protest Against Killing," *The Boston Globe*, November 7, 1965, 49.

83 Ryan, "The One Who Burns," 18, 22.

84 Feminism and Nonviolence Study Group, *Piecing It Together: Feminism and Nonviolence* (Feminism and Nonviolence Study Group, 1983), 36.

85 For example, Sara Rosen's sensitive portrayal of Kurdish women's self-immolation illuminates that the act is one of the few forms of suicide accessible to women in some parts of the world. Sara Rosen, "Self-Immolation: A Desperate Protest Against the Patriarchy," *Blind Magazine*, January 17, 2022.

86 Quang Minh Thich, "Vietnamese Buddhism in America," (PhD diss., Florida State University, 2007), 164.

87 "Rites Set for Torch Victim, 82," *Detroit Free Press*, March 30, 1965, 21.

88 "In Memoriam—Alice Herz," SCPC Alice Herz Papers, Alice: Biographical Information.

89 Letter from Anna Louise Strong to Lucy Haessler, June 15, 1965, SCPC Alice Herz Papers, Alice: Biographical Information.

90 Letter from Keiko Takizawa to Women Strike for Peace, undated, SCPC WSP Records, ACC 92A-118:1, Alice Herz.

91 Letter from New Japan Women's Association to Dagmar Wilson, SCPC WSP Records, ACC 92A-118:1, Alice Herz.

92 Letter from Shingo Shibata to Sir Bertrand Russell, February 27, 1967, SCPC Alice Herz Papers, Alice: Biographical Records; "Report and Appeal of the Alice Herz Peace Fund, June 1971," SCPC Alice Herz Papers, Alice: Biographical Records; Coburn, "I Have Chosen."

93 Letter from Mitsuko Kumagai to Women Strike for Peace, undated, SCPC WSP Records, ACC 92A-118:1, Alice Herz.

94 Letter from Keiko Takizawa to Women Strike for Peace, undated, SCPC WSP Records, ACC 92A-118:1, Alice Herz.
95 "Letter from Alice Herz to Shingo Shibata, December 28, 1955," in Shibata, *Phoenix*, 92–93.
96 "Let us Fulfil Mrs. Herz's Dying Wishes," *Akahata Japanese Communist Daily*, May 17, 1966, SCPC Alice Herz Papers, Alice: Biographical Materials.
97 Qiang Zhai, "Opposing Negotiations: China and the Vietnam Peace Talks, 1965–1968," *Pacific Historical Review* 68, no. 1 (1999): 42.
98 Felix Greene, "Ho Interviewed: Raps LBJ, But Silent on Cong Aid," *The Boston Globe*, December 19, 1965, 8–9.
99 Anne Morrison Welsh, *Held in the Light: Norman Morrison's Sacrifice for Peace and his Family's Journey of Healing* (Orbis Books, 2008): 33.
100 Sallie B. King, "They Who Burn Themselves for Peace: Quaker and Buddhist Self-Immolators During the Vietnam War," *Buddhist–Christian Studies* 20 (2000): 142.
101 David Hunt, "Propaganda and the Public: The Shaping of Opinion in the South Vietnamese Countryside During the Second Indochina War," *Journal of Social Issues in Southeast Asia* 31, no. 2 (2016): 497–531; Alice Steinbach, "Of Norman Morrison: Thirty Years Ago a Baltimore Quaker Set Himself On Fire to Protest the War In Vietnam. Did It Make a Difference?" *Baltimore Sun*, July 30, 1995; Coburn, "I Have Chosen."
102 "Mary Clarke," in James W. Clinton, ed., *The Loyal Opposition: Americans in North Vietnam, 1965–1972* (University of Colorado Press, 1995), 2.
103 Lorraine Gordon, *Alive at the Village Vanguard: My Life In and Out of Jazz Time* (Hal Leonard, 2006), 154.
104 "Mary Leona Clarke," SCPC WSP Records, ACC 90A-015:1, Djakarta 1965.
105 Mary Hershberger, *Traveling to Vietnam: American Peace Activists and the War* (Syracuse University Press, 1998), 8.
106 Estepa, "Taking the White Gloves Off" (PhD diss.), 193.
107 Swerdlow, *Women Strike for Peace*, 214–15.
108 Gordon, *Alive at the Village Vanguard*, 152; "Mary Clarke," in *The Loyal Opposition*, 1.
109 "Concerning the Jakarta Meeting, July 14–19," SCPC WSP Records, ACC 92A-113:5, Jakarta Meeting with Vietnamese Women A First July 1965.
110 Letter from Margaret Russell to WSP Steering Committee and Other National Contacts, June 17, 1965, SCPC WSP Records, ACC 92A-113:5, Jakarta MTG With Vietnamese Women a First 1965 July; "Concerning the Jakarta Meeting, July 14–18," SCPC WSP Records, ACC 92A-113:5, Jakarta MTG With Vietnamese Women a First 1965 July, 2.
111 "Role of San Francisco Women for Peace in the US War Against Vietnam," UCB WFP Records, 1:8, Historical Information for Vietnam Women's Association, 1984.
112 Hershberger, *Travelling to Vietnam*, 5, 101.
113 Letter from Dagmar Wilson to Friends, June 20, 1965, SCPC WSP Records, ACC 92A-113:5, Jakarta Meeting with Vietnamese Women A First July 1965.
114 Swerdlow, *Women Strike for Peace*, 215–16.
115 Jessica M. Frazier, *Women's Antiwar Diplomacy During the Vietnam War Era* (University of North Carolina Press, 2017), 12.
116 There was a long tradition of citizen diplomacy enacted internationally through women's voluntary associations, but WSP's efforts in Vietnam were notable for engaging with people whose country was actively at war with the US. See, e.g., Dayo F.

Gore, *Radicalism at the Crossroads: African American Women Activists in the Cold War* (New York University Press, 2011); Helen Laville, *Cold War Women: The International Activities of American Women's Organisations* (Manchester University Press, 2002).

117 "Michael Myerson," in *The Loyal Opposition*, 8.

118 "Role of San Francisco Women for Peace in the US War Against Vietnam," UCB WFP Records, 1:8, Historical Information for Vietnam Women's Association, 1984.

119 Frazier, *Women's Antiwar Diplomacy*, 49; Ethel Taylor interview, October 5, 1987, ARS.0056.

120 Judy Tzu-Chun Wu, *Radicals on the Road: Internationalism, Orientalism, and Feminism During the Vietnam Era* (Cornell University Press, 2013), 99.

121 "Women Score U.S. at Jakarta Talks," *The New York Times*, July 19, 1965.

122 "LA WISP, August 1965," SCPC WSP Records, ACC 92A-113:5, Jakarta Meeting with Vietnamese Women, A First, 1965 July.

123 Hershberger, *Travelling to Vietnam*, 13.

124 "American Women Report on Meeting with Vietnamese Women RE Ending War, by Ruth Ehrlich," SCPC WSP Records, B1:3, Trip to Djakarta 1965. Emphasis in the original.

125 "Letter from Southern California WSP to Ann Arbor WFP, June 1965," SCPC WSP Records, B1:3, Trip to Djakarta, 1965; "Jakarta Meeting with Vietnamese Women, a First, July 1965," SCPC WSP Records, B1:3, Trip to Djakarta, 1965

126 Hershberger, *Traveling to Vietnam*, 7; Jessica M. Frazier, "Collaborative Efforts to End the War in Viet Nam: The Interactions of Women Strike for Peace, the Vietnamese Women's Union, and the Women's Union of Liberation, 1965–1968," *Peace and Change*, Vol. 37, No. 3 (July 2012): 342.

127 "Memo: Jan–Feb 1969, 2–5," UWS SWAP Records, 3:13, Women Strike for Peace, 1962–2000.

128 Letter from Dagmar Wilson to Friends, August 1, 1967, SCPC WSP Records, ACC 92A-113:3, Dagmar Wilson Trip to Hanoi, Summer1967.

129 Frazier, *Women's Antiwar Diplomacy*, 49; Taylor, *We Made a Difference*; Taylor interview, October 5, 1987, ARS.0056.

130 Frazier, *Women's Antiwar Diplomacy*, 11; Taylor, *We Made a Difference*, 35–39.

131 Madeleine Duckles interview, November 22, 1985, ARS.0056.

132 Swerdlow, *Women Strike for Peace*, 214–18.

133 "Role of San Francisco Women for Peace in the US War Against Vietnam—Hazel Grossman's response to letter from Vietnamese Women's Union," UCB WFP Records, 1:8, Historical Information for Vietnam Women's Association, 1984.

134 Frazier, *Women's Antiwar Diplomacy*, 14–15, 39.

135 Frazier, *Women's Antiwar Diplomacy*, 100.

136 "Mary Clarke, 1972," SCPC WSP Records B1:7, Working Documents 1965–date, 10.

137 Frazier, *Women's Antiwar Diplomacy*, 15.

138 Frazier, "Collaborative Efforts," 349, 356.

139 "Dear WSPer, 1965," SCPC WSP Records, D2, Philadelphia, March 1964–1965.

140 "2,500 Women Pacifists Storm Pentagon Door," *The Boston Globe*, February 16, 1967, 5; "Pentagon Bars Viet Pickets," *Chicago Tribune*, February 16, 1967, A5; "2,500 Women Storm Pentagon Over War," *The Washington Post*, February 16, 1967, A1.

141 Swerdlow, *Women Strike for Peace*, 135; Estepa, "Taking the White Gloves Off" (PhD thesis), 153.

142 Zaroulis and Sullivan, *Who Spoke Up?* 103.

143 "Cops, 'Peace' Women in Bloody Melee," *Chicago Tribune*, September 21, 1967, B6.
144 Taylor, *We Made a Difference*, 79–89.
145 Taylor, *We Made a Difference*, 89.
146 Nadine Brozan, "Women's Group Began as One Day Protest 4,215 Days Ago," *The New York Times*, May 16, 1973, 52. See also, Taylor, *We Made a Difference*, 85–86; ACC 94A-005:1, April 13, 1971—WSP Women Chain Themselves to the White House Fence; "For Immediate Release—May 11, 1972," SCPC WSP Records, May 11, 1972—Sit-in In Carl Albert's Office;
147 Letter from Anci Koppel to Jo Friedman, March 23, 1967, SCPC WSP Records, A3:10, 1967 Jan–June. Emphasis in original.
148 "Washington WSP 'Retreat' Meeting at Folly Fodor's, Saturday, October 5, 1968," SCPC WSP Records, A1:2, Washington WSP Retreat—October 5 1968, 23, 45.
149 "Anci Koppel Statement, September 15, 1968," UWS SWAP Records, 2:3, American Peace Delegation to the Soviet Union.
150 "WSP & Resistance Story—Speech at Celebration, June 8, 1975," UCB WFP Records, 1:9, Historical Sketches by Members, 1982, 1985.
151 Estepa, "Taking the White Gloves Off" (PhD diss.), 268.
152 Memo, October 1967, UCB WFP Records, Newsletters, Memo Vol. 5, No. 1–12, 1966–1967, 5.
153 "3 Are Convicted in Contempt Case," *The New York Times*, April 9, 1965, 68.
154 "Role of San Francisco Women for Peace in the US War Against Vietnam." UCB WFP Records, 1:8, Historical Information for Vietnam Women's Association, 1984.
155 Duckles interview, November 22, 1985, ARS.0056.
156 Harriet Hyman Alonso, *Peace as a Women's Issue: A History of the U.S. Movement for World Peace and Women's Rights* (Syracuse University Press, 1993), 204, 231.
157 Estepa, "Taking the White Gloves Off" (PhD diss.), 86.
158 Goedde, *The Politics of Peace*, 149.
159 Stephanie Gilmore, *Groundswell: Grassroots Feminist Activism in Postwar America* (Routledge, 2013), 128.
160 Laura E. Nym Mayhall, "Defining Militancy: Radical Protest, the Constitutional Idiom, and Women's Suffrage in Britain, 1908–1909," *Journal of British Studies* 39, no. 3 (2000): 342.
161 For example, Wesley G. Phelps, "Women's Pentagon Action: The Persistence of Radicalism and Direct-Action Civil Disobedience in the Age of Reagan," *Peace and Change* 39, no. 3 (2014); Louise Krasniewicz, *Nuclear Summer: The Clash of Communities at the Seneca Women's Peace Encampment* (Cornell University Press, 1994).
162 David A. Snow and Remy Cross, "Radicalism within the Context of Social Movements: Processes and Type," *Journal of Strategic Security* 4, no. 4 (2011): 118–19.
163 Mayhall, "Defining Militancy," 341–42.
164 Zaroulis and Sullivan, *Who Spoke Up?* 83, 113.
165 Harvey, *American Anti-Nuclear Activism*, 71.
166 This is despite Amy Swerdlow arguing this point in 1993's *Women Strike for Peace.*
167 Hershberger, *Travelling to Vietnam*, 5.
168 "Issues for Discussion—Pre-Conference, scheduled for Oct. 21–24, 1965," SCPC WSP Records, A1:3 National Conference—1965, San Francisco CA, 3.
169 "Steering Committee Meeting Minutes, February 22, 1967," SCPC WSP Records, A1:2, Minutes of Steering Committee—1965–1970.

170 "March 4, 1967, Washington, D.C.," AU WSP Records, Box 19, FOIA FBI Files—100–39566 Vol. 17 (1), 2; "February 22, 1967, Washington, D.C.," AU WSP Records, Box 19, FOIA FBI Files—100–39566 Vol. 17 (1), 2.
171 "Strike Three," *The Washington Post*, September 22, 1967, A24.
172 "To SAC WFO (100–39566) from SA Philip H. Wilson, Oct 24 1966," AU WSP Records, Box 19, FOIA FBI Files—100–39566, Vol. 15 (1).
173 Zaroulis and Sullivan, *Who Spoke Up?* 113.
174 Schneidhorst, *Building a Just and Secure World*, 119.
175 "March 9, 1967, Washington, D.C.," AU WSP Records, Box 19, FOIA FBI Files—100–39566 Vol. 17 (1).
176 "Letter from Mary Clarke to Jean Shulman, February 17, 1967," SCPC WSP Records, ACC 92A-113:3, Antidraft Action.
177 UCB WFP Records, 5–7, Office Files: The Whitehorn Case, 1968.
178 "Important Information and Warning to All Volunteers RE: End-the-Draft Caravans," ACC 92A-113:3, Antidraft Work.
179 "Minutes: WSP Draft Counseling Service Workshop, December 9, 1967," SCPC WSP Records, ACC 92A-113:3, End the Draft Week 12-4-9-67; Swerdlow interview, September 25, 1987, ARS.0056.
180 Swerdlow, *Women Strike for Peace*, 186.
181 Estepa, "Taking the White Gloves Off" (PhD diss.), 256.
182 Swerdlow, *Women Strike for Peace*, 162, 164, 177.
183 Michael S. Foley, *Confronting the War Machine: Draft Resistance During the Vietnam War* (University of North Carolina Press, 2003): 169, 178–84.
184 Schneidhorst, *Building a Just and Secure World.*
185 "Lucy Haessler," in *Peacework*, 144–45.
186 Taylor interview, October 5, 1987, *ARS.0056.*
187 "Role of San Francisco Women for Peace in the US War Against Vietnam," UCB WFP Records, 1:8, Historical Information for Vietnam Women's Association, 1984.
188 Thanks to editor Ellen Goldstein for this turn of phrase.

Chapter Four

1 "Washington WSP 'Retreat' Meeting at Folly Fodor's, Saturday, October 5, 1968," Swarthmore College Peace Collection, WSP Records SCPC-DG-115 (hereafter SCPC WSP Records), A1:2, Washington WSP Retreat—October 5, 1968.
2 "Women for Peace Outline", UCB WFP Records, 1:3 Chronologies, 1960–1983, 4–5.
3 Stephanie Gilmore, *Groundswell: Grassroots Feminist Activism in Postwar America* (Routledge, 2013), 4. See also Harriet Hyman Alonso, "Dissension in the Ranks: The New York Branch of WILPF vs. the National Board, 1914–1955," *Peace Review* 8, no. 3, (1996): 337–42.
4 Byron A. Miller, *Geography and Social Movements: Comparing Antinuclear Activism in the Boston Area* (University of Minnesota Press, 2000), 172.
5 Existing WSP histories, notably that by Amy Swerdlow provide rich and detailed focus to WSP branches on the East Coast and throughout out the Midwest—often at the expense of more detailed histories of the branches on the West Coast. This chapter focuses on San Francisco WFP specifically as a correction to that. However, the author recognizes that a deeper dive into the local histories of WSP branches

elsewhere—such as the Midwest, which were a party to some of the divisions discussed later—would be just as interesting. For more information on these histories, Swerdlow's *Women Strike for Peace* remains a fantastic resource.

6 Lisa McGirr, *Suburban Warriors: The Origins of the New American Right* (Princeton University Press, 2015), 52; Michelle Nickerson, *Mothers of Conservatism: Women and the Postwar Right* (Princeton University Press, 2012).

7 Jonathan Bell, "Social Democracy and the Rise of the Democratic Party in California, 1950–1964," *The Historical Journal* 49, no. 2 (2006): 514.

8 "Eleanor Garst: Chapter 1, Who Are These Women?" Wisconsin Historical Society WSP Records (hereafter WHS WSP Records), M83–327, Working Papers for Ch 1, 2, WSP Formation, Test Ban Efforts, 24.

9 Letter from Janet Stevenson to Margaret Russell, October 12, 1961, SCPC WSP Records A3:6, 1961; "Eleanor Garst: Chapter 1, Who Are These Women?" WHS WSP Records, M83–327, Working Papers for Ch 1, 2, WSP Formation, Test Ban Efforts, 24; Robbie Lieberman, *The Strangest Dream: Communism; Anticommunism, and the U.S. Peace Movement, 1945–1963* (Syracuse University Press, 2000), 166; Kathleen L. Endres, "La Wisp," in *Women's Periodicals in the Unites States: Social and Political Issues*, ed. Kathleen L. Endres and Therese L. Lueck (Greenwood Press, 1996), 151.

10 Fred Fejes, *Gay Rights and Moral Panic: The Origins of America's Debate on Homosexuality* (Palgrave Macmillan, 2008), 187; Brian G. Casserly, "Puget Sound's Security Codependency and Western Cold War Histories, 1950–1984," *Pacific Historical Review* 80, no. 2 (2011): 268–93; Letter from Anci Koppel to President Jimmy Carter, March 9, 1977, University of Washington, Seattle, Seattle Women Act for Peace Records, 4073 (hereafter UWS SWAP), 1:6, General Correspondence, 1967–1977; "Trident is a First-Strike Weapon! Bangor Is Not Just 'Another Base,'" UWS SWAP Records, 3:6, Trident Protests (May 22nd), 1978.

11 "Biographical Notes, August 31, 1981," UWS SWAP Records, 1–36, Speeches and Writings, 1955–Feb 1982.

12 "Thorun Ingibjorg Johannson Robel," WHS WSP Records, 2:34, Robel, Thorun; Susan Paynter, "Can Brigade Still Acting Up in Behalf of World Peace," *Seattle Times*, January 26, 1998, B1; "A Fond Farewell, Thorun Johannsson-Robel," WHS WSP Records, 2:34, Robel, Thorun.

13 Katherine Turk, *The Women of NOW: How Feminists Built an Organization that Transformed America* (Farrar, Straus and Giroux, 2023), 120.

14 Anthony Ashbolt, *A Cultural History of the Radical Sixties in the San Francisco Bay Area* (Routledge, 2016), 4.

15 Peter Cole, *Dockworker Power: Race and Activism in Durban and the San Francisco Bay Area* (University of Illinois Press, 2018).

16 Gilmore, *Groundswell*, 99.

17 "International League to Hold Convention Here," *San Francisco Examiner*, July 6, 1955, 19; Claire Leeds, "An International Conference in S.F.," *San Francisco Examiner*, January 16, 1962, 20.

18 "Read as Spokesman for Women for Peace to Mayor Christopher, November 1, 1961," SCPC WSP Records, B1:7, Working Documents 1961–1964.

19 "Frannie: A Profile of Frances W. Herring," UCB WFP Records, 17:27, 43–45; "Photo," University of California, Berkely, San Francisco Women for Peace Records BANC

MSS 89/132 c (hereafter UCB WFP Records), 18:35, Oslo Conference on Nuclear Weapons, 1961 May.

20 Letter from Frances Herring to Philip Noel-Howard, July 17, 1961, UCB WSP Records, 18:35, Oslo Conference on Nuclear Weapons, 1961 May.

21 For example, "WSP & Resistance Story—Speech at Celebration, June 8, 1975," UCB WFP Records, 1:9, Historical Sketches by Members, 1982, 1985; Endres, "La Wisp," 149.

22 Myrna Oliver, "Alice Hamburg, 96; Activist Began Women's Peace Group," *Los Angeles Times*, November 19, 2001; Judith Scherr, "Local activist, Alice Hamburg, dies at 95," *Berkeley Daily Planet*, November 14, 2001. Hamburg's obituaries differed on her age; however, she was 95 at the time of her death.

23 Carl Nolte, "'Black Friday,' birth of U.S. protest movement," *San Francisco Chronicle*, May 13, 2010.

24 "Hazel's 70th Birthday Celebration, 6/23/83," UCB WFP Records, 17–22, Grossman, Hazel, and Grossman, Aubrey, 1967–2000; "Fire Hoses Douse 200 S.F. Rioters," *Los Angeles Times*, May 14, 1960; James Paddison, "San Franciscans for Academic Freedom and Education and the Bay Area Opposition to HUAC, 1959–1960," *California History* 78, no. 3 (1999): 188–201.

25 "Role of San Francisco Women for Peace in the US War Against Vietnam," UCB WFP Records, 1:8, Historical Information for Vietnam Women's Association, 1984.

26 "Alice Hamburg Introducing Madeline Duckles at AFSC Program 'Two Lifetimes of Peace Work,' 10/27/2000," UCB WFP Records, Duckles, Madeline, and Duckles, Vincent, 1985, n.d.

27 "Madeline Taylor Duckles," in *Peacework: Oral Histories of Women Peace Activists, ed.* Judith Porter Adams (Twayne, 1991), 160; "Madeline Taylor Duckles, May 19, 1916–Nov. 23, 2013," *San Francisco Chronicle*, December 8, 2013.

28 "Women for Peace San Gabriel Valley Section, November 20, 1961," UCB WFP Records, 1:19, WSP National and Other Cities Beginnings; "Notes on WILPF-WFP Meeting, September 27, 1979," UCB WFP Records, 1:10, SF WFP-SF WILPF Members Meeting Concerning Relationship.

29 For example, "WSP & Resistance Story—Speech at Celebration, June 8, 1975," UCB WFP Records, 1:9, Historical Sketches by Members, 1982,1985; Endres, "LA WISP," 149.

30 Raymond A. Mohl, "'Some of Us Were There Before Betty': Jewish Women and Political Activism in Postwar Miami," in *A Jewish Feminine Mystique?: Jewish Women in Postwar America*, ed. Hasia R. Diner, Shira Kohn, and Rachel Kranson Rutgers University Press, 2010), 25. Mohl explains that, under the stewardship of Thalia Stern and Gertrude Leiner, Miami WSP was religiously inclined in a way not seen in other parts of the country.

31 Plastas, *A Band of Noble Women*, 241.

32 "Women Strike for Peace, Minutes December 2, 1961," WHS WSP Records, M83-327, Working Papers for Ch 1, 2, WSP Formation, Test Ban Efforts.

33 "Mount Prospect Women Set for Fashion Show," *The Daily Herald*, Wednesday May 8, 1985, 4-Section 2; "Making Peace," SCPC WSP Records, ACC 90A-028:6, Ambler Branch Activities.

34 "Seattle Women Act for Peace—Our Second Year, 1963," UWS SWAP Records, 3:12, Women Strike for Peace, 1963–1997, n.d.

35 Letter from Rosina Woodhouse to Gladys Farber, June 8, 1965, SCPC WSP Records, B1:3, Mary Clarke Trip to Djakarta, 1965.

36 "Agenda Items for Nov. 29 East Coast Phila. Conference Via D.C., Nov. 20 1990," UWS SWAP Records, 1:17, General Correspondence, Jan 1990—Aug 1991.

37 For example of branches developing their own founding stories, see "Mailer from Gunhilt Hozelitz, Chicago Women for Peace, n.d." UCB WFP, 1:19, WSP National and Other Cities Beginnings; "Example of Mailer Sent to Trudi Young from San Antonio Women for Peace, 1970," SCPC WSP Records, A3:4, Branch File—Texas (1970); "Letter by Anci Koppel, 1992," UWS SWAP Records, 1:34.

38 "Role of San Francisco Women for Peace in the US War Against Vietnam—Hazel Grossman's Response to Letter from Vietnamese Women's Union," UCB WFP Records, 1:8, Historical Information for Vietnam Women's Association, 1984.

39 Rose Dellamonica interview, September 10, 1985, ARS.0056, Stanford University Archive of Recorded Sound.

40 "WSP & Resistance Story—Speech at Celebration, June 8, 1975," UCB WFP Records 1:9, Historical Sketches by Members, 1982, 1985.

41 "Peace . . . It's Wonderful," *San Francisco Examiner*, February 7, 1962, 7; Judith Scherr, "Local activist, Alice Hamburg, dies at 95," *Berkeley Daily Planet*, November 14, 2001.

42 "Guide to the San Francisco Women for Peace Records, 1943-[on-going]," *Online Archive of California*, https://oac.cdlib.org/findaid/ark:/13030/kt000000k5/. Last accessed February 11, 2025.

43 *Communist Activities in the Peace Movement*, 2190.

44 SCPC WSP Records, B1:1, Minutes, Conference Reports 1961 and 1962, "Minutes of the Meeting of the Women's Strike for Peace, November 27, 1961."

45 Letter from Anci Koppel to Irene Wall, April 1982; Letter from Anci Koppel to Ted Koppel, October 28, 1982; Letter from Anci Koppel to Senate State Government Committee, February 23, 1982, UWS SWAP Records, 1:10, General Correspondence, Oct 1981–Dec 1982; "Seattle Women Act for Peace Business Card," UWS SWAP Records, 1:1, Historical Features; "Position Statement Pert. Air Strike on Libya, April 15, 1986," UWS SWAP Records, 1:37, Speeches and Writings—Misc., Sept 1982–Mar 1990.

46 "Women! Act Together for Peace! November 1, 1961," UCB WFP Records, 1:1 Beginnings, 1961 Oct.–Dec.; "San Francisco Women Acting for Peace, Statement of Precedents, Draft," SCPC WSP Records, B2:2, 1962 San Francisco and East Bay WFP Memos, Minutes, Finances.

47 Taylor, *We Made a Difference*, x.

48 Wendy B. Sharer, "The Persuasive Work of Organizational Names: The Women's International League for Peace and Freedom and the Struggle for Collective Identification," *Rhetoric Review* 20, nos. 3 and 4 (2001): 234–50.

49 Midge Decter, "The Peace Ladies," *Harper's Magazine*, March 1963.

50 "Washington WSP 'Retreat' Meeting at Folly Fodor's, Saturday, October 5, 1968," SCPC WSP Records, A1:2, Washington WSP Retreat—October 5 1968; *Communist Activities in the Peace Movement*, 2189.

51 Alice Sachs Hamburg, *Grass Roots: From Prairie to Politics: The Autobiography of Alice Sachs Hamburg* (Creative Arts Books Company, 2001), 173.

52 "Draft Agenda for Second Annual National Conference of Women Strike for Peace and Women for Peace," SCPC WSP Records, A1:3, National Conference—1963, Champaign, IL.

53 "A New Film Documentary, 1962", UCB WFP Records, 15:9, Women's Peace Office—Activities and Campaigns, 1970–1979.
54 "Women's Peace Office, Save the Date: 1986," UCB WFP Records, 15;10, Women's Peace Office—Activities and Campaigns, 1980–1989; "Dear Friend of Peace, November 15, 1981," "WFP Anniversary, 11/16/86," UCB WFP Records, 15:10, Women's Peace Office—Activities and Campaigns, 1980–1989.
55 "Women Strike for Peace Annual National Conference, Saturday October 1, 1982," SCPC WSP Records, A1:3, National Conference—1982, Philadelphia PA.
56 Letter from Mabel S. Proctor to Trudi Young, November 9, 1970, SCPC WSP Records, A3:4, Washington 1965, 1968–1970.
57 Amy Swerdlow, *Women Strike for Peace: Traditional Motherhood and Radical Politics in the 1960s* (University of Chicago Press, 1993).
58 "Peace . . . It's Wonderful," 7.
59 Alice Richards and Harvey Richards, dirs., with narration from Frances Herring. *Women Strike for Peace* (WSP, 1962).
60 "San Francisco Women for Peace, August 1983," UCB WFP Records, 9:26, University of California Nuclear Weapons Labs Conversion Project and Livermore Action Group 1983; "Dear Peacemaker, February 5, 1987," UCB WFP Records, 11:1, Missouri Campaign, 1987; "Resolution Adopted by San Francisco Board of Supervisors, February 10, 1969," UCB WFP Records, 5:23, Bay Area Coalition, Save Angel Island Campaign.
61 "Resolution Adopted by San Francisco Board of Supervisors, February 10, 1969," UCB WFP Records, 5–23, Bay Area Coalition, Save Angel Island Campaign.
62 "What About Food for Disaster," *San Francisco Examiner*, March 26, 1964, 16.
63 "Historical Data, Issued June 1990, July 19, 1991," UWS SWAP Records, 1:1, Historical Features; "Fond Memories of Ruth Pool—Anci Koppel," UWS SWAP Records, 1:37, Speeches and Writings—Misc., Sept 1982–Mar 1990.
64 Madeleine Duckles interview, November 21, 1985, ARS.0056.
65 "California WFP/WSP Statewide Conference, March 10–11, 1963," SCPC WSP Records, B2:2, 1963 Early WFP Activity Against Vietnam War.
66 "Statement from Peninsula Women for Peace, October 31, 1963," UCB WFP Records, B3:1, Other CA Area Offices Literature.
67 "S.F. Women for Peace to Confront Madame Nhu, October 28, 1963," SCPC WSP Records, B2:2, 1963, Early WFP Activity Against Vietnam War.
68 "S.F. Women Snubbed on Viet Protest," *San Francisco Examiner*, October 19, 1963, 36.
69 "WSP & Resistance Story—Speech at Celebration, June 8, 1975," UCB WFP Records, 1:9, Historical Sketches by Members, 1982, 1985.
70 "S.F. Women Snubbed," 36.
71 Esther Newill interview, February 23, 1980, ARS.0056.
72 "Issues for Discussion No.5, October 22, 1963," WHS WSP Records, MSS 433, 2:10, Ephemera.
73 Swerdlow, *Women Strike for Peace*, 80.
74 "Artist Paints Rural, Forgotten Loudoun," *Loudoun Times-Mirror*, November 12, 1987, Section D.
75 Charles DeBenedetti and Charles Chatfield, *An American Ordeal: The Antiwar Movement of the Vietnam Era* (Syracuse University Press, 1990), 85; Mitchell K.

Hall, *Because of Their Faith: CALCAV and Religious Opposition to the Vietnam War* (Columbia University Press, 1990), 2.

76 "Draft Agenda for Second Annual National Conference of Women Strike for Peace and Women for Peace, Champaign, Illinois," SCPC WSP Records, A1:3, National Conference—1963, Champaign IL; Swerdlow, *Women Strike for Peace*, 129; "Position Paper," SCPC WSP Records, A1:3, National Conference—1965, San Francisco CA.

77 Justin David Suran, "Coming Out Against the War: Antimilitarism and the Politicization of Homosexuality in the Era of Vietnam," *American Quarterly* 53, no. 3 (2001): 484 n43. Though Proposition P suffered a heavy defeat, it demonstrated San Francisco antiwar voters' ability to force elected officials and the general public to confront opposition to the conflict. "P Vote Seen as 'No Surrender'," *San Francisco Examiner*, November 8, 1967, 1-A.

78 "Easter Peace Walk, April 1963," SCPC WSP Records, D2, Philadelphia, 1962–1964; "Portland Women for Peace Steering Committee Meeting, July 9, 1963," D3:1, Oregon; Letter from C. Clark Kissinger to Dagmar Wilson, June 5, 1965, SCPC WSP Records, A3:10, 1965 Jan.–Aug.; Letter from Dagmar Wilson to C. Clark Kissinger, 1965, SCPC WSP Records, A3:10, 1965 Sept.–Dec.; Amy Swerdlow interview, September 25, 1987, ARS.0056.

79 "Madison Square Garden Rally to End the Vietnam War Now!" SCPC WSP Records, ACC 92A-113:2, 1966 Dec 8—SANE & WSP Rally Madison Square Garden; Swerdlow interview, September 25, 1987, ARS.0056.

80 Andrea Estepa, "Taking the White Gloves Off: Women Strike for Peace and the Transformation of Women's Activist Identities in the United States, 1961–1980," (PhD diss., Rutgers University, May 2012), 309.

81 "Issues for Discussion—Pre-Conference, Scheduled for Oct 21–24, 1965," SCPC WSP Records, A1:3, National Conference—1965, San Francisco, CA.

82 Swerdlow interview, September 25, 1987, ARS.0056.

83 Letter from Henrietta Levine to Barbara Bick, November 27, 1968, SCPC WSP Records, A3:11, 1968 Oct.–Dec.; "Washington WSP 'Retreat' Meeting at Folly Fodor's, Saturday, 5 October 1968," SCPC WSP Records, A1:2, Washington WSP Retreat—October 5 1968, 25; Letter from Roz Buchalter and Shirley Margolin to NY CCC and North Shore Women for Peace, 22 October 1968, SCPC WSP Records, A3:11, 1968 Oct.–Dec.; "4/29/67, New Orleans, Louisiana," AU WSP Records, FOIA FBI Files—100-39566 Vol. 18; Letter from Liaison Committee to Expanded NCC and Chapters, February 18, 1971, SCPC WSP Records, A1:1, National Consultative Committee Minutes and Memos—Aug 1970–1973.

84 "Vietnam House, Saigon, for the Committee of Responsibility," UCB WFP Records, 4:39 Committee of Responsibility.

85 Duckles interview, November 21, 1985, *ARS.0056*.

86 Michael S. Foley, *Confronting the War Machine: Draft Resistance During the Vietnam War* (University of North Carolina Press, 2003): 76–79; Suran, "Coming Out Against the War," 461.

87 "Role of San Francisco Women for Peace in the US War Against Vietnam," UCB WFP Records, 1;8, Historical Information for Vietnam Women's Association, 1984.

88 "Celebrate, Celebrate, Celebrate," UCB WFP Records, 15:10, Women's Peace Office—Activities and Campaigns, 1980–1989.

89 Swerdlow, *Women Strike for Peace*, 174–75.

90 "Celebrate, Celebrate, Celebrate," UCB WFP Records, 15:10, Women's Peace Office—Activities and Campaigns, 1980–1989.
91 "Newsletter Item from East Bay WFP RE: NCC Meetings and WSP Member Groups, 6 July 1970," SCPC WSP Records, A3:5, About National Coordinating Committee Meetings, 1968–1970.
92 Gilmore, *Groundswell*, 99.
93 Martin Klimke, *The Other Alliance: Student Protest in West Germany and the United States in the Global Sixties* (Princeton University Press, 2010), 41.
94 Eric Brazil, "Alice Hamburg—Peace Activist for 5 Decades," *San Francisco Chronicle*, November 17, 2001.
95 "Take the Moratorium Home," *Synapse: The UCSF Student Newspaper* 14, no. 10, December 15, 1969, 8.
96 Brazil, "Alice Hamburg."
97 "Role of San Francisco Women for Peace in the US War Against Vietnam—Hazel," UCB WFP Records, 1:8, Historical Information for Vietnam Women's Association, 1984.
98 Estepa, "Taking the White Gloves Off" (PhD diss.), 309.
99 "For National WSP Conference—Boston, May 19–23, 1971," UCB WFP Records, 6:2, Office Files—National, 1971.
100 "WSP Lobby for Poor People's Campaign, July 15–16, 1968," UCB WFP Records, 5:1, Civil Rights-Social Welfare, 1968.
101 "Celebrate, Celebrate, Celebrate," UCB WFP Records, 15:10, Women's Peace Office—Activities and Campaigns, 1980–1989.
102 Gilmore, *Groundswell*, 98–99.
103 Russ Cone, "Sex and City Hall: Struggle Shapes Up," *San Francisco Examiner*, November 1, 1966.
104 Turk, *The Women of NOW*, 119–21.
105 "Information Page," *Sisters: By and For Gay Women* (Daughters of Bilitis), November 1973.
106 Mina Carson, *Ava Helen Pauling: Partner, Activist, Visionary* (Oregon University Press, 2013), 137; Frances Herring interview, June 1, 1985, ARS.0056; "25th Women for Peace Birthday Celebration, November 16, 1986," SCPC WSP Records, B2:1, 1961–date, 50 Oak St.
107 Swerdlow, *Women Strike for Peace*, 50–51.
108 "Kay Boyle Report on Cambodia," UCB WFP Records, 15:9, Women's Peace Office—Activities and Campaigns, 1970–1979.
109 Letter from Hazel Grossman to Senator Alan Cranston, January 29, 1972, SCPC WSP Records, B2:5, Peace Poll Electoral Activity Wonder Bread 1972.
110 Hamburg, *Grass Roots*, 175.
111 "Women for Peace Newsletter," UCB WFP Records, 1:8, Historical Information for Vietnam Women's Association, 1984.
112 Hamburg, *Grass Roots*, 177; Alice Hamburg, WILPF: A History of Outreach and Achievement," UCB WFP Records, 1:12, SF WILPF History by Alice Hamburg, 1985–1986.
113 "Dear Friend of Peace," Summer 1971, UCB WFP Records, 15:9, Women's Peace Office—Activities and Campaigns, 1970–1979.
114 "Dear Friend of Peace," Fall of 1972, UCB WFP Records, 15:9, Women's Peace Office—Activities and Campaigns, 1970–1979.

115 "Dear Friend of Peace, June 1976," UCB WFP Records, 15:9, Women's Peace Office—Activities and Campaigns, 1970–1979.
116 "Celebrate, Celebrate, Celebrate," UCB WFP Records, 15:10, Women's Peace Office—Activities and Campaigns, 1980–1989.
117 Letter from Hazel Grossman to Board Member of AGAPE, March 8, 1985, UCB WFP Records, 1:5, Collections, n.d.
118 David Steinberg, "Aging Myths, and How Some Are Defying Them," *San Francisco Examiner*, June 15, 1991, 19.
119 "Notes on WILPF-WFP Meeting, September 27, 1979," UCB WFP Records, 1:10, SF WFP-SF WILPF Members Meeting Concerning Relationship.
120 "Notes on WILPF-WFP Meeting, September 27, 1979," UCB WFP Records, 1:10, SF WFP-SF WILPF Members Meeting Concerning Relationship.
121 "Women's Peace Office, Save the Date: 1986," UCB WFP Records, 15:10, Women's Peace Office—Activities and Campaigns, 1980–1989; "WFP Anniversary, 11/16/86," UCB WFP Records, 15:10, Women's Peace Office—Activities and Campaigns, 1980–1989.
122 "25th Women for Peace Birthday Celebration, November 16, 1986," SCPC WSP Records, B2:1, 1961–date, 50 Oak St.
123 "WFP Anniversary, 11/16/86," UCB WFP Records, 15:10, Women's Peace Office—Activities and Campaigns, 1980–1989.
124 "Dear Friends, August 1985," UCB WFP Records, 15:10, Women's Peace Office—Activities and Campaigns, 1980–1989; Letter from Hazel Grossman to Board Member of AGAPE, March 8, 1985, UCB WFP Records, 1:5, Collections, n.d.
125 Guide to the San Francisco Women for Peace Records, 1943-[ongoing], UC Berkeley Bancroft Library, https://oac.cdlib.org/findaid/ark:/13030/kt0000000k5/. Last accessed February 11, 2025.
126 Georgina Denton, "Mothers Joining Together in Sisterhood: Women Strike for Peace and the National Welfare Rights Organization in the 1960s and 1970s," *Journal of the Motherhood Initiative* 3, no. 2 (2012): 122.
127 Mohl, "Some of Us Were There Before Betty," 25.
128 Peter Laine and Robert Feldkamp, "War, Race Haunt New Congress," *Miami Herald*, January 16, 1968, 1.
129 Sara M. Evans, *Tidal Wave: How Women Changed America at Century's End* (Free Press, 2003), 27–28.
130 Ruth Rosen, *The World Split Open: How the Modern Women's Movement Changed America* (Penguin Books, 2001), 201–3.
131 Catherine Foster, *Women for All Seasons: The Story of the Women's International League for Peace and Freedom* (University of Georgia Press, 1989), 44.
132 Harriet Hyman Alonso, *Peace as a Women's Issue: A History of the U.S. Movement for World Peace and Women's Rights* (Syracuse University Press, 1993), 221–22.
133 Foster, *Women for All Seasons*, 44–46.
134 "Statement Adopted at the Special NY WSP CCC meeting 11/14/67," SCPC WSP Records ACC 92A-113:1, Jeannette Rankin Brigade.
135 "San Francisco Branch Hosts Large El Salvador Meeting," UCB WFP Records 15:17, WILPF—Bay Area Material.
136 Jacqueline Castledine, *Cold War Progressives: Women's Interracial Organizing for Peace and Freedom* (University of Illinois Press, 2012), 7.
137 Carolyn Lewis, "Brigade Ponders Value of March," *The Washington Post*, January 17, 1968, D3.

138 Letter from Lynda Stein to Mrs. Arthur S. Johnson, April 27, 1966, SCPC WSP Records, A3:4, Branch File—Other States.

139 Letter from Lynda Barrett to Prudy Leib, December 13, 1967, SCPC WSP Records, A3:4, Washington, DC, 1966–1969.

140 Letter from Kay Johnson to Fon Vestal, November 18, 1964, SCPC WSP Records, A3:4, Branch File—Florida (1964).

141 Letter from Lynda Stein to Mrs. Arthur S. Johnson, April 27, 1966, SCPC WSP Records, A3:4, Branch File—Other States.

142 "Minutes of the National Consultative Committee Meeting, January 17, 1968," SCPC WSP Records, A1:1, National Consultative Committee Minutes and Memos—1965–July 1970; "Proposed Budget Given to Annual Conference, 8 June 1963," SCPC WSP Records, A1:2, Financial Data.

143 "Statement of Income and Expenses for the Year Ending Dec. 31, 1964," "Statement of Income and Expenditures for the Period January 1, to September 30, 1965," SCPC WSP Records, A1:2, Financial Data; "Statement of Income and Expenses for the Year Ending December 31, 1968," "Memo from Trudi Young/Joni Phillips, WSP National Office to Expanded NCC, December 2, 1970," SCPC WSP Records, A1:1, National Consultative Committee Minutes and Memos—Aug 1970–1973.

144 Jo Reger, "Debating US Contemporary Feminism," *Sociology Compass* 8, no. 1 (2014): 43–51.

145 Zarnow, *Battling Bella*, 55.

146 Jo Freeman, "The Tyranny of Structurelessness," *The Second Wave* 2, no. 1 (1972): 1–6; see also Carol Hanisch, "Struggles Over Leadership in the Women's Liberation Movement," in *Leadership in Social Movements*, ed. Colin Barker et al. (Manchester University Press, 2001), 77–95.

147 Swerdlow, *Women Strike for Peace*, 75; Harriet Hyman Alonso, "Review," review of *Women Strike for Peace: Traditional Motherhood and Radical Politics in the 1960s*, by Amy Swerdlow, *The American Historical Review* 99, no. 5 (1994): 1774; Letter from Lynda Stein to National Consultative Committee, 1965, SCPC WSP Records, A1:1, National Consultative Committee Minutes and Memos—1965–July 1970; Unsigned letter to Lynda Stein, Donna Allen, National Consultative Committee, and 'Whoever,' December 2, 1965, SCPC WSP Records, A3:10, 1965 Sept.–Dec.

148 "Suggestions for Officers and Steering Committee," UCB WFP Records 2:35, Meeting Agenda, Notes.

149 Letter from Vivian Raineri to Henrietta Levine, July 22, 1971, SCPC WSP Records, A3:13, 1971 Apr.–Dec.; "Newsletter Item from East Bay WFP REL NCC Meetings and WSP Members Groups, July 6, 1970," SCPC WSP Records, A3:5, About National Coordinating Committee Meetings 1968–1970.

150 Letter from Barbara Bick to WSP National Steering Committee and Contact List, September 30, 1968, UCB WFP Records, 5:54, WSP National Conference, St. Louis, 1968.

151 Letter from Anci Koppel to NCC, September 27, 1968, SCPC WSP Records, A1:1, National Consultative Committee Meeting Minutes and Memos—1965–July 1970; Letter from Barbara Bick to WSP National Steering Committee and Contact List, September 30, 1968, UCB WFP Records, 5:54, WSP National Conference, St. Louis, 1968.

152 "Speaking Date Reports," SCPC WSP Records, B1:3, Trip to Djakarta 1965, 3; "Memo Concerning the Jakarta Proposal from Ann Arbor Women for Peace, June 1965,"

SCPC WSP Records, ACC 91A-113:5, Jakarta MTG with Vietnamese Women a First 1965 July; Duckles interview, November 22, 1985, ARS.0056; Letter from Carolyn Marks to Margaret Russell, June 18, 1965, SCPC WSP Records, A3:10, 1965 Jan.–Aug.

153 Letter from E. Elkind to WSPers, July 4, 1965, SCPC WSP Records, ACC 92A-113:5, Jakarta MTG with Vietnamese Women a First 1965 July.

154 "To National Consultative Committee from Lynda Stein, 1965," SCPC WSP Records, A1:1, National Consultative Committee Minutes and Memos—1965–July 1970.

155 Newill interview, February 23, 1980, ARS.0056.

156 "Eleanor Garst: Chapter 1: Who Are These Women?" WHS WSP Records, M83–327, Working Papers for Ch 1, 2, WSP Formation, Test Ban Efforts, 29; "Proposal Number Two: WISP??," SCPC WSP Records, B2:1, San Francisco Literature Undated.

157 "Problems of the National Office, As Related to Washington WSP and Solutions, 1968," SCPC WSP Records, A1:2, Documents Describing WSP History; Letter from Daryl Stewart to Lynda Barrett and Washington WSP, May 2, 1967, SCPC WSP Records, A3:4, Washington, DC, 1966–1969.

158 Swerdlow, *Women Strike for Peace*, 75–77.

159 "Memo from National Office to NCC, May 7, 1970," SCPC WSP Records, A1:1, National Consultative Committee Meeting Minutes and Memos—1965–July 1970.

160 Taylor, *We Made a Difference*, x, 45; "Newsletter Item from East Bay WFP RE: NCC Meetings and WSP Member Groups, July 6, 1970," A3:5, About National Coordinating Committee Meetings, 1968–1970.

161 "Suggestions for Officers and Steering Committee," UCB WFP Records 2:35, Meeting Agenda, Notes; Memo from Henrietta Levine to Barbara Bick and Lynda Barrett, December 15, 1967, SCPC WSP Records, A3:5, About National Coordinating Committee Meetings 1968–1970.

162 "9-27-62," WHS WSP Records, M83–327, Other WSP Acts, 1961.

163 Letter from Anci Koppel to Lynda Barrett, April 7, 1968, SCPC WSP Records, A3:11, 1968 Apr.–Sept.

164 Letter from Anci Koppel to Mabel S. Proctor, October 4, 1970, SCPC WSP Records, A3:4, Washington 1965, 1968–1970.

165 Letter from Mabel S. Proctor to Dagmar Wilson, October 18, 1967, SCPC WSP Records, SCPC WSP Records, A3:1, West Coast Tour 1967.

166 "Pentagon Is Stormed by 2,500 Women," *The New York Times*, February 16, 1967, 4; "Demonstrators for Peace Shout and Shove," *Globe and Mail*, September 21, 1967, W4.

167 "Instructions to Local Coordinators from Jeannette Rankin Brigade," SCPC WSP Records, ACC 92A-113, Jeannette Rankin Brigade.

168 Letter from Anci Koppel to NCC, September 27, 1968, SCPC WSP Records, A1:1, National Consultative Committee Meeting Minutes and Memos—1965–July 1970.

169 "Minutes of Planning Meeting for 1966 National Conference," SCPC WSP Records, A1:3, National Conference—1966, Chicago, IL.

170 Letter from Harriet M. Avery to Barbara Bick, December 28, 1967, SCPC WSP Records, A3:5, About National Coordinating Committee Meetings 1968–1970.

171 One in Michigan (1962), six in Illinois (1963, 1964, 1966, 1968, 1971, 1973), one in Washington, DC (1967), one in Pennsylvania (1969), one in Wisconsin (1970), and two in New York (1974, 1975), SCPC WSP Records, A1:3.

172 "Special—Please Note, 9/1965," SCPC WSP Records, B2:1, 1961–date, 50 Oak St.

173 Letter from Mabel S. Proctor to Lynda Fanning, September 26, 1965, SCPC WSP Records, A3:10, 1965 Sept.–Dec.

174 Letter from the Women of Southern California WSP Council, September 25, 1968, SCPC WSP Records, A3:11, 1968 Apr.–Sept.
175 Letter from Barbara Bick to NCC Members, August 23, 1968, SCPC WSP Records, A1:1, National Consultative Committee Meeting Minutes and Memos—1965–July 1970.
176 Letter from Ethel Taylor to Barbara Bick, August 23, 1968, SCPC WSP Records, A3:11, 1968 Apr.–Sept.
177 Memo from Barbara Bick to NCC Members, September 4, 1968, SCPC WSP Records, A1:1, National Consultative Committee Meeting Minutes and Memos—1965–July 1970.
178 Amy C. Schneidhorst, "'Little Old Ladies and Dangerous Women': Women's Peace Activism and Social Justice in Chicago, 1960–1975," *Peace & Change* 26, no. 3 (2001): 385; David T. Dellinger, *From Yale to Jail: The Life Story of a Moral Dissenter* (Pantheon Books, 1993).
179 "WSP mailer to NCC Representatives, April 29, 1968," SCPC WSP Records, A1:1, National Consultative Committee Minutes and Memos—1965–July 1970.
180 WSP employed the talents of numerous volunteers in a national secretary role since 1961. Kay Johnson, Lynda Stein/Barrett, Barbara Bick, Sally Bortz, Vicki King, and Dagmar Wilson (with various assistants) all turned their hands to the task. Trudi Young was the first to occupy that position officially.
181 Martin Weil, "War Protesters Plan New Offensive Feb. 21," *The Washington Post*, February 10, 1970, A2; "March 'Comply-In' Mapped to Tie Up Draft Boards' Work," *The New York Times*, March 3, 1970, 12; "Foes of War Elated at Antidraft Week," *The New York Times*, March 21, 1970, 28.
182 "Dear COLers, June 25, 1970," SCPC WSP Records, ACC 94A-051:2, POW Liaisons.
183 Letter from Trudi Young to Carolyn Berger, July 1, 1970, SCPC WSP Records, A3:5, About National Coordinating Committee Meetings 1968–1970; Letter from Didi Halkin to Trudi Young, May 7, 1971, SCPC WSP Records A3:13, 1971 Apr.–Dec.
184 Letter from Trudi Young to Jean Kovner, April 20, 1971, SCPC WSP Records, A3:13, 1971 Jan.–Mar.
185 Letter from Trudi Young to Shelby Grantham, March 19, 1971, SCPC WSP Records, A3:13, 1971 Jan.–Mar.
186 Letter from Trudi Young to Jean Kovner, April 20, 1971, SCPC WSP Records, A3:13, 1971 Apr.–Dec; Letter from Trudi Young to WSP Members, May 1, 1971, UCB WFP Records, 6:2, Office Files—National 1971.
187 Letter from Trudi Young to WSP Members, May 1, 1971, UCB WFP Records, 6:2, Office Files—National 1971.
188 Letter from Bernice Crane to WSP Activists, May 21, 1971, SCPC WSP Records, A1:1, National Consultative Committee Meeting Minutes and Memos—Aug 1970–1973; Richard Halloran, "30,000 Protesters Routed in Capital," *The New York Times*, May 3, 1971, 1; William R. MacKaye, "Many Church Leaders Assail New Bombings," *The Washington Post*, December 23, 1972, A6.
189 Telegraph from Anci Koppel to Trudi Young, March 18, 1971, SCPC WSP Records, A3:13, 1971 Jan.–Dec.
190 Plastas, *A Band of Noble Women*, 241.
191 Susan K. Freeman, "From the Lesbian Nation to the Cincinnati Lesbian Community: Moving Toward a Politics of Location," *Journal of the History of Sexuality* 9, nos. 1 and 2 (2000), 137–74.

192 "Newsletter Item from East Bay WFP RE: NCC Meetings and WSP Member Groups, July 6, 1970," A3:5, About National Coordinating Committee Meetings, 1968–1970.

193 Alonso, *Peace as a Women's Issue*; Swerdlow's *Women Strike for Peace* confines WSP's history to the 1960s and early 1970s.

Chapter Five

1 "Progress Report on WSP Research," Swarthmore College Peace Collection, WSP Records SCPC-DG-115 (hereafter SCPC WSP Records), C1:3, Research on WSP by Amy Swerdlow.

2 See, for example, Jon Coburn, "Basically Feminist: Women Strike for Peace, Maternal Peace Activism, and Memory of the Women's Peace Movement," *Journal of Women's History* 33, no. 2 (2021): 136–62; Petra Goedde, *The Politics of Peace: A Global Cold War History* (Oxford University Press, 2019), 140.

3 Ruth Rosen, "The Day They Buried 'Traditional Womanhood': Women and the Politics of Peace Protest," in *The Legacy: The Vietnam War in the American Imagination*, ed. D. Michael Shafer (Beacon Press, 1990), 238; Amy C. Schneidhorst, *Building a Just and Secure World: Popular Front Women's Struggle for Peace and Justice in Chicago during the 1960s* (Bloomsbury Publishing, 2011); Andrea Estepa, "Taking the White Gloves Off: Women Strike for Peace and the Transformation of Women's Activist Identities in the United States, 1961–1980," (PhD diss., Rutgers University, May 2012), 84–112; Jessica M. Frazier, *Women's Antiwar Diplomacy During the Vietnam War Era* (University of North Carolina Press, 2017).

4 See, for example, Sara Ruddick, *Maternal Thinking: Toward a Politics of Peace* (The Women's Press, 1989).

5 Taylor, *We Made a Difference*, 111. WSP had, in the 1960s, advanced a campaign that declared "the Women's Vote is the Peace Vote," which reflected a desire for more political involvement by WSP's supporters. The tone and sentiment towards women's politics was, however, noticeably stronger later.

6 For example, see Alice Echols, "'We Gotta Get Out of This Place': Notes Toward a Remapping of the Sixties," in *Shaky Ground: The Sixties and its Aftershocks*, ed. Alice Echols (Columbia University Press, 2002): 62; Dorothy Sue Cobble, Linda Gordon, and Astrid Henry, *Feminism Unfinished: A Short, Surprising History of American Women's Movements* (Liveright Publishing Corporation, 2014), xiv.

7 Taylor, *We Made a Difference*, 2.

8 Red Chidgey, *Feminist Afterlives: Assemblage Memory in Activist Times* (Palgrave Macmillan, 2018); Red Chidgey and Joanne Garde-Hansen, *Museums, Archives and Protest Memory* (Palgrave Macmillan, 2024).

9 Estepa, "Taking the White Gloves Off" (PhD diss.), 304.

10 Letter from Leona Grant to Dagmar Wilson, December 10, 1964, Wisconsin Historical Society WSP Records (hereafter WHS WSP Records), MSS 433, 2:7, Correspondence of Dagmar Wilson 1961–1964; "Eleanor Garst: Chapter 1, Who Are These Women?" WHS WSP Records, M83-327, Working Papers for Ch 1, 2, WSP Formation, Test Ban Efforts, 12–13.

11 "Corrections for Amy," SCPC WSP Records, ACC 2013-050:17, Draft Chapters 1–5, Amy Swerdlow's Dissertation with Dagmar's Biographical Corrections, 1981.

12 Letter from Dr. Isidore Zifferstein to Dagmar Wilson, June 15, 1967, SCPC WSP Records, A3:4, Washington, DC, 1966–1969.

13 Richard Dudman, "Dagmar Wilson: Striking for Peace," *The Washington Post Potomac* [magazine section], April 13, 1966.

14 "Corrections for Amy," SCPC WSP Records, ACC 2013–050:17, Draft Chapters 1–5, Amy Swerdlow's Dissertation with Dagmar's Biographical Corrections, 1981.

15 Wilson's secretary explained that the leader had, for all intents and purposes, "retired" in 1964 following the passage of the Partial Test Ban Treaty. Reply to Mrs. Harold J. Stein from Dorothy Maund, Secretary to Dagmar Wilson, February 6, 1964, SCPC WSP Records, A3:1, D. Wilson Files—Invitations to Speak, etc. (1964); "Lady Pacifist Visits Hanoi Women," *The Boston Globe*, April 13, 1968, 3.

16 "Dagmar Wilson: Striking for Peace," WHS WSP Records, MSS 433, 2:11, Biographical Data on Dagmar Wilson.

17 "Dagmar Wilson: Striking for Peace," WHS WSP Records, MSS 433, 2:11, Biographical Data on Dagmar Wilson; "Corrections for Amy," SCPC WSP Records, ACC 2013–050:17, Draft Chapters 1–5, Amy Swerdlow's Dissertation with Dagmar's Biographical Corrections, 1981.

18 Dagmar Wilson interview, April 15, 1989, ARS.0056, Stanford University Archive of Recorded Sound.

19 "3 Are Convicted in Contempt Case," *The New York Times*, April 9, 1965, 68; "2 in Women's Peace Unit and Editor Deny Contempt," *The New York Times*, January 9, 1965, 3; Donna Allen interview, April 26, 1989, ARS.0056; "Court Crowd Cheers 3 Held for Contempt," *The Washington Post*, January 9, 1965, B3; "400 Honor 3 Defendants Cited by House Committee," *The New York Times*, April 7, 1965, 87.

20 "Defenders of 'Three Against HUAC,'" WHS WSP Records, MSS 433, 1:12.

21 "Eleanor Garst: Chapter 1, Who Are These Women?" WHS WSP Records, M83–327, Working Papers for Ch 1, 2, WSP Formation, Test Ban Efforts, 12:13.

22 "Dagmar Wilson: Striking for Peace," WHS WSP Records, MSS 433, 2:11, Biographical Data on Dagmar Wilson.

23 Marjorie Hunter, "Arms Race Opposed—Response Cheers Head of 'Strike,'" *The New York Times*, November 22, 1961, 4; "Washington WSP 'Retreat' Meeting at Folly Fodor's, Saturday, October 5, 1968," SCPC WSP Records, A1:2, Washington WSP Retreat—October 5 1968, 4; Allen interview, April 29, 1989.

24 "Washington WSP 'Retreat' Meeting at Folly Fodor's, Saturday, October 5, 1968," SCPC WSP Records, A1:2, Washington WSP Retreat—October 5 1968, 4, 46.

25 "Keynote address given by Dagmar Wilson to the National Conference of Women Strike for Peace in Chicago (Evanston) Illinois, November 9, 1968," SCPC WSP Records, A1:3, National Conference—1968, Winnetka, IL, 2. Emphasis in original transcript.

26 "Keynote address given by Dagmar Wilson to the National Conference of Women Strike for Peace in Chicago (Evanston) Illinois, November 9, 1968," SCPC WSP Records, A1:3, National Conference—1968, Winnetka, IL, 5.

27 "Report on a Trip to the USSR, Representing Women Strike for Peace at Conference with Soviet Peace Committee—no.7–17, 1968, by Anci Koppel," University of Washington, Seattle, Seattle Women Act for Peace Records, 4073 (hereafter UWS SWAP), 2:3, American Peace Delegation to the Soviet Union.

28 Herbert H. Denton, "Inaugural Protesters Win Site," *The Washington Post, Times Herald*, January 4, 1969, D4; "Women Use Chains in Antiwar Protest," *The Washington*

Post, April 14, 1971, B2; Letter from Taylor Adams to Sally Bortz, April 19, 1969, SCPC WSP Records, A3:4, Washington, DC, 1966–1969; Letter from Anci Koppel to Mabel Proctor, October 4, 1970, A3:4, Washington 1965, 1968–1970.

29 Letter from Sue Oppenheimer to Trudi Young, 26 June 1970, SCPC WSP Records, A3:4, Branch File—Texas (1970).

30 Letter from Jean Shulman, July 3, 1974, University of California, Berkely, San Francisco Women for Peace Records BANC MSS 89/132 c (hereafter UCB WFP Records), 7:2, Office Files—1974, National; Letter from Mary Clarke to Dagmar Wilson, December 30, 1978, SCPC WSP Records, ACC 2013-050:11, Women Strike for Peace Friends Personal Correspondence.

31 "Women's Strike for Peace (WSP) National Conference, Santa Barbara, California, December 8–11, 1972," American University DC Office of the Women Strike for Peace Records (hereafter AU WSP Records), Box 19, FOIA FBI Files—100-39566 Vol. 7.

32 Letter from Jean Shulman, July 3, 1974, UCB WFP Records, 7:2, Office Files—1974, National.

33 Letter from Jean Shulman to Ethel Taylor, July 25, 1974, SCPC WSP Records, ACC 01A-005:6, Ethel Taylor.

34 "My Trip to WSP and On the West Coast, Ethel Taylor," SCPC WSP Records, ACC 01A-005:9, Philadelphia Women Strike for Peace.

35 "Women Strike for Peace National Newsletter, 25 June 1976," SCPC WSP Records, ACC 96A-040:2, Carter 1976 Election.

36 "My Trip to WSP and On the West Coast, Ethel Taylor," SCPC WSP Records, ACC 01A-005: 9, Philadelphia Women Strike for Peace.

37 Verta Taylor and Alison Dahl Crossley, "Abeyance Cycles in Social Movements," in *Movements in Times of Democratic Transitions* eds. Bert Klandermans and Cornelius van Stralen (Temple University Press, 2015), 64–87.

38 Betty Friedan, *The Feminine Mystique* (Penguin Classics, 2010); Daniel Horowitz, *Betty Friedan and the Making of the Feminine Mystique* (University of Massachusetts Press, 1998).

39 President's Commission on the Status of Women, *American Women: Report of the President's Commission on the Status of Women, 1963* (Government Printing Office, 1963).

40 Katherine Turk, *The Women of NOW: How Feminists Built an Organization that Transformed America* (Farrar, Straus and Giroux, 2023); Kelsy Kretschmer, *Fighting for NOW* (University of Minnesota Press, 2019).

41 Leandra Ruth Zarnow, *Battling Bella: The Protest Politics of Bella Abzug* (Harvard University Press, 2019), 39, 45, 51.

42 Amy Swerdlow, *Women Strike for Peace: Traditional Motherhood and Radical Politics in the 1960s* (University of Chicago Press, 1993), 108.

43 Rhodri Jeffreys-Jones, *Peace Now! American Society and the Ending of the Vietnam War* (Yale University Press, 1999), 143–44; Zarnow, *Battling Bella*, 65.

44 Swerdlow, *Women Strike for Peace*, 22.

45 "Women Strike for Peace, Minutes December 2, 1961," WHS WSP Records, M83-327, Working Papers for Ch 1, 2, WSP Formation, Test Ban Efforts.

46 Lisa Brush, "Review: Love, Toil, and Trouble: Motherhood and Feminist Politics," *Signs* 21, no. 2 (1996), 429–54.

47 "Middle-Class Masses," by Eleanor Garst, from *Magazine of the Fellowship of Reconciliation*, September 1962, SCPC WSP Records, B1:7, Working Documents 1961–1964. Emphasis mine.
48 "Peace de Resistance: A Cook Book, Volume II," SCPC WSP Records, B1:1, Beginnings of LA WSP (1961).
49 Marian Mollin, *Radical Pacifism in Modern America: Egalitarianism and Protest* (University of Pennsylvania Press, 2006), 96.
50 Swerdlow, *Women Strike for Peace*, 72–73.
51 Jeanne Molli, "Women's Peace Group Uses Feminine Tactics," *The New York Times*, April 19, 1962, 26.
52 Swerdlow, *Women Strike for Peace*, 81.
53 "We Stand by Our Record," December 7, 1962, Chicago History Museum Women for Peace (Chicago, IL) Records (hereafter CHM WFP Records), 2:11 WFP HUAC Hearings 1962.
54 Goedde, *The Politics of Peace*, 140.
55 Catherine Foster, *Women for all Seasons: The Story of the Women's International League for Peace and Freedom* (University of Georgia Press, 1989): 40.
56 "For the Sake of Our Sons," SCPC WSP Records, ACC 92A-113:2, Xmas Card Campaign Xmas Pilgrimage to DC 1965.
57 Anne Eaton, "Hathaway Brown School Commencement Address, June 12, 1970," SCPC WSP Records, ACC 2013–050:15, Women Strike for Peace History.
58 Nancy Skelton, "Can One Man—Even a Governor—Out-Talk 200 Women?" *Sacramento Bee*, March 30, 1967, 15; 29, WFP East Bay—Clippings, Notes, Correspondence, 1961–1969.
59 Another Mother for Peace mobilized hundreds of thousands of people to antiwar protest in the late 1960s, in large part because of its popularity with Hollywood figures such as Donna Reed, Patty Duke, Debbie Reynolds, and Paul Newman. It is, though, perhaps most remembered for its striking logo, a cartoon image of a sunflower with the slogan "War is Not Healthy for Children and Other Living Things." Harriet Hyman Alonso, *Peace as a Women's Issue: A History of the U.S. Movement for World Peace and Women's Rights* (Syracuse University Press, 1993), 216–19.
60 Judy Tzu-Chun Wu, *Radicals on the Road: Internationalism, Orientalism, and Feminism During the Vietnam Era* (Cornell University Press, 2013), 202.
61 "Trip to Hanoi, Cora Weiss," 1969, SCPC Cora Weiss, 1 Women Strike for Peace, '62–'72, 6.
62 Alonso, *Peace as a Women's Issue*, 5–8. Alonso also classified women's peace action as feminist if it "stressed the importance of education for women who needed to make wise lobbying and electoral choices" and "maintained the female power structure and feminist networking that had been used in suffrage organizations and scorned working with men." WSP unevenly demonstrated some of these attributes during the 1960s.
63 Estepa, "Taking the White Gloves Off" (PhD diss.), 307–11.
64 Jo Freeman, "On the Origins of the Women's Liberation Movement from a Strictly Personal Perspective," in *The Feminist Memoir Project: Voices from Women's Liberation*, ed. Rachel Blau DuPlessis and Ann Barr Snitow (Three Rivers Press, 1998), 179.
65 "Alice Hamburg's History of San Francisco Women's Peace Office," UCB WFP Records 1:13, Women's Peace Office (WPO) History, 7.

66 Jeannette Rankin Brigade News Release, January 3 1968, SCPC WSP Records ACC 92A-113:1, Jeannette Rankin Brigade.
67 Alice Echols, "'Women Power' and Women's Liberation: Exploring the Relationship Between the Antiwar Movement and the Women's Liberation Movement," in *Give Peace a Chance: Exploring the Vietnam Antiwar Movement (Essays from the Charles DeBenedetti Memorial Conference)*, ed. Melvin Small and William D. Hoover (Syracuse University Press, 1992), 175–77.
68 Ruth Rosen, "The Day They Buried 'Traditional Womanhood': Women and the Politics of Peace Protest," in *The Legacy: The Vietnam War in the American Imagination*, ed. D. Michael Shafer (Beacon Press, 1990), 238.
69 Shulamith Firestone, "The Jeannette Rankin Brigade: Woman Power?" *Notes from the First Year: New York Radical Women* (June 1968): 18; Swerdlow, *Women Strike for Peace*, 138.
70 Swerdlow, *Women Strike for Peace*, 138; Firestone, "The Jeannette Rankin Brigade," 18.
71 Estepa, "Taking the White Gloves Off" (PhD diss.), 316.
72 Ruth Rosen, *The World Split Open: How the Modern Women's Movement Changed America* (Penguin Books, 2001), 203.
73 Swerdlow, *Women Strike for Peace*, 241; Alice Echols, *Daring to Be Bad: Radical Feminism in American, 1967–1975* (University of Minnesota Press, 1989): 246; Freeman, "Origins of the Women's Liberation Movement," 179.
74 Wu, *Radicals on the Road*, 194.
75 Described by Judy Wu as "War at a Peace Conference." *Radicals on the Road*, 219–43.
76 Wu, *Radicals on the Road*, 245.
77 Letter from Trudi Young to Sisters, May 1, 1971, UCB WFP Records, 6:2, Office Files—National, 1971.
78 Swerdlow, *Women Strike for Peace*, 228–30.
79 Barbara Burris, "The Fourth World Manifesto," in *Notes from the Third Year: Women's Liberation* (1971), 102–19.
80 Wu, *Radicals on the Road*, 231; Echols, *Daring to Be Bad*, 245.
81 Swerdlow, *Women Strike for Peace*, 137.
82 "Report on Planning Sessions for Revolutionary People's Plenary Scheduled for September 4–7," SCPC WSP Records, A1:1, National Consultative Committee Minutes and Memos—Aug. 1970–1973.
83 "Our Women in Hanoi, 12/71," SCPC WSP Records ACC 94A-005:1, Trip to Hanoi—Amy Swerdlow and Irma Zigas; "Amy Swerdlow Reports on her Trip to Hanoi," SCP WSP Records ACC 94A-005:1, Trip to Hanoi—Amy Swerdlow and Irma Zigas.
84 "Our Women in Hanoi, 12/71," SCPC WSP Records ACC 94A-005:1, Trip to Hanoi—Amy Swerdlow and Irma Zigas; "Amy Swerdlow Reports on her Trip to Hanoi," SCP WSP Records ACC 94A-005:1, Trip to Hanoi—Amy Swerdlow and Irma Zigas.
85 "Mary Clarke, 1972," SCPC WSP Records B1:7, Working Documents 1965–date, 9.
86 "Trip to Hanoi, Cora Weiss," 1969, SCPC Cora Weiss, 1, Women Strike for Peace '62–'72, 6.
87 Rosemary Curb, "In the Eye of the Storm: Feminist Research and Action in the 90's," *off our backs* 22, no. 8 (1992): 20.
88 "Press Release," SCPC WSP Records, C1:3, WSP Related Material About-By Bella Abzug; "WSP Played a Major Role," SCPC WSP Records, C1:3, WSP Related Material About-By Bella Abzug.

89 "National Conference Planning Committee, September 17, 1970," SCPC WSP Records, A1:1, Misc. Minutes.
90 "Report from Liaison Committee to WSP Groups and National Conference Participants," October 28, 1971, SCPC WSP Records, A1:3, National Conference—1971, Evanston, IL.
91 Among these were Ethel Taylor, Mary Clarke, Shirley Lens, Alice Hamburg, and Edith Villastrigo.
92 "March International Women's Day 1975," SCPC WSP Records, ACC 96A-949:3, International Women's Day Year 1975.
93 "Pam Block, Motherhood in WSP, 1961–1973," SCPC WSP Records, ACC 01A-005:12, National WSP Historical Material.
94 Barbara Ryan, *Feminism and the Women's Movement: Dynamics of Change in Social Movement Ideology and Activism* (Routledge, 1992), 55; Estepa, "Taking the White Gloves Off" (PhD diss.), 319, 330–331.
95 Jane Alpert, *Mother Right: A New Feminist Theory* (Know, Inc., 1974).
96 Echols, *Daring to Be Bad*, 250–54.
97 "Minutes: National Conference, WSP, 1974," SCPC WSP Records, A1:3, National Conference—1974, New York NY, 8; Barbara J. Love ed., *Feminists Who Changed America, 1963–1975* (University of Illinois Press, 2006), 453.
98 Dagmar Wilson interview, April 15, 1989, ARS.0056.
99 "Letter from Nadine Vesel to Joyce Dinsmore, October 19, 1977," CHM WFP Records, 7:10, WFP Correspondence 1977–1978.
100 Myra Macpherson, "Bella Abzug, Champion of Women," *The Washington Post*, April 2, 1998, B1; "Bella Abzug," *The New York Times*, April 1, 1998, A22; Judy Klemesrud, "The Lesbian Issue and Women's Lib," *The New York Times*, December 18, 1970, 60.
101 Jonathan Bell, "'To Strive for Economic and Social Justice': Welfare, Sexuality, and Liberal Politics in San Francisco in the 1960s," *Journal of Policy History* 22, no. 2 (2010): 193–225.
102 Linda K. Schott, *Reconstructing Women's Thoughts: The Women's International League for Peace and Freedom Before World War II* (Stanford University Press, 1997) 10, 124
103 Taylor, *We Made a Difference*, 111.
104 Swerdlow, *Women Strike for Peace*, 242.
105 "Women's Declaration of Liberation from Military Domination, March 18, 1970," SCPC WSP Records, ACC 94A-005:1, 31/8/70 WSP Demo Women's Declaration of Liberation from Military Domination.
106 "Suggested Agenda for October 4, 5, and 6," UCB WFP Records, 7–2, Office Files—National, 1974; "Minutes—East Coast WSP Conference, January 24, 1975," SCPC WSP Records, A1:3, Regional Conferences; "Women's Plea for Survival," SCPC WSP Records, ACC 96A-040:2, International Women's Year Coalition 1975.
107 "Women Call Upon US Women to Stop Nuclear Arms Race, May 9 1975," SCPC WSP Records, ACC 96A-040:1, Launching of Women Strike for Peace and Survival 5/14/75; Women Strike for Peace and Survival 1975, SCPC WSP Records, ACC 96A-040:1, Launching of Women Strike for Peace and Survival 5/14/75.
108 Ethel Taylor, "Women: Get Politically Involved," *Philadelphia Inquirer*, May 9, 1975, SCPC WSP Records, ACC 96A-040:1, Launching of Women Strike for Peace and Survival 5/14/75.
109 "Kaleidoscope: Tribune of International Women's Year," CHM WFP Records, 5:11, WFP Women 1975.

110 Letter from Judith Joseph to Hazel Grossman, August 1, 1975, UCB WFP Records, 7:22, World Congress for International Women's Year, 1975.
111 "Geographical Index of the U.S. Delegation, World Congress for International Women's Year," UCB WFP Records, 7:22, World Congress for International Women's Year, 1975.
112 Taylor, *We Made a Difference*, 107–14.
113 National Commission on the Observance of International Women's Year, *The Spirit of Houston: The First National Women's Conference*—An Official Report to the President, the Congress, and the People of the United States (U.S. Government Printing Office, 1978), 243–49.
114 "Dear Friend of Peace, Fall 1977," UCB WFP Records, 15:9, Women's Peace Office—Activities and Campaigns, 1970–1979; Taylor, *We Made a Difference*, 107.
115 *The Spirit of Houston.*
116 Doreen J. Mattingly and Jessica L. Nare, "'A Rainbow of Women': Diversity and Unity at the 1977 U.S. International Women's Year Conference," *Journal of Women's History* 26, no. 2 (2014): 88–112; Caroline Bird, *What Women Want: From the Official Report to the President, the Congress and the People of the United States* (Simon & Schuster, 1979); Taylor, *We Made a Difference*, 107–14; Lindsy Van Gelder, "Flashback: From Seneca Falls to Houston," *Ms.* 12, no. 3 (2002): 96–98; Erin M. Kempker, "Battling 'Big Sister' Government: Hoosier Women and the Politics of International Women's Year," *Journal of Women's History* 24, no. 2 (2012): 144–70.
117 Marjorie J. Spruill, "Gender and America's Right Turn," in *Rightward Bound: Making America Conservative in the 1970s*, ed. Bruce J. Schulman and Julian E. Zelizer (Harvard University Press, 2008), 75.
118 Mattingly and Nare, "'A Rainbow of Women'" 90; Bird, *What Women Want*, 123.
119 Van Gelder, "Flashback," 96.
120 Bird, *What Women Want*, 123.
121 Dominic Sandbrook, *Mad as Hell: The Crisis of the 1970s and the Rise of the Populist Right* (Anchor Books, 2011), 262; Bruce Schulman, *The Seventies: The Great Shift in American Culture, Society, and Politics* (Da Capo Press, 2002), 186.
122 Donald T. Critchlow, *Phyllis Schlafly and Grassroots Conservatism: A Woman's Crusade* (Princeton University Press, 2005), 244–48; Seth Dowland, "'Family Values' and the Formation of a Christian Right Agenda," *Church History* 78, no. 3 (2009): 624–27; Carol Felsenthal, *The Sweetheart of the Silent Majority: The Biography of Phyllis Schlafly* (Doubleday, 1981); Sandbrook, *Mad as Hell*, 260–62; Ronnee Schreiber, *Righting Feminism: Conservative Women and American Politics* (Oxford University Press, 2008), 21–22; Judy Klemesrud, "Houston Hosts, If Not Toasts, Feminists," *The New York Times*, November 18, 1977, 48; Marlene Cimons, "Phyllis Schlafly Heads for Houston," *Los Angeles Times*, November 11, 1977, H1.
123 Meg O'Connor and Jon Margolis, "Women's Meet Backs Abortion and Gay Rights," *Chicago Tribune*, November 21, 1977, 3; Sandbrook, *Mad as Hell*, 260.
124 "Home from Houston," *The Washington Post*, November 27, 1977, 74.
125 Ethel Taylor, "Women: Get Politically Involved," *Philadelphia Inquirer*, May 9, 1975, SCPC WSP Records, ACC 96A-040:1, Launching of Women Strike for Peace and Survival 5/14/75.
126 "Message to American Women—International Women's Year—1975," SCPC WSP Records, ACC 96A-040:2, International Women's Year Coalition 1975.
127 "A Message to Ms./Miss/Mrs. Everywoman," AU WSP Records, 17, Women and Peace, 1967–1971, 1977–1994.

128 "Kaleidoscope: Tribune of International Women's Year," CHM WFP Records, 5:11, WFP Women 1975; Arvonne S. Fraser, "Becoming Human: The Origins and Development of Women's Human Rights," *Human Rights Quarterly* 21, no. 4 (1999): 894; Cynthia Salzman Mondell and Allen Mondell, dirs., *Sisters of '77* (PBS, 2005).
129 "National Women's Conference November 18–21, Houston, Tentative Agenda," SCPC WSP Records, D1:5, Subject File: National Women's Conference (1977), 3; Taylor, *We Made a Difference*, 111.
130 "Proposed National Plan of Action," SCPC WSP Records, D1:6, National Women's Conference 1977; Bird, *What Women Want*.
131 Taylor, *We Made a Difference*, 111.
132 WHS WSP Records, M83–327, Working Papers for Ch1, 2, WSP Formation, Test Ban Efforts; Working Papers for Ch 3 on WISP, Jan 1962; Ch 3 Working Papers on Geneva Conference, Clippings, 1962; Ch 4 Working Papers on High Altitude Testing, Clippings, April 1962; Working Papers for Chapter 7, Test Ban Treaty, Initial Stand Against Vietnam War, Anti-Nuclear Dem in Netherlands, May 1964.
133 "Women Strike for Peace Minutes December 2, 1961," WHS WSP Records, M83–327, Working Papers for Ch1, 2, WSP Formation, Test Ban Efforts.
134 Gerda Lerner, "New Approaches to the Study of Women in American History," *Journal of Social History* 3, no. 1 (1969): 53–62; Gerda Lerner, "Placing Women in History: Definitions and Challenges," *Feminist Studies* 3, nos. 1and 2 (1975): 5–14; Joan Kelly, "The Doubled Vision of Feminist Theory: A Postscript to the 'Women and Power' Conference," *Feminist Studies* 5, no. 1 (1979): 216–27.
135 Lara Leigh Kelland, *Clio's Foot Soldiers: Twentieth-Century U.S. Social Movements and Collective Memory* (University of Massachusetts Press, 2018): 6, 71.
136 Card from Mary Clarke to Dagmar Wilson, SCPC WSP Records, ACC 2013–050:11, WSP Friends Personal Correspondence.
137 "Memo—Special Commemorative Issue, 1970," UWS SWAP Records, 3:13, WSP 1962–2000, 1–3.
138 "Minutes of WSP National Conference, December 8–11, 1972, Santa Barbara, California," UCB WFP Records, 6:13, Office Files—National Conference, Santa Barbara, 1972.
139 "Keynote Address by Ethel Taylor at WSP National Conference, Chicago, Illinois, October 1973," SCPC WSP Records, A1:3, National Conference—1973, Chicago, IL.
140 "WSP National Conference November 10–11, 1982," SCPC WSP Records, A1:3, National Conference—1982, Berkeley, CA.
141 Timothy Kubal and Rene Becerra, "Social Movements and Collective Memory," *Sociology Compass* 8, no. 6 (2014): 871.
142 Timothy B. Gongaware, "Collective Memories and Collective Identities: Maintaining Unity in Native American Educational Social Movements," *Journal of Contemporary Ethnography* 32, no. 5 (2003): 484–85.
143 "National WSP Conference, Dec. 8–11, 1972, Santa Barbara, Calif. Remarks by Mary Clarke," SCPC WSP Records, A1:3, National Conference—1972, Santa Barbara, CA.
144 "Keynote Address by Ethel Taylor at WSP National Conference, Chicago, Illinois, October 1973," SCPC WSP Records, A1:3, National Conference—1973, Chicago, IL.
145 Timothy B. Gongaware, "Keying the Past to the Present: Collective Memories and Continuity in Collective Identity Change," *Social Movement Studies* 10, no. 1 (2011): 39–54.

146 "Minutes of WSP National Conference, December 8–11, 1972, Santa Barbara, California," UCB WFP Records, 6:13, Office Files—National Conference, Santa Barbara, 1972.

147 "National WSP Conference, Dec. 8–11, 1972, Santa Barbara, Calif. Remarks by Mary Clarke," SCPC WSP Records, A1:3, National Conference—1972, Santa Barbara, CA. Emphasis in the original.

148 Sarah Diamondstein, "Women Still Strike for Peace," *The New York Times*, January 29, 1978, WC12.

149 "WSP Commemorative Journal, 1961–1979," SCPC WSP Records, A1:2, Documents Describing WSP History.

150 Suzanne Braun Levine and Mary Thom, eds., *Bella Abzug: How One Tough Broad from the Bronx Fought Jim Crow and Joe McCarthy, Pissed Off Jimmy Carter, Battled for the Rights of Women and Workers, Rallied Against War and for the Planet, and Shook Up Politics Along the Way* (Farrar, Straus and Giroux, 2007), 4; see also Sato Masaya, "Bella Abzug's Dilemma: The Cold War, Women's Politics, and the Arab-Israeli Conflict in the 1970s," *Journal of Women's History* 30, no. 2 (2018): 112–35.

151 "Celebrating the Remarkable Life of Bella Abzug," AU WSP Records, 2, Leadership, 1975, 1979, 1982–1987, 1990–1998, n.d.

152 Peter Dreier, *The 100 Greatest Americans of the 20th Century: A Social Justice Hall of Fame* (Nation Books, 2012), 317.

153 Alan H. Levy, *The Political Life of Bella Abzug, 1920–1976: Political Passions, Women's Rights, and Congressional Battles* (Lexington Books, 2013), 62.

154 Leandra Zarnow, "The Legal Origins of 'The Personal is Political': Bella Abzug and Sexual Politics in Cold War America," in *Breaking the Wave: Women, Organizations, and Feminism, 1945–1985*, ed. Kathleen A. Laughlin and Jacqueline Castledine (Routledge, 2011), 28–29.

155 Zarnow, *Battling Bella*, 15.

156 Zarnow, *Battling Bella*, 41–43.

157 Laura Mansnerus, "Bella Abzug, 77, Congresswoman and a Founding Feminist, Is Dead," *The New York Times*, April 1, 1998, A1; "Bella Abzug," *The New York Times*, April 1, 1998, A22.

158 Levy, *The Political Life of Bella Abzug*, 64.

159 Braun Levine and Thom, *Bella Abzug*, 63.

160 Zarnow, *Battling Bella*, 43.

161 Braun Levine and Thom, *Bella Abzug*, 63.

162 Zarnow, *Battling Bella*, 42; Braun Levine and Thom, *Bella Abzug*, 62.

163 Rhodri Jeffreys-Jones, *Changing Differences: Women and the Shaping of American Foreign Policy, 1917–1994* (Rutgers University Press, 1995), 60; Braun Levine and Thom, *Bella Abzug*, 86.

164 Braun Levine and Thom, *Bella Abzug*, 61, 86.

165 Jeffreys-Jones, *Changing Differences*, 135.

166 Estepa, "Taking the White Gloves Off" (PhD diss.), 306; Swerdlow, *Women Strike for Peace*, 146.

167 Estepa, "Taking the White Gloves Off" (PhD diss.), 306; Swerdlow interview, September 25, 1987, ARS.0056.

168 Levy, *The Political Life of Bella Abzug*, 66.

169 Based on an archival review of *The New York Times*, *The Washington Post*, *Chicago Tribune*, *The Boston Globe*, and *Los Angeles Times* from 1960 to 1970, Bella Abzug appeared in articles concerning WSP activity only twice, both coming in the first half of 1969.
170 "Summary of Report to Political Action Panel, New York WSP Conference 11/18/67," SCPC WSP Records B1:7, Working Documents 1965–date.
171 "A Decade of Frustrations and Success," SCPC WSP Records ACC 94A-005:1, Judy Lerner's Trip to Japan and Hanoi.
172 Braun Levine and Thom, *Abzug*, 97, 99; Levy, *The Political Life of Bella Abzug*, 109–10.
173 Charles DeBenedetti and Charles Chatfield, *An American Ordeal: The Antiwar Movement of the Vietnam Era* (Syracuse University Press, 1990), 331.
174 Love, *Feminists Who Changed America*, 3.
175 Braun Levine and Thom, *Bella Abzug*, 110.
176 "Bella Abzug, March 18, 1973," SCPC WSP Records, A1:1, National Consultative Committee Minutes and Memos—Aug 1970–1973.
177 "Kaleidoscope: Tribune of International Women's Year," CHM WFP, 5:11, WFP Women 1975.
178 Myra Macpherson, "Bella Abzug, Champion of Women," *The Washington Post*, April 2, 1998, B1.
179 Dreier, *The 100 Greatest Americans of the 20th Century*, 319.
180 "Memo—Special Commemorative Issue, 1970," UWS SWAP Records, 3:13, WSP 1962–2000, 21.
181 "Press Release, 70," SCPC WSP Records, C1:3, WSP Related Material About Bella Abzug.
182 Swerdlow, *Women Strike for Peace*, 153; WSPers, Congress, Jail, SCPC WSP Records ACC 94A-005:1, May 11, 1972—Sit in in Rep Carl Albert's Office.
183 "Message to WSP National Conference, California, December 9, 1972," UCB WFP Records, 6:6, Office Files—National Conference, Santa Barbara, 1972.
184 WSPers, Congress, Jail, SCPC WSP Records ACC 94A-005:1, May 11, 1972—Sit in in Rep Carl Albert's Office.
185 "Bella: Our Woman of the Year," SCPC WSP Records, C1:3, WSP Related Material About Bella Abzug.
186 Nadine Brozan, "Chronicle: Looking Back at a Spontaneous Moment in the History of Women," *The New York Times*, December 6, 1993, B7.
187 Based on a digital archival review of *The New York Times*, *The Washington Post*, *Chicago Tribune*, *The Boston Globe*, and *Los Angeles Times* from 1960 to 1970. Bella Abzug appeared in articles concerning WSP activity only twice, both coming in the first half of 1969.
188 Zarnow, *Battling Bella*, 39.
189 John J. Goldman, "Former N.Y. Rep. Bella Abzug Dies at 77," *Los Angeles Times*, April 1, 1998, A10; Laura Mansnerus, "Bella Abzug, 77, Congresswoman and a Founding Feminist, Is Dead," *The New York Times*, April 1, 1998, A1; Claudia Levy, "Feminist, Congresswoman Bella Abzug Dies at 77," *The Washington Post*, April 1, 1998, B6; Zarnow writes that Abzug "rarely corrected those who assumed she had been there from the start," *Battling Bella*, 39.
190 "Guide to the Seattle Women Act for Peace Records," University Libraries, University of Washington, Seattle. https://archiveswest.orbiscascade.org/ark:80444/xv49597. Last accessed January 9, 2025; "Women Strike for Peace," Jewish Women's Archive. https://jwa.org/thisweek/nov/01/1961/wsfp. Last accessed February 12, 2025.

191 Love, *Feminists Who Changed America*, 3.
192 Nancy F. Cott, "What's in a Name? The Limits of 'Social Feminism;' or, Expanding the Vocabulary of Women's History?" *The Journal of American History* 76, no. 3 (1989): 821.
193 Claire Goldberg Moses, "'What's in a Name?" On Writing the History of Feminism,' *Feminist Studies* 38, no. 3 (2012): 765.
194 Goldberg Moses, "'What's in a Name?" 767.
195 Goldberg Moses, "'What's in a Name?" 757–79.
196 Swerdlow, *Women Strike for Peace*, 54.
197 Ellen Malos, "Introduction," in *The Politics of Housework*, ed. Ellen Malos (Allison & Busby, 1980): 1.
198 Pat Mainardi, "The Politics of Housework," *Ms.* 2, no. 6 (1992): 40–41.
199 Simone de Beauvoir, "Simone de Beauvoir Talks about Sartre," *Ms.* 12 (August 1983): 87–90; Micaela Di Leonardo, "Morals, Mothers, and Militarism: Antimilitarism and Feminist Theory," *Feminist Studies* 11, no. 3 (1985): 615. Intriguingly, de Beauvoir's criticism followed her earlier expression of "solidarity" with WSP, "Message from Simone de Beauvoir, 1964," SCPC WSP Records, ACC 01A-005, National WSP Statements About, "Message from Simone de Beauvoir, 1964."
200 Di Leonardo, "Morals, Mothers, and Militarism," 599–617.
201 Di Leonardo, "Morals, Mothers, and Militarism," 602, 612; Velma García-Gorena, *Mothers and the Mexican Antinuclear Power Movement* (University of Arizona Press, 1999): 121–22.
202 Ruddick, *Maternal Thinking*; Sara Ruddick, "Preservative Love and Military Destruction: Some Reflections on Mothering and Peace," in *Mothering: Essays in Feminist Theory*, ed. Joyce Trebilcot (Rowman & Littlefield, 1983), 231–62; Jean Keller, "Rethinking Ruddick and the Ethnocentrism Critique of Maternal Thinking," *Hypatia* 25, no. 4 (2010): 834–51. See also, Jodi York, "The Truth(s) About Women and Peace," *Peace Review* 8, no. 3 (1996): 323–29; Nancy Scheper-Hughes, "Maternal Thinking and the Politics of War," in *The Women and War Reader*, ed. Lois Ann Lorentzen and Jennifer Turpin (New York University Press, 1998), 227–33.
203 Alice Echols, "'Women Power' and Women's Liberation: Exploring the Relationship Between the Antiwar Movement and the Women's Liberation Movement," in *Give Peace a Chance: Exploring the Vietnam Antiwar Movement*, ed. Melvin Small (Syracuse University Press, 1992), 176.
204 Wesley G. Phelps, "Women's Pentagon Action: The Persistence of Radicalism and Direct-Action Civil Disobedience in the Age of Reagan," *Peace and Change* 39, no. 3 (2014): 352.
205 "Highlights from November 5–6 Minneapolis Meeting of Women's Peace Presence," SCPC Women's Peace Presence to Stop Project ELF.
206 "Agenda for UPFA WILPF Meeting 10/9 in Ithaca," SL WEFPJ, 1.2 Minutes, agendas, etc., 1982–July 1983.
207 Love, *Feminists Who Changed America*, 453; Letter from Mary Clarke to Dagmar Wilson, March 8, 1974, SCPC WSP Records, ACC 2013–050:11, WSP Friends Personal Correspondence; Alice Kessler-Harris, "Keynote address to Fifteenth Annual Women's History Month Conference" (Paper Presented at the Fifteenth Annual Women's History Month Conference, Sarah Lawrence College, New York, March 1, 2013).
208 Swerdlow, *Women Strike for Peace*, 233–34.
209 Swerdlow, "Ladies' Day at the Capitol," 516.

210 Ruth Milkman and Rayna Rapp, "Preface," *Feminist Studies* 8, no. 3 (1982): 491.
211 "Progress Report on WSP Research," SCPC WSP Records, C1:3, Research on WSP by Amy Swerdlow.
212 "WSP Commemorative Journal, 1961–1979," SCPC WSP Records, A1:2, Documents Describing WSP History.
213 Amy Swerdlow, "'Pure Milk, Not Poison': Women Strike for Peace and the Test Ban Treaty of 1963," in *Rocking the Ship of State: Toward a Feminist Peace Politics*, ed. Adrienne Harris and Ynestra King (Westview Press, 1989), 227.
214 Nadine Brozan, "Chronicle: Looking Back at a Spontaneous Moment in the History of Women," *The New York Times*, December 6, 1993, B7.
215 Swerdlow, *Women Strike for Peace*, 233; Love, *Feminists Who Changed America*, 453.
216 Naomi Goodman, "Review: WSP: Traditional Motherhood and Radical Politics in the 1960s, by Amy Swerdlow," *Fellowship* (July/August 1994): 27.
217 "An Open Letter to the Women's Pentagon Action, 1981," SCPC Women's Pentagon Action
218 "Alice Hamburg's History of San Francisco Women's Peace Office," UCB WFP Records 1:13, Women's Peace Office (WPO) History, 6.
219 Judith Scheer, "Local Activist, Alice Hamburg, Dies at 95," *The Berkeley Daily Planet*, November 14, 2001.
220 Taylor, *We Made a Difference* 2, 111.
221 Eleanor Garst, "A Memory of Ava Helen Pauling," SCPC WSP Records, ACC 96A-012:1.
222 "Trip to Hanoi, Cora Weiss," 1969, SCPC Cora Weiss, 1, Women Strike for Peace '62–'72, 6.
223 Wilson interview, April 15, 1989, ARS.0056.
224 Alonso, *Peace as a Women's Issue*, 204–31.
225 Chidgey, *Feminist Afterlives*; Chidgey and Garde-Hansen, *Museums, Archives and Protest Memory*.
226 For example, see Echols, "'We Gotta Get Out of This Place,' 62; Cobble, Gordon, and Henry, *Feminism Unfinished*, xiv.
227 Francesca Polletta and James M. Jasper, "Collective Identity and Social Movements," *Annual Review of Sociology* 27 (2001): 283–305.
228 Swerdlow, *Women Strike for Peace*, 234.
229 Levy, *The Political Life of Bella Abzug*, 67.
230 "Feminist Revolutionary Force for Change," in *We Are Ordinary Women: A Chronicle of the Puget Sound Women's Peace Camp* (Seal Press, 1985) 17; Kyle Harvey, *American Anti-Nuclear Activism, 1975–1990: The Challenge of Peace* (Palgrave Macmillan, 2014).

Chapter Six

1 Ruth Pinkson interview, October 1987, ARS.0056, Stanford University Archive of Recorded Sound.
2 "Unsigned letter to WSP Branch Leaders, March 28, 1989," Swarthmore College Peace Collection, WSP Records SCPC-DG-115 (hereafter SCPC WSP Records), 90A-028:4, Comprehensive Test Ban Correspondence.

3 Robert Scheer, *With Enough Shovels: Reagan, Bush, and Nuclear War* (Random House, 1982), 18–26, 138–40; "The Dirt on T. K. Jones," *The New York Times*, March 19, 1982, A30; Carol Cohn, "'Clean Bombs' and Clean Language," in *Women, Militarism, and War: Essays in History, Politics and Social Theory*, ed. Jean Bethke Elshtain and Sheila Tobias (Rowman & Littlefield, 1990), 34.

4 "1949 Test Linked to Radiation in Northwest," *The New York Times*, March 9, 1986, 35; Judith Miller, "4 Veterans Suing U.S. Over Exposure in '54 Atom Test," *The New York Times*, September 20, 1982, B15.

5 Pinkson interview, October 1987, ARS.0056.

6 Taylor, *We Made a Difference*, 155.

7 Paul Valentine, "The Decline of the Demonstration," *The Washington Post*, July 14, 1973, A18; Rose De Wolf, "New War Protest Is Attacked by Apathy," *The Evening Bulletin*, April 27, 1973.

8 "To SAC, WFO (100–39566) from SA Joseph A. Connors Jr., 11/9/66," American University DC Office of the Women Strike for Peace Records (hereafter AU WSP Records), Box 19, FOIA FBI Files—100–39566 Vol. 15 (1).

9 Lawrence S. Wittner, "The Forgotten Years of the World Nuclear Disarmament Movement, 1975–1978," *Journal of Peace Research* 40, no. 4 (2003): 440; Milton S. Katz, *Ban the Bomb: A History of SANE, The Committee for a SANE Nuclear Policy, 1957–1985* (Greenwood Press, 1986), 136–38.

10 "Ethel Taylor's Address NCC 3/12/73," SCPC WSP Records, A1:1, National Consultative Committee Minutes and Memos 1970–1973.

11 Letter from Ethel Taylor to WSPers, May 2, 1975, SCPC WSP Records, ACC 01A-005:9, Philadelphia Women Strike for Peace.

12 "Minutes: National Conference, Women Strike for Peace, 1974," SCPC WSP Records, A1:3, National Conference—1974, New York, NY.

13 "Minutes: National Conference, Women Strike for Peace, 1974," SCPC WSP Records, A1:3, National Conference—1974, New York, NY; Wittner, "The Forgotten Years" 436; Thomas Borstelmann, *The 1970s: A New Global History from Civil Rights to Economic Inequality* (Princeton University Press, 2011), 236; Jerome Price, *The Antinuclear Movement* (Twayne, 1982), 9.

14 "Minutes: National Conference, Women Strike for Peace, 1974," SCPC WSP Records, A1:3, National Conference—1974, New York, NY.

15 Borstelmann, *The 1970s*, 231; Jonathan H. Adler, "Fables of the Cuyahoga: Reconstructing a History of Environmental Protection," *Fordham Environmental Law Journal* XIV (2002): 90; Adam Rome, "'Give Earth a Chance': The Environmental Movement and the Sixties," *Journal of American History* 90, no. 2 (2003): 525–554; Gene Marine, "Politics of the Environment," *The Nation*, January 26, 1970; Raymond R. Coffey, "Teach-In On the Environment," *The Nation*, April 6, 1970; Nicholas Lemann, "When the Earth Moved," *New Yorker*, April 15, 2013.

16 J. Brooks Flippen, *Nixon and the Environment* (University of New Mexico Press, 2000); Richard Reeves, *President Nixon: Alone in the White House* (Touchstone, 2001), 163; Bruce Schulman, *The Seventies: The Great Shift in American Culture, Society, and Politics* (Da Capo Press, 2002), 30–31.

17 Thomas Raymond Wellock, *Critical Masses: Opposition to Nuclear Power in California, 1958–1978* (University of Wisconsin Press, 1998), 21; Price, *The Antinuclear Movement*,

12; Wittner, "The Forgotten Years," 443. See also Toshihiro Higuchi, *Political Fallout: Nuclear Weapons Testing and the Making of a Global Environmental Crisis* (Stanford University Press, 2020).

18 "Memo—Special Commemorative Issue, 1970," University of Washington, Seattle, Seattle Women Act for Peace Records, 4073 (hereafter UWS SWAP), 3:13, Women Strike for Peace 1962–2000, 22.

19 Letter from Anci Koppel to Ralph Nader, June 25, 1979, UWS SWAP Records, 1:7, General Correspondence, 1978–1979; Letter from Shirley Lens to Kankakee Area Chapter National Audubon Society, December 6, 1974, Chicago History Museum Women for Peace (Chicago, IL) Records (hereafter CHM WFP Records), 7:9, WFP Correspondence 1960–1975; "Memo—Special Commemorative Issue, 1970," UWS SWAP Records, 3:13, Women Strike for Peace 1962–2000; "Press Conference, June 3, 1977," CHM WFP Records, 8:8, WFP Press Releases 1971–1977; "Letter from Hazel Grossman to National Center to Slash Military Spending, April 20, 1976," University of California, Berkely, San Francisco Women for Peace Records BANC MSS 89/132 c (hereafter UCB WFP Records), 7:24, Office Files—General, 1976.

20 Letter from Hazel Grossman to National Center to Slash Military Spending, April 20, 1976, UCB WFP Records, 7–24, Office Files—General, 1976.

21 Letter from Mary Clarke to Dagmar Wilson, August 26, 1977, SCPC WSP Records, ACC 2013-050:11, Women Strike for Peace Friends Personal Correspondence.

22 Edith Villastrigo interview, October 1987, ARS.0056; Taylor, *We Made a Difference*.

23 Letter from Helen Mills to Hazel Grossman, undated, UCB WFP Records, 7:24, Office Files—General, 1976; Letter from Helen Mills to Hazel Grossman, April 9, 1976, UCB WFP Records, 7:30, Nuclear Weapons, 1976; "Women Strike for Peace National Newsletter, June 25, 1976," SCPC WSP Records, ACC 96A-040:2, Carter 1976 Election.

24 Strobe Talbot, *Endgame: The Inside Story of SALT II* (Harper and Row Publishers, 1980).

25 Taylor, *We Made a Difference*, 103–5.

26 James T. Patterson, *Restless Giant: The United States from Watergate to Bush v. Gore* (Oxford University Press, 2005), 121–23.

27 Burton I. Kaufman, *Presidential Profiles: The Carter Years* (Facts on File, 2006), 5.

28 Letter from Anci Koppel to Jimmy Carter, June 14, 1979, UWS SWAP Records, 1–6, General Correspondence, 1967–1977.

29 "Women's Group Charges Administration with Nuclear Insanity, August 21, 1980"; "For Immediate Release, December 13, 1979," SCPC WSP Records, D1:1, Literature 1979–1985.

30 "Ethel Taylor, January 18," SCPC WSP Records, ACC 01A-040, National Conference 1978—SALT II.

31 Robert Surbrug, Jr., *Beyond Vietnam: The Politics of Protest in Massachusetts, 1974–1990* (University of Massachusetts Press, 2009), 258; Gerard J. De Groot, *The Bomb: A Life* (Harvard University Press, 2004), 303.

32 "Women Strike for Peace Urges Carter to Move on SALT II," SCPC WSP Records, D1:1, Literature 1979–1985.

33 Robert Scheer, "Bush Assails Carter Defense Strategy," *Los Angeles Times*, January 24, 1980, B1; Wade Greene, "Rethinking the Unthinkable," *The New York Times*, March 15, 1981, SM12; John Trinkl, "Struggles for Disarmament in the USA," in *Reshaping*

the US Left: Popular Struggles in the 1980s, ed. Mike Davis and Michael Sprinker (Verso, 1988), 51.

34 Alexander Cockburn and James Ridgeway, "The Freeze Movement Versus Reagan," *New Left Review* 137 (January–February 1983), 6; Lawrence S. Wittner, "The Nuclear Freeze and Its Impact," *Arms Control Association.*

35 Frances B. McCrea and Gerald E. Markle, *Minutes to Midnight: Nuclear Weapons Protest in America* (Sage Publications, 1989), 97.

36 Randall Forsberg, *Call to Halt the Nuclear Arms Race: Proposal for a Mutual US-Soviet Nuclear-Weapon Freeze* (American Friends Service Committee, 1980).

37 Bradford Martin, *The Other Eighties: A Secret History of America in the Age of Reagan* (Hill and Wang, 2011), 4.

38 McCrea and Markle, *Minutes to Midnight*, 108.

39 Jonathan Schell, "Reflections: The Fate of the Earth—A Republic of Insects and Grass," *New Yorker*, 1 February 1, 1982, 47–113; "Reflections: The Fate of the Earth—The Second Death," *New Yorker*, February 8, 1982, 48–109; "Reflections: The Fate of the Earth—The Choice," *New Yorker*, February 15, 1982, 45–107; Jonathan Schell, *The Fate of the Earth and the Abolition* (Stanford University Press, 2000); John Leonard, "Books of the Times: The Fate of the Earth," *The New York Times*, April 8, 1982, C15; Richard Rhodes, "Schell's Timely Nuclear Nightmare Right on Target," *Chicago Tribune*, April 18, 1982, H1.

40 Tom Shales, "'The Day After' Approaches," *The Washington Post*, October 11, 1983, C1; John Corry, "'The Day After': TV as a Rallying Force," *The New York Times*, November 20, 1983, H1; Kenneth J. Cooper, "For Some Viewers, a Sleepless Night After Watching TV's 'The Day After'," *The Boston Globe*, November 22, 1983, 6.

41 SCPC Greenham Common Women's Peace Camp, Collection of High Schools Students' Notes.

42 "Warning on Utah Fallout is Termed Inadequate," *The New York Times*, September 22, 1982, A20; "1949 Test Linked to Radiation in Northwest," *The New York Times*, March 9, 1986, 35; "Excess of Leukemia Detected in Fallout Zones, Doctor Says," *The New York Times*, September 18, 1982, 7.

43 Judith Miller, "4 Veterans Suing U.S. Over Exposure in '54 Atom Test," *The New York Times*, September 20, 1982, B15; Judy Mann, "Atomic Victims," *The Washington Post*, April 20, 1983, C1; "Reagan's Advisers Push Veto of 'Atomic Veterans' Measure," *Chicago Tribune*, May 3, 1988, 16; Howard Ball, "In the 1950s, the Government said its atomic tests in Nevada were safe. Now, faced with a high cancer rate, people living downwind of the test sites are disillusioned. Did Washington lie?" *The New York Times*, February 9, 1986, SM33; George Raine, "Expert Faults U.S. on 50's Atom Tests," *The New York Times*, October 10, 1982, 32; Thomas H. Saffer and Orville E. Kelly, *Countdown Zero* (Putnam, 1982); Tod Ensign and Michael Uhl, *G.I. Guinea Pigs: How the Pentagon Exposed Our Troops to Dangers More Deadly Than War* (Playboy Press, 1980); Harvey Wasserman and Norman Solomon, *Killing Our Own: The Disaster of America's Experience with Atomic Radiation* (Delacorte Press, 1982); Leslie J. Freeman, *Nuclear Witnesses: Insiders Speak Out* (Norton, 1981); Howard L. Rosenberg, *Atomic Soldiers: American Victims of Nuclear Experiments* (Beacon Press, 1980).

44 Paul J. Crutzen and John W. Birks, "The Atmosphere After a Nuclear War: Twilight at Noon," *Ambio* 2, no. 2–3 (1982): 114–25; Carl Sagan, "The Nuclear Winter," *The Boston Globe*, October 30, 1983, SMA4.

45 Scheer, *With Enough Shovels*, 18; Terry Atlas, "A Grim Picture of Nuclear War," *Chicago Tribune*, October 31, 1983, 8; Philip Shabecoff, "Grimmer View Is Given of Nuclear War Effects," *The New York Times*, October 31, 1983, A16; Philip J. Hilts, "Scientists Say Nuclear War Could Cause Climactic Disaster," *The Washington Post*, November 1, 1983, A1.

46 Figures vary from 750,000 to over one million—Paul Boyer, Promises to Keep: The United States Since World War II (Wadsworth, 2005), 330; Vincent Intondi, *Saving the World from Nuclear War: The June 12, 1982, Disarmament Rally and Beyond* (Johns Hopkins University Press, 2023); Wittner, *Toward Nuclear Abolition*, 176.

47 Paul L. Montgomery, "Throngs Fill Manhattan to Protest Nuclear Weapons," *The New York Times*, June 13, 1982, 1.

48 "We Come to Mourn, Rage & Defy!: Statement of Unity," *Peace News*, December 12, 1980, 8.

49 Phelps, "Women's Pentagon Action," 340.

50 Jon Coburn, "'It Provoked the Question: Did Women Do Anything for Peace Before?": Historical Amnesia and the Disappearing Memory of Women's Antinuclear Activism,' *DEP* 54 (December 2024): 166–85; Louise Krasniewicz, *Nuclear Summer: The Clash of Communities at the Seneca Women's Peace Encampment* (Cornell University Press, 1994); Sasha Roseneil, *Common Women, Uncommon Practices: The Queer Feminisms of Greenham* (Cassell Publishing, 2000); Niamh Moore, "Remembering an Eco/Feminist Peace Camp," in *Feminism and Protest Camps: Entanglements, Critiques and Re-Imaginings*, ed. Catherine Eschle and Alison Bartlett (Bristol University Press, 2023) 237; Alison Bartlett, "Sites of Feminist Activism: Remembering Pine Gap," *Continuum* 30, no. 3 (2016): 307–315; "Upstate Feminist Peace Alliance Meeting, October 9, Ithaca 1982," Schlesinger Library, Records of the Women's Encampment for a Future of Peace & Justice (hereafter SL WEFPJ), 1.2 Minutes, agendas, etc., 1982—July 1983; Ann Arbor Women's Peace Camp Resource Handbook, October 1983, SCPC Ann Arbor Women's Peace Camp, Oct 1983; "Why a Minnesota Women's Peace Camp? 1983" SCPC Minnesota Women's Camp for Peace and Justice; "Phila. Women's Peace Encampment," SCPC Philadelphia Women's Encampment, Box 1, Outreach and Coalition Work.

51 De Groot, *The Bomb*, 322.

52 Phelps, "Women's Pentagon Action," 352.

53 Kyle Harvey, *American Anti-Nuclear Activism, 1975–1990: The Challenge of Peace* (Palgrave Macmillan, 2014), 78.

54 "Congressional Action Alert, January 20, 1986," American University DC Office of the Women Strike for Peace Records (hereafter AU WSP Records), Box 16, WAND (Women's Action for Nuclear Disarmament), 1984–1993.

55 Johanna Brenner, "Beyond Essentialism: Feminist Theory and Strategy in the Peace Movement," in *Reshaping the US Left: Popular Struggles in the 1980s*, ed. Mike Davis and Michael Sprinker (Verso, 1988), 104.

56 Harriet Hyman Alonso, *Peace as a Women's Issue: A History of the U.S. Movement for World Peace and Women's Rights* (Syracuse University Press, 1993), 240.

57 Wittner, *Confronting the Bomb*, 153, 156.

58 "Dear Sisters Newsletter, August 1982," SCPC WSP Records, ACC 2013-050:17, Women Strike for Peace 1981–1983.

59 Judy Mann, "Stop the Arms Race: It Seems So Simple," *The Washington Post*, May 8, 1981, B1.

60 "Minutes of Conference," SCPC WSP Records, ACC 90A-028:1, Conference 1983; Letter from Edith Villastrigo to Janet Harrell, December 29, 1983, AU WSP Records, Box 8, Greenham Common Women, 1983–1987; Letter from Hazel Grossman to 'Fellow Peace Workers,' August 1983, UCB WFP Records, 9:26, University of California Nuclear Weapons Lab Conversion Project and Livermore Action Group 1983.
61 "An Open Letter to the Women's Pentagon Action, 1981," SCPC Women's Pentagon Action.
62 Ruth Rosen, "Next Time, Listen to Mother," *Los Angeles Times*, August 7, 1997.
63 Colman McCarthy, "Mothers, Sons and America's 'War Fever'," *The Washington Post*, February 3, 1980, H10.
64 "Reports from Branches (Highlighted)," SCPC WSP Records, A1:3, National Conference—1982, Philadelphia, PA.
65 Colin S. Gray and Keith Payne, "Victory is Possible," *Foreign Policy* 39 (Summer 1980): 14–27; Wade Greene, "Rethinking the Unthinkable," *The New York Times*, March 15, 1981, SM12.
66 "I Refuse to be One of 20 Million 'Acceptable' Dead," UCB WFP Records, 9:20, "I Refuse to be One of 20 Million Acceptable Dead" Campaign, 1982; "Reagan Will Be the Death Of Us!" AU WSP Records, Box 14, Reagan Policy, 1980–1987.
67 Taylor, *We Made a Difference*, 132.
68 Note from Mariene River, UCB WFP Records, 9:20, "I Refuse to be One of 20 Million Acceptable Dead" Campaign, 1982.
69 *The Bulletin of the Atomic Scientists*, February 1983, 55.
70 Cohn, "'Clean Bombs' and Clean Language," 34.
71 Don Oberdorfer, *The Turn: How the Cold War Came to an End: The United States and the Soviet Union, 1983–1990* (Jonathan Cape, 1992), 25; De Groot, *The Bomb*, 313.
72 Boyer, *Promises to Keep*, 394; Edmund Morris, *Dutch: A Memoir of Ronald Reagan* (HarperCollins, 2000), 477–8, 594–9.
73 "Stop Star Wars: A Campaign of Women Strike for Peace," SCPC WSP Records, ACC 90A-028:3, WSP Internal Notes, Goals etc. Star Wars.
74 "Stop Star Wars: A Campaign of Women Strike for Peace," SCPC WSP Records, ACC 90A-028:3, WSP Internal Notes, Goals etc. Star Wars.
75 "A Basic Primer on Star Wars for the Legitimately Confused," SCPC WSP Records, ACC 01A-076, Material from Refile Box (1992), i, 7.
76 Letter from Ethel Taylor, SCPC WSP Records, ACC 90A-028:3, Slide Show—Final Script and Packet.
77 "Star Wars: A Short Course for the Legitimately Confused," SCPC WSP Records, ACC 90A-028:3, Slide Show—Final Script and Packet.
78 Letter from Sister Diane Edwards IHM, SCPC WSP Records, ACC 90A-028:3, Primer Promotion Religious Orders.
79 "Stop Star Wars: A Campaign of Women Strike for Peace," SCPC WSP Records, ACC 90A-028:3, WSP Internal Notes, Goals etc. Star Wars; Ethel Taylor interview, October 5, 1987, ARS.0056.
80 Attendance at the 1962 national conference was 105; 82 participated in 1964; 76 WSP activists took part in 1966; while 82 travelled to Santa Barbara in 1972, at a time many considered the group to be at a nadir. SCPC WSP Records, A1:1; SCPC WSP Records ACC 90A-028:1.
81 Taylor, *We Made a Difference*, 129.

82 Letter from Noreen Warnock, CHM WFP Records, 8:11, Misc. Administration Materials.
83 Unsigned letter to Dagmar Wilson, March 8, 1983, SCPC WSP Records, ACC 2013-050:17, 21st Annual National Conference.
84 "Minutes National Conference 1984," SCPC WSP Records, ACC 90A-028:1, Conference 1984.
85 "Minutes National Conference 1984," SCPC WSP Records, ACC 90A-028:1, Conference 1984.
86 "A Summary of New York WSP Report Made at Conference 1986," SCPC WSP Records, ACC 90A-028:1, 1986 National Conference.
87 "Memo—Special Commemorative Issue, 1970," UWS SWAP Records, 3:13, Women Strike for Peace 1962–2000, 22.
88 Taylor, *We Made a Difference*, 151, 153.
89 Trinkl, "Struggles for Disarmament in the USA," 56–58.
90 WAND Education Fund, *Turnabout: The Emerging New Realism in the Nuclear Age* (WAND Education Fund, 1986), 1.
91 Trinkl, "Struggles for Disarmament in the USA," 56.
92 Cockburn and Ridgeway, "The Freeze Movement Versus Reagan," 11.
93 Martin, *The Other Eighties*, xiv–xv.
94 "Sunday Afternoon, October 3, 1982," SCPC WSP Records, A1:3, National Conference—1982, Philadelphia, PA.
95 "The WSP Foundation: Women Strike for Peace Research & Education Fund, Inc." SCPC WSP Records, ACC 2013-050:21st Annual National Conference.
96 "I Refuse to be One of 20 Million 'Acceptable' Dead," UCB WFP Records, 9–20, "I Refuse to be One of 20 Million Acceptable Dead" Campaign, 1982.
97 Unsigned letter to Dagmar Wilson, March 8, 1983, SCPC WSP Records, ACC 2013-050:17, 21st Annual National Conference; "In Preparation for 1983 WSP Conference: Issue for Discussion—Reexamination of WSP Membership Policy," SCPC WSP Records, ACC 2013-050:17, 21st Annual National Conference.
98 Letter from Ruth Tabak to Dagmar Wilson, December 23, 1982, SCPC WSP Records, ACC 2013-050:17, 21st Annual National Conference; "Procedures for Funding Requests Made to the WSP Research & Education Fund, Inc." SCPC WSP Records, ACC 2013-050:17, 21st Annual National Conference.
99 Unsigned letter to Dagmar Wilson, March 8, 1983, SCPC WSP Records, ACC 2013-050:17, 21st Annual National Conference; "In Preparation for 1983 WSP Conference: Issue for Discussion—Reexamination of WSP Membership Policy," SCPC WSP Records, ACC 2013-050:17, 21st Annual National Conference; Note from Edith Laub to Edith Villastrigo, April 22, 1983, AU WSP Records, Box 2, History 1961–1994.
100 "In Preparation for 1983 WSP Conference: Issue for Discussion—Reexamination of WSP Membership Policy," SCPC WSP Records, ACC 2013-050:17, 21st Annual National Conference.
101 Note from Edith Laub to Edith Villastrigo, April 22, 1983, AU WSP Records, Box 2, History 1961–1994.
102 Unsigned letter to Women Strike for Peace, October 19, 1987, SCPC WSP Records, ACC 90A-028:1, Miscellaneous Correspondence; Letter from Ethel Taylor to Helen, November 4, 1987, SCPC WSP Records, ACC 90A-028:1, Miscellaneous Correspondence.

103 "Report to May WSP Board Meeting, Libby Frank," AU WSP Records, Box 1, Board—1988–1989, 1992.
104 Wittner, *Confronting the Bomb*, 156.
105 "In Preparation for 1983 WSP Conference: Issue for Discussion—Reexamination of WSP Membership Policy," SCPC WSP Records, ACC 2013-050:17, 21st Annual National Conference; "Minutes National Conference 1984, Presentation of Organizational Matters by Pat Gross," SCPC WSP Records, ACC 90A-028:1, Conference 1984.
106 Marilyn Gittell and Teresa Shtob, "Changing Women's Roles in Political Volunteerism and Reform of the City," *Signs* 5, no. 3 (1980): S77; National Organization for Women, *Task Force on Volunteerism, Position Paper* (National Organization for Women, 1973); Peggy Petrzelka and Susan E. Mannon, "Keepin' This Little Town Going: Gender and Volunteerism in Rural America," *Gender and Society* 20, no. 2 (2006): 236–58.
107 "Meeting Notes for Thurs, 5/4/88," UCB WFP Records, 11:8, Office Files—General, 1988.
108 Katz, *Ban the Bomb*, 162; McCrea and Markle, *Minutes to Midnight*, 112.
109 Geraldine Ferraro, *Ferraro: My Story* (Northwestern University Press, 2004), 311.
110 Swerdlow interview, September 25, 1987, *ARS.0056*.
111 McCrea and Markle, *Minutes to Midnight*, 112.
112 Robert Surbrug, Jr., *Beyond Vietnam: The Politics of Protest in Massachusetts, 1974–1990* (University of Massachusetts Press, 2009), 169.
113 Letter from Hazel Grossman, March 16, 1984, UCB WFP Records, 10:3, Office Files—General, 1984.
114 "Minutes National Conference 1984," SCPC WSP Records, ACC 90A-028:1, Conference 1984.
115 "Ethel Taylor Speech to 23rd Anniversary," UCB WFP Records, 10:4, Office Files—National, 1984.
116 Rose Dellamonica interview, September 10, 1985, ARS.0056.
117 "The House: Test-Ban Treaty," *Los Angeles Times*, March 4, 1986, 2.
118 "Statement of Support for J. J. Res. 3 by Women Strike for Peace to the Subcommittee on Arms Control, International Security and Science, May 8, 1985," UCB WFP Records, 10:13, Office Files—WSP National, 1985.
119 Ronald Reagan, *An American Life: The Autobiography* (Simon and Schuster, 1990), 219–20.
120 Ronald Reagan, "Address to the Veterans of Foreign Wars Convention in Chicago," August 18, 1980. University of California, Santa Barbara, *The American Presidency Project*. https://www.presidency.ucsb.edu/documents/address-the-veterans-foreign-wars-convention-chicago. Last accessed January 9, 2025.
121 Mary McGrory, "Viet Talk Hurting Reagan," *The Boston Globe*, August 24, 1980, A7.
122 Daniel Abramson, "Maya Lin and the 1960s: Monuments, Time Lines, and Minimalism," *Critical Inquiry* 22, no. 4 (1996): 679–709; Robin Wagner-Pacifici and Barry Schwartz, "The Vietnam Veterans Memorial: Commemorating a Difficult Past," *American Journal of Sociology* 97, no. 2 (1991): 376–420.
123 John Bodnar, *Remaking America: Public Memory, Commemoration, and Patriotism in the Twentieth Century* (Princeton University Press, 1992), 3–12; Tom Carhart, "Insulting Vietnam Vets," *The New York Times*, October 24, 1981, 23.

124 Jack Mabley, "A Life-Death Matter: Nuclear 'Folly' Haunts Election," *Chicago Tribune*, August 21, 1980, 4; Rowland Evans and Robert Novak, "Making Reagan 'Fail-Safe'," *The Washington Post*, August 22, 1980, A15; Joseph Kraft, "Reagan Shoots a Hole in His Defense Policy," *The Boston Globe*, August 21, 1980, 19; Lou Cannon, "Reagan: 'Peace Through Strength'," *The Washington Post*, August 19, 1980, A1; UPI, "Powell: Reagan Is 'Trying to Have It Both Ways'," *The Washington Post*, August 19, 1980, A4.

125 Phillip Jenkins, *Decade of Nightmares: The End of the Sixties and the Making of Eighties America* (Oxford University Press, 2006), 11.

126 Bradford Martin, *The Other Eighties: A Secret History of America in the Age of Reagan* (Hill and Wang, 2011), x.

127 Todd Gitlin, *The Sixties: Years of Hope, Days of Rage* (Bantam Books, 1993), 435; Tom Hayden, *Reunion: A Memoir* (Random House, 1988), 501–7.

128 Peter Collier and David Horowitz, *The Destructive Generation: Second Thoughts About the Sixties* (Summit Books, 1989); Gil Troy, *Morning in America: How Ronald Reagan Invented the 1980s* (Princeton University Press, 2005), 145.

129 David T. Dellinger, *More Power Than We Know: The People's Movement Toward Democracy* (Anchor Press, 1975); Mary McGrory, "Women's Strike for Peace Finally Makes It," *New York Post*, March 8, 1977, 24; Letter from Amy Swerdlow, 78/79, SCPC WSP Records, A3:13, 1974–1979.

130 Jill Liddington, *The Road to Greenham Common: Feminism and Anti-Militarism in Britain Since 1820* (Syracuse University Press, 1991), 2–3. The peace camp movement was distinctively interested in both learning and recording its history. See Coburn, "The Question Was Asked," 178–83.

131 "A Call to Action, Seneca Army Depot Summer 1984," AU WSP Records, Box 14, Seneca Women's Peace Encampment, 1983–1984.

132 Mima Cataldo et al., *The Women's Encampment for a Future of Peace and Justice* (Temple University Press, 1987)10–13.

133 "Why a Women's Peace Camp?" AU WSP Records, Box 14, Seneca Women's Peace Encampment, 1983–1984.

134 "Women in the Peace Movement: Conference on the Fate of the Earth, September 22, 1984," AU WSP Records, Box 14, Seneca Women's Peace Encampment, 1983–1984.

135 Letter from Amy Swerdlow, 78/79, SCPC WSP Records, A3:13, 1974–1979.

136 "Women in the Peace Movement," AU WSP Records, Box 8, Greenham Common Women, 1983–1987.

137 "San Francisco Women for Peace Newsletter, April 1983," UCB WFP Records 1:39, Newsletters 1981–1983.

138 Letter from Cora Weiss, April 1984, UCB WFP Records, 1:8, Historical Information for Vietnam Women's Association, 1984.

139 Letter from Hazel Grossman to Cora Weiss, January 29, 1985, UCB WFP Records, 1:8, Historical Information for Vietnam Women's Association, 1984; Letter from Hazel Grossman to Anne Spake, May 25, 1984, UCB WFP Records, 1:8, Historical Information for Vietnam Women's Association, 1984.

140 *Peacework: Oral Histories of Women Peace Activists, ed.* Judith Porter Adams (Twayne, 1991), 1–7; Jonathan Manton, "Celebrating 100 years of the Women's International League for Peace and Freedom," *Stanford University Libraries*. http://library.stanford.edu/blogs/stanford-libraries-blog/2015/04/celebrating-100-years-womens-international-league-peace-and.

141 "Women for Peace Newsletter," UCB WFP Records, 1:8, Historical Information for Vietnam Women's Association, 1984.
142 "Women's Peace Office (WPO) History—The Peace Movement in Transition by Alice Hamburg," UCB WFP Records, 1:12, SF WILPF History by Alice Hamburg, 1985–1986.
143 SCPC WSP Records, ACC 2013-050:4, MD (Draft of Ethel Taylor's Book), 1996; Taylor interview, October 5, 1987, ARS.0056; UWS SWAP Records, 2:31, Oral History Class at Seattle Central Community College, 1979, n.d.
144 Swerdlow interview, September 25, 1987, ARS.0056; Wilson interview, April 15, 1989, ARS.0056; Villastrigo interview, October 1987, ARS.0056; Duckles interview, November 22, 1985, ARS.0056.
145 Letter from Amy Swerdlow, 78/79, SCPC WSP Records, A3:13, 1974–1979; Letter from Amy Swerdlow to Dagmar Wilson, February 9, 1982, SCPC WSP Records, ACC 2013-050:17, Draft Chapters 1–5, Amy Swerdlow's Dissertation with Dagmar's Biographical Corrections 1981.
146 Letter from Amy Swerdlow, 78/79, SCPC WSP Records, A3:13, 1974–1979
147 "San Francisco Women for Peace Newsletter October 1985," UCB WFP Records 2:3, Guide to Peace and Action 1985–1987, 3.
148 Letter from Amy Swerdlow to Dagmar Wilson, July 31, 1981, SCPC WSP Records, ACC 2013-050:15, Women Strike for Peace History.
149 Letter from Amy Swerdlow to Dagmar Wilson, December 14, 1981, SCPC WSP Records, ACC 2013-050:17, Draft Chapters 1–5, Amy Swerdlow's Dissertation with Dagmar's Biographical Corrections 1981; Letter from Amy Swerdlow to Dagmar Wilson, February 9, 1982, SCPC WSP Records, ACC 2013-050:17, Draft Chapters 1–5, Amy Swerdlow's Dissertation with Dagmar's Biographical Corrections 1981.
150 Letter from Amy Swerdlow to Dagmar Wilson, July 31, 1981, SCPC WSP Records, ACC 2013-050:15, Women Strike for Peace History.
151 Letter from Cora Weiss, April 1984, UCB WFP Records, 1:8, Historical Information for Vietnam Women's Association, 1984.
152 Letter from Hazel Grossman to Orah, May 29, 1984, UCB WFP Records, 1:8, Historical Information for Vietnam Women's Association, 1984.
153 Letter from Hazel Grossman to Anne Spake, May 25, 1984, UCB WFP Records, 1:8, Historical Information for Vietnam Women's Association, 1984 Letter from Anci Koppel to Amy Swerdlow, March 16, 1994, UWS SWAP Records, 1:21, General Correspondence, May 1993–1994.
154 Boyer, *Promises to Keep*, 394.
155 Thomas G. Goodnight, "Reagan, Vietnam, and Central America: Public Memory and the Politics of Fragmentation," in *Beyond the Rhetorical Presidency*, ed. Martin J. Medhurst (Texas A&M University Press, 2004), 127, 151.
156 Goodnight, "Reagan, Vietnam, and Central America," 123; Villastrigo interview, October 1987, ARS.0056; "Minutes of Meeting: Women Strike for Peace Annual National Conference 11/10/83–11/13/83," SCPC WSP Records, ACC 90A-028:1, Conference 1983.
157 Swerdlow interview, September 25, 1987, ARS.0056.
158 Pinkson interview, October 1987, ARS.0056; Allen interview, April 26, 1989, ARS.0056.
159 Todd Gitlin, *The Sixties: Years of Hope, Days of Rage* (Bantam Books, 1993), 435;

Tom Hayden, *Reunion: A Memoir* (Random House, 1988), 435; "No Weapons, No Advisers, No Vietnam in El Salvador," CHM WFP Records, 2:1, WFP El Salvador 1981–1982.

160 Martin, *The Other Eighties*, xii.

161 "Dear Friend of Peace, November 15, 1981," "WFP Anniversary, 11/16/86," UCB WFP Records, 15:10, Women's Peace Office—Activities and Campaigns, 1980–1989.

162 "Dear Friends, August 1985," UCB WFP Records, 15:10, Women's Peace Office—Activities and Campaigns, 1980–1989.

163 Newill interview, February 23, 1980, ARS.0056.

164 Esther Newill Presentation on Santa Rita Prison, Livermore Protests, August 1983, Women's International League for Peace and Freedom Collection ARS.0056.

165 Swerdlow interview, September 25, 1987, ARS.0056.

166 Taylor interview, October 5, 1987, ARS.0056.

167 Villastrigo interview, October 1987, ARS.0056.

168 Taylor interview, October 5, 1987, ARS.0056.

169 Taylor interview, October 5, 1987, ARS.0056; Villastrigo interview, October 1987, ARS.0056.

170 William L. Howarth, "Some Principles of Autobiography," *New Literary History* 5, no. 2 (1974), 363–381; Martha Solomon, "Autobiographies as Rhetorical Narratives: Elizabeth Cady Stanton and Anna Howard Shaw as 'New Women,'" *Communication Studies* 42, no. 4 (1991): 354–70.

171 Solomon, "Autobiographies as Rhetorical Narratives," 355.

172 Taylor interview, October 5, 1987, ARS.0056; Villastrigo interview, October 1987, ARS.0056; Howarth, "Some Principles of Autobiography," 363–81.

173 Taylor, *We Made a Difference*, xvi.

174 Taylor, *We Made a Difference*, x, 49.

175 Swerdlow, *Women Strike for Peace*, 4–5.

176 Ruth Milkman and Rayna Rapp, "Preface," *Feminist Studies* 8, no. 3 (1982): 491–92.

177 Taylor, *We Made a Difference*, 115.

178 Taylor interview, October 5, 1987, ARS.0056; Adams ed., *Peacework*, 18.

179 Taylor, *We Made a Difference*, 103–5.

180 Taylor interview, October 5, 1987, ARS.0056.

181 Taylor, *We Made a Difference*, 154.

182 Boyer, "From Activism to Apathy"; Robert A. Jacobs, *The Dragon's Tail: Americans Face the Atomic Age* (University of Massachusetts Press, 2010); Wittner, "The Nuclear Threat Ignored," 439–60; Swerdlow, *Women Strike for Peace*, 127.

183 Joshua W. Busby, *Moral Movements and Foreign Policy* (Cambridge University Press, 2010), 49–50, 59–60; William A. Gamson, *The Strategy of Social Protest* (The Dorsey Press, 1975), 35; Katz, *Ban the Bomb*, 169.

184 Taylor interview, October 5, 1987, ARS.0056.

185 "Keynote Address by Ethel Taylor at WSP National Conference, Chicago, Illinois, October 1973," SCPC WSP Records, A1:3, National Conference—1973, Chicago, IL.

186 Villastrigo interview, October 1987, ARS.0056.

187 Taylor interview, October 5, 1987, ARS.0056.

188 "Report to May WSP Board Meeting, Libby Frank," AU WSP Records, Box 1, Board—1988–1989, 1992; Taylor, *We Made a Difference*, 153–54.

189 Unsigned letter to WSP Branch Leaders, March 28, 1989, SCPC WSP Records, 90A-028:4, Comprehensive Test Ban Correspondence.

190 "Meeting Notes for Thurs, 5/4/88," UCB WFP Records, 11:8, Office Files—General, 1988; "Message from Ethel Taylor to 2/7/90 Meeting," SCPC WSP Records, ACC 01A-005:11, Co-ordinating Committee Meeting National 2-7-90.
191 "Message from Ethel Taylor to 2/7/90 Meeting," SCPC WSP Records, ACC 01A-005:11, Co-ordinating Committee Meeting National 2-7-90.
192 Letter from Anci Koppel, February 5, 1990, UWS SWAP Records, 1:17, General Correspondence, Jan. 1990–Aug. 1991.
193 Letter from Ethel Taylor, February 20, 1990, SCPC WSP Records, ACC 01A-005:12, Closing Philadelphia Office; "Message from Ethel Taylor to 2/7/90 Meeting," SCPC WSP Records, ACC 01A-005:11, Co-ordinating Committee Meeting National 2-7-90.
194 Letter from Ethel Taylor, February 20, 1990, SCPC WSP Records, ACC 01A-005:12, Closing Philadelphia Office.
195 "Message from Ethel Taylor to 2/7/90 Meeting," SCPC WSP Records, ACC 01A-005:11, Co-ordinating Committee Meeting National 2-7-90.
196 "WSP Coordinating Committee Notes—4/18/90 Transitional Coordinating Committee," SCPC WSP Records, ACC 01A-005:11, Co-ordinating Committee Meeting National 2-7-90.
197 "Making the Connection—The Test Ban and Iraq," AU WSP Records, Box 8, Iraq—1990–1992; "Letter from Ethel Taylor to Editor, December 2, 1990," SCPC WSP Records, ACC 01A-005:11, Iraq, Kuwait.

Conclusion

1 Amy Swerdlow, *Women Strike for Peace: Traditional Motherhood and Radical Politics in the 1960s* (University of Chicago Press, 1993), 12; Amy Swerdlow, "Ladies' Day at the Capitol: Women Strike for Peace Versus HUAC," *Feminist Studies* 8 no. 3 (1982), 493.
2 Sybil Oldfield, *Women Against the Iron Fist* (Oxford: Basil Blackwell 1989); Alonso, *Peace As a Women's Issue*; Liddington, *The Road to Greenham Common.*
3 Noreen O'Donnell, "Peace studies gains popularity on campuses," *The Reporter Dispatch*, November 18, 1993, 34; "Peace: Sweeping Campuses," *The Daily Times*, November 18, 1993, 6A.
4 Ethel Taylor interview, October 5, 1987, ARS.0056, Stanford University Archive of Recorded Sound.
5 Taylor, *We Made a Difference.*
6 For example, see the introductions to Judy Tzu-Chun Wu, *Radicals on the Road: Internationalism, Orientalism, and Feminism During the Vietnam Era* (Cornell University Press, 2013), and Petra Goedde's *The Politics of Peace: A Global Cold War History* (Oxford University Press, 2019).
7 Taylor, *We Made a Difference.*
8 Ann Davidon, "Women Strike for Peace in the 1960s: A Turning Point in the Feminist Drive," *Philadelphia Inquirer*, February 6, 1994, 109.
9 Rose DeWolf, "A Mother's Book Recalls Four Decades of Activism," *Philadelphia Daily News*, November 3, 1998.
10 Wu, *Radicals on the Road*, 194.
11 Lara Track, *Frieden und Frauenrechte im Kalten Krieg: Women Strike for Peace und die amerikanische Frauenrechtsbewegung im Spiegel transnationaler Kooperationen, 1961–1990* (Transcript Publishing, 2024).

12 "Washington DC sent out the call," University of Washington, Seattle, Seattle Women Act for Peace Records, 4073 (hereafter UWS SWAP), 1:39, Speeches and Writings—Misc., April 1990–1998, n.d.

13 "Letter from Alice Hamburg to Medea Benjamin, July 27, 1996, University of California, Berkely, San Francisco Women for Peace Records BANC MSS 89/132 c (hereafter UCB WFP Records), 16:46, Global Exchange [includes travel to Cuba], 2000–2001.

14 Taylor, *We Made a Difference*, 155.

INDEX

www.ingramcontent.com/pod-product-compliance
Lightning Source LLC
Chambersburg PA
CBHW030531230426
43665CB00010B/842